A Field Guide to Birds' Nests

Also by Bruce Campbell (illustrated by Donald Watson)

The Oxford Book of Birds

Bruce Campbell
and James Ferguson-Lees

A Field Guide to Birds' Nests

with the assistance of
Henry Mayer-Gross

Bird drawings by
D. I. M. Wallace

Constable London

First published in Great Britain 1972
by Constable and Company Ltd
10 Orange Street London WC2H 7EG

ISBN 0 09 458350 1

Set in Monotype Baskerville
Printed in Great Britain by
The Anchor Press Ltd
and bound by
Wm Brendon & Son Ltd
both of Tiptree Essex

Contents

Photographs

between pages 18 and 19

‘Ge beag an t-ugh thig eun as’
Though the egg be small, a bird will come out of it

Gaelic proverb

Foreword and Acknowledgements

The years since BC's *Finding Nests* appeared in 1953 have seen great changes in British ornithology. The Bird Protection Acts of 1954 and 1967 have introduced an approval system under which the nests even of rare birds may be examined for scientific purposes, while pressure on the natural environment has brought all interested in our bird life much closer together. First came co-operation between wildfowlers and conservationists; more recently, responsible oologists have ceased to collect eggs in Britain except under licence and have endeavoured to restrain the 'wild men', much as wildfowlers condemn the 'marsh cowboys' of the shooting world.

In presenting what is virtually a completely new book under a new title, we have therefore enlisted the help of the Jourdain Society, and especially of R J Connor, who has farmed out sections of the text to different members for their comments; and much valuable advice has been received from them. Shortly after the publication of *Finding Nests*, Andrew Pierssené drew our attention to the late Major H T Gosnell's *The Science of Birdnesting* and in 1966 Clive Simson published *A Bird Overhead*: hints from both these books have been incorporated by us, and Brigadier Simson has given further help as President of the Jourdain Society. The specific accounts for the waders have also been seen by I E Hills. Two articles in *The Ringer's Bulletin*, by P G Davis and G O Stephens, also contain some useful new material. But our main debt must be to Henry Mayer-Gross who, both as organiser of the Nest Records Scheme for the British Trust for Ornithology from 1959 to 1971 and as a tireless field-worker, has amassed an enormous knowledge of nesting habits and has put this freely at our disposal. N W Orr has kindly given us notes on a number of rare species. M A Ogilvie and David Glue also gave us valuable help in defining the seasons for wildfowl and owls respectively. R K Murton provided information on the share of the sexes in building by pigeons and doves. The basis of the data on which the distribution maps for each species were compiled has been J L F Parslow's paper (1967–8) in *British Birds* on changes in status among breeding birds in Britain and Ireland and the maps which subsequently appeared in *Book of British Birds*. We are very grateful to John Parslow, H F & G Witherby, William Collins Sons & Co., and the *Reader's Digest* for permission to use these sources. In fact, many maps have been altered and 37 completely revised in consultation with J T R Sharrock, organiser of the BTO and Irish Wildbird Conservancy's *Atlas of Breeding Birds* project; the map for the Collared Dove has also been checked by Robert Hudson. The maps and the breeding season diagrams were drawn for us with the greatest care by Robin Prytherch, who partly designed the diagram, and Karen Rayner.

Acknowledgements made at the beginning of *Finding Nests* also remain apposite: to the late Arthur Whitaker, whose records of 21,620 nests (now in the Edward Grey Institute at Oxford) BC was able to study through the kindness of the late Mrs Whitaker and of Mrs Angela Hughes; to the late W B Alexander for much good advice; to *Birdsnesting* by J G Black; and to a previous generation of Campbells, whose knowledge was mostly gained round Bedford. IJF-L has also done much of his field work in this area; from an earlier period in Sussex he owes a special debt to the late Jock Walpole-Bond, both for passing on some of his vast knowledge at first hand and for the three volumes of *A History of Sussex Birds*, a repository of valuable nesting hints. Many other ornithologists are acknowledged in the text and there is a bibliography on pages 534–6.

The total of 234 species covered by the book includes all that have been recorded as breeding or attempting to breed, in a wild or established feral state, in Britain and Ireland during historic times to the end of 1971.

Overleaf: a typical nest record card (with acknowledgements to the British Trust for Ornithology)

OBSERVER Bruce Campbell

SPECIES Swallow (1a)

YEAR 1971

B.T.O.Ref.

NO. of EGGS or YOUNG at each visit. Record here stage of building; if bird sitting; if eggs warm; age of young; ring nos. etc.

DAY	MTH.	B.S.T.	EGGS	YNG.	
9	June				Building
17	"	10.50	1		
19	"	13.15	4		
21	"	18.00	5		Warm
3	July		5		~~Adult flies off~~
6	"	12.00	3	2	Hatching
11	"	02.10			Adult on
11	"	18.15		5	
18	"			5	Ringed HC69551-5
24	"	12.15		2+?	PTO
26	"				Empty

Further visits, notes on outcome, etc. – ON BACK

COUNTY Oxon

If this record is entered on ATLAS CARD put ✓ in box: ✓

Office Use Only: D, C, H, F

LOCALITY (place-name) Hordley Woodstock

Grid Ref SP447193

ALTITUDE above sea level 250 ft.

HABITAT Delete those inapplicable:- RURAL / ~~SUBURBAN~~ / ~~URBAN~~

Buildings (garage) in farmland

NEST SITE Old nest against beam built up with a few layers of new mud.

Height above ground or cliff-base 10 ft.

NEST RECORD CARD

BRITISH TRUST FOR ORNITHOLOGY, BEECH GROVE, TRING, HERTS.

Please consult instruction leaflet for method of completing cards, advice on visiting nests, and what observations are most useful.

A few reminders:-

1. Clubs and schools should give their name as well as the observer's.
2. Use one card for each nesting attempt, even if a nest is used twice.
3. To avoid mistakes, please write the month, e.g. 5 Apr., not 5/4.
4. Accurate counts of eggs and young are important, but if there is uncertainty put a ✓ , or put brackets round the probable number.
5. Do not forget to record any eggs remaining unhatched.
6. Final visit: please enter details in the normal way overleaf, and indicate your findings under "Outcome of Nest" below. The central space below can be used for further visits and/or notes.

RECORD ONLY WHAT YOU OBSERVE: PLEASE MAKE NO GUESSES

24 July Did not go close for fear of premature dispersal of brood

OUTCOME OF NEST

If you have positive evidence that the young left safely, or of failure, please put a cross (☒) in the appropriate box or boxes below. Otherwise mark the appropriate "Outcome Unknown" box.

OUTCOME UNKNOWN
- Because evidence for or against success is inconclusive☐
- Because observations on nest were not continued☐

EVIDENCE FOR SUCCESS
- Young old enough at previous visit to leave if disturbed☐
- Young: seen leaving naturally☐ left when approached☐
- Young seen and/or heard near nest☐
- Parent bird(s): giving alarm calls☐ carrying food☐
- In nest: hatched shells☐ feather scale☐ droppings☒
- Any other evidence:-

EVIDENCE FOR FAILURE
- Nest: empty☐ damaged☐ fallen☐ flooded☐ removed☐
- Eggs: damaged☐ deserted☐ all infertile or addled☐
- Young: all dead, uninjured☐ all dead, 1 or more injured☐
- Any other evidence (e.g. type of weather causing failure, species of predator if seen, etc.):-

Introduction

Finding nests

There are four main reasons why ornithologists want to find nests: to make a record of each one, if possible from building right through to fledging; to make observations (including tape-recordings) on the behaviour of the adults and young; to mark the brood, at the right age, with rings; and to photograph the birds. Another object is for such studies as the *Atlas of Breeding Birds* to be published by the British Trust for Ornithology and the Irish Wildbird Conservancy after five years' field work in 1968–72. Although proof of breeding is accepted on other evidence, for example the carrying of food or faecal sacs, the actual discovery of the nest with eggs or young is absolutely conclusive.

At the end of 1970 the total of cards in the Nest Records collection of the British Trust for Ornithology was over 300,000, referring to 193 species. The origins, history and development of the scheme have been described by Henry Mayer-Gross (1970). Suffice to say here that, as the Hatching and Fledging Enquiry, it was started in 1939 by Sir Julian Huxley and the late James Fisher and that, when *Finding Nests* was published, only two papers analysing nest record data had appeared. By the end of 1970 about 55 analyses and other papers had made use of the data in various ways. The scheme is an indispensable tool for students of breeding biology and has been copied in at least 13 other countries. An example of the card now in use is shown on pages xii and xiii and indicates the amount and type of information that can be recorded. Special cards and sheets for visits to colonies are also in use.

Data on many nests can also be used to give extensive support to intensive observations on a few nests by one worker or a small team. This type of research is particularly associated with Professor Niko Tinbergen's comparative ethological studies of gulls and terns, whose nests normally need little skill to find, but has also been applied to small passerines.

The marking with rings of young in the nest has to some extent been overshadowed, especially since the introduction of the mist net in 1956, by the catching of full grown birds, but it is essential for studies of vital statistics: a nestling ringed before fledging supplies accurate information on age and place of hatching.

The motives of bird photographers are not always scientific, but the superb results they have achieved have, through magazines, books, exhibitions, films and television programmes, been the means of interesting hundreds of thousands of people in birds, in their protection and encouragement, and in the conservation of nature in general.

There may be four stages in finding a nest. First, the observer must be in the breeding range of the species; second, he must locate the right habitat; third, he must be able to recognise suitable sites; finally comes the actual discovery of the nest. In this book we have combined a section on distribution and habitat for each bird, and we have combined information on nest-site and nest with details of eggs, clutch size, incubation and fledging periods; and a specially designed diagram indicates the limits of the breeding season.

It may be argued that the point at which habitat becomes site is sometimes difficult to determine; for example, a bird of prey may nest in an isolated crag or a clump of trees but range and feed over moorland. How should its breeding habitat be correctly described? We have confined site to the immediate surroundings of the nest, though the actual area will naturally vary with the size of the bird and its nest. It is in a knowledge of the likely sites for each species that much success in nest-finding lies; the breeding habitat is only a general guide. 'Site sense' is largely a matter of experience, either acquired at first hand or passed on in the field; it is often extremely hard to identify in words the little indications that reveal a possible site, indications at once apparent when pointed out on the spot. But we have tried to make suggestions.

Every year accounts of freak nesting sites find their way into the papers. These are almost always those of very common birds, because it is usually only when a species is numerous that pressure on available sites leads to odd choices. The remnant stocks of rare birds tend to breed in the optimum habitat and in the most advantageous sites. It is therefore harder to find all the nests of a common bird than of a rare one over a given area, because there will be often one or two pairs of the common species which defeat the observer by freak selection. What experienced nest-finder looks for Robins' nests in the saddle-bags of bicycles, or for Blackbirds' and Song Thrushes' nests on the buffers of rolling stock?

The majority of pairs of each species, however, show recognisable preferences for certain types of site. These preferences may vary regionally, and this is something on which the accumulation of nest record cards is beginning to give information, and why each card is important even if it only contains a single date entry of nest contents.

There are two main ways in which a nest is found: by getting the birds to show it, or by searching. The second method can be divided into 'cold' searching, when the aim is to find the nest itself, and 'hot' searching, when the aim is to flush the sitting bird. Finding by searching is cruder than finding by watching, which Gosnell called 'the use of science'. It requires less knowledge of the birds and far less patience, but it demands a keen appreciation of site preferences. For a study involving finding the nests of all species in a particular area, searching is the most useful method if time is limited, as a look-out can be kept for different specific sites, and the ground covered and time spent can be assessed. Opportunities to find a nest by watching can be taken in the middle of the search, if a bird is seen carrying food (to the nest) or a faecal sac (from the nest) or otherwise behaving suspiciously. G O Stephens records finding the occupied nests of Blackbird, Lesser Whitethroat, Bullfinch and Linnet inside a 3-metre circle in a 'thorn and bramble thicket', and the searcher must be on the alert for such possibilities.

Time, which reared its head in the previous paragraph, is often the limiting factor in nest-finding success. Any nest of any bird can be found if the clock has not to be watched, and the advice given on methods for each species assumes this ideal condition, under which the oologists of more spacious days seem often to have worked.

The hour of the day is another very important factor. Birds are most active early in the morning, and this is easily the best time to watch building in progress and to locate territories by song. Feeding the young may continue all day, but many species show peaks of activity in early morning and late afternoon. The middle of the day is the dead period for movement but is a good time to search; the vegetation should be dry and less likely to reveal the observer's tracks; it is also easier when the sun is high to look into bushes and through hedgerows. Fine, still weather is best for all observations on birds; both wind and rain make watching and searching difficult, though showers have the effect of driving ground-nesting species back to their eggs.

Locating the birds is a preliminary to any systematic searching or watching; for this a knowledge of habitats is necessary and some hours of field work spent early in the spring or even, with some residents, in winter may save a lot of time later when it is vital. This is particularly important in the study of a single species over a large area. Song or display by the male is a good guide to the neighbourhood of the territory. Sometimes both male and female are seen showing attachment to a particular locality; sometimes the actual selection of a site can be watched, though it may not be the one ultimately used.

When the birds begin nesting, their behaviour often gives a clue to the stage which they have reached in the breeding cycle. Some species show a remarkable change when the eggs are near hatching. Close-sitting waders, for example, previously only visible at the change-over on the nest, become shrieking aerial demons mobbing the observer. Song is often marked during the nest-building of those species in which the males take little or no part, then declines almost to nothing during the incubation and nestling periods, to revive if there is a second nest. When the young are about to leave the nest there is sometimes another change in behaviour or fresh alarm notes come into use, and the bird-ringer knows that he is too late to attempt to mark that brood.

Success in cold searching goes to those who spend the longest time looking in the largest number of likely places; it is a question of persistence rather than of skill or scientific observation, and is most useful at the beginning of the season before the leaves come out and the ground vegetation grows up. As all ecologists know, the edge between two habitats carries the richest variety of species; this is practically expressed by Gosnell's remark that many nests are built near tracks, for these create artificial interfaces. It is usually advisable to have the sun and wind behind the observer, as in bird-watching, but when searching, for example, along hedgerows and round clumps of bushes, the sun should be on the other side so that nests appear as dark patches among the transparent foliage (Plate 1). A stick is always useful for parting the leaf cover to give a view inside (Plate 2). The positions of nests should be marked carefully in relation to features that can be seen from outside; otherwise it may be necessary to go round a clump three or four times to examine a nest which looks obvious from inside the canopy.

It is nearly always better to look upwards rather than downwards when searching hedges, banks or cliffs. This is because arrangements of the vegetation, for example the leaves at the entrance to many Robins' nests, or the smoothed way into a Pied Wagtail's nest, cannot easily be seen from above. This is also true of most cliff nests, though it is often necessary to get above them to see their contents. Results are usually better when walking at some distance from a bank or cliff, the distance increasing in proportion to the height. This improves chances of spotting the indicators of a nest-site: detached material, tracks and approaches to holes, and the green patches which betray ancestral eyries of the bigger species, though fresh droppings of excreta may be misleading, indicating only perches or roosts. If there is a ditch beside a hedge, J G Black's good advice is to walk along it while searching.

A stick is the indispensable tool for hot searching, enormously increasing the observer's range, though it should not be so long that it is difficult to control or gets in the way in thick cover; something rather over a metre ($3\frac{1}{2}$ to 4 feet) is quite long enough even for a full-grown man. If an inspection mirror (Plate 3) is fixed to the end, anything much longer becomes hard to manipulate; telescopic metal sticks have been on the market, though neither of us has used them. But the Rye Meads Ringing Group find that a light pole, 4 to 5 m long, effectively increases the range of hot searching when looking for Sedge Warblers and other species along the edges of pools. When trying to flush birds, the stick should be used gently; light touches and taps secure the best results and do not frighten the birds so much. After tapping low growth of bushes, stand back and listen: the sitting bird may not show itself and only its movement through the twigs and stems gives it away. Dead leaves dislodged by the tap make much the same noise and lead to many false alarms. Unless the nest can be found within a minute of the bird's leaving, retreat and try again later. The longer the search, the greater the disturbance of the site, which may lead enemies to the nest and in any case is bad field work.

Dragging a rope over open country is an old device, used by David Lack and L S V Venables in their surveys of heathland; in these they were concerned only to flush birds, not find their nests. The limitation of the rope is that it catches in bushes, boulders or even big anthills and becomes almost useless, but it can be used in uniform grassland, heaths or sedgy ground with fair success; a third man walking behind the two carrying the rope watches for birds rising and can free it when it catches. P E Brown suggests white tags at intervals along the rope as markers; when a bird rises, the drag stops, the rope is laid down quietly and the observers concentrate on the mark. The rope is dragged in a curve and odd corners of fields can be worked by one observer standing still and the other going round the edges. It is even possible to use a rope single-handed, by pegging one end and dragging the other round in a circle. The longer the rope, the heavier the drag, but 40 m of climbing rope is quite manoeuvreable in grassland, where BC has had some success with it for finding Skylarks' nests. The method is not dangerous either to birds or nests; the vegetation keeps the rope well off the ground, and even the most exposed nests are usually slightly sunk in a hummock.

The flushing of close-sitting birds in cliffs or trees is often surprisingly difficult. A sharp noise can be tried – gamekeepers used to fire a shot when cartridges were cheaper – but may put birds off from places not being watched. Clapping is therefore most useful when there is a wide view, as on cliffs, less so in woodland. Claps with the hands well cupped so that palm and fingers are almost at right-angles to each other are the most effective. To get a reaction from a nest high in a tree, the trunk may be scraped or tapped with the stick.

If a bird sits lightly in thick cover, its departure will not be seen at all (though birds of prey are sometimes betrayed by small birds mobbing them) and the nest must be found by cold searching. Light-sitting birds in open country are a better proposition, but must be carefully marked. If the observer is alone, he must not let his eye leave the mark and must try to relate it to other features in the surroundings: large tufts, flowerheads, prominent stones. Results are much better with two observers; one marks the bird, the other walks out and is directed on to the mark, where he plants his stick and begins searching. This is particularly useful for marks made through field-glasses, which distort perspective. If using field-glasses on his own, the observer must combat this by looking alternately through the glasses and then with the naked eye, until he is familiar with features which he can use as marks. Black and Stephens both suggest two partners range-finding from different points and then converging, but even this simple manoeuvre is hard to synchronise in some habitats, though useful when walking in line over moorland.

All purposeful searching for nests depends on a knowledge of habitats and site-preferences, but, when nests are found by watching the actions of the birds, the observations are more obviously 'ornithological' and this method appeals most strongly to experienced bird-watchers, for it enables them to collect data on the birds' behaviour which is often as important as finding the nest. Bird's-nesting small boys do not bother to watch the bird; indeed they hardly seem aware of its connection with the nest, and all searching, however skilful, can be criticised for its lack of emphasis on the movements of the bird, except as a momentary blur when flushed from the nest.

When many birds are building or have young, not much patience is needed to find their nests by watching. Sometimes they even attract attention by calling as they move towards the site. This applies mainly to passerine species, for which P G Davis has worked out a system of approximate location by watching the birds building, then returning to ring the brood after calculating the necessary time interval; 'half an hour of patient observation' usually enables him to walk to the nest. But the nests of other important groups – ducks, waders, gulls and game-birds – cannot be found like this, since they do not build at all in the sense that passerines do, and their young leave the nest almost immediately after hatching. Watching ducks and game-birds back to their eggs requires almost unlimited time and patience; waders and gulls are easier but success depends very much on whether there is a suitable hiding place from which to watch. It is easy to lie up in sand-dunes and wait for Ringed Plovers, Oystercatchers and terns nesting on the shore to return to their nests, but to tackle Golden Plovers, Curlews or even Common Gulls on open moorland is another matter: if the observer lies down he cannot see the birds; if he stands up, even a long way away, they can see him. Among small passerines whose females incubate there is a fairly regular pattern of behaviour, the male coming to the vicinity of the nest when his mate leaves it to feed; often he appears to call her off. *Cherchez l'homme* and follow him seems to be the way to success with these species.

Another general point, which seems to hold good when watching most species back to the nest, is that they are much more reluctant, and in some cases will refuse to return, if at the same time they have to move towards the observer. Naturally it is not always easy to know where to lie up at first, but if, after five or ten minutes, the bird shows no inclination to return to where the nest is believed to be, then it can usually be assumed either that it is under no strong compunction to return at all, or that the observer is somewhere on its line of approach. In either event nothing can be lost by moving, but to avoid such an initial mistake, hide as far from the bird as possible while still keeping it under observation, which means that field-glasses are almost essential for successful watching back in open country.

The top of a tree is the best natural hide, giving a commanding view and eliminating the watcher from the suspicion of the bird, which associates the human enemy with ground level. Rocks are a good substitute in highland country, but complete concealment is not usually necessary with passerines, provided the stance is far enough off their line to the nest.

Specially constructed tall hides are coming into use at bird reserves and observatories and are ideal for watching the whole life of the locality unseen by the birds. At the other extreme, P G Davis uses a tiny collapsible hide (70 cm × 70 cm × 1 m high) with a canvas stool. Hinged at all corners and at the centres of the cross members, it folds into a bundle 20 cm × 1 m. No companion is required: 'for Skylarks and Meadow Pipits all that is necessary is to watch flying birds until one comes along carrying food, then erect the hide more or less where it settles. It is usually possible to follow the movements of the bird through the herbage at such close range.' On the other hand, for large species, Black advocated the accepted bird-photographer's technique of having one or more partners, who see the observer into the hide and then walk away to distract the birds' attention. But birds of many species quickly accept such an apparently unusual object as a motor car in their habitat, returning to their nests even when it is bulging with bird-watchers and their visual aids only a few yards away (Plate 4). Unfortunately there is a limit to the places to which even an ornithologist is prepared to drive his car.

Given patience and a good vantage point, the technique of watching back is simple to describe: find the bird that shows a disposition to return – with some practice the signs of anxiety are quite easy to recognise – and stick to it until it reveals the nest either by going to it or by flitting repeatedly over the same spot. Sometimes the final dart to the nest is difficult to see; the spot must be marked and the nest found by flushing the bird, as in hot searching. When birds are watched back during building, it is advisable not to look at the nest but to mark it carefully for a future visit.

One development of the watching back technique has been suggested by the work of Stuart Smith, Eric Hosking and George Edwards with stuffed Cuckoos, which elicit violent attacks from several small passerines. In the intervals of these, one or both parents, showing a reaction surprisingly like the feminine trait of which Sherlock Holmes made use in 'A Scandal in Bohemia', go to or near the nest, apparently to reassure themselves of its safety. Therefore, by placing a stuffed Cuckoo in the vicinity of a suspected nest, it is possible to attract the birds and then to find the nest. Other stimuli probably act similarly with a variety of species, and some references will be found in the individual accounts.

Related species tend to resemble each other in their nesting habits and behaviour, so some general advice can be given about the larger groups, to be read in conjunction with the Methods section for each species.

Divers and Grebes (pp. 40–55) All species nest by or on sheets of fresh water or slow-moving rivers. The three divers and the Great Crested Grebe do not conceal their presence and can be located well before they begin to lay; the three smaller grebes, however, become very retiring once nesting starts, and thorough searches of beds of aquatic vegetation may have to be made for a complete census. This is highly inadvisable for the two rare species. The usually inconspicuous nests of divers are invariably made close to water, with access slides, and often on islands. Divers and grebes generally lay at 2-day intervals, probably at any time of day.

Seabirds (Petrels and Shearwater) (pp. 56–63) Although the locations of the principal colonies of these birds are now known, an accurate census or a reasonable estimate of their numbers is very hard and time-consuming to make, even for the Fulmar which normally nests in exposed sites. The areas occupied by the other species may be honeycombed with tunnels, which are briefly visited by night. The problem of establishing breeding in new localities, where only a few pairs are involved, is even harder and involves watching and listening by night, combined with a keen nose for inspecting possible sites. Some Fulmars at least lay their single eggs by night.

Seabirds (Cormorants and Gannet) (pp. 64–9) The Gannet colonies round the coasts of Britain and Ireland are well known (though Operation Seafarer discovered a new one on the Flannan Isles). So are most Cormorant colonies, which also occupy exposed sites: but look out for tree-nesting in Ireland and Scotland. Shags, often nesting under cover and scattered along a stretch of sea cliffs, are more difficult to count accurately. Cormorants and Shags lay their eggs at intervals of one to three days.

Waterfowl (pp. 76–119) Nearly all species breed near fresh water, Shelducks and Eiders being the only regular salt-water nesters, though several others are found along sea lochs and estuaries; and, with the exception of the hole-nesting ducks and some Mallards, all build on the ground, though their nests are poorly developed apart from the lining of down. Material, even for bulky swans' nests, may be collected within reach of the sitting bird. This means that there is virtually no building or nestling period and that nests must normally be found during laying, which is always difficult, especially as the eggs are left covered, or during incubation. Ducks are extremely wary when returning, so watching back is not much use unless the observer is prepared to spend a great deal of time on each nest. Most nests therefore are found by intensive searching after location of the pair, though a family predilection for islands in lochs and lakes may cut the time short, provided transport is available. The outstanding example in Britain is St Serf's Island in Loch Leven where in a recent year, on 20 hectares (50 acres), nests of 557 Mallards, 452 Tufted Ducks, 47 Gadwalls, 35 Wigeons, 10 Shovelers, 4 Teal and one Shelduck were found. Swans usually lay at intervals of more than a day, geese and ducks on consecutive days; and all waterfowl tend to lay early in the morning. There is a propensity, especially among Mallard and Tufted Duck, for more than one ♀ to lay in the same scrape; such 'clutches' are usually deserted.

Birds of Prey (pp. 120–59) General reference: Brown and Amadon (1968). The harriers invariably and the Merlin regularly nest on the ground, and several other species do so occasionally or in special habitats; but to reach the majority of nests of this group some kind of climbing is necessary (see pp. 23–7), their owners relying rather on inaccessibility than on concealment in their choice of sites, which they (especially the falcons) advertise in the early stages of the breeding cycle though many may become unobtrusive during incubation. The hardest nests to find are those of buzzards and hawks in thick woodland. The height at which birds of prey nest (or take over the old nests of other species) varies from bushes to sea cliffs hundreds of feet high; and there is local variation according to habitats: Buzzards nest indifferently in trees or rocks in the same district, whereas the Kestrel normally nests in rocks (or even on the ground) in highland country and in old nests or holes in trees and buildings in the lowlands. Eggs are normally laid at intervals of 2 or 3 days, sometimes more, occasionally less, but varying even within a species. Probably most eggs are laid between sunrise and mid-morning, with an extension to early afternoon, at least by some species. Several birds of prey do not normally lay a repeat clutch if the first one is lost.

Game-Birds (pp. 160–78) Great numbers of nests of Pheasant, partridges and grouse are found by gamekeepers every year when laying is in progress. Keepers are sometimes helped by dogs, but much of their success is due to highly developed site-sense. They have usually much more time at their disposal than most amateur ornithologists, know their ground intimately and have relatively dense populations to deal with. In areas where game-birds are scarce and unkeepered, their nests are among the hardest to find unless the off-nest feeding routine is studied. Where there is a pair bond, the behaviour of the ♂ may be a guide, but this is not much help with the Quail: unless the reaper takes a hand, this is perhaps the hardest of all British nests to find. Eggs are laid on consecutive days in the evening (pheasants) or at longer intervals up to 48 hours (average 36) and at any time of day (Red Grouse and Ptarmigan).

Crakes, Moorhen and Coot (pp. 180–9) This small nidifugous group includes one of the easiest (Coot) and one of the hardest (Spotted Crake) of British nests to find. Although often prodigal with their calls, the crakes and rails normally nest in very thick or extensive homogeneous cover, giving little or no opportunity for watching back. The nests of Moorhens are usually very easy to find, though they too may favour dense cover as well as remarkably obvious sites. Elsewhere in its wide range the species is as secretive as its relations. All species usually lay on consecutive days; some by night as well as by day.

Waders (pp. 191–248) No family of British birds has a greater attraction for the bird-watcher than the waders, and this applies to their nests as well. Although some nests may be well concealed (Snipe, Dunlin), waders as a rule avoid thick cover and physical obstacles which hinder the observer's approach. Instead they rely on placing their nests somewhere in large, often vast areas of uniform and usually open habitat, and it is up to the searcher either to exhaust himself by methodical quartering or to find some entry into the mind of the bird and get it to betray the nest site.

Waders, like ducks and game-birds, have virtually no building (and no nestling) period so that, unless a nest can be found when the clutch is incomplete, accurate data on the length of incubation are hard to obtain. Some British waders begin to sit before the clutch is complete or brood the first one or two eggs intermittently, but the chances against finding the nest by watching them at this stage are heavy, unless the ground can be visited regularly at dusk. Location of the birds at the site selection stage, followed by close observation and searching, may result in the discovery of the finally chosen scrape, though there is always the risk of desertion if the observer is seen to visit the spot.

Nest-finding during incubation gives some information on breeding seasons by back calculation from the hatching date. At this stage some species (Ringed and Little Ringed Plovers, Oystercatcher) are easy to watch back, others require highly individual techniques (Greenshank), while a few can hardly be found in this way at all (Woodcock). The Dotterel is relatively easy to watch back, but initial location of a pair may take hours or even days.

The general technique of watching back has been described, but it may be stressed here that there seems to be a critical point at which the bird decides to return or not to return at that particular attempt. Physically this point may be a hundred metres or more from the actual site and it is most important that the observer should be as far away from where he supposes the nest may be as is consistent with a general view of the habitat. Many of the difficulties in finding waders' nests arise in this way: either the observer remains too close in his effort to keep the bird in the field of his glasses, or he is forced to go so far away that he cannot see the final stages of its return. The photographer's device of having one or two people walk away ostentatiously while the observer stays concealed near the site may speed things up considerably. Black considered that the chance of a quick return, or of the bird sitting closer, was much increased on a wet day or when a sudden shower began, and he also recommended searching at dusk to get closer marks at species which normally rise a long way off.

The typical wader clutch is of four pyriform and cryptically coloured eggs placed with their points together in an open or partly covered scrape: sometimes this catches the eye from some metres away. There is a great range in laying intervals among the group, from consecutive days (Black-tailed Godwit) to 4 days (Curlew); the majority probably vary between 24 and 48 hours. Some vary the interval even within a clutch, and laying may take place at any time of day, sometimes even at night. The nidifugous young are also cryptically coloured; good descriptions of their plumage are given in *The Handbook* and other standard works.

Seabirds (Skuas, gulls, terns) (pp. 250–77) Methods vary from those advocated above for cliff-nesting seabirds to the watching back recommended for waders when pairs are nesting scattered over moorland or beaches. In general, colonies of all species can be located fairly easily and all return to their nests more readily than do most waders. Look out for nests on buildings, even in town centres (Herring Gull, Lesser Black-backed Gull and, over water, Kittiwake). Parents often feed young away from the nest. The interval between eggs varies from consecutive days (Little Tern) to as much as a week for some bigger gulls; time of laying also variable, from morning to evening.

Seabirds (Auks) (pp. 278–85) The four British species have fairly distinctive site preferences. Razorbills may overlap with Guillemots on exposed ledges, but some prefer shelter in a crevice or below boulders, where Black Guillemots may also be found, though their sites are generally more concealed. The Puffin resembles the petrels in using burrows or deep recesses in rocks, but its diurnal habits make its numbers a little easier to estimate. No information on time of day when eggs are laid.

Pigeons and Doves (pp. 287–98) The five British breeding doves occupy niches in all except the barest moorland and normally nest well off the ground in bush, tree, rock or building. All flush noisily and fairly readily and all have the habit of sitting on empty nests. Many nests can be found during incubation and the early nestling stages by searching likely habitats, but a better method, to get full nest records, is to watch for the displays that go on near chosen sites. The three *Columba* species are easy to locate at this stage (which, owing to their protracted season, keeps recurring right through the year); so is the Collared Dove, though it is liable to desert if put off an empty nest. The Turtle Dove is the most elusive of the group and has a much shorter season. The laying interval between the 2 eggs of the clutch varies from 36 to 48 hours.

Owls (pp. 302–13) A very difficult group about which to generalise. Nesting areas can be approximately located from calling at night; then, for the nocturnal species which use cavities or old nests, it is a question of searching at likely places. Sometimes, however, the male can be located when he is mobbed by small passerines, and this may narrow the area to be searched, though he can be nowhere near the nest. Eggs may be laid at 2-day intervals, or with as much as a week between; no information on time of laying. When the young are hatched, both parents present mobbing targets.

Near-Passerines (pp. 314–29) Such a diverse group can hardly be commented on generally, except to point out that both sexes of the hole-nesting species tend to be most unobtrusive during the laying and incubation periods, though sometimes ridiculously easy to follow when feeding young, which may themselves be very noisy. Initial location during the display period may narrow down the search; during excavation of the nest by woodpeckers the noise made by the bird may lead to the site, which is revealed by the fresh chippings below. Several species tend to return to the same site or its vicinity the following year. Most species lay on consecutive days, but the Nightjar has a 36-hour interval and the Cuckoo normally lays every 48 hours in the afternoon. The Swift lays between 8 and 11 a.m. (D Lack).

Passerine Groups

Crows (pp. 343–59) The nests of most of this family are easy to see or to locate in cavities, as the birds make little attempt to hide their visits to them, except for the Crow, which usually builds conspicuously anyway, and the Jay, which favours denser and lower cover. The Raven lays at 2-day intervals, but eggs are normally laid early in the morning on consecutive days by all passerines.

1 Searching against the light from inside leaf canopy

2 Examination of thick cover with stick and hand

3 Use of mirror on stick to examine Mistle Thrush nest

4 The car as a hide

5 Descent from Heron's nest with use of rope

6 Recording nest contents with 'electronic notebook'

7 Two 'blue riband' waders of wild country: a, Dotterel; b, Greenshank

8a A new regular breeding species: Redwing

8b Typical of bank-nesting passerines: Rock Pipit

Tits and allies (pp. 360–81) Like other cavity-nesting birds, most of this group are hardest to locate when laying or during incubation, except by learning the calls and following the off-nest bird on a feeding foray. But at both the building and nestling stages the parents can be watched to the site without too much trouble. The early morning is, of course, the best time to see building in progress.

Thrushes (pp. 390–424) **and Flycatchers** (pp. 463–8) This from the nest-finding angle is a miscellaneous group, including the two most frequently found non-colonial nests in Britain (Song Thrush and Blackbird) and the difficult Stonechat, Whinchat and Wheatear. They are adapted to more open environments whereas the Nightingale is usually found in dense cover. Generally the species in this group are ground and bush nesters, occupying a wide range of niches from rabbit holes to the tallest shrubs; and the thrushes build in trees to considerable heights. Redstarts and flycatchers resemble each other in nesting on ledges or in holes, and may be difficult to find during incubation, though fairly easy when selecting sites, building and feeding young.

Warblers and Kinglets (pp. 425–62) Thirteen warblers now breed regularly in Britain and, as regards their nesting, may be divided into three groups: the riparian species of the genera *Acrocephalus* and *Locustella* usually associated with wet situations, in which each favours a characteristic site; the genus *Sylvia* which build somewhat similar nests over much the same height range in hedges, copses, commons and gardens; and the three leaf warblers of the genus *Phylloscopus* building dome-shaped nests usually on or near the ground. Only the Lesser Whitethroat builds at all frequently above the height to which a man can reach, so the warblers are pre-eminently birds of the shrub and herb layers of the vegetation, especially where these meet: where grasses and nettles grow up into the lower branches of bushes and the whole is traversed by trailers of brambles, briars or honeysuckle. Their nests are generally light and dainty and hence do not require the stout forks favoured by finches; some have evolved ingenious suspensions from the vegetation, others rest on a junction of stems and are tenuously woven to them. The ground-nesting leaf warblers build more solidly. The two kinglets build comparatively large and compact nests normally attached to the underside of a horizontal branch.

The best way to find warblers' nests is to watch them building; this leads to least disturbance of the site. But in practice the great majority of nests of all except the leaf warblers are found by hot or cold searching though, when flushed, these birds make off much more elusively than finches or buntings, and may need to be flushed more than once before the nest is found. Indeed, Grasshopper and Savi's Warblers run off through the cover like mice. The leaf warblers are easy to track back during incubation owing to their repeated call-notes, but none of the others are so helpful until they have young. The song of the ♂ is a good guide when locating territories, at least up to the early stages of incubation, but some species have several distinct song areas and it is not always easy to pick the right one.

Larks (pp. 330–4), **Pipits and Wagtails** (pp. 471–85)
These are mainly ground-nesting birds, their sites ranging from an arable field to a wall, rock face or quarry. Nests may be well hidden by foliage, even in a crevice (Pied Wagtail) or very exposed (both larks), but many sites are revealed, especially when there are young, by a track leading to them or by a smoothed appearance at the entrance. Pipits and wagtails are not easy to watch when building, and may desert if the unfinished nest is found; larks are even more difficult because they gather most of their material near the

site. Watching back is useful but requires great patience, especially when pipits have large young. Searching likely areas after locating birds is probably how most larks' and pipits' nests are found, but this is a crude method compared to those suggested under Woodlark and Tree Pipit.

Finches, Buntings and Sparrows (pp. 491–533) Finches in Britain and Ireland nest anywhere from ground level (Twite) to 20 m up in trees (Siskin). But, on the whole, they prefer bushes and small trees, so they are more birds of hedgerow, garden, orchard and common than of woodland or moorland. They therefore tend to thrive in habitats strongly modified by man, though some are very susceptible to human interference. Several like sites on horizontal branches (Hawfinch, Crossbill) and some at the ultimate spray of foliage (Goldfinch, Siskin). Some of the most attractive and compact British nests are built by finches and others, if not compact, are light and elegant. The ♂♂ do not as a rule help in building but their habit of accompanying the ♀♀ to the site is a useful pointer, and happens at all stages in the cycle. Most finches show a fearless solicitude for the nest and will come close to the observer when he is in its vicinity, calling continually. This is a good 'hot or cold' indicator. All finches are liable to desert if the nest is examined closely during building; the Hawfinch is the most tricky of all, even deserting during incubation, and the greatest care should be used when examining nests; this is equally true when the nestlings are feathered and liable to 'explode' if approached.

The ground or bush-nesting buntings are often seen carrying material and build relatively bulky nests. Methods range from intensive watching back (Corn Bunting) to intensive search after locating the singing ♂ (Cirl Bunting). Many nests of Yellowhammers and Reed Buntings are found by hot searching, the sitting bird flying off at easy range; but they can be watched back too.

Although both our sparrows are normally colonial species, it may not be easy to find individual sites in crevices of walls or holes in trees, as both can be very shy at returning, even when with young.

Looking at Nests

Once a nest has been found, its contents are not necessarily revealed and to examine them often needs considerable effort and care, if its future is not to be prejudiced. Indeed, as a general rule we would say: do not attempt to look into a nest if this is bound to attract attention to it or lead to permanent disturbance of its surroundings, or if you have reason to believe that it contains large young which may 'explode' prematurely. Henry Mayer-Gross gives detailed advice on visiting nests for the purposes of the Nest Record Scheme.

The contents of nests on cliffs can sometimes be seen through field-glasses. Nests on water or in trees overlooked by cliffs can also be examined at a distance, but there is the risk that an egg is hidden by the near side of the nest if it has a deep cup. It is even harder to count young through binoculars, but some large birds with flat nests and small broods—herons, buzzards, eagles—can be dealt with in this way.

A stick is useful, almost essential, for examining nests in thick vegetation, allowing it to be parted with the least disturbance. A mirror fixed to the end gives an extension of vision, both in height and laterally into hedges and bushes. Not only does it save disturbance but clothes and skin as well and is certainly worth the trouble of rigging up. The mirror can be mounted on a ball-joint or attached by means of clamps: if the observer is not mechanically skilled, he should consult a gadget-minded friend. The disadvantage of the mirror is that it is not easy to count small young or very large clutches of eggs through it, and this difficulty increases with the length of the stick used, though abroad mirrors have been used to look into nests at the tops of trees.

A torch should be carried for looking into hole nests; do not fiddle about with the entrance: if the wood is at all rotten, it may break away. An ordinary torch has its limits if the hole is deep or narrow, but one is now marketed which has the bulb on a flexible neck; Whitaker used to mount a bulb on the end of a flex and dangle it in the hole. Corners, as in woodpecker holes, can sometimes be circumvented by using a very small mirror in conjuction with the torch.

For regular inspections of nests in holes and burrows, trap doors can be cut, glass panels inserted and whole hides fitted in position. The photographers have taken the lead in this technique, which does not really come within our scope. But we must praise the skill and ingenuity shown by Ron and Rosemary Eastman, who constructed a perfect nesting bank for their Kingfishers, and have gone on to other successes.

The nests of a number of species can only be examined by climbing a tree, cliff or wall. Tree-climbing has not grown into a sport in its own right like rock-climbing, but is a skill which requires serious training. The muscles, especially those of the arms and thighs, should be kept in tone throughout the winter by regular exercise; this avoids the humiliation and handicap of a torn or strained muscle early in the season. Elbows and knees play an important part in tree-climbing, providing short alternatives to hands and feet. As general safety rules, always have two and if possible three limbs well supported when moving the fourth, get support as close to the trunk as possible and always face the trunk. Practice looking down as well as up: it is essential to get used to seeing the ground twenty metres below.

Swarming is a necessary accomplishment for the tree-climber and can be learnt on a gymnasium rope. Although sometimes hugging the trunk cannot be avoided, the body should be kept away from the tree and the climber should be able to lean out like a woodpecker to study his next move. Never slide down trees; swarm down them. It takes less off the bark—and the skin.

The horizontal bough is one of the most difficult obstacles, but crows and birds of prey often nest at the ends of sloping branches. With practice in balancing, it is possible to walk along flat boughs, using other branches and twigs as supports; for those that slope upwards a form of swarming must be used. Downward-sloping boughs near the ground can be used to avoid swarming up a thick trunk, sometimes by climbing up, sloth-like, underneath them, sometimes by swinging and then heaving the body on top of them. Any difficult climb should be studied carefully from the ground at some distance from the foot of the tree before it is attempted: false starts are expensive in energy and morale.

The most useful tool to assist scaling a tree or building is an extending ladder. The majority of small passerine nests in Britain are less than 10 metres above the ground and within its range; a ladder also gives a valuable start up the limbless base of a tree. But ladders cannot be carried far afield and other devices must be used. Climbing irons are the simplest, though they may be difficult to come by nowadays and, however carefully used, are bound to score the trunk slightly. They are therefore not to be recommended for trees of economic or amenity value. Short irons are much easier to carry about than the long type that used to be favoured by Post Office engineers, though they give less support. Even with irons an initial boost from a companion ensures a good start, though the climber must be careful not to spike him in the process. Going up with irons is fairly easy, moving one foot at a time and clapping it smartly against the trunk with a slight downward movement so that the point of the iron digs in sufficiently. The body should be held as far from the trunk as possible: to embrace the tree shows lack of confidence. The harder part is coming down, because the point of the iron must be lifted upward out of the notch before lowering the foot to make a new one; if the climber is hurried or tired, there is a tendency to tear the point out, making ugly marks on the trunk. Irons are also rather a nuisance among the branches, and it is quite feasible to remove and throw them down, descending the bare trunk by swarming; this cannot be done on very big trees.

Really large trees demand more complex techniques, of which the simplest is a haul up to the first bough by rope. First throw a stone or shoot an arrow attached to a length of string over a suitable branch. This may be as hard as Mrs Beeton's hare to catch (for an amusing account of the problem, read the second chapter of Clive Simson's *A Bird Overhead*). Once this is achieved, one end of the rope is tied to the string and pulled over the branch. The climber ties himself to the other end of the rope (which should be at least twice as long as the height of the first bough) and swarms or irons his way up. Owing to friction against the bark there is, except on smooth beeches, very little hauling in actual practice, but the rope consolidates every inch gained and enormously lessens the effort required. On reaching the branch over which the rope is running, the climber can either untie himself, secure the end of the rope for use in his descent and continue in free climb or, provided the rope is long enough, he can go on climbing with it round his waist, moving spirally round the trunk so that the rope acts as a safety line if he slips, because it is threaded over several branches (Plate 5).

About forty years ago Myles North was working on this and other forms of assisted climbing, which he later summarised in a short paper in *Ibis* (85: 43–54). But his ingenious methods, based on those of Canadian loggers, have now been superseded by the use of the Swiss tree-bicycle and safety line as described by D T Seal, J D Matthews and R T Wheeler. Anyone seriously interested in ascents of tall trees should buy this Forestry Commission leaflet; it gives detailed instructions on climbing with the help of strops and the safety line, after the tree bicycle, which does the same job as climbing irons, has been parked on reaching the crown. The technique is used by foresters for cone collection and is described entirely in terms of conifers; but it can easily be adapted to hardwoods. Readers with a knowledge of German should also consult the section on 'Das Besteigen von Baumen' in the revised edition of Hans Bub's *Vogelfang und Vogelberingung*, which contains illustrated descriptions of various methods, involving both climbing irons and ropes.

Difficult trees may sometimes be avoided by using the next tree for the actual ascent, and looking across to the nest, perhaps with a mirror. Each species of tree has its own problems, which are solved by experience. Isolated, flat-topped pines are tedious and painful with their innumerable dead twigs once the crown is reached; the other conifers are relatively simple, having plenty of branches at convenient intervals. Oak is the classic hardwood, usually with sound boughs, but long intervals between them. English elms which develop holes interesting to owls, Jackdaws, Kestrels and Stock Doves are likely to be treacherous and it is worth taking considerable trouble to bring a ladder to them. A cover of ivy adds to the difficulty of any tree and is very exhausting to negotiate, as well as leaving tell-tale evidence for human or other predators to find.

The simplest method to examine nests in rock faces which cannot safely be approached unassisted is to lower the observer on a rope (or a doubled rope to reduce spinning), with another line separately and securely attached to a crowbar at the top for him to handle when necessary. Two firmly seated anchor-men are desirable; the front man has the rope round his back and over his elbows so that he can lock it instantaneously; the second has the body rope round him with spare coiled alongside ready to pay out. Rope can be brought on from behind with the right hand and let out forward with the left. It is useful also to have a link man on a point of vantage to convey messages from the climber, who goes down using the hand-line and leaning back as far as possible. If there is no link, it may be necessary to arrange a system of signals on the handline.

Simson uses a very similar method and illustrates it with one hair-raising example of what can happen when a climber attempts a traverse without a sling or rope round his body and relies on the hand-line, in this instance fortunately passed through his belt. When the climber slipped, he was able to hold on to the life-line and the friction of the rope on his belt decreased the speed of his fall. He escaped with badly 'burnt' hands and a severely bruised side when the life-line ran out and he fell on the boulders below. But it is normally a very safe method for non-alpinists. Climbing up is usually easier than climbing down and on a low cliff a rope can be used to assist, much as for tree-climbing, by pulling from the top. But with portable tackle a man cannot be hauled up a climb as a dead weight. Practice in team-work is essential before using ropes, and the spread of mountaineering knowledge, e.g. of abseiling, is all to the good for the more venturesome ornithologist.

For very soft marshes pattens are sometimes advisable: these are flat surfaces which strap on the footwear and give a good spread. They seem to be very local in their use; generally it is easier to strip off and put on old trousers and rubber shoes. Concealment of tracks is not usually so important in such habitats and by treading sideways and using what vegetation there is as platforms for the feet, progress is usually not too difficult. But one must be prepared to sink in occasionally, and it is essential that any field ornithologist should be able to swim. Incidentally, it may be difficult to take notebook and pencil into soft marshes or over the water, and a midget tape-recorder or electronic notebook can be held in one hand or slung round the neck (Plate 6). It is also very useful for making notes in moving vehicles.

Once a nest is found, some sort of marking is necessary against future visits. In localities safe from disturbance artificial guides can be used: sticks in the ground, coloured wool or string tied to bushes, broken ends of twigs. But in many places discretion is needed and the best method for a nest in the open is to align it between natural features, pace the distances involved and jot them down in the field notebook. Or compass bearings can be taken on the nest from various points. Nothing is more annoying than not to be able to re-find a nest, and it is worth taking trouble to mark its position carefully, bearing in mind that the pattern of vegetation can change in a matter of days.

After finding and marking the nest comes a most important act: leaving it tidily. Although there is some evidence that human tracks to a nest do not lead animal predators to it—they have other methods of finding them—there is no harm in taking precautions in wild country, and it is vital to do so in a populous countryside. Care when going to a nest is just as important as when leaving it, and this is where the mirror-stick is so useful, since it avoids opening up the site at all. If the verge of a road has to be crossed, start from a point not directly opposite the nest and take as few steps as possible, lifting the feet high each time. Use the same footmarks when coming away, raising the trodden grass with the stick on the retreat; in this way and by painstakingly putting the grass back into position, it is often possible to remove traces of the visit and thus avoid attracting unwelcome attention to the site. The same procedure applies to nests in bushes; if taking photographs or making long observations from a hide, do not cut the vegetation but tie it back or peg it down, to be replaced after each session.

Finally, there is the legal necessity under the Protection of Birds Act 1967 (which makes it an offence wilfully to disturb rare species at the nest) to get approval to photograph, ring or make nest records of any species on Schedule 1 (the specially protected list) or of any protected bird in a sanctuary or nature reserve. Approval is given by the Natural Environment Research Council to serious observers and it is a good idea to ask the advice of the British Trust for Ornithology, Beech Grove, Tring, Hertfordshire, before applying. Applications must be made afresh each year.

Approval covers all species designated as 'general', but must be sought individually for those on the 'special' list.

The species on Schedule 1 in 1972 are:

Birds designated as 'Special'

Black-throated Diver
Great Northern Diver
Slavonian Grebe
Black-necked Grebe
Bitterns (all species)
Spoonbill
Scaup
Goldeneye
Long-tailed Duck
Velvet Scoter
Whooper Swan
Eagle (all species)
Goshawk
Kite
Honey Buzzard
Harriers (all species)
Osprey
Hobby
Peregrine
Spotted Crake
Kentish Plover
Dotterel
Black-tailed Godwit
Wood Sandpiper
Temminck's Stint
Ruff
Avocet
Black-winged Stilt
Red-necked Phalarope
Black Tern

Snowy Owl
Bee-eater
Hoopoe
Wryneck
Golden Oriole
Bearded Tit
Fieldfare
Redwing
Bluethroat
Savi's Warbler
Marsh Warbler
Dartford Warbler
Firecrest
Red-backed Shrike
Serin
Brambling

Birds designated as 'General'

Red-throated Diver
Garganey
Common Scoter
Sparrowhawk
Merlin
Quail
Corncrake
Little Ringed Plover
Whimbrel
Greenshank
Stone Curlew
Roseate Tern
Little Tern
Barn Owl
Kingfisher
Woodlark
Chough
Crested Tit
Black Redstart
Crossbill
Snow Bunting

How to use this book

The species are listed 1 to 234 simply for the purpose of this book: they are arranged in the order used in *A Species List of British and Irish Birds* published by the British Trust for Ornithology (1972) and adopted by the national conference of editors of bird reports. Orders, families and genera are not given in the text, but an indication of the main groupings is given in the Introduction (pp. 11–22). The scientific names follow the BTO list.

Measurements throughout are metric, using the following abbreviations (with approximate equivalents in brackets):

km—kilometre (5 furlongs)	cm—centimetre ($2\frac{1}{2}$ to the inch)
m—metre (39 inches)	mm—millimetre (25 to the inch)
ha—hectare (2.5 acres)	

Other abbreviations are: ♂ for male and ♀ for female
BB for *British Birds* journal
Handbook for *The Handbook of British Birds*

References to papers in journals are given in brief in the text, as are the surnames of constantly quoted authorities (e.g. Lewis, Walpole-Bond, Whitaker), of those who have given us personal communications, and of individuals quoted in *The Handbook*. Where there is a monograph in English on a species to which we have referred, author and year of publication are given at the end of the Methods section, and a full citation in the bibliography (pp. 534–6).

The first section in the account of each species begins with a summary of its British and Irish **breeding distribution** according to information available to us at 31 December 1971. The first words give the status according to the categories adopted by J L F Parslow (1967–8). The numerical basis of each category is the 'possible number of breeding pairs in Britain and Ireland':

Very scarce: 1 to 100	Fairly numerous: 10,000 to 100,000
Scarce: 100 to 1,000	Numerous: 100,000 to 1 million
Not Scarce: 1,000 to 10,000	Abundant: over 1 million

In a few cases, e.g. Puffin, we have altered Parslow's rating to agree with up-to-date information.

On the accompanying maps for 185 species, **black areas** are those in which each breeds regularly in some numbers; **stippled areas** are those in which it breeds regularly but is local or sparsely distributed; in the **white areas** it breeds sporadically or not at all. Colonies of some seabirds are indicated by **black dots,** as are all breeding records (even single occurrences) for the Isles of Scilly, the St Kilda group and Fair Isle between Orkney and Shetland. The maps for the following 37 species are based almost entirely on preliminary maps published in *BTO News* from data supplied for the *Atlas of Breeding Birds* to be published by the BTO and the Irish Wildbird Conservancy:

28 Mandarin, 48 Buzzard, 49 Sparrowhawk, 58 Hobby, 63 Ptarmigan, 73 Water Rail, 88 Woodcock, 94 Common Sandpiper, 103 Stone Curlew, 108 Herring Gull, 126 Stock Dove, 130 Collared Dove, 132 Barn Owl, 136 Long-eared Owl, 138 Nightjar, 140 Kingfisher, 144 Great Spotted Woodpecker, 145 Lesser Spotted Woodpecker, 147 Woodlark, 154 Carrion/Hooded Crow, 163 Crested Tit, 164 Marsh Tit, 165 Willow Tit, 171 Dipper, 180 Stonechat, 181 Whinchat, 184 Nightingale, 187 Grasshopper Warbler, 201 Wood Warbler, 205 Pied Flycatcher, 211 Grey Wagtail, 215 Hawfinch, 218 Siskin, 220 Twite, 221 Redpoll, 230 Cirl Bunting, 234 Tree Sparrow.

After the distribution come the **habitat** details for each species; as far as possible technical ecological terms are avoided, but some generic or specific names of plants are given to assist recognition.

The section on **Nest** starts with a bracket indicating the share of the sexes in building; thus (♀♂) means that both take part, (♀) that only the ♀ builds, (♂♀) that the ♂ takes the major part. Sometimes there is an expanded statement, e.g. (♀, ♂ brings material). Where considered relevant the inner diameter of the nest cup is given in cm in the same bracket. Details of the shape and structure of the nest follow, then a summary of **nest-sites,** usually including some exceptional ones, though we have not attempted an exhaustive catalogue of these; they are rather intended to alert readers to possibilities. An indication of solitary (e.g. Robin), social (e.g. Lapwing) or colonial (e.g. Gannet) breeding comes next. After **Eggs** is given the usual clutch size, followed by the extremes in brackets, by a general description of the ground colour and markings and by the average dimensions of the egg, rounded off from those given in *The Handbook*. **Incubation** is followed by the share of the sexes in brackets and by the average incubation period for Britain and Ireland. **Fledging** is followed by the share of the sexes in feeding and caring for the brood, by the terms nidicolous (remaining in the nest for some or all of the fledging period), nidifugous (leaving the nest within 24 hours of hatching) or semi-nidifugous (remaining in or near the nest for several days) and by the average fledging period. Finally the **number of broods** is given. The majority of British birds will replace a clutch lost in the early stages of incubation and some even when eggs are hard set or young hatched; only where this is not the case have we indicated it (e.g. Golden Eagle).

The **seasonal diagram** is placed below the map (eight species without maps also have diagrams). The **upper black band** shows the main period when eggs may be expected in the nest, while the **lower black band** shows the main fledging period. The sloped extensions at either end indicate the dates within which not more than 5 per cent of eggs or young may be found, either in early or late seasons or in the geographical extremities of the country; verbal comments are added for some species.

The section on **Methods** usually starts by recommending ways of locating a pair of the species early in the season and follows the breeding cycle, suggesting appropriate tactics at each stage.

List of species

NOTE: A single asterisk indicates seasonal chart but no distribution map; two asterisks indicate no chart or map; all other species have both chart and map.

1 Black-throated Diver
**2 Great Northern Diver
3 Red-throated Diver
4 Great Crested Grebe
5 Slavonian Grebe
*6 Black-necked Grebe
7 Little Grebe
8 Fulmar
9 Manx Shearwater
10 Storm Petrel
11 Leach's Petrel
12 Gannet
13 Cormorant
14 Shag
15 Grey Heron
**16 Night Heron
**17 Little Bittern
18 Bittern
**19 White Stork
**20 Spoonbill
21 Mallard
22 Teal
23 Garganey
24 Gadwall
25 Wigeon
26 Pintail
27 Shoveler
28 Mandarin
**29 Red-crested Pochard
**30 Scaup
31 Tufted Duck
32 Pochard
**33 Goldeneye
**34 Long-tailed Duck
**35 Velvet Scoter
36 Common Scoter
37 Eider
**38 Ruddy Duck
39 Red-breasted Merganser
40 Goosander
41 Shelduck
**42 Egyptian Goose
43 Greylag Goose
44 Canada Goose
45 Mute Swan
**46 Whooper Swan
47 Golden Eagle
48 Buzzard
49 Sparrowhawk
**50 Goshawk
51 Red Kite
**52 White-tailed Eagle
*53 Honey Buzzard
54 Marsh Harrier
55 Hen Harrier
56 Montagu's Harrier

*57 Osprey
58 Hobby
59 Peregrine
60 Merlin
61 Kestrel
62 Red Grouse
63 Ptarmigan
64 Black Grouse
65 Capercaillie
66 Red-legged Partridge
67 Partridge
68 Quail
69 Pheasant
**70 Golden Pheasant
**71 Lady Amherst's Pheasant
**72 Crane
73 Water Rail
*74 Spotted Crake
**75 Baillon's Crake
76 Corncrake
77 Moorhen
78 Coot
**79 Great Bustard
80 Oystercatcher
81 Lapwing
82 Ringed Plover
83 Little Ringed Plover
**84 Kentish Plover
85 Golden Plover
86 Dotterel
87 Snipe
88 Woodcock
89 Curlew
90 Whimbrel
91 Black-tailed Godwit
**92 Green Sandpiper
93 Wood Sandpiper
94 Common Sandpiper
95 Redshank
96 Greenshank
**97 Temminck's Stint
98 Dunlin
*99 Ruff
100 Avocet
**101 Black-winged Stilt
102 Red-necked Phalarope
103 Stone Curlew
104 Great Skua
105 Arctic Skua
106 Great Black-backed Gull
107 Lesser Black-backed Gull
108 Herring Gull
109 Common Gull
**110 Mediterranean Gull
111 Black-headed Gull
112 Kittiwake
**113 Black Tern
**114 Gull-billed Tern
115 Common Tern
116 Arctic Tern
117 Roseate Tern
118 Little Tern
119 Sandwich Tern
120 Razorbill
**121 Great Auk
122 Guillemot
123 Black Guillemot

124 Puffin
**125 Pallas's Sandgrouse
126 Stock Dove
127 Rock Dove
128 Woodpigeon
129 Turtle Dove
130 Collared Dove
131 Cuckoo
132 Barn Owl
**133 Snowy Owl
134 Little Owl
135 Tawny Owl
136 Long-eared Owl
137 Short-eared Owl
138 Nightjar
139 Swift
140 Kingfisher
**141 Bee-eater
**142 Hoopoe
143 Green Woodpecker
144 Great Spotted Woodpecker
145 Lesser Spotted Woodpecker
146 Wryneck
147 Woodlark
148 Skylark
149 Swallow
150 House Martin
151 Sand Martin
**152 Golden Oriole
153 Raven
154 Carrion/Hooded Crow
155 Rook
156 Jackdaw
157 Magpie
158 Jay
159 Chough
160 Great Tit
161 Blue Tit
162 Coal Tit
163 Crested Tit
164 Marsh Tit
165 Willow Tit
166 Long-tailed Tit
167 Nuthatch
168 Treecreeper
**169 Short-toed Treecreeper
170 Wren
171 Dipper
172 Bearded Tit
173 Mistle Thrush
**174 Fieldfare
175 Song Thrush
176 Redwing
177 Ring Ouzel
178 Blackbird
179 Wheatear
180 Stonechat
181 Whinchat
182 Redstart
183 Black Redstart
184 Nightingale
**185 Bluethroat
186 Robin
187 Grasshopper Warbler
*188 Savi's Warbler
**189 Moustached Warbler

190 Reed Warbler
191 Marsh Warbler
192 Sedge Warbler
**193 Icterine Warbler
194 Blackcap
195 Garden Warbler
196 Whitethroat
197 Lesser Whitethroat
198 Dartford Warbler
199 Willow Warbler
200 Chiffchaff
201 Wood Warbler
202 Goldcrest
*203 Firecrest
204 Spotted Flycatcher
205 Pied Flycatcher
206 Dunnock
207 Meadow Pipit
208 Tree Pipit
209 Rock Pipit
210 Pied/White Wagtail
211 Grey Wagtail
212 Yellow/Blue-headed Wagtail
213 Red-backed Shrike
214 Starling
215 Hawfinch
216 Greenfinch
217 Goldfinch
218 Siskin
219 Linnet
220 Twite
221 Redpoll
**222 Serin
223 Bullfinch
224 Crossbill
**225 Parrot Crossbill
226 Chaffinch
**227 Brambling
228 Corn Bunting
229 Yellowhammer
230 Cirl Bunting
231 Reed Bunting
*232 Snow Bunting
233 House Sparrow
234 Tree Sparrow

Accounts of each species

I **BLACK-THROATED DIVER**

Gavia arctica

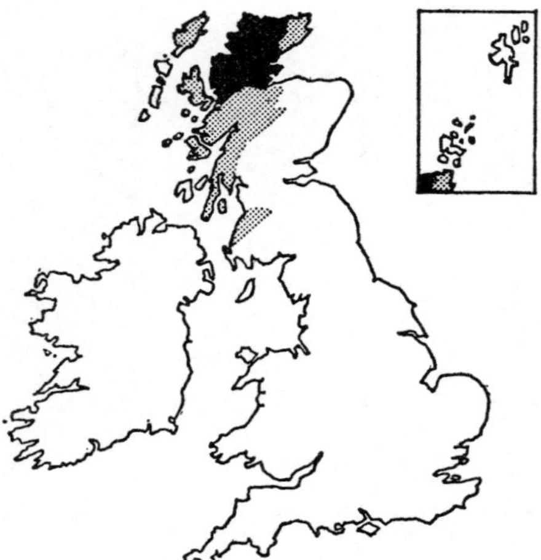

Very local and scarce (under 100 pairs); mainly from Argyll and north Perth northwards, but extension since 1950's to Arran and south Ayrshire. Generally restricted to large freshwater lochs, usually with islets, in both treeless and forested country, from sea-level to 500 m in central Highlands.

Nest (♀♂) Open scrape, sometimes lined with rotting vegetation. Usually on islet but occasionally on shore of large loch and rarely by tarn (normally habitat of Red-throated); may be on bare ground or among short heather or rushes, very close to water and slightly above it, with slide worn to shore. Solitary. Eggs 2 (1 to 3) olive to umber with sparse black spots and blotches (84 × 53 mm). Incubation (♀♂) from first egg, 29 days. Fledging (♀♂) nidifugous, about 8 to 9 weeks. One brood.

Methods Listen for wailing and mewing calls on likely waters. Pairs often visit other lochs near that on which they are nesting and sometimes, perhaps when water-level unsuitable, they will summer without nesting. But presence of single bird often indicates mate on nest in vicinity. Sitting bird slips off eggs, submerges, and surfaces from a few to 50 or more metres away: sudden appearance near islet or low headland justifies immediate search, but otherwise watch back or wait for change-over.

2 GREAT NORTHERN DIVER

Gavia immer

Pair and 2 young on loch in Wester Ross late June and early July 1970 (Eric N Hunter, *Scottish Birds* 6: 195) first satisfactory breeding record; same loch July 1971 bird identified as hybrid Great Northern × Black-throated seen with normal Black-throated and accompanied by well-grown chick; so important to establish, when breeding suspected, that both parents are Great Northern. Obviously worth watching for in Scotland in summer and observing carefully if seen: species often recorded in breeding season, sometimes in pairs, in West Highlands and particularly Shetland, Orkney and Outer Hebrides. Pair by island on loch in Assynt 1868, but observers had no boat (J A Harvie-Brown, *Zoologist* 26: 1309–10); families of adults and juveniles sometimes seen second half August, at least once previously where breeding recorded 1970, and assumed to be early migrants from Iceland, but adults there normally desert young on breeding grounds. Large freshwater lochs and lakes in both highlands and lowlands, and in treeless or forest country, often but not necessarily with islands and usually with low marginal vegetation, e.g. rushes and grasses.

Nest (♀♂) Usually little more than flattened scrape at outset, but sitting bird gathers surrounding grass, rushes, even twigs, and nest may become quite bulky by hatching time. Generally within 30 cm of water where deep enough to dive immediately, on island if possible, otherwise promontory or, less often, sheltered shoreline; normally in short vegetation, exceptionally on bare earth or rock or, conversely, in tall grass, scrub, even among trees; sites and nest often wet and sometimes in floating bog or surrounded with water, perhaps after level has risen. Solitary. Eggs 2 (1 to 3) greenish or olive to dark brown, occasionally almost unmarked, usually sparingly spotted dark brown or blackish (90 × 58 mm) from end May or early June. Incubation (♀♂) from first egg, 29 days. Fledging (♀♂, sometimes only one) nidifugous, 10 to 11 weeks. One brood.

Methods As for Black-throated, but again possibility of non-breeding pairs summering. Breeding cries by day or night loud and carrying: long-drawn, mournful wail rising and falling again, sometimes almost with quality of scream, or pleasant laughing sound. One of pair does most incubation and, when time for change-over, calls repeatedly until mate appears. Same nest-site, or within metre or two, often used in successive years.

3 **RED-THROATED DIVER**
Gavia stellata

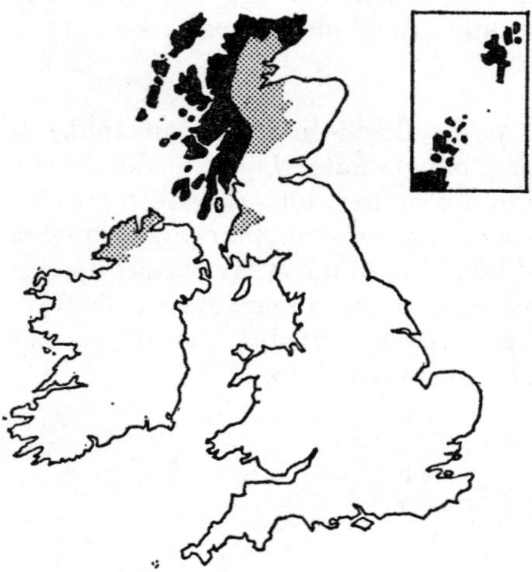

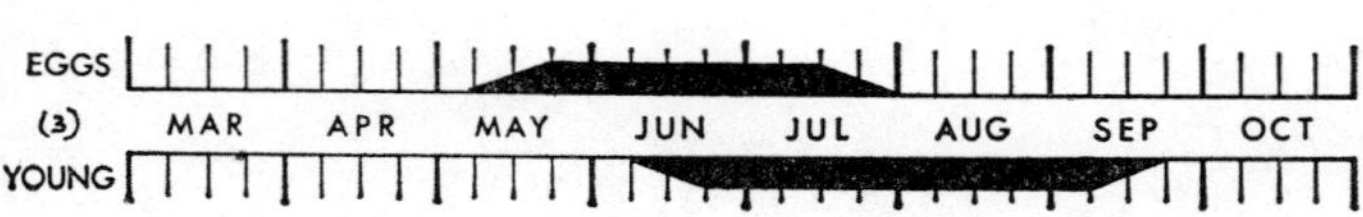

Scarce (but locally common) with similar range to Black-throated, mainly from Argyll and Perth northwards, and likewise breeds Arran; has bred Ayr and probably Kirkcudbright; a few pairs also in Donegal. Nests on quite small lochans, as well as larger lochs, with or without islands, in both open and wooded country, from near sea-level to 500 m or more, visiting larger lochs or sea to fish.

Nest (♀♂) Varies from open scrape, with or without lining of rotten vegetation, on islet or shore of large or small loch (see also Black-throated) to substantial platform of aquatic vegetation and wet moss built up in shallow water; such platforms may be left high and dry if water level recedes during incubation. Solitary. Eggs 2 (1 to 3) yellowish-olive to dark umber, spotted and blotched rather sparsely with blackish-brown (75 × 48 mm). Incubation (♀♂) from first egg, 24 to 29 days. Fledging (♀♂) nidifugous, about 8 weeks. One brood.

Methods As for Black-throated and usually easier to find, owing to small size of waters frequented, but same caveat about non-breeding pairs. Sometimes overlooked, if off-nest bird is away on neighbouring water and sitting mate slips off unobtrusively, perhaps emerging only as snake-like head under bank (S Sloan Chesser).

4 GREAT CRESTED GREBE
Podiceps cristatus

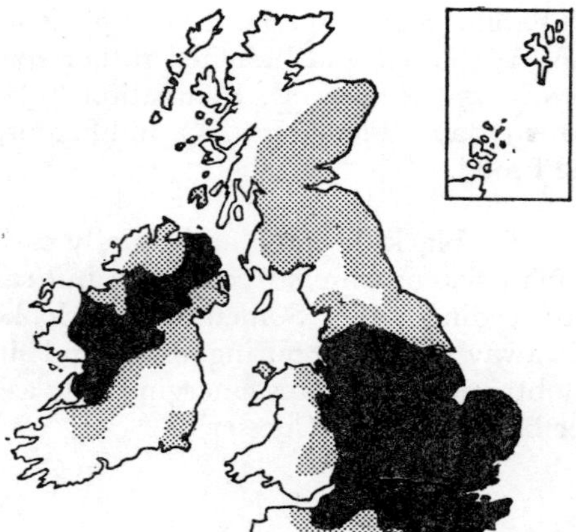

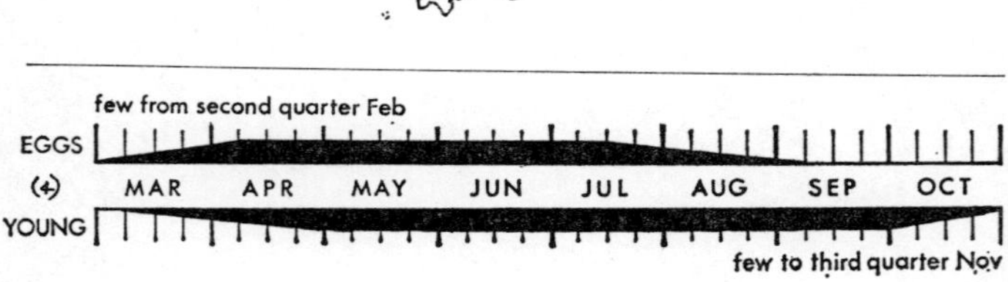

Not scarce (2,000+ pairs) and widely distributed, but absent south-west England, parts of Ireland and north Scotland, and local in Wales and rest of Scotland. Increase helped in much of England by spread of reservoirs and flooded gravel pits, as well as 'flashes' occurring after subsidence in north and Midlands. Breeds on medium to large sheets of shallow fresh water (minimum 1 ha, but usual territory 2 to 3 ha) with plentiful aquatic vegetation, such as reeds, sedges, water bistort and horsetails with weeping branches of trees sometimes acting as substitute. At times very little cover suffices and presence of open water seems more important. Surroundings of lake may be wooded or bare; occasionally on stretches of slow-flowing rivers.

Nest (♂♀) Soggy heap, normally floating, of locally available decaying and green aquatic plants, often with some sticks or twigs in foundations, becoming quite solidified, with central depression for eggs but no lining; in shallow water may be built up from bottom and, if water level falls, left high and dry on mud or reservoir masonry; material added during incubation. Typically built in clump of aquatic plants or anchored to weeping branches, and usually well hidden, but may show up prominently in low vegetation or when growth late, and nests in open by no means rare. In thick beds circular area may be cleared all round nest. Distance from shore very variable and in extensive beds in shallow water may be many metres out and normally nearer open water than bank. Nests occasionally quite close together, even forming colonies. Eggs 3 to 5 (1 to 9) chalky white becoming stained to buff and later dark brown or rusty (55 × 37 mm). Incubation (♀♂) from first egg, 27 to 29 days. Fledging (♀♂) nidifugous, 9 to 10 weeks. Sometimes two broods.

Methods Birds easily located on breeding waters and may be watched to nest-site when building (averaging one load of weed per minute for long periods) or incubating (off-duty bird visits nest about three times an hour; sexes change over every 2 to 2½ hours). When disturbed, sitting bird often seen to swim away, but sometimes, if cover is thick, pair remain hidden. Searching certain to succeed eventually if less exhausting methods fail. Eggs generally covered on leaving nest but may be glimpsed from side.

Some birds not illustrated individually: left from top, Gull-billed Tern (p. 267), two Black Terns (p. 267) and pair of Little Bitterns (p. 72); right, two White Storks (p. 75) and Night Heron (p. 72)

5 **SLAVONIAN GREBE**
Podiceps auritus

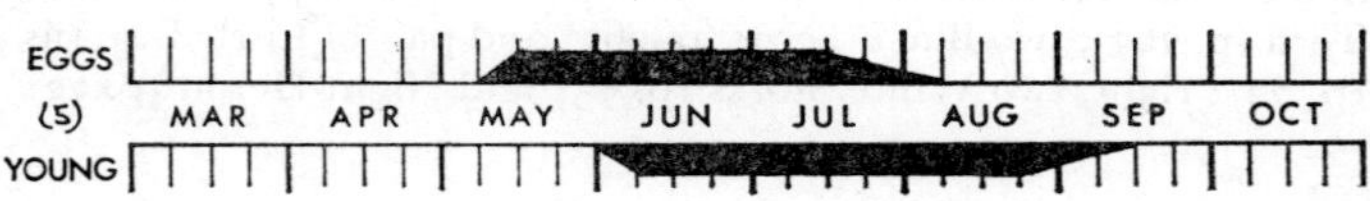

Scarce (probably under 150 pairs) in Inverness, Sutherland and Caithness and, more recently, in Moray and Aberdeen. Increasing and spreading slowly. Restricted to lochs and meres (but on Continent also slow-moving rivers) with variable, sometimes very scanty cover of reeds, rushes and, especially, mare's tails and sedges.

Nest (♀♂) Soggy floating heap like other grebes (see Great Crested), but mud occasionally used and whole structure bulkier than nest of Black-necked: about 35 to 45 cm in diameter at water level and 8 to 12 cm in height above water; material added during incubation. In Scotland nests a few yards from shore in beds of aquatic plants in small bays of lochs, sometimes very exposed. Solitary or social, even colonial. Eggs 4 to 5 (3 to 6, and even up to 10 abroad) chalky-white becoming stained to rich chocolate or even orange-red where iron deposit (47 × 31 mm). Incubation (♀♂) from first egg, 22 to 25 days. Fledging (♀♂) nidifugous, period unknown. Usually one brood.

Methods As Great Crested Grebe and usually easier to find, because cover generally thinner and lower and area of search more restricted. Often covers eggs on leaving nest.

6 BLACK-NECKED GREBE

Podiceps nigricollis

Very scarce (probably under 20 pairs) and regular breeding now confined to two or three sites in central Scotland, though single pairs and small colonies occasionally appear for a year or two elsewhere in Scotland and in England and Wales (in five such counties south to Kent and west to north Wales in the ten years 1957–66); formerly bred in four or five counties of Ireland, particularly Roscommon where 250 pairs at Lough Funshinagh during 1929–32 and up to 15 pairs near Briarfield up to 1957, but now apparently extinct through drainage. Found on lochs, meres, reservoirs and large ponds with extensive reeds, bulrushes and sedges, and probably satisfied with smaller areas of open water than Great Crested and Slavonian; abroad also on quiet stretches of river and adjacent flooded areas.

Nest (♀♂) Soggy floating heap like other grebes (see Great Crested), but, whereas Slavonian builds unusually bulky nest nearer in size to those of larger species, the similar-sized Black-necked makes a relatively small nest which is difficult to tell from that of Little Grebe; about 22 to 33 cm in diameter at water level and 5 to 8 cm above water; built in about three hours and material less likely to be added during incubation. Nest-site overlaps with those of other grebes, but is usually well hidden and often in denser aquatic vegetation than some species will tolerate (such as tall, dense reeds). Typically social and colonial where common, but single nests likely in Britain. Eggs 3 to 5 (2 to 8) chalky white becoming stained dark chocolate (43 × 30 mm). Incubation (♀♂) from first egg, 20 to 22 days. Fledging (♀♂) nidifugous, period unknown. Sometimes two broods.

Methods Location more difficult than other grebes as birds more silent and nests in denser cover, but where several pairs are present off-duty birds gather in small parties near nesting area. Useless to attempt to find colony, let alone single nest, from bank and better to take boat. Sitting bird slips off without trace, but probably less prone than other grebes to cover eggs. On Continent often in association with terns and, especially, Black-headed Gulls, which was apparently the case at Lough Funshinagh and other Irish sites. Solitary pairs in thick cover may need careful observation, even after nest is found, to establish identity.

7 **LITTLE GREBE**
Tachybaptus ruficollis

Not scarce and generally distributed, though rarer in north-west Scotland and absent Pembroke and Shetland. Much more catholic than other grebes in its choice of breeding habitat, being found on all kinds of ponds, lochans (but not with rocky shores), meres, lakes, reservoirs, slow-running rivers and streams and waterlogged marshes, and quite often on lakes in urban parks. Cover similarly varies from reeds (often in dense beds) to sedges, bulrushes, bogbean, bistort and flags through weeping branches to submerged hedges and bushes with little other protection.

Nest (♀♂) Soggy floating heap like other grebes (see Great Crested), but often made largely of dead leaves as well as water plants. In variety of cover, usually close to shore and even in narrow streams, but sometimes right out in open water anchored to submerged bush or hidden vegetation. Social or solitary. Eggs 4 to 6 (1 to 10) chalky white becoming stained buff and later dark sepia, reddish-brown or orange red where iron deposit (38 × 26 mm). Incubation (♀♂) from first egg, 19 to 20 days. Fledging (♀♂) nidifugous, period unknown. Two, occasionally three broods.

Methods Cold search necessary more often than with other grebes. As Great Crested in many habitats, but in extensive reed beds and other dense vegetation birds are located only when they call and exhaustive search would be necessary to find all nests. Sitting bird covers eggs when leaving nest, usually so well that they cannot be seen at all.

8 **FULMAR**

Fulmarus glacialis

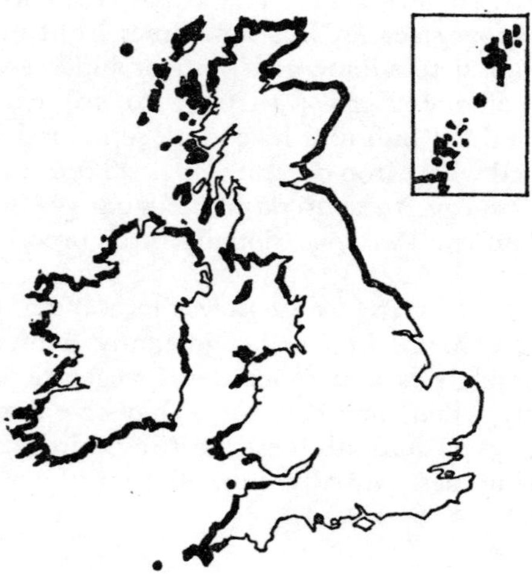

Numerous (probably over 100,000 occupied sites) at about 500 colonies on most suitable cliffs except south-east England; commonest St Kilda, Shetland, Orkney and other parts of north Scotland, scaling down southwards; prospects and occasionally nests in areas other than those shown on map. Typically sea cliffs with outcrops in terraces, exposed earth ledges and steep grassy or earthy slopes, but also on precipitous cliffs and in great expansion has taken to all sorts of littoral habitats: talus slopes and scree, steep banks, sand-dunes, beaches, ruins and houses; also on one or two crags several kilometres inland.

Nest (♀) None when on bare rock, but fairly deep scrape in earth or sand; frequently, in sites where surrounded by luxuriant vegetation and in more open places, sitting bird may arrange small stones around it, but any nest lining at best vestigial and probably accidental. Mainly on fairly broad ledges, and so in all sorts of hollows and even in recesses in banks and buildings; in isolated areas and especially small islands many nest sites often on low and practically flat ground. Highly colonial. Eggs 1 (1 to 2) white becoming marked with excreta (74 × 51 mm). Incubation (♀♂ in alternate spells mostly of 4 to 5 days) 41 to 57 days. Fledging (♀♂) nidicolous, about 6½ weeks. One brood and no repeat if egg lost.

Methods Chief difficulty is to know when species is really breeding, as new sites are prospected and occupied for average 4 to 5 years (J Fisher) before any eggs are laid. Census of occupied sites in late June recommended; late count of large nestlings also possible, but this only records successful breeding. Some large colonies almost impossible to count without unlimited time, as many sites hidden from above and below and even offshore. Monograph: Fisher (1952).

9 MANX SHEARWATER

Puffinus puffinus

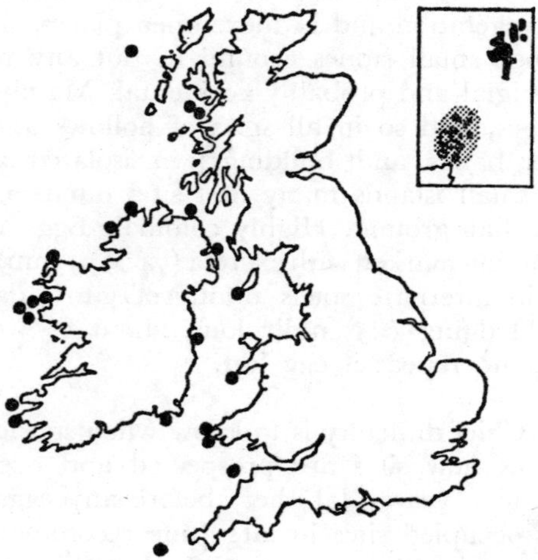

Numerous; local south-west England (notably Scilly), Wales (chiefly Pembroke and Caernarvon), Ireland (particularly Kerry, Galway and other parts of west coast, but also east coast), Isle of Man, and west Scotland north to Shetland. Turf-topped rocky islands and headlands, sometimes also scree slopes and sometimes to considerable heights above sea level (e.g. over 700 m on hill-tops of Rum).

Nest (♀♂) Chamber, usually lined with a few bits of dry grass, bracken or heather, at end of excavated burrow in turf-covered slope; sometimes rabbit hole adapted or even shared; length of burrow depends at times on presence of rocks and rabbit workings and may be as little as 45 to 60 cm, but normally 90 to 180 cm. Highly colonial and large colonies show honeycomb effect. Only one egg, dull white becoming stained (61 × 42 mm). Incubation (♀♂ in alternate spells of 3 to 5 days, but 1 to 16 days recorded) 52 to 54 days. Fledging (♀♂) nidicolous, 10½ weeks; young not fed for last 10 days. One brood and no repeat if egg lost.

Methods Nocturnal crowing and aerial evolutions often occur where there are no nests (even 5 to 6 km inland), so can be no more than general guide to possible areas. Nevertheless, small groups of nests and new sites can only be located in this way and then confirmed by seeing birds enter burrows or hearing crowing from them; a good torch and much patience needed. By day large colonies revealed by masses of burrows with smoothed entrances (late in season young deposit down at entrance on their nocturnal excursions). An extremely difficult species to census, but see *Skokholm Bird Observatory Report* for 1967 for advice on methods. Monograph: Lockley (1942).

10 **STORM PETREL**
Hydrobates pelagicus

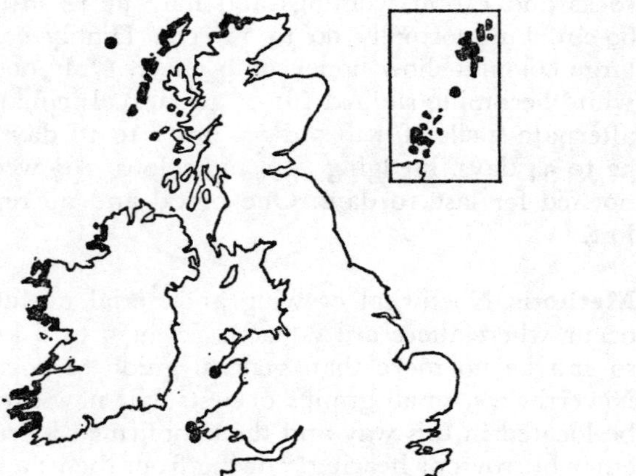

Numerous; local south-west England (especially Scilly), Wales (chiefly Pembroke), west Ireland (particularly Kerry, Galway, Mayo and Donegal) and west Scotland north to Shetland. Chiefly on bare and rocky oceanic islands, normally with substantial turf cap, but also occasionally on ecologically similar headlands.

Nest (♀♂?) Chamber or cavity in excavated burrow in peaty turf, like Leach's Petrel, but far more often in crack or crevice of rock, under boulder, among loose stones or in old wall or ruined building; in Scilly some nests on sandy floor under boulders close to high tide line (Whitaker); nests in turf usually quite well lined with dry grass, but in many other sites no material used. Loosely colonial. Only one egg (two if one addled from previous year) dull white, often zoned with reddish-brown spots at larger end (28 × 21 mm). Incubation (♀♂ in alternate spells of 2 to 3 days) 38 to 40 days. Fledging (♀♂) nidicolous, 8 to 9 weeks; young usually not fed for last 3 or 4 days. One brood and probably no repeat if egg lost.

Methods Area of colony can be located by musical creaking call used in courtship chases, and by glimpses of flying birds in torch beams, but much less noisy on wing than Leach's Petrel. More effective and audible at 50 to 100 m is characteristic purring (with associated *chikka* note) from nesting holes and this, as well as *peet-peet* of young, helps to pinpoint occupied sites. Checking by day by noting musty smell and by hearing occasional soft purring; Connor suggests that sitting bird will utter 'an uneasy murmuring' if boulder near likely hole is sharply tapped. Care, however, should be taken not to disturb sites unnecessarily and census-makers must usually be content with estimated order of abundance.

11 LEACH'S PETREL
Oceanodroma leucorhoa

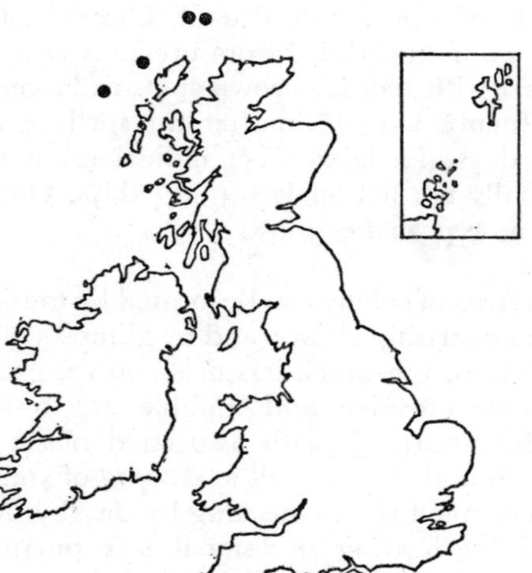

Not scarce (2,000+ pairs), but chiefly on four remote island groups off north-west Scotland (St Kilda, Flannans, Sula Sgeir and North Rona); perhaps also on Foula, Shetland, and possibly elsewhere in Hebrides and off western Ireland, though no recent records. Restricted to turfy and rocky oceanic islands, sometimes overlapping with Storm Petrels, though the colonies are distinct.

Nest Chamber of cavity excavated by ♂, then lined with grass or other locally obtained dry vegetation, but sometimes with little or no lining; under boulders, in scree or in ruins, like Storm Petrel, but more often in excavated burrow on open turf, in bank or under bracken; nests on North Rona in ruined village and in burrows (see J A Ainslie and R Atkinson, *BB* 30: 234–48, and M J H Robson, *Scottish Birds* 5: 130–3). Whitaker described St Kilda burrows as like rat holes 60 to 120 cm long in turf close to rocky outcrops, their entrances often masked by grass. Ainslie and Atkinson found length might be as great as 180 cm with nests of several different pairs in chambers at ends of lateral offshoots. Often, however, chamber is not right at end of burrow. Loosely colonial. Only one egg, dull white and usually with zone of fine reddish spots at larger end (33 × 24 mm). Incubation (♀♂ in alternate spells of about 4 days and up to 6) 41 to 42 days. Fledging (♀♂) nidicolous, 9 to 10 weeks. One brood, and probably no repeat if egg lost.

Methods Area of colony revealed at night by high-pitched staccato flight calls ending in a slurred trill, and by glimpses of flying birds in torch beams. Occupied sites can then be located by hearing these calls and continuous crooning (distinct from purring of Storm Petrel) coming from burrows, as well as plaintive *peee-peee-peee* of young. Soft crooning can sometimes be heard by day when characteristic smell (though indistinguishable from that of Storm Petrel) also helps to pinpoint sites.

12 **GANNET**
Sula bassana

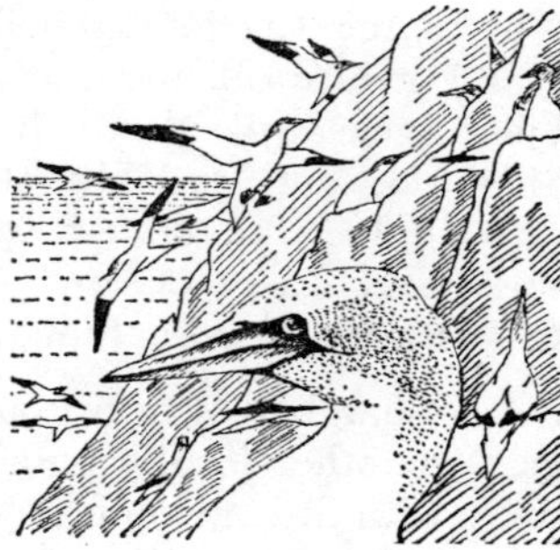

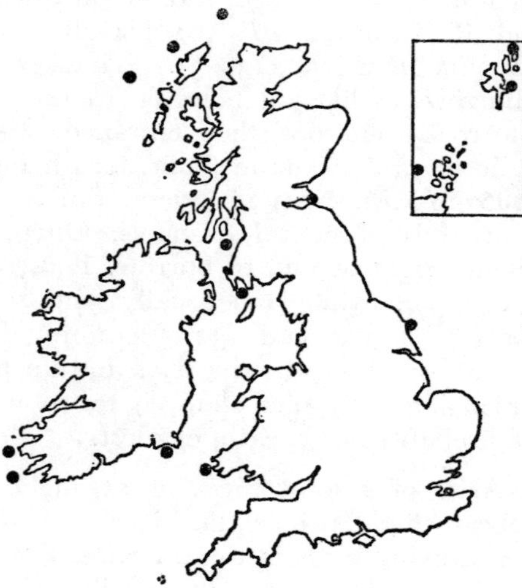

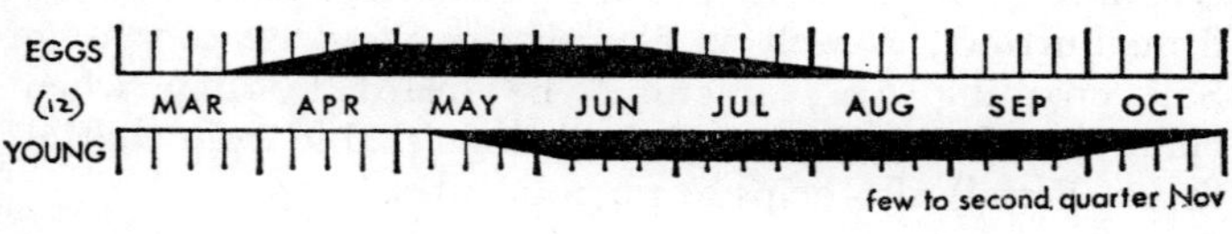

Fairly numerous (about 100,000 pairs) and increasing at 13 island colonies and one small mainland one: St Kilda, Flannans, Sula Sgeir, Noss, Hermaness, Sule Stack, Bass Rock, Ailsa Craig and Scar Rocks in Scotland; Great Saltee, Little Skellig and Bull Rock in Ireland; Grassholm in Wales; and Bempton Cliffs (Yorkshire) in England. Restricted to rocky and usually precipitous islands and headlands.

Nest (♀♂) Heap of seaweed, such as *Laminaria* and *Fucus* (*Handbook*), with addition of local vegetation and any oddments lying about or washed up; whole becomes very white as youngster develops. Typically on ledges and brackets of rock faces, but island colonies tend to spill over on to cliff-top slopes. Highly colonial and nests often so close together as to touch; the intruding observer may be within pecking radii of several sitting birds. Eggs 1 (1 to 2) bluish undershell patchily covered with chalky white deposit which becomes stained yellow and brown, even dark brown (78 × 49 mm). Incubation (♀♂) 43 to 45 days. Fledging (♀♂) nidicolous, 14 to 15 weeks. One brood.

Methods Presence of birds at any new site in breeding season should be carefully checked, as there have been isolated attempts to nest outside known colonies and species has colonised Channel Islands and Breton coast in last 30 years. Nest-finding hardly arises in known colonies, but problem of accurate counts best solved by photography.

13 **CORMORANT**
Phalacrocorax carbo

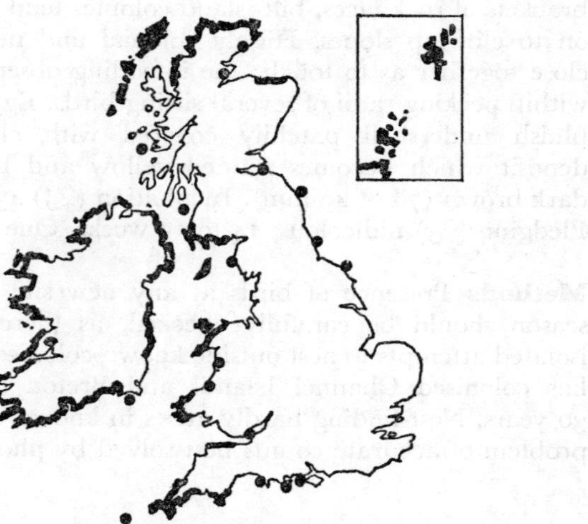

Not scarce; widely distributed on coasts of north and west, more local in east, with certain well-defined gaps from Peterhead to Forth, Flamborough to Wight, Dee to St Bees Head, and mainland Ayr to Ross; single inland colonies in Wigtown (Castle Loch) and Merioneth (Craig-yr-Aderyn), several in Ireland and recently in Kent. Usually sea cliffs or rocky islets; Irish colonies on islands in fresh water loughs are in trees, as in many places on the Continent.

Nest (♀♂) Flattish structure, usually mainly of seaweeds on coast, but at inland sites various materials, such as stalks of tree-mallow and other large herbs, sticks and heather, lined with rushes, straw, grass and oddments, while tree nests contain many more sticks; whole becomes profusely whitened by young. Normally on cliff-faces or rocky islets and stacks with many small ledges or shelves, tending therefore to be at top of cliff, but sometimes at bottom where shelving occurs below huge overhang; or inland in trees, often dead, at heights of 2 to 10 m. Highly colonial and nests often less than a metre apart. Eggs 3 to 4 (3 to 6) pale blue undershell patchily covered with chalky white deposit (66 × 41 mm). Incubation (♀♂) 27 to 29 days. Fledging (♀♂) nidicolous, about 7 weeks. Usually one brood, but perhaps occasionally two.

Methods Passage of birds to and fro a good guide and then search of likely cliff-faces with binoculars. Probably easiest seabird to census owing to conspicuous sites and limited size of colonies. But do not dismiss possibility of isolated nests, both coastal and inland, and in trees as well as rocks.

14 **SHAG**
Phalacrocorax aristotelis

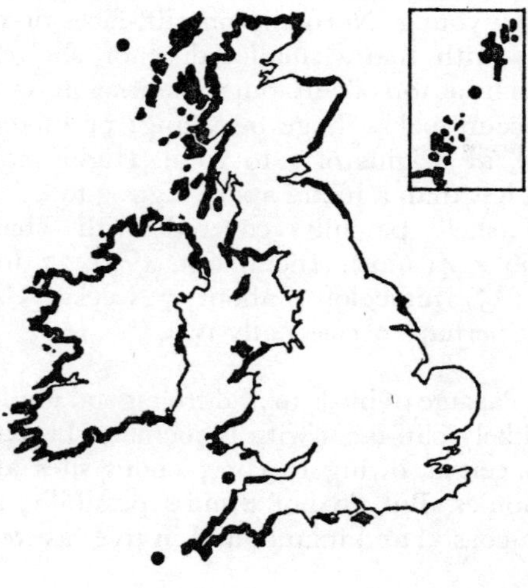

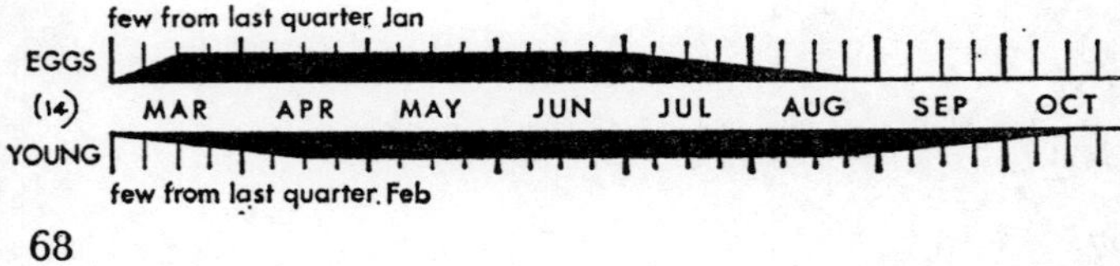

Fairly numerous; widely distributed on coasts of north and west, more local in east, with well-defined gaps from Farnes and Flamborough to Wight, Dee to Solway, and most of Down to Wexford; never breeding on fresh water. Recent marked increase, particularly in east Scotland and north-east England. Rocky coasts and islands, especially with sea caves, crevices and talus slopes.

Nest (♀♂) Flattish structure, mainly of seaweeds, but also heather and sticks used where available, with lining of dry grasses, leaves and all sorts of oddments; whole becomes white and foul during nestling period. Typically on small ledges and rock brackets inside or at entrance of sea caves, also overlapping with normal Cormorant sites on larger ledges and shelves; but a second type is well concealed under boulder or in crevice and this may be either at foot of sea cliff, as at Cló Mor (I D Pennie), or on top of it below secondary line of crags, as at Luinga, Treshnish. Colonial, but nests often more scattered than Cormorants'. Eggs 3 (1 to 6) pale blue undershell patchily covered with chalky white deposit (63 × 38 mm). Incubation (♀♂) 30 to 31 days. Fledging (♀♂) nidicolous, 7 to 8 weeks. Probably nearly always one brood.

Methods Passage of birds to and fro a useful guide to occupied sites, then search with binoculars. Complete census of cave or boulder nests hard to make, though sitting Shags utter continuous grunts when observer is near (e.g. on talus slopes) and entrances to boulder sites usually wide enough to see bird and nest. Shags use traditional perches on apparently suitable cliffs without ever nesting: they may breed eventually, but we know of one site used for over 40 years where they have not.

15 **GREY HERON**

Ardea cinerea

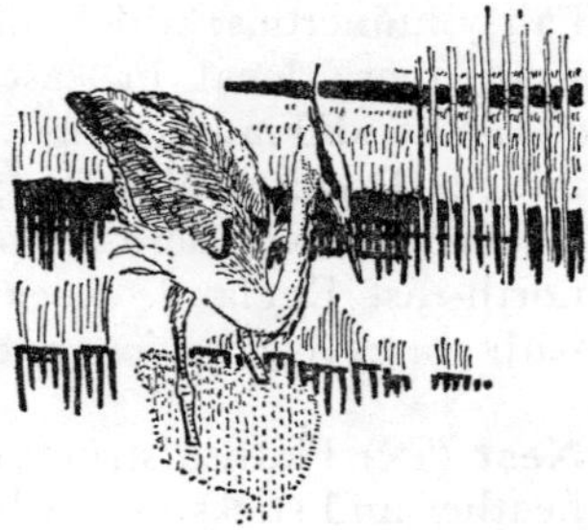

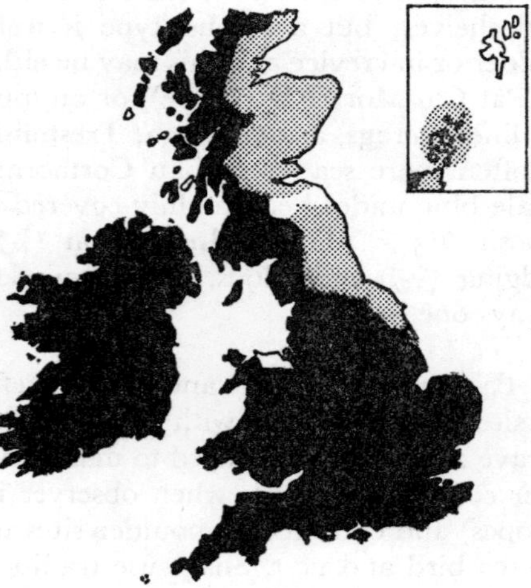

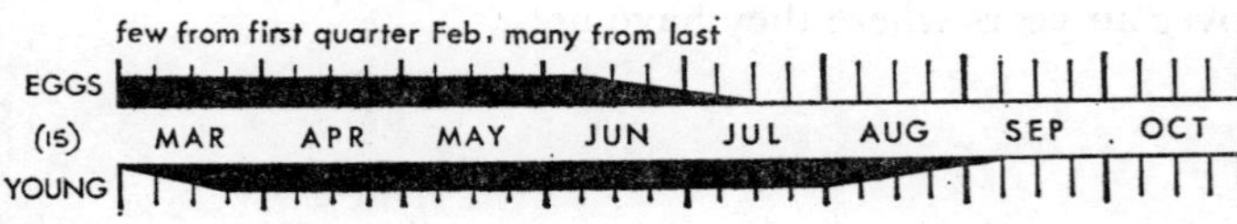

Not scarce; nesting in all counties except Shetland, five in south-east Scotland, Denbigh and Flint in Wales. Well-watered country of all types, including vicinity of lakes, ponds and marshes, valleys of large rivers, rocky (even cliff-bound) coasts and muddy shores backed by tree-clad hinterland; but some sites several kilometres from water.

Nest (♂ carries to ♀) Slightly built saucer of small branches with twigs, roots, dead bracken and grass as lining, but added to every year until very deep and bulky, providing nest-sites in bottom for both House and Tree Sparrows and even Jackdaws; nests in reed beds entirely of adjacent material; whole structure becomes whitened during nestling period. Situation variable from tops of tall trees (up to 25 m) down to ground level in reed beds, on small islets and exceptionally on beaches, among rocks or inside woods, as well as on ledges of sea cliffs; great variety of trees used but oaks and conifers favoured, while nests in north-west Scotland, Ireland and Wales may be in low scrub (birch, rowan, alder or sallow); by Hebridean lochs even in 'feral' currant bushes (J W Campbell), rhododendrons and long heather. Colonial, but pairs may nest singly. Eggs 3 to 5 (2 to 7) greenish-blue (60 × 43 mm). Incubation (♀♂) 25 days. Fledging (♀♂) nidicolous, 7 to 8 weeks. Usually one brood, but occasionally two.

Methods Vast majority of heronries in England and Wales now known as result of long-term population study, but still possible to find new ones and others that have escaped notice for years, while Scotland and Ireland have been less closely worked. In spite of colonial habits and large size, breeding herons surprisingly difficult to locate, especially in conifers and wooded glens, while single nests easily missed. Not easy to make accurate count of occupied nests. Best plan, particularly in conifers, is to make ground count and then check from vantage point above, preferably by climbing one or more well-placed trees. In difficult sites at least three counts should be made and mean taken. Advisable to make counts when majority of nests have young, owing to risk of predation on exposed eggs. Monograph: Lowe (1954).

16 NIGHT HERON
Nycticorax nycticorax

Nearest and most northerly natural colony is in Netherlands, but free-flying birds nest at Edinburgh Zoo Park (D F Dorward, *Scottish Naturalist* 69: 32–6; *BB* 60: 313) and pairs might spread. Builds flimsy nest of radiating twigs in bushes or trees near water, or occasionally in reeds. Eggs 3 to 4 (3 to 5) light blue-green (50 × 35 mm); from late April in southern Europe to June.

17 LITTLE BITTERN
Ixobrychus minutus

No published record of proven breeding, but probably nested sporadically in Norfolk and Suffolk in 19th century, in two counties of southern England in 1947 and again in East Anglia in recent years; pair also summered in Surrey in 1956. Nest of reeds and sedges, sometimes with a few twigs, in reed beds or low in trees growing in water or on bank (sometimes as high as 3 to 4 m): usually rather slight, but in reeds may have considerable foundation under water. Eggs 5 to 6 (4 to 10) white (35 × 26 mm); from early May onwards.

18 **BITTERN**
Botaurus stellaris

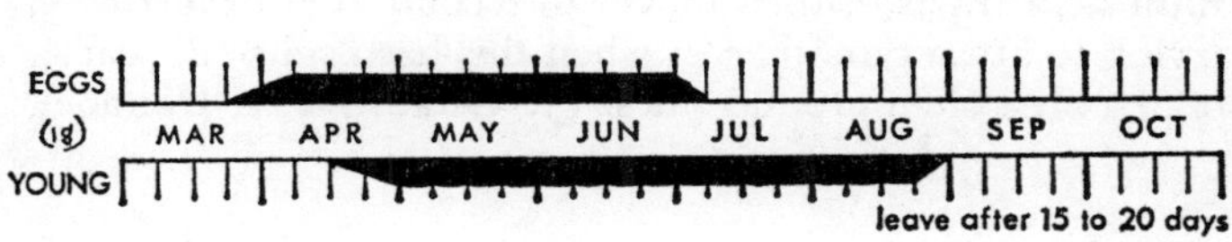

Very local and scarce (under 100 pairs); mainly in East Anglia with isolated pockets in Kent, Lancashire, and Anglesey; has bred in at least four other counties since 1940. Greatly diminished in 1963 winter, but now increasing and spreading again. Restricted to extensive reed beds, swamps and fens.

Nest (♀) Untidy and rather flat structure of reeds and sedges taken from immediate vicinity, with very shallow cup lined with finer vegetation or short pieces of reed; about 35 to 40 cm in diameter, size of some Coots' nests. Built among previous year's reeds or sedges to height of 15 to 20 cm above water, occasionally in drier areas, exceptionally on tussock in open water (*Handbook*). Eggs 4 to 6 (3 to 7) dull olive-brown, sometimes with fine brown speckles at larger end and characteristic striations down whole length (53 × 39 mm). Solitary. Incubation (♀) from first egg, 25 days. Fledging (♀) nidicolous for about 15 days, flying after about 8 weeks. One brood, but ♂ sometimes pairs with second ♀ after first has begun to incubate (*Handbook*).

Methods Listen for booming of ♂ (February to June) and watch for ♀ flying near nest-site. May feed several hundred metres from nest and fly straight back or by stages over periods up to half an hour. ♂ may also visit nest. When approximate position located, approach quietly and ♀ will crawl off and then fly at about 12 m range, after which final cold search can seldom be avoided; this should not be lightly undertaken and needs great care. In Poland, where numerous, ♂ often booms from one limited area until he attracts ♀, then moves to second area in territory, trying to attract another ♀; when this has occurred, search of first area often produces nest (J. Witkowski *per* Connor).

19 **WHITE STORK**
Ciconia ciconia

Nested on St Giles's Cathedral, Edinburgh, in 1416. Though decreasing in Europe and therefore even more unlikely to nest in Britain—indeed, the species is now only a rare vagrant – there was an influx in spring 1967 and a pair spent the rest of the year in Norfolk. Builds a bulky stick nest on building or in a tree. Eggs 3 to 5 (1 to 7) chalky white (73 × 52 mm); from April and early May.

20 **SPOONBILL**
Platalea leucorodia

Formerly nested in high trees in Norfolk and Suffolk to mid 17th century. Now only regular visitor to East Anglia and elsewhere, but breeds in Netherlands and, as individuals and apparent pairs sometimes stay for varying periods, nesting could take place again. Bulky nest 30 to 45 cm deep, of reeds or twigs in dense reed beds or bushes and trees. Eggs 4 (3 to 6) dull white smeared with rusty brown (67 × 45 mm); from April and early May.

21 **MALLARD**
Anas platyrhynchos

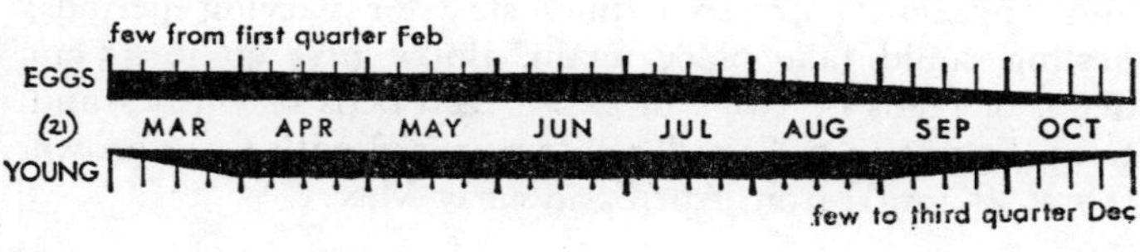

Numerous and generally distributed. Neighbourhood of all kinds of fresh water from marshes, bogs and pools to rivers and large lakes, in open country, woodland or towns; also sea lochs, estuaries, and coastal islands; and sometimes well away from any water.

Nest (♀) Hollow or scrape lined with dead leaves, grasses, rush stems and other local material and built up with down (brown with large indistinct light centres and light tips) and breast feathers (whitish buff with brown centres and single or double spot on either side). Not necessarily close to water and seldom actually on water's edge; in natural habitats shows typical duck preference for islands in lakes or lochs, but also nests on hillsides 2 km or more from nearest water. Usually in fairly thick cover of riparian vegetation, nettles, sedge and grass tussocks, rushes, brambles, gorse, bracken and heather or under bushes and hedgerows; other ground sites almost bare, as in thin growth of marram on dunes, while freak urban nests recorded in roof gardens of buildings, on artificial islets in small ponds and in other man-made cover. In some southern districts largely or almost exclusively in tops of pollard willows and also in holes of trees and old Crows' and other nests up to 10 m or higher. Quite often lays in same scrape as Pheasant. Not really social but nests may be only a metre or two apart and several hundred pairs nest on St Serf's Island, Loch Leven. Eggs 9 to 12 (7 to 16) greenish-grey or greyish-buff, but occasionally white or pale blue (57 × 41 mm). Incubation (♀) about 28 days. Fledging (normally ♀) nidifugous, about 7½ weeks. Only one brood in wild, but in sheltered conditions may rear two. Some late clutches laid by early maturing ♀♀ in their first autumn.

Methods Pairs can be located early in season and, where population dense, many nests can be found by searching likely habitats. Incubating ♀♀ sit very close, but may rise at 10 to 20 m range. Nevertheless, to find all nests in large marsh or moorland area would be extremely difficult.

22 **TEAL**

Anas crecca

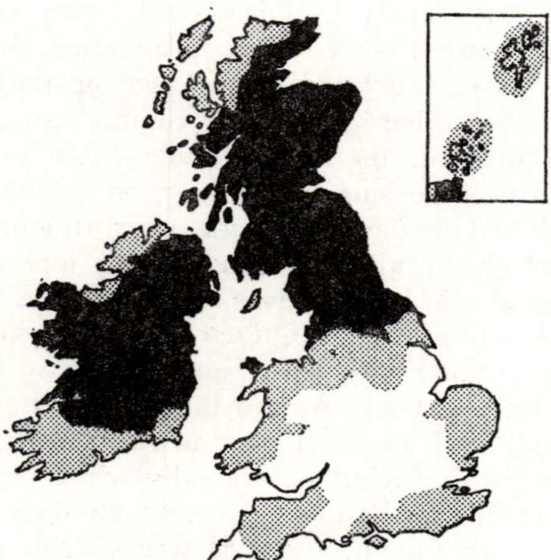

Not scarce and widely distributed, but more local and even sporadic in most parts of south and central England and south-east Wales. Characteristically in rushy moorland and peat mosses with small pools and lochans, streams and burns, but also often well away from water; elsewhere marshes, sewage farms, water meadows and lakes and islands with good cover.

Nest (♀) Lined hollow like other ducks (see Mallard) but with generally dark down (variable but usually with light centres and no white tips as Garganey) with distinctive breast feathers (whitish with diffuse buff side marks and tips which wash over most of feather). Up to 150 m from water which even then may be only narrow stream; fairly well hidden in heather and associated vegetation, rushes, bog myrtle, nettles, bracken and grass tussocks, usually on but occasionally just off ground, and normally in open but sometimes within edge of woodland; may be under hedge, bush or sapling conifer or in overgrown ditch. Typical site of this and other ducks nesting in peat mosses is mossy hummock through which lank heather grows and surrounded by sphagnum-filled runnels. Solitary. Eggs 8 to 10 (6 to 16) pale stone to light greenish-buff or even greenish (45 × 33 mm). Incubation (♀) 21 to 22 days. Fledging (normally ♀) nidifugous, up to 6 weeks. One brood.

Methods Where numerous, nests can be found by searching likely areas, but very hard to find where only pair or two present, owing to variable sites; though isolated ♂ is usually near sitting ♀, this is not of great assistance in extensive mosses and other large habitats. ♀ flushes generally at several metres' range, but she covers eggs when off nest or laying and it can then be found only by chance.

23 GARGANEY

Anas querquedula

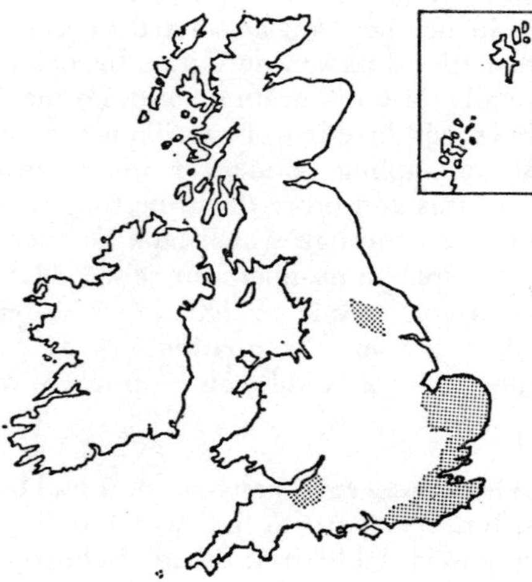

Very scarce and rather sporadic, breeding mainly in six counties of south-east England (Norfolk to Sussex), Yorkshire and Somerset, but also sporadically elsewhere and nested in 12 other counties 1953–65; has bred very occasionally in Scotland, Wales and Ireland. Neighbourhood of shallow fresh waters such as water meadows, fens, broads, rushy bogs, marshes (sometimes near sea) and sewage farms.

Nest (♀) Lined hollow like other ducks (see Mallard) but with distinctive down (usually dark brown but greyer brown in repeat clutches, with pale centres and prominent white tips) and breast feathers (whitish with golden-buff tips and large oval of dark brown in centre). Typically in medium to long coarse grass near water meadow or open pool, but usually on dry ground and sometimes at side of bank; distance from water variable, but often 20 to 50 m, though recorded in large rush tussock surrounded by water (*Handbook*); in small birch thicket with bog myrtle, heather and 'tangled grass' (Lewis). Solitary. Eggs 10 to 11 (7 to 14) warm creamy-buff without greenish tinge of Teal (45 × 33 mm). Incubation (♀) 21 to 23 days. Fledging (♀) nidifugous, 5 to 6 weeks. One brood.

Methods Pair should be located early in season and later, owing to open habitat, sometimes possible to watch ♀ back to nest from company of ♂ during laying period or after feeding. Presence of ♂ no guide once incubation has started as he usually swims and feeds far from nest; but ♀ when flushed usually flies to nearest water and may then be joined by him.

24 **GADWALL**

Anas strepera

Scarce (about 200 pairs); very local and patchy distribution largely as result of scattered introductions in England. But some 20 to 40 pairs of wild origin breed on Loch Leven, Kinross, and smaller numbers on nearby waters in Fife and Perth; has bred recently several other Scottish areas including Strathspey, Skye, Outer Hebrides and Orkney but nowhere else regularly. Similarly very small numbers have nested in four northern Irish counties since 1933 without becoming established. Main centre is East Anglia after introductions about 1850 and small numbers breed elsewhere, following introductions or escapes, particularly in Essex, Kent, Surrey, Somerset, Gloucester, Yorkshire and Scilly (Tresco). Usually secluded sheets of fresh water, slow-running rivers and adjacent marshes with small pools, especially with good cover of reeds and rank vegetation.

Nest (♀) Lined hollow like other ducks (see Mallard) but with distinctive down (dark with small light centres and greyish-white extreme tips) and breast feathers (whitish with buff lateral patches and dark central tips). Generally close to water and well hidden in rough tussocky grass, sedges, nettles, brambles or other vegetation. Sometimes nests socially on islands (e.g. St Serf's, Loch Leven). Eggs 8 to 12 (7 to 16) warm creamy buff (54 × 39 mm). Incubation (♀) 27 to 28 days. Fledging (♀) nidifugous, about 7 weeks. One brood.

Methods Pairs can be located on open water and pointer to position of nest obtained by prolonged watching until ♀ flies off to incubate. Zone of search then more limited than for many ducks, as nest seldom more than 15 to 20 m from water and often less. ♀ will usually flush at short range, but will sometimes sit very close and careful search then needed as she may be completely invisible from above.

25 **WIGEON**
Anas penelope

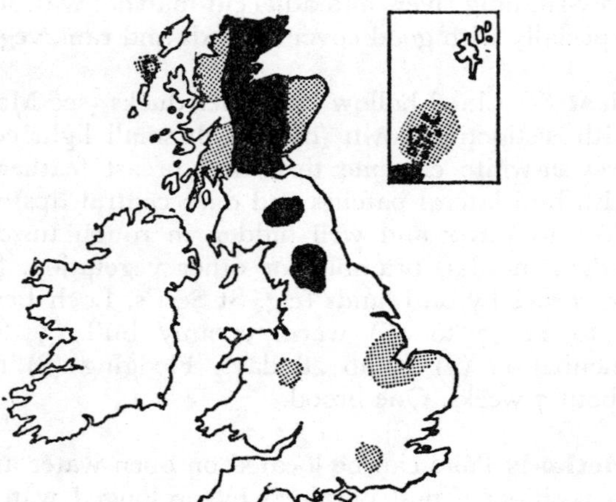

Scarce (about 350 pairs); fairly widespread in Scotland from Argyll, Stirling and Kinross (up to 40 pairs on Loch Leven) northwards; also south Scotland (has nested eight counties, though chiefly Selkirk) and north England south to north-west Yorkshire; sporadically elsewhere in England and Wales, where at least some records may involve escaped or injured birds, and twice in Ireland (Armagh and Antrim). Lochs, pools and rivers in moorland, marsh and wooded country, favouring islands and adjacent bracken-clad hillsides, but not tidal waters; farther south near marshland, pools and other fresh water with adjacent rough ground.

Nest (♀) Lined hollow like other ducks (see Mallard) but with characteristic down (dark with indistinct light centres and pale tips which are not as white as Garganey) and breast feathers (white, sometimes with buffish-grey in middle). On ground in heather, bracken, rushes or rough grass, at varying distances from water; may be close by, particularly when on island, or 150 m or more away on bracken-covered slopes above loch. Sometimes social, especially on St Serf's Island, Loch Leven. Eggs 7 to 8 (6 to 10) creamy-buff (54 × 38 mm). Incubation (♀) 24 to 28 days. Fledging (♀) nidifugous, 6 to 6½ weeks. One brood.

Methods When pairs located on open water, patient watching until ♀ flies off to incubate may reveal general position of nest. Presence of apparent pairs does not necessarily mean breeding, but one or two ♂♂ loafing close to land often indicate sitting ♀♀. If searching loch or pool, any island should be first choice and then surrounding slopes. ♀ flushes at short range like other species, but if leaving naturally covers eggs when off nest.

26 **PINTAIL**
Anas acuta

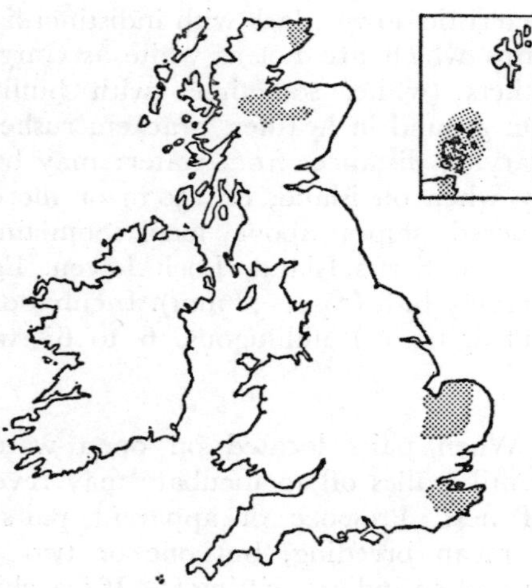

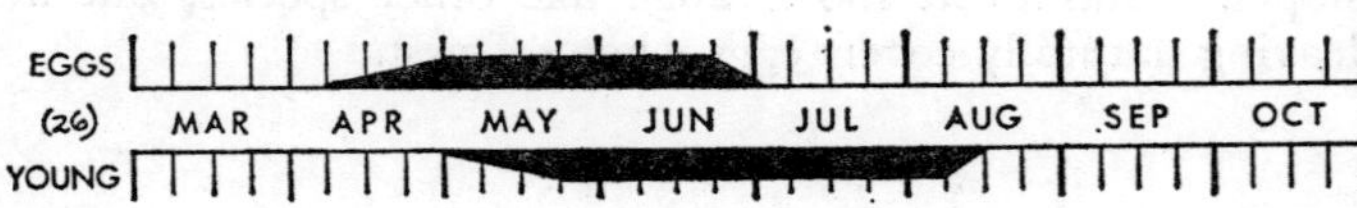

Scarce; curiously scattered and sporadic, breeding for some years in a locality, then disappearing; in Scotland has recently bred Orkney, Caithness, Inverness, Aberdeen and more irregularly elsewhere, e.g. Kinross (Loch Leven) and Kirkcudbright; in England breeds fairly consistently East Anglia and Kent, and has nested several other counties; in Ireland has bred sporadically in four northern and two central counties. May prefer moorland pools, lochs and lakes with drier shores, but nests in extensive marshland in East Anglia.

Nest (♀) Lined hollow like other ducks (see Mallard) with rather indeterminate down (brown with light centres) but more distinctive breast feathers (dusky with light tips and often cream diagonal bar on each side). Generally more exposed than other ducks and often on open ground with short grass or on dunes with scanty marram, but also in heather, rushes and long grass, while Whitaker described nests at one Scottish locality in 'soft, tussocky grass'; attracted to islets, but on mainland may be 50 to 200 m from water. May nest socially on islands. Eggs 7 to 9 (6 to 12) yellowish-green or yellowish-cream, but also occasionally bluish (54 × 37 mm). Incubation (♀) 23 to 24 days. Fledging (♀ with ♂ attending) nidifugous, 6 to 7 weeks. One brood.

Methods Location of pairs on open water, patient watching until ♀ flies off to incubate, and flushing her by searching, as for other species; but tendency for ♂ to remain in vicinity of nest and use of more exposed sites make this easier than some to find. Sitting ♀ may rise from nest at considerable distance (Whitaker).

27 **SHOVELER**
Anas clypeata

Not scarce; widespread, if somewhat local, throughout Britain and Ireland; numerous in Fens, Breckland and Broads but scarce or absent in west, central and north Scotland (has bred Shetland but not established), much of Wales and south-west England, being found in isolated pockets in most of these areas (e.g. several pairs at Chew Valley Lake, Somerset). More restricted to shallow, muddy, weedy sheets of fresh water, such as reed-fringed meres, pools in marshland, sewage farms and water-logged ground.

Nest (♀) Lined hollow like other ducks (see Mallard) with indeterminate down (dark brown or greyish-brown with light centres and variable white extreme tips confusable with Pintail and even Wigeon) but more distinctive breast feathers (almost white to golden buff with circular patch of brown in centre or larger feathers of rich golden buff with circular to oval patch of umber sometimes broken); sitting ♀ has habit of working grass around into canopy over nest (Whitaker). Generally much more open sites than other ducks, particularly in or among tufts of short grass on flat and dry meadows or grazed marshland, but sometimes also in thicker cover, such as long grass by hedges, clearings in reed beds and dry heather and gorse; seldom more than 40 m from water or wet ground and sometimes in tussock at water's edge. Solitary. Eggs 8 to 12 (7 to 14) buffish white sometimes with tinge of green (52 × 37 mm). Incubation (♀) 23 to 25 days. Fledging (♀ with ♂ sometimes attending) nidifugous, 6 to 6½ weeks. One brood.

Methods Location of pairs on open water, patient watching until ♀ flies off to incubate, and flushing her as for other species, but in some localities sitting ♀♀ can be picked out from a distance with binoculars as nests are so open. ♀ may rise up to 20 m away, or sit tight if eggs well incubated, and then fly round joined by ♂, whose presence indicates that observer is warm. Covers eggs when off nest.

28 **MANDARIN**
Aix galericulata

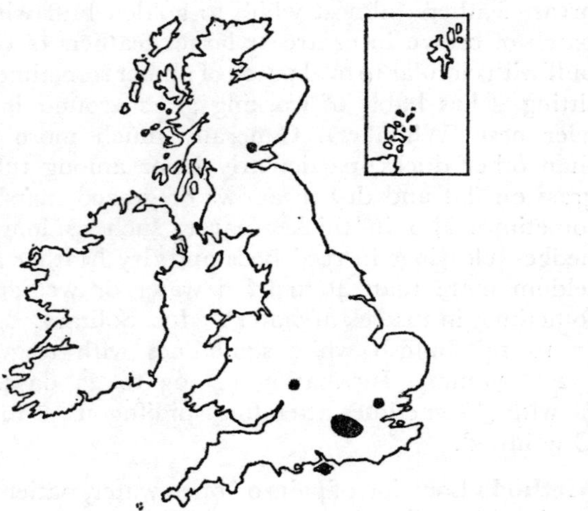

Scarce (probably over 250 pairs) and local, established from introduced stock from China in 20th century; main centre Surrey and east Berkshire, but a few East Anglia and one or two other small feral groups, including about twenty pairs on Tay at Perth. Generally small pools in open woodland, especially of oak and beech, with rhododendron shrub-layer.

Nest (♀) In hole of tree, hollow or scrape like other ducks (see Mallard), lined with vegetable material, particularly rotten wood, and white down. Usually about 6 to 7 m up, not necessarily in wood and often several hundred metres from water. Solitary. Eggs 9 to 12 (9 to 14) pale buff (51 × 37 mm). Incubation (♀) 28 to 30 days. Fledging (♀) nidifugous, about 6 weeks. One brood.

Methods Very difficult nest to find except by chance sighting of ♀ flying to hole in tree. Could no doubt be induced to use nestboxes at suitable heights like related Wood Duck *Aix sponsa*, which has been re-established in many parts of USA by these means, and which may now also be breeding ferally in England. Monograph: Savage (1952).

29 **RED-CRESTED POCHARD**

Netta rufina

The only British breeding records (Lincoln 1937, Essex 1958, Gloucester 1969–70) are considered to involve escapes from waterfowl collections – there is, for example, full-winged 'colony' on lake at St James's Park, London – but this species colonised Denmark in 1940 and Netherlands about 1942, spreading from north Germany, and has since established itself in these countries, so that genuine spread across North Sea is always possibility. Nest a hollow or scrape, always on ground, lined with reeds and other local material and characteristic down (brownish with small light centres) and breast feathers (greyish-white with dusky circle in centre and yellowish-white tips); deeply hidden in cover and in partial darkness at end of tunnel. Eggs 6 to 12 (6 to 21, high number product of two ♀♀) light stone to pale green (58 × 42 mm); from mid-May.

30 **SCAUP**

Aythya marila

Has bred sporadically north Scotland and Northern Isles since end 19th century and ♀ and brood were seen Lincoln in 1944 (*BB* 38: 192–3). Since 1945 has nested Orkney (one or two pairs Papa Westray 1954–9, North Ronaldsay 1965, Mainland 1969), Outer Hebrides (North Uist 1969), Wester Ross, Perth (three nests 1970: S Sloan Chesser) and perhaps elsewhere; infertile clutches laid Suffolk 1967 to 1971; for earlier records see *BB* 2: 85, 132, 209, 283, 416; 6: 368; 7: 147. Moorland lochs, pools and rivers.

Nest (♀) Lined hollow like other ducks (see Mallard, though nests of diving ducks noticeably larger than surface-feeders) but with distinctive down (sooty brown with inconspicuous white centres) and breast feathers (white). Sometimes open, sometimes well hidden by heather, blaeberry, grass and tall plants; usually on island, sometimes on shore of loch or river. Nests socially in main part of range. Eggs 7 to 11 (6 to 13, 19 to 22 probably product of two ♀♀) greenish to olive-grey (63 × 44 mm); in Scotland from early May into June. Incubation (♀) 27 to 28 days. Fledging (♀ sometimes joined by ♂) nidifugous, 5 to 6 weeks. One brood.

Methods Pairs can be located early in season and, as nests are usually on small islands, area of search probably limited. Once incubation has started, however, ♂ often goes some distance away, even to other waters, but at recent Perthshire nests the three ♂♂ were together on water only 400 m away. *Handbook* states that ♀ seldom leaves nest, but experience in Finland suggests that she may go down to water at least twice a day, usually walking each way, and if island is reasonably bare she can thus be watched back. Nests on mainland probably within 40 m of water.

31 **TUFTED DUCK**
Aythya fuligula

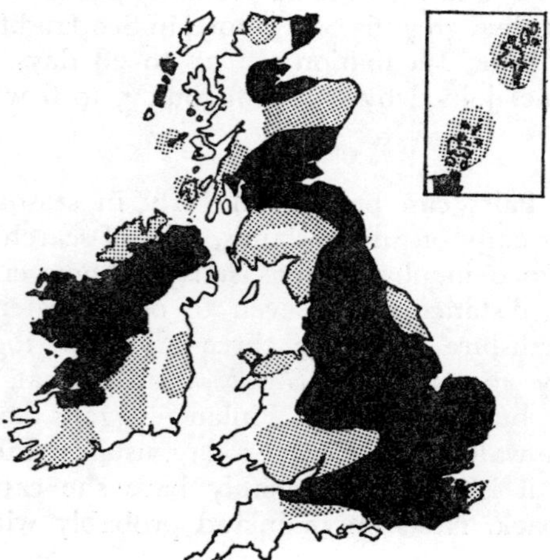

Not scarce and widely distributed Britain and Ireland, though absent or very scarce south-west England, parts of Wales, north-west Scotland (very local Shetland), Man and some counties of east and south-east Ireland; increasing, particularly in England. Flooded gravel pits, lakes and lochs, with or without islands, but usually with good cover, and sometimes by slow-flowing rivers or in very wet marshes; not usually on small pools and lochans, but has colonised lakes in urban parks where protected.

Nest (♀) Lined hollow like other ducks (see Mallard and Scaup) with characteristic down (sooty-brown with ill-defined greyish-white centres and some wholly greyish) and breast feathers (mainly off-white with vague greyish or brownish marks, but some mottled blackish and some sooty-brown with whitish tips); often dome or canopy effect of grasses overhead. Sometimes in tussock over water, when it has such a solid base of sedges or reeds that it looks like nest of Coot or Moorhen with down added; recorded in old Coot nests by Black and Whitaker. Usually, however, on shore very close to and seldom more than 10 m from water, hidden in riparian cover of all kinds; also under bush, but sometimes quite exposed, even on wall (*Handbook*). Often social, especially on islands. Eggs 7 to 12 (6 to 18, and even 20 to 28 when several ♀♀ lay in same nest) greenish-grey (58 × 41 mm). Incubation (♀) 23 to 27 days. Fledging (♀) nidifugous, about 6 weeks. One brood.

Methods Initial location by presence of birds, though this does not necessarily mean that any are nesting as they will not breed if conditions not just right. ♂♂ remain on water and, when number of visible ♀♀ drops, search of all thick cover within 10 m of edge often successful, though in large beds of *Glyceria maxima* nests may be farther from open water. Search needs to be intensive as ♀ will sit tight, particularly in later stages of incubation. ♂ occasionally flies over sitting ♀ 'as if calling her off to feed' (Lewis).

32 **POCHARD**

Aythya ferina

Scarce (250 to 300 pairs) and local, though widespread; most numerous Kent and East Anglia; otherwise chiefly eastern and central areas north to Orkney; increasing England but some apparent decrease Scotland; largely absent south-west England, Wales, west Scotland and Ireland, though breeds or has bred occasionally in various counties in these and other areas. Habitat more restricted than Tufted Duck and limited to large pools, lakes and slow-flowing rivers with thick but not necessarily broad zone of reeds, sedge tussocks, rushes, flags and other riparian vegetation or with islands similarly overgrown; sometimes in wet marshes with comparable cover.

Nest (♀) If on dry land, lined hollow like other ducks (see Mallard and Scaup) but usually rather deeper, with down variable in colour and amount (greyish-brown to dark brown with light centres, and sometimes so little that it is mixed with other nest material) and breast feathers (greyish-brown in middle with cinnamon-brown edges and, often, white tips); more frequently nest is in water-logged area on platform of sedges and other aquatic plants to keep it above water, when surprisingly substantial, resembling large Coot's nest. Usually close to or actually surrounded by water in tussock of sedges or rushes, sometimes with slide of dead plants down to water; nests on bank usually well hidden by surrounding reeds, rushes, flags or under bushes, notably gorse, up to 10 m from water. Generally solitary. Eggs 8 to 11 (6 to 15 and even 18) greenish-grey (61 × 44 mm). Incubation (♀) 24 to 26 days. Fledging (♀) nidifugous, 7 to 8 weeks. One brood.

Methods Initial location by presence of birds, though, like Tufted Duck, this does not necessarily mean they are nesting; they will not breed if plant growth is inadequate or if frequently disturbed. If breeding, narrow zone in which nest placed makes it easier to find by searching than those of most other ducks. Incubating ♀♀ sit tight.

33 GOLDENEYE

Bucephala clangula

Said to have bred Cheshire 1931–2 (*Bulletin British Oologists' Association* 59: 5–7). Despite nestboxes put up round Scottish lochs where birds stay late each spring, no other record until 1970, when two reports of suspected breeding and ♀ with 4 young seen on small loch in central Highlands. Nestboxes erected and in 1971, after agitated ♀ seen in summer, used nest with shells and two unhatched eggs found in box, brood presumed taken by predator or otherwise failed.

Nest (♀) In tree hole, of wood chips mixed with down (very pale grey, tinged bluer than Smew, with lighter centres) and white breast feathers. Usually by lake or river in tree, stump, old Black Woodpecker boring or nestbox; height from near ground level to 10 m or more (Cheshire nests were in rabbit burrows). Solitary. Eggs 6 to 15 (larger numbers probably from 2 ♀♀) bright bluish-green when fresh (59 × 43 mm); probably from mid-May in Scotland. Incubation (♀) 26 to 30 days. Fledging (♀) nidifugous, 8 to 8½ weeks. One brood.

Methods Initial location by presence of birds, but pairs sometimes summer in Scotland without breeding. When prospecting for nest-site ♀ perches freely on branches, but later flies directly in and out of hole. ♂ remains near incubating ♀, so hot search close to water may be successful where he is seen, as suitable sites likely to be limited.

34 LONG-TAILED DUCK

Clangula hyemalis

Eggs reported taken in Shetland at least three times in 19th century and in Orkney in 1911 and probably 1912 (see *Handbook* and Venables 1955). Nesting suspected Outer Hebrides 1969 and this species undoubtedly worth watching for in north Scotland and islands. Nest a hollow, always on ground, lined with little grass or heather and down (dark sooty-brown with marked light centres) and breast feathers (white or off-white with ash-brown tips). Eggs 6 to 8 (5 to 11) greenish-blue to olive-buff (54 × 38 mm); from late May and June.

35 VELVET SCOTER

Melanitta fusca

Reported to have bred several times in Scotland in 19th and early 20th centuries, but evidence unsatisfactory; probably nested Shetland 1945 (see *Handbook* and Venables 1955); clearly worth watching for in north Scotland and islands. Nest a hollow, always on ground, lined with grasses, leaves and twigs as well as down (dark brown with indistinct light centres, similar to Common Scoter) and breast feathers (grey to grey-brown, sometimes with whitish edges); in long grass, heather and other vegetation, under bush or at foot of small tree, particularly on marine islands but also on moorland and in lightly wooded areas near lakes and rivers. Eggs 5 to 8 (5 to 14) buff to creamy (71 × 48 mm); from late May and early June.

36 COMMON SCOTER
Melanitta nigra

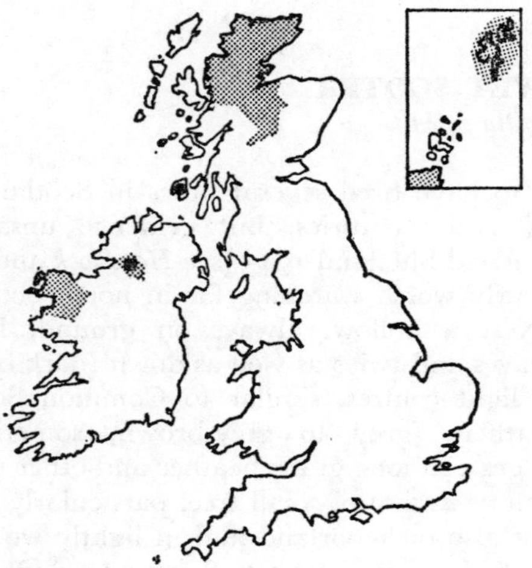

Scarce and restricted to Scotland (particularly Sutherland and Ross, south to north Perth and Islay) and north-west Ireland (two localities, totalling over 70 pairs, in Fermanagh and Mayo). Vicinity of small lochs in high moorland, but in Ireland on large loughs with both heathery and tree-clad islets.

Nest (♀) Hollow, always on ground, lined with grasses, heather sprays, moss and lichens together with down (dark brown with rather indistinct light centres) and breast feathers (grey, often with whitish tips). Usually in heather within 20 m of lake shore, often on headland, though sometimes up to 100 m from water; also on small islands with variety of vegetation, but these are not necessarily first choice. Often social, particularly on islands. Eggs 5 to 10 (5 to 12) creamy to buff (65 × 45 mm). Incubation (♀) 27 to 28 days. Fledging (♀) nidifugous, 6 to 7 weeks. One brood.

Methods Initial location of pairs before breeding starts. Nests on islets fairly easily found by searching and, though Scoters prefer surrounds of lakes, even then they tend to choose promontories; moreover, well-worn track through vegetation can be located at water's edge and followed to nest (Connor); ♀ may also be watched back. During later stages of incubation she may sit very tight and be missed. ♂ tends to leave vicinity after incubation begins.

37 **EIDER**

Somateria mollissima

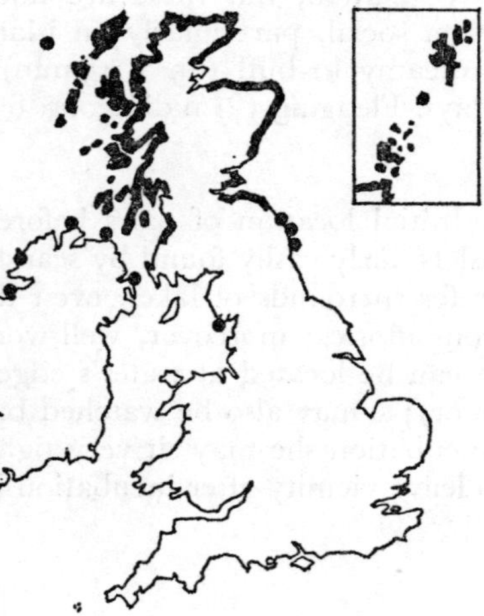

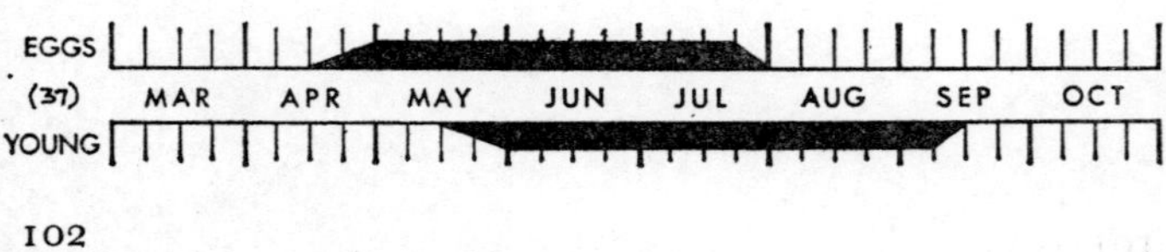

Not scarce and still increasing on islands and coasts of Scotland (practically whole coastline except Moray and neighbouring firths, and parts of Forth, Clyde and Solway), north England (only Northumberland and Walney, Lancashire) and north Ireland (Down, Antrim, Donegal and Sligo). Almost entirely marine, mainly on offshore islands and along coast varying from rocks (even cliff-bound) to sands and saltings; also by estuaries and sea lochs and, more rarely, in Shetland and Hebrides, on fresh-water lochs; up to 300 m on St Kilda, and now several kilometres inland in East Lothian (D Jenkins).

Nest (♀) Hollow like other ducks (see Mallard and Scaup) with foundation of grass and, particularly, seaweed, lined with abundant down (light grey-brown with indistinct light centres) and characteristic breast feathers (cinnamon-buff barred with black-brown and with variable lighter tips). Site varies greatly and perhaps regionally: in West Highlands nearly always well hidden in heather, bracken, brambles, woodrush, even among young trees, but in Shetland and along east coast may be very exposed on short thrift turf or marram grass on dunes; sometimes sheltered by or even recessed in rocks or old building; in sugar-beet in East Lothian (Jenkins). Social or even colonial, particularly on islands, but many solitary nests. Eggs 4 to 6 (3 to 10 and even up to 19) pale greenish-grey to buff, sometimes green and rarely deep blue (77 × 51 mm). Incubation (♀) 27 to 28 days. Fledging (any ♀) nidifugous, 8½ to 10½ weeks. One brood.

Methods Searching on islets usually successful where Eiders common. Isolated nests on shore can be hard to find in thick cover though general area sometimes located by watching ♀ back off water; presence of down on surrounding vegetation may be guide to exact position. ♂ tends to remain in vicinity while ♀ incubating, especially at isolated nests.

38 **RUDDY DUCK**

Oxyura jamaicensis

Very scarce and local, becoming established through escapes from North American stock; in recent years small numbers have begun to breed Somerset (Chew Valley Lake), Gloucester (Frampton) and Stafford (Belvide reservoir and Copmere); pair nested Hertford (Tring reservoirs) 1965; further spread and colonisation seems likely. Present habitat marshy surrounds of reservoirs and flooded gravel pits.

Nest (♀) In North America 'a bulky buoyant structure, often basket-like . . . Often canopying rushes are bent over by the bird' (Headstrom 1949) and not always lined with down (Chester A Reed). Usually in aquatic vegetation, sometimes floating and sometimes on solid ground; one British nest in rushes by reservoir (B D Bell). Solitary? Eggs 6 to 10 (5 to 20) greyish white to buffish white (62 × 46 mm); only dated British nest completed clutch end May. Incubation (♀) 20 to 25 days. Fledging (♀) nidifugous, 7 to 8 weeks. One brood.

Methods British breeding records to date have mostly involved young seen with ♀♀. Perhaps careful watching of pair on water, then searching where ♀ disappears would be most promising.

39 **RED-BREASTED MERGANSER**

Mergus serrator

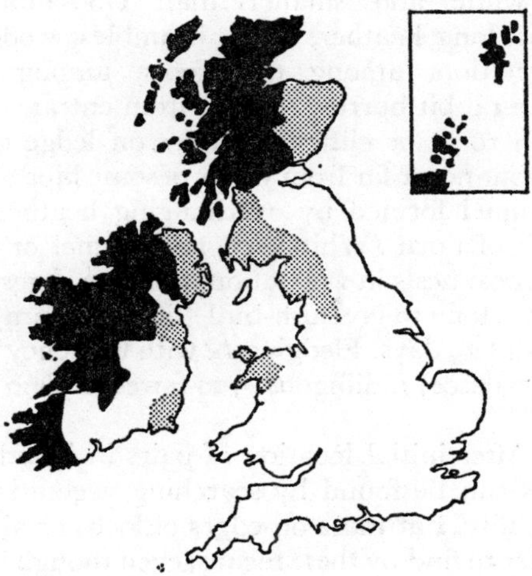

Not scarce, breeding north, west and south-west Scotland (including islands), most of Ireland (except parts of east and south), English Lake District and north-west Wales, having spread to last two areas since 1950; nested Lincoln in 1961. Commonest on sheltered sea lochs with numerous islets, but also on medium to large freshwater lochs and lakes and clear rivers in both bare and wooded country, often far inland and up to 300 m or higher.

Nest (♀) Hollow in humus or earth with little gathered material apart from some grass and a few leaves, but abundant down (darker than Goosander, grey with brown tinge and more distinct light centres and tips) and breast feathers (white and smaller than Goosander). Well-sheltered in long heather, grass, brambles, woodrush and other vegetation, among tree roots, among or under boulders, in rabbit burrow (not far from entrance), in crack or recess in rocks or cliff, sometimes on ledge or bank of little crag, but never far from water of some kind; in Orkney often in tunnel formed by overhanging heather and turf along bank of burn (Whitaker), and tunnel or runway a feature of most nests in vegetation. Solitary. Eggs 7 to 12 (7 to 17 or 19) stone to greenish-buff (66 × 45 mm). Incubation (♀) about 29 days. Fledging (♀ with tendency for several broods to coalesce) nidifugous, 5 to 6 weeks. One brood.

Methods After initial location of pairs in breeding areas, many nests can be found by searching vegetation caps of islets in vicinity, but those on edges of lochs or along rivers much harder to find by these means, even though likely zone is fairly narrow. Pair may fly over and ♀ descend to nest but ♂ often absent after incubation has started. Like other sawbills, ♀ spends quite long periods off nest (see Goosander), swimming quietly and feeding by herself; on loch, but not river, fairly easy to keep her under observation and watching back to general area often possible.

40 **GOOSANDER**
Mergus merganser

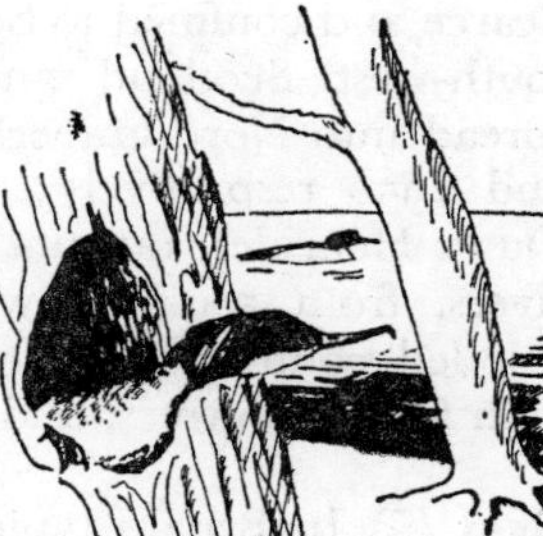

Scarce and confined to Scottish Highlands (not Caithness), south-west Scotland and Border counties whence has spread into Northumberland and Cumberland since 1941 and 1950 respectively; occasional records in Inner and Outer Hebrides, but not Northern Isles. Larger lochs and rivers, from 500 m down to near coast and usually in wooded country, but occasionally smaller lochs or areas with few or no trees, and sometimes by sea lochs.

Nest (♀) In Britain typically in hollow tree, with no nest material except bits of rotten wood lying in cavity and abundant down (pale grey, recalling Goldeneye) and breast feathers (white and larger than Goldeneye); often also in holes in rocks and banks to depths of one or more metres, among heather and tree roots, under boulders and rarely on cliff ledge (Connor); in Fenno-Scandia occasionally in nestboxes and ruined buildings. Pine and birch are favoured trees and holes often up to 7·5 m above ground; generally fairly near water but not possible to give precise range. Solitary. Eggs 7 to 13 (7 to 19) creamy-white (66 × 46 mm). Incubation (♀) 34 to 35 days. Fledging (♀) nidifugous, 5 to 6 weeks. One brood.

Methods Initial location of pairs in breeding areas, but searching for nests well above ground in wooded country very difficult. Like other sawbills, ♀ fortunately spends long periods off nest, keeping eggs warm by covering them in thick lining of down and debris, so that there is more opportunity to watch her back; but patience needed and not easy to keep ♀ under observation on tree-lined river, though usually possible on loch. ♂ may remain in general vicinity, but normally flocks with other ♂♂; so watch for ♀ swimming quietly alone until she returns to nest. When searching, wisps of down at entrance may reveal hole. Once found, site should be revisited in subsequent years as often used again and again.

41 **SHELDUCK**
Tadorna tadorna

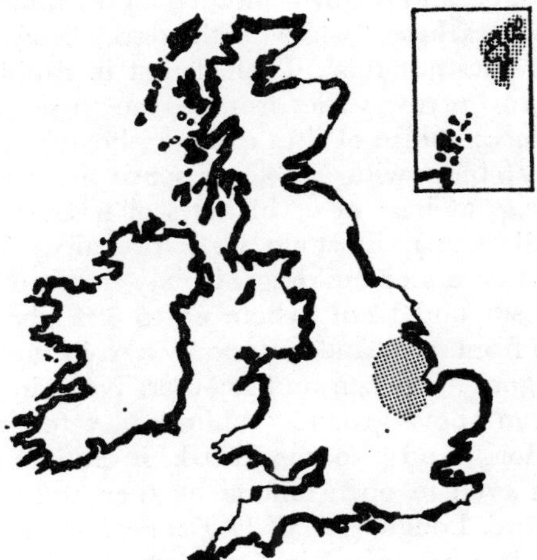

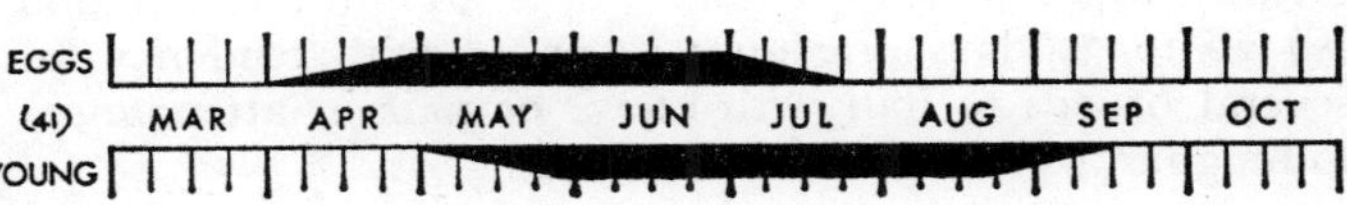

Fairly numerous, breeding in coastal areas and estuaries in almost every maritime county in Britain and Ireland (not certainly Berwick, Banff and Leitrim); also increasingly well inland in parts of England (Nottingham, Cambridge, Huntingdon). Typically on sandy shores and estuaries with dunes and warrens, but also some 3 km from water in woods and on commons, heaths and farmland where plenty of brambles, rabbit holes and old trees; less commonly on quite rocky highland coasts and sea lochs with islets and cairns of loose stones.

Nest (♀) In tunnel or hole with some vegetable material (e.g. marram grass) and abundant down (pale grey with brownish tinge and slightly mottled appearance in bulk) and breast feathers (white with dark brown or, less commonly, chestnut tips). Typical nest in rabbit or other subterranean burrow varies from 60 cm to several metres from entrance; choice of sites catholic, however, including 'almost any object with a hole or space in or beneath it' (J Hori), e.g. at base of or in holes of trees (particularly Suffolk and Kent), in stone walls or cairns and under boulders, in or under buildings, in hay or straw stacks (at least in Sussex and Kent, where up to 8 m above ground and 5 m in from face) and commonly also in tunnels under brambles, gorse, bracken and heather. Nests in trees may be up to 2 m above ground (Whitaker), 3 to 5 m in elms in Kent (Hori), and 3 to 7 m in oaks in Suffolk (Connor). Some nests even in open among heather and rushes, e.g. on Strangford Lough (*per* C D Deane). Usually solitary but up to six nests found in 'communes' in one haystack (Hori) and two to three in holes in one tree (Connor). Eggs 8 to 10 (3 to 17 or up to 50 by two or more ♀♀) creamy white with little gloss (66 × 48 mm). Incubation (♀) 26 to 31 days. Fledging (♀ or ♀♂ with tendency for several broods to join with one ♀ or pair in attendance) nidifugous, 6½ to 8 weeks. One brood.

Methods ♂ remains in general neighbourhood of nest and calls ♀ off once to six times a day to feed; afterwards he usually sees her back to nest and they often circle above site before ♀ drops to ground or flies straight into high sites. Nevertheless observer needs to be concealed and well-positioned to see general area. Nests in sand-dunes may sometimes be found by footmarks and by bits of down caught in entrance, and down also possible guide to other tunnel sites, but ♀ often visits a number of holes before and during egg-laying and down may then be left outside unused sites. Where pairs nest scattered over wide area inland in all sorts of sites, location must be largely matter of luck as ♀ may be very difficult to flush from hole or tunnel site by hot searching, and many nests have alternative exits or 'escape tunnels', but ♀♀ often hiss on nest (Hori), a useful indication when examining likely holes. Same site may be used in successive, even up to 30, years. See J Hori, *Ibis* 106: 333–60, and *Wildfowl* 20: 5–22.

42 **EGYPTIAN GOOSE**
Alopochen aegyptiacus

Scarce and local, established from stock introduced during and since 18th century; mainly in Norfolk (especially in Holkham Park and on Broads), but also elsewhere in East Anglia and some other parts of England. Lakes and pools in wooded and parkland areas.

Nest (♀) Conglomeration of grass and reeds, well lined with smoky-grey down. British breeding has attracted no attention, but in Africa nests in variety of sites, particularly in holes in trees and old nests of other birds, sometimes in burrows or holes in cliffs, less often on ground or in piles of flood debris. Eggs 5 to 10, yellowish-white (69 × 50 mm); no details of British season. Incubation (♀) 28 to 30 days. Fledging (♀♂) nidifugous, 10 to 14 weeks. One brood.

Methods Pair keeps close together when ♀ is off nest which should not be difficult to find by searching neighbourhood of frequented waters.

43 GREYLAG GOOSE
Anser anser

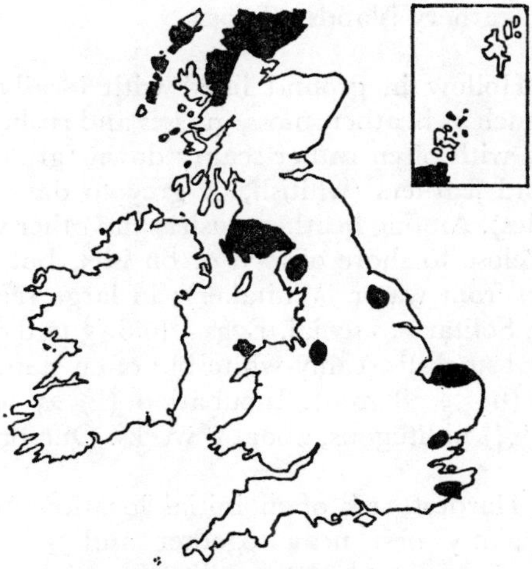

Hebridean and some mainland Scottish birds wild, rest feral

Indigenous population scarce (probably under 200 pairs) and very local, confined to Outer Hebrides and north Scotland (Caithness, Sutherland and Wester Ross). In some parts of north Scottish mainland, however, numbers reinforced by feral stocks also present in Inner Hebrides, four counties of south-west Scotland, Norfolk and Essex, and recently established also in Lake District, Yorkshire, Kent, Anglesey and elsewhere. Feral populations present in variety of habitats, ranging from Broads and other large sheets of open water to gravel pits, but natural breeding areas of indigenous birds include moorland (especially boggy 'flow ground' with small lochans), vicinity of large lochs and heathery islands off coast.

Nest (♀) Hollow in ground lined with locally available material (such as heather, moss, grasses and rushes) rimmed and mixed with often rather scanty down (grey with light centres) and feathers (whitish, or grey to dark grey with whitish sides). Among heather, rushes and other vegetation, and often close to shore of loch or on islet, but sometimes 40 to 50 m from water (Whitaker); in large reed beds on Continent. Solitary to social. Eggs 4 to 6 (3 to 8 or up to 15 among feral stocks) creamy-white but often stained yellowish-brown (85 × 58 mm). Incubation (♀) 27 to 28 days. Fledging (♀♂) nidifugous, about 8 weeks. One brood.

Methods Hardest task often initial location, but several pairs frequently nest near together and ♂♂ remain in general vicinity (though not standing by nest) while ♀♀ are incubating. ♀♀ flush at few metres' range and so nests fairly easy to find by searching once locality is known, but great care should be taken not to disturb indigenous population unnecessarily as they will easily desert eggs.

44 CANADA GOOSE
Branta canadensis

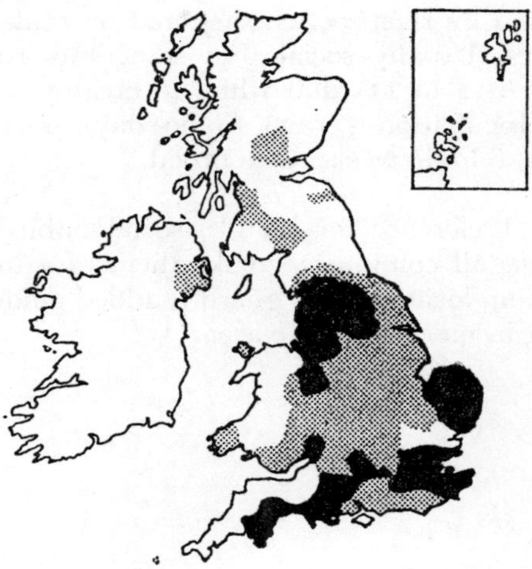

Not scarce and widely distributed in England with smaller numbers in Wales (the south and Anglesey), Scotland (north to Perth) and Northern Ireland (Antrim and Down) as result of introductions since 17th century; stronghold still Norfolk where as many as 1,500 to 2,000 birds in largest colony at Holkham. Vicinity of lakes, meres and flooded gravel pits, including surrounding marshes, grassland, parkland and even open woodland.

Nest (♀) Hollow in ground lined with any local materials (grass, reeds, dead leaves) as well as down (dark greyish-brown with light centres and tips) and feathers (whitish-grey to grey with square tips). Generally close to water, particularly on islands in lakes and gravel pits, but also in marshes and by rivers; often sheltered by rank vegetation and bushes. Usually social, but sometimes single pairs. Eggs 5 to 6 (2 to 11) dull white to creamy-white (86 × 58 mm). Incubation (♀) 28 to 30 days. Fledging (♀♂) nidifugous, 6 to 6½ weeks. One brood.

Methods Preference for islands, social habits and large size of nests all combine to make them easy to find once pair or group located. ♂ on guard is added guide in case of single nest in more extensive area.

45 **MUTE SWAN**

Cygnus olor

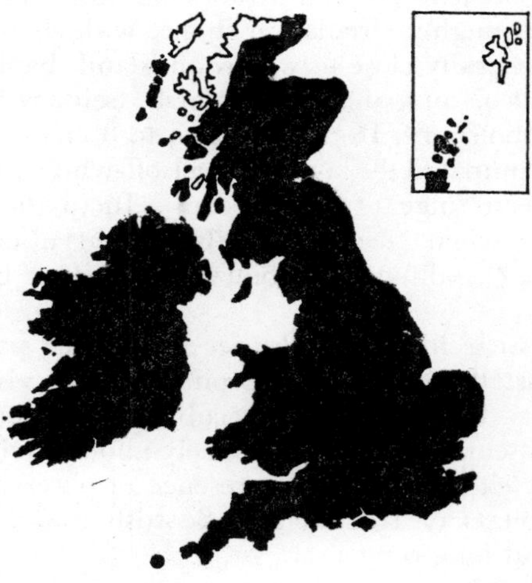

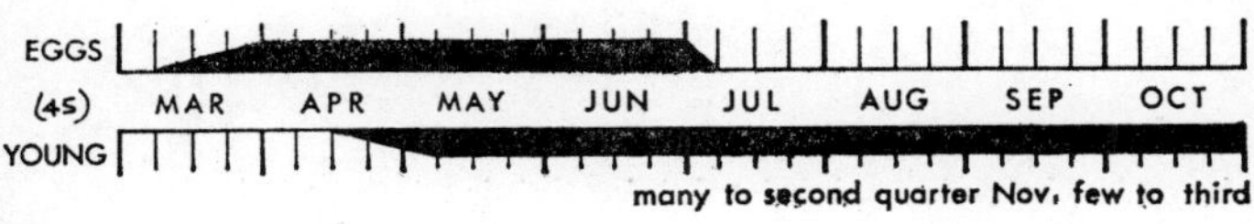

Not scarce and widely distributed in Britain (particularly southern England) and Ireland, but not Shetland and some parts north-west Scotland. Almost any type of fresh or salt water with subaqueous vegetation, ranging in size from small ponds and gravel pits to largest lakes, sea lochs, estuaries and other sheltered tidal waters, as well as along slow-moving rivers and on marshes in river valleys and near sea, in urban and rural settings, but less commonly on some wilder lochs and tarns.

Nest (♀ assisted by ♂) Huge pile of locally collected dead and live water plants (especially reeds, rushes and roots of waterweeds), as well as grasses, sticks and other vegetable material, odd feathers and little or no down, unlike ducks and geese; roughly circular in shape, with shallow cup in middle. Generally close to water, on island, bank or shore, in reed bed or on waterlogged marsh. Solitary to colonial (e.g. at Abbotsbury, Dorset). Eggs 3 to 8 (1 to 12 or more when two unmated ♀♀ lay together) off-white with greyish to blue-green tinge (115 × 74 mm). Incubation (mainly ♀, but also ♂ when ♀ feeding, chiefly at night) about 35 days. Fledging (♀♂) nidifugous, about 13 weeks. One brood.

Methods Searching scarcely necessary once pair located as this must be one of most prominent and visible of all British nests (though those on scrub-clad islets in lochs can be hard to see). ♂ swims aggressively about territory while ♀ normally sits unmoved by presence of observers, but in wilder habitats of Ireland and Scottish islands she may leave nest at long range.

46 **WHOOPER SWAN**
Cygnus cygnus

Has nested sporadically north Scotland but rarely successfully and since 1939 recorded only for Benbecula in 1947 (Nethersole-Thompson 1971), though reputed 'Scotland' in 1968 (BOU 1971) and there may be others which have not been published. Moorland lochs and tarns up to 300 m and possibly rivers or marshes.

Nest (♀ assisted by ♂) Large heap of mosses and aquatic plants partly solidified with mud and with some white down and feathers; roughly circular with variable depression in middle. Close to water on islet or shore, or on drier patch in marsh. Solitary. Eggs 3 to 5 (3 to 8) creamy-white but soon becoming stained (113 × 72 mm); probably from mid-May in Scotland. Incubation (♀) 35 to 42 days. Fledging (♀♂) nidifugous, about 9 weeks. One brood.

Methods Some former Scottish sites were by large lochs or quite close to habitations, but it might take a long time to locate an unknown pair on a small and unfrequented hill loch, though birds very vocal during courtship and their calls carry a long way (Simson).

47 **GOLDEN EAGLE**
Aquila chrysaetos

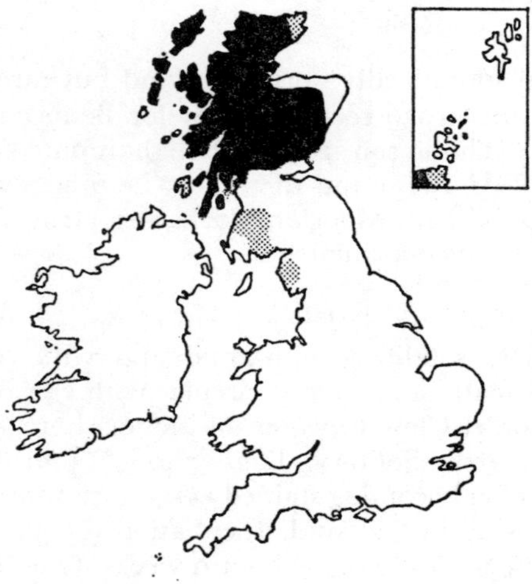

Scarce (250 to 300 pairs); breeds Scottish Highlands, Inner and Outer Hebrides, a few south-west Scotland; one pair English Lake District laid eggs 1969, reared young 1970–1; formerly resident England south to Derby, many parts Wales, and Ireland where last nested Mayo about 1912, then one pair Antrim 1953–60. Hill and mountain country, mainly between 300 and 700 m (locally up to 1,000 m) but rather lower in west, thus including fairly gentle slopes with natural pine forest and new conifer plantations, steep crags rising out of lochs and broken country or large areas of moorland, and mountains separated by wide glens, but seldom now sea cliffs.

Nest (♀♂) Bulky structure of sticks and branches (up to 4 cm thick), heather stems and bracken, sometimes mixed, sometimes almost entirely one material; lined and decorated to various thicknesses with grass, woodrush, *Vaccinium*, ferns and fresh greenery from conifers or broadleaves. On cliff ledge or in tree: ledge nests often boldy situated, scorning overhang protection, though still very difficult of access, but some on wooded crags and others in west Scotland low and easily reached; tree nests usually in Scots pines, sometimes near crags, but birch also recorded; new nests on ledges may be no more than ring of sticks with scanty lining, but with repeated use become huge agglomerations up to 3 m across and 1 to $1\frac{1}{2}$ m deep; long-established tree nests may be much deeper (one over 5 m deep). Solitary. Eggs 2 (1 to 3) dull white, freckled, spotted or blotched various shades of red-brown and underlying ashy: some very lightly marked, others so heavily that little white ground shows; often one egg paler than other (77 × 59 mm). Incubation (♀♂) from first egg, 43 to 45 days. Fledging (♀♂) nidicolous, 65 to 70 days (occasionally 80 or more); in about 80 per cent of nests elder kills younger eaglet. One brood. Repeat clutch exceptional if first is lost.

Methods Scottish eagles are resident and, though some move down from higher ground in winter, many remain in vicinity of eyries throughout year and, in good weather, indulge in aerial displays at any season. One bird (occasionally both) dives down 20 to 30 m, swoops up again, flaps wings a few times in level flight, then continues for dozen or more dives; in breeding season both will soar together, sometimes with mewing calls, and dive to much greater distances on half-closed wings before swooping up again; or ♂ will dive at ♀, who rolls over and presents claws; sometimes display ends by ♀ swooping to nest crag or wood, followed by ♂. Thus initial location not difficult and, though home range in Scotland varies from 44 to 72 sq km, each pair has favoured areas within it. Usually two or three alternative nests (occasionally up to ten) added to each year before final selection. Sometimes same nest used several consecutive years, but alternating more usual; successive generations inherit sites. Nests added to throughout season, exceptionally in November (Seton Gordon), so worth tracking bird carrying branch. Most traditional eyries unfortunately all too well known locally and many visible a long way off, but some difficult to find if tucked away in wooded glen. Incubating bird flies off conspicuously when nesting cliff approached from below. ♀ also normally leaves nest to feed, often in afternoon, but ♂ sometimes brings food, chiefly early morning. For first 3 weeks after eggs hatch, ♀ stays by nest, often brooding, and ♂ sometimes broods; for next 3 weeks she is usually perched or soaring nearby, but after that spends more time away, often taking major share in catching and bringing prey. Desertion risk high during laying and incubation, and eyries should only be inspected at long range until eaglets visible. See Leslie H Brown and Adam Watson, *Ibis* 106: 78–100. Monograph: Gordon (1955).

48 **BUZZARD**
Buteo buteo

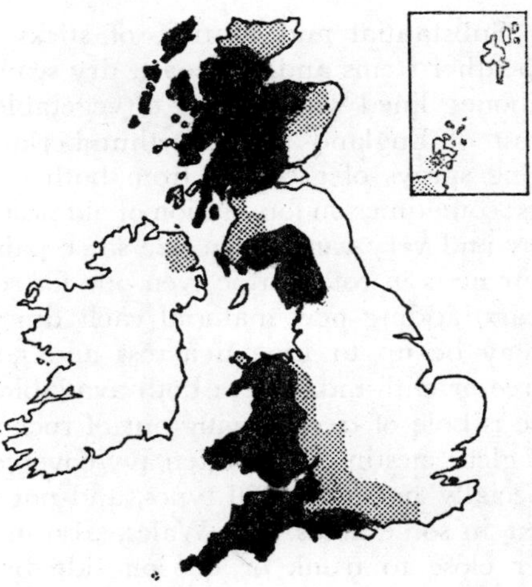

Not scarce; breeds widely western England (Lake District and west Yorkshire, Welsh border east to west Stafford, Worcester and Gloucester, south-west counties to west Sussex and probably Surrey), Wales and Scotland (Hebrides, Highlands, west Lowlands); absent Man but has bred Northern Ireland since 1950's (mainly Antrim); irregular rest of England (e.g. Northumberland, Derby, Kent) where widespread up to mid 19th century. In many areas confined to moorland, scrub-woods and both coastal and inland cliffs from sea level to 350 m in upland regions, but also well-wooded heaths, farmland and, on Continent, forest land with some open ground, even up to 3,000 m and more.

Nest (♀♂) Substantial and flattish, of sticks and small branches, heather stems and, on coast, dry seaweed, often also a few bones, lined wide variety of vegetable material, irregular rest of England (e.g. Northumberland, Derby, and adorning sprays of greenery from both conifers and broadleaves; sometimes on foundation of old nest of another bird or drey and very variable in size since pair often use three or four nests in rotation or even one for several consecutive years, adding new material each time: resulting structure may be up to 120 cm across and 50 cm deep. Either in tree or cliff and, where both available, favourite compromise is bole of tree growing out of rock face, often in wooded glen; nesting trees often ivy-covered in small woods, especially hangers of all types, and not necessarily at edge; but in some areas, e.g. Wales, also in hedgerow trees, either close to trunk or out on side branch with height range 5 to 20 m; cliff sites often within 30 m of top and in ivy if present (may use same site as Raven but usually less overhung); occasionally on ground or broken hillside sheltered by bushes. Solitary. Eggs 2 to 3 (1 to 6) dull white, sometimes tinged bluish, blotched and smeared with red-brown to chocolate and underlying lilac; markings few or heavy and evenly distributed or, more often, zoned or concentrated at big end (57 × 45 mm). Incubation (♀♂) from first or second egg, 33 to 35 days. Fledging (♀♂) nidicolous, 40 to 45, sometimes up to 50 days. One brood. Repeat clutch usual if first lost when fresh.

Methods Territory varies from 50 ha to 2 sq km or more, average perhaps 1¼ sq km, usually occupied February, after which birds easily located as they circle and call repeatedly, wings held more steeply above back than normal; if both in air together, usually face each other with ♂ slightly higher; they also dive on half-closed wings followed by upward swoops, even looping the loop. Once pair located, search before leaves open, though nest sometimes surprisingly hard to see in ivied tree or conifer. J H Owen considered right nest could be recognised from below with practice, though indications like feathers on rim, even bird flying off, sometimes misleading. Nor is view from above conclusive as several nests may be lined afresh. But incubating birds easily flushed. Nests with young very hard to find in large woods after leaves open, as seldom visited by parents. Once nest found, worth visiting in subsequent years as likely to be one of three or four used in rotation.

49 **SPARROWHAWK**

Accipiter nisus

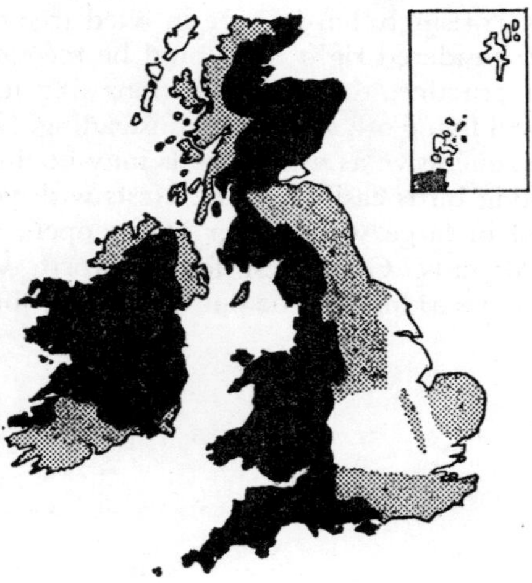

Not scarce; widespread western England, Wales, mainland Scotland and Ireland, absent Shetland, Orkney, Outer Hebrides, and, following marked decrease since 1955, very local eastern two-thirds England; undoubtedly commoner formerly, though long persecuted, and increased during 1939–45 war. Woodland of many kinds, particularly conifers and mixed, but also pure stands of broadleaves; cultivated areas with scattered woods, copses and shelter belts, also large remnant forests (e.g. Dean, Wyre) where woodland broken by open ground; western scrubwoods and where scrub degenerates to bushes, as on some Welsh hillsides, and in overgrown orchards and quarries (Ian Newton).

Nest (♀♂) Flat, untidy, loosely built platform of locally available twigs, especially larch or birch, broken off with beak; shallow central hollow sometimes lined bark, decayed wood or fine twigs; size variable and from ground can be confused with Woodpigeon; unlike compact corvid nests, larger twigs often laid all one way and trail down one side; small feathers catch on twigs and, as incubation proceeds, white down deposited all round rim and nearby twigs; normally new nest started each year, but old ones sometimes repaired or used as foundations and occasionally old nests of crows, pigeons, birds of prey or squirrels form base. Most commonly in conifers, especially spruce, pine, larch, also frequently in oak or birch, sometimes in variety of other trees, e.g. apple in Somerset (Lewis), and bushes; usually close to main trunk, often supported by two or more branches of conifer whorl, but sometimes out on horizontal bough: height very variable from 1½ to 35 m, usually 6 to 15 m; often sited in glade, or quite near road or ride, but some in dense conifer stands; low nests in moorland and downland bushes and osier-beds. Solitary. Eggs 5 to 6 (3 to 7, up to 10 with 2 ♀♀) bluish-white to whitish or pale greenish, sometimes unmarked but generally blotched, spotted and streaked chocolate-brown, often zoned or concentrated at one end (40 × 32 mm). Incubation (almost entirely ♀) from second or third egg, occasionally later, 32 to 36 days, usually 35. Fledging (♀♂) nidicolous, 24 to 30 days, even 21, but usually 26 to 28. One brood. One, even two repeat clutches (Walpole-Bond).

Methods Spends much time among trees so easily overlooked, but breeding area, distinct from feeding range of ♂, which may be up to 3 km from nest (Newton), may be located by display flights March to May, even December to June, when one or both of pair, or even three or four birds, soar in wide circles with spread tails or fly to and fro with slow wing-beats: sometimes ♂ swoops repeatedly at ♀; performance ends by headlong plunge from height into nesting wood. ♂ tolerates strange ♀♀ within territory and bigamous matings occur. Building starts February or March and usually takes about 4 weeks, though nest finished except for lining may remain empty for some time. Built mostly early mornings, chiefly by ♀, though ♂ brings materials and sometimes adds them when ♀ not present. Similar rituals to Goshawk may apply. During incubation ♂ brings food to vicinity two or three times a day, calling *kew-kew-kew;* ♀ leaves nest to receive prey which she eats before returning. ♀ broods newly hatched young continuously for 4 to 5 days, and regularly up to 8 or 10 days, then remains on or near nest until young well-feathered at about 3 weeks. ♂ brings food to nest six or seven times daily at first, later 10 times or more. Nests fairly easy to find by searching, even in conifers, and feathers on edge good guide to use. Even with persecution, pairs return faithfully to same glade or strip of woodland, where several nests may persist at the same time. Sitting ♀ usually flushes quite readily, so silent approach essential; she then often flies round calling.

50 GOSHAWK
Accipiter gentilis

Very scarce (wild status uncertain); has bred recently six or more areas in Scotland, Wales and England, probably regularly in at least two, but not known how many are truly wild or birds liberated by or escaped from falconers (e.g. ♀ of pair nesting Shropshire 1951 certainly escaped); bred sporadically 19th century and apparently regularly before that; up to 3 pairs bred Sussex 1938 (perhaps as early as 1921) until 1951. Coniferous, mixed and broad-leaved (especially beech) woodland in lowlands and mountains, particularly adjacent to large clearings or open country, including cultivation.

Nest (♂♀) Large, rather flat-topped, usually built by birds themselves of sticks and twigs broken or bitten off tops of trees; shallow cup lined and ringed green conifer sprays, beech leaves or bark; often same nest used several years in succession, ♀ doing much of refurbishing; but ♂ does most building of new nest; sometimes old nest of Buzzard or other large predator taken over and added to. Perhaps most commonly in pine or beech, but wide variety of trees used, usually in fork close to main trunk, sometimes out on side branch, from 8 to 30 m (normally 12 to 20 m); nests on ground recorded. Eggs 3 to 4 (1 to 5) pale blue or dull white, generally plain but occasionally marked light reddish-brown; chalk-like covering sometimes conceals colour (57 × 44 mm); from early April to June. Incubation (largely ♀) from first, second or later egg, 36 to 38 days. Fledging (♀♂) nidicolous, about 45 days, but can take to branches from 35 days. One brood. Repeat clutch probable if first lost when fresh.

Methods Like Sparrowhawk spends much time among trees, so easily overlooked but at least from March to May (also in autumn) display flights may be seen, one or both birds soaring over breeding area with white undertail-coverts conspicuously fanned, or flying to and fro with slow, harrier-like wingbeats; less commonly series of steep dives and almost vertical upward swoops by ♂, sometimes ending by plunge from great height into nesting wood. Limits of territory ill-defined and alternative sites may be several kilometres apart. In early spring ♀ attracts ♂ to previous year's site by uttering harsh screams, though new nest not necessarily built anywhere near. Once started, pair roosts nearby with screaming duet from about 40 minutes before sunrise, ♀'s voice hoarser and deeper than ♂'s; period of building follows until about 10 a.m., ♀ often screaming from perch when ♂ brings sticks. Six or seven weeks may pass before nest complete and first egg laid; usually daily interruption when ♂ goes off to hunt. On return with prey, he screams, ♀ answers, then flies to meet him, often taking food in air. In afternoon pair remain near nest until ♂ hunts again, with same ritual on return. Once incubation started, ♀ more silent, but leaves nest to take prey from ♂; later sits tighter and ♂ leaves prey in fork or old nest nearby. He occasionally covers eggs during laying period and while ♀ feeds; otherwise, except when hunting, spends most of day perched near nest. Once young hatched, ♂ hunts much more while ♀ at first broods closely; when young 10 to 15 or 20 days old she watches them from perch, and regularly adds green sprays to nest. ♂ brings food 3 to 5 times a day, in low (below tree level) laboured flight. Once food deposited, ♀ utters choked screams until he leaves; prey plucked and beheaded before being brought to nest, at posts within 30 to 150 m radius. From about 16 days young start to chirrup in nest. After location during display period, listen and watch, particularly in early mornings, for clue to favoured vicinity; search should reveal bulky nest, sometimes with long tail of incubating ♀ projecting over edge.

51 **RED KITE**

Milvus milvus

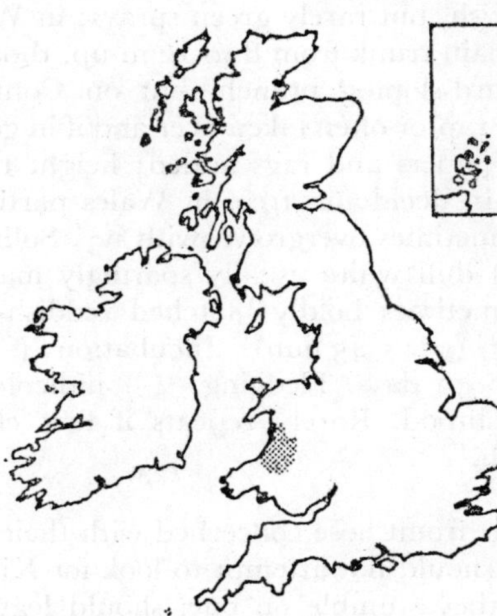

Very scarce; confined to central Wales where recorded numbers have fluctuated e.g. 4 to 6 pairs 1905–10, 10 to 12 pairs 1910–19, 3 to 7 pairs 1921–49, 15 pairs 1951–3 and since then slight increase to 20 to 25 pairs early 1970's; nested Devon 1913 (probably also 1947) and Cornwall 1920; formerly common in many parts of Britain. Mature woodland in Wales, often on steep sides of valleys, but on Continent usually in lowland areas or even parkland with scattered, generally deciduous trees; nests in pines in Corsica and formerly Scotland.

Nest (♀♂, 75 to 90 cm across) Nearly flat-topped, of sticks solidified with earth and lined rags, wool, paper and other rubbish, but rarely green sprays; in Wales often built close to main trunk from 8 to 12 m up, though sometimes on upward-sloping branch, but on Continent old nest of Crow or raptor often taken over and if in good repair no more than papers and rags added; height range 6 to 30 m. Usually in deciduous tree, in Wales particularly in slender oak, sometimes overgrown with ivy. Solitary. Eggs 2 to 3 (1 to 5) dull white usually sparingly marked with brown, but sometimes boldly blotched reddish-brown or purplish-brown (57 × 45 mm). Incubation (♀?♂) from first egg, 28 to 30 days. Fledging (♀♂) nidicolous, 45 to 54 days. One brood. Rarely repeats if first clutch lost, even when fresh.

Methods Apart fromt hose concerned with their conservation, observers should not attempt to look for Kite nests in Wales and, if they stumble on one, should leave vicinity quickly without trying to reach it, because Welsh population very prone to desert and in any case is still so small that disturbance must be kept to minimum. We include full details, not merely for completeness, but because odd pairs may be found nesting outside Wales and because we hope this book will also be used abroad. Initial location of Kites in breeding area not difficult as they spend much time in the air, either hunting or soaring and calling in display, which often takes place at great height and particularly in fine weather (it seems to be inhibited in cold and wet), birds crisscrossing in sky, sometimes hovering; then one or both may dive towards wood where nest is or will be, either flying straight into it or at last moment swooping up again. During building, twigs broken off trees either in flight or when perched, mostly within 70 m of nest, but up to 300 m away. Same territory may be used year after year, but this may vary from 250 m to 10 km across and alternative woods may be considerable distance apart. Shrill whinnying calls may be pointer that observer is near nest. During incubation ♀ may be watched leaving and returning and this becomes easier when young hatched for a fortnight, as both parents then bring food; visits less frequent when young well-grown, perhaps every hour or so.

52 **WHITE-TAILED EAGLE**
Haliaeetus albicilla

Well distributed 200 years ago in Scotland and Ireland (also bred Lake District, Man and probably Wight), but by late 19th century reduced to handful; last bred Ireland in Kerry and Mayo early 20th century, in Shetland about 1910, Scottish mainland about 1911 and Skye 1916; now rare vagrant with only four or five recorded during 1958–70 (none since 1962). Unlikely to recolonise as adults sedentary in Scandinavia and Iceland; attempted reintroduction of four immatures at Fair Isle 1968 was unsuccessful. Nests in Norway generally below 300 m and in Iceland restricted to coast: on cliffs, crags, rock columns, lava outcrops, rocky slopes, even level ground and inshore islets, also trees; same sites used on and off for many years (one in Iceland at least 160 years old) and result in conglomerations of birch, heather, juniper, even seaweed and driftwood, lined finer twigs, grass and moss, though nests in Iceland often little more than lined scrapes. Eggs 2 to 3 (1 to 4) chalky-white, sometimes becoming marked with yellow stains (76 × 59 mm); March to May.

53 **HONEY BUZZARD**
Pernis apivorus

Very scarce; breeds very locally southern and central England, at least occasionally to Welsh Border and almost certainly in Fife 1949; rather more widespread but still rare in 19th century when nesting recorded from south and west England north to Durham, Ross and Aberdeen. Mature woodland, especially beech but also other broad-leaves, sometimes mixed or occasionally even in pure conifers; usually where trees well spaced or broken up with glades, or in clumps and small woods in agricultural land.

Nest (♀♂, 60 to 80 cm wide and 20 to 25 cm deep) Of sticks, thickly lined and decorated with green sprays of beech or other trees, often on side branch or in fork; when built entirely by pair not particularly large for bird of prey, but frequently old nest of Crow, Buzzard or other species forms foundation, and whole structure much larger. Usually in beech, oak or other broadleaf, less commonly in spruce or pine, at wood edge or near clearing or ride, from 10 to 25 m. Solitary. Eggs 2 (1 to 3) white or pale buff very heavily freckled, smeared or blotched reddish-brown to deep purplish-red or even chocolate which may cover whole surface; rarely unmarked (50 × 41 mm). Incubation (♀♂) from first egg, 30 to 35 days. Fledging (♀♂) nidicolous, 40 to 44 days. One brood.

Methods Because it obtains almost all its food (nests of wasps and bees, other large insects, small mammals, snakes, lizards and frogs) on ground, Honey Buzzard spends much less time in air than many other raptors and is easily overlooked. Forages up to 3·5 km from nest, but may be located by distinctive display flights, often at considerable height, in which pair soars in undulating fashion with ♂ higher and repeatedly diving down and swooping up again or hovering and clapping wings above back. Territory may be about 10 sq km in extent, so much watching necessary to establish breeding area. Nest-building lasts 10 to 15 days and green sprays continue to be added throughout incubation, particularly in evening, but both birds remain unobtrusive, even when feeding young. Once general area established, search for likely nests best method, but as many are not very large this can be time-consuming, and undue disturbance should be avoided at all stages. Off-duty bird during incubation, or ♀ after young about week old, spends much time near nest, so worth looking where bird is put out of tree. When flushed, sitting bird flies off through trees silently, even with young. Old nests may be recognised by remains of honeycombs and wasps' nests and there is tendency to return to same vicinity (though not often same site) in successive years.

54 MARSH HARRIER

Circus aeruginosus

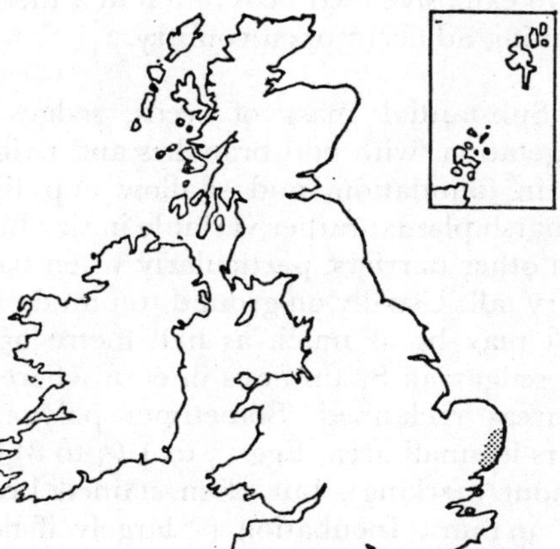

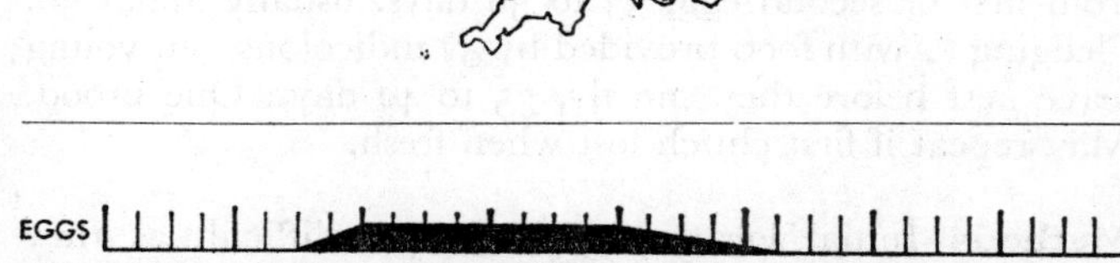

Very scarce; now probably Britain's rarest breeding raptor with less than five pairs in Suffolk and one other English county, though pairs have recently summered in one more area of England and in Scotland; in 18th century rather widespread in England and Ireland, but by mid-19th century reduced to handful which became extinct in England in 1890's and in Ireland by 1917; bred occasionally Norfolk from 1908 and re-established 1920's, in Suffolk in 1930's or early 1940's and in Dorset by 1951, as well as breeding sporadically in four or five other counties in England and one in Wales; by late 1950's probably nearly 20 pairs in all, then came slump with no breeding Norfolk since 1959 nor Suffolk apart from Minsmere since 1961. Restricted to extensive reed beds, often in a metre of water, though hunting adjacent open country.

Nest (♀) Substantial mass of reeds, sedges and other aquatic vegetation, with odd branches and twigs of willow and alder in foundation, and shallow cup lined grasses and finer marsh plants; rather variable in size but generally larger than other harriers, particularly when base in water or reeds very tall. Usually on ground (on mud or in shallow water), but may be as much as half metre up on clump of reeds or sedges; in Spain nests in corn where traditional breeding areas reclaimed. Sometimes polygamous; also several pairs in small area. Eggs 5 to 4 (3 to 8) dull bluish-white without markings, but often stained brown if nest wet (50 × 39 mm). Incubation (♀ largely if not entirely) from first or second egg, 33 to 38 days, usually about 36. Fledging (♀ with food provided by ♂) nidicolous, but young leave nest before they can fly, 35 to 40 days. One brood. May repeat if first clutch lost when fresh.

Methods Initial location of birds not difficult as they reveal presence when hunting, while soaring displays, with diving and somersaulting by ♂ and rolling over by ♀, conspicuous. But, except by chance, nest can only be found by watching unless possible area very small; in different parts of range territories vary from as little as 1 to 200 ha, in Britain probably at least 50 ha. ♀ builds nest but ♂ constructs supplementary platforms which may be some distance away; during incubation he adds material to nest; both birds pull up material with bill, but carry it in feet, so not difficult to see. ♂ obtains food for ♀, sometimes visiting her at nest but more often calling her off to take food by aerial pass; she may call loudly from nest before flying up. After taking food, she may return direct to nest or may eat it on perch or elsewhere among reeds. When marked down, she can be flushed at reasonably easy range of 5 to 15 m but is then likely to desert, particularly off fresh eggs, so better to wait until she is away from site. ♀ sometimes remains at nest for first 5 to 10 days after young hatch, particularly in wet or cold weather, and ♂ continues to call her off for food; but later she hunts as well. ♂ visits young in nest more often than other harriers and drops food for them when older, but does not apparently feed them. Both ♂ and ♀ may be very demonstrative when observer near nest (N W Orr). Young out of nest may be fed in reeds some distance away before they can fly.

55 **HEN HARRIER**

Circus cyaneus

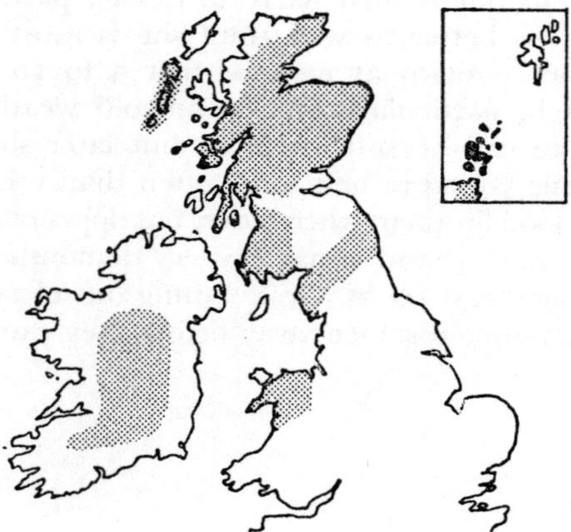

Scarce; breeds many parts Scotland, including Orkney (long main stronghold), Outer Hebrides, much of Highlands and south to Ayr, Galloway and other areas; has now spread to two English counties, one or two in Wales, and six more in Ireland: a dramatic increase since about 1940, though still not as widespread as in 19th century. Mainly moorland, often with areas of rush or sedge, but also in young conifers, particularly when overgrown and on damp ground; on Continent in wider variety of habitats, including reed and other marshes, fens and cornfields.

Nest (♀, ♂ brings material) Variable pad of reeds, sedges, grasses and some heather or twigs (particularly birch) with shallow cup lined finer materials; in dry areas may be only 30 to 40 cm across and 8 to 25 cm thick, in wetter sites as much as 60 to 90 cm across and 45 cm high. On ground on small open space flattened or cleared in low, quite thick vegetation, usually long heather or gorse mixed with reeds or rushes, but also young conifers up to 1½ or 2 m high; on Continent in reed beds, corn and other crops and swamps with straggly alder and willow. Very loosely social where numerous, sometimes polygamous with nests 200 to 1,500 m apart, otherwise solitary. Eggs 4 to 6 (3 to 12) bluish-white, usually unmarked but sometimes with spots and streaks of rusty red-brown (46 × 36 mm). Incubation (♀) from second (sometimes first) or subsequent egg (laid at intervals of 48 to 96 hours, even up to 8 days) 29 to 39 days, usually 29 to 30. Fledging (♀, food provided by ♂) nidicolous, but young crawl out of nest increasingly from about 15 days and fly at 35 to 42. One brood. Often repeats if first clutch lost when fresh.

Methods Location in open moorland even easier than other harriers; ♂♂ occupy territories up to 3 weeks before ♀♀ and begin characteristic display flights, climbing rapidly with body vertical and powerful wing-beats to 20 or 30 m, then diving within 2 or 3 m of ground before swooping up again and rolling or even somersaulting; this may be repeated 20, 30, even 70 times, and continues after ♀ arrives. Pair then spar, sometimes quite high, or both swoop and plunge, or ♂ dives at ♀ who rolls over and shows claws. Both bring material to nest from 30 to 150 m away, usually in feet, sometimes in bill. Open habitat with comparatively low cover makes this easiest harrier nest to find by searching (though territory may be 600 to 1,500 m across): white droppings at perch are pointer and ♀ flushes at easy range up to 40 m. Chivvying of crows and other raptors good indication of nest area. During incubation ♂ hunts and calls ♀ off to take food pass, usually dropping prey above her to catch in air, or she may snatch it from his feet with her talons, then eat it on ground before returning to nest; may also hunt for herself, then ♂ sometimes visits nest briefly. Routine continues for 10 to 20 days after hatch, though in bigamous pairings ♀ has to spend more time hunting. Watching ♀ return to nest with food for young, whether or not provided by ♂, usually reasonably easy, though she may pluck it elsewhere first. Same general area, but not site, occupied in successive years. During display and when nest threatened, ♂♀ utter rapid chatter, ♀'s noticeably higher-pitched than ♂'s and less on one note; this helps to narrow area of search (Connor, S Sloan Chesser).

56 MONTAGU'S HARRIER

Circus pygargus

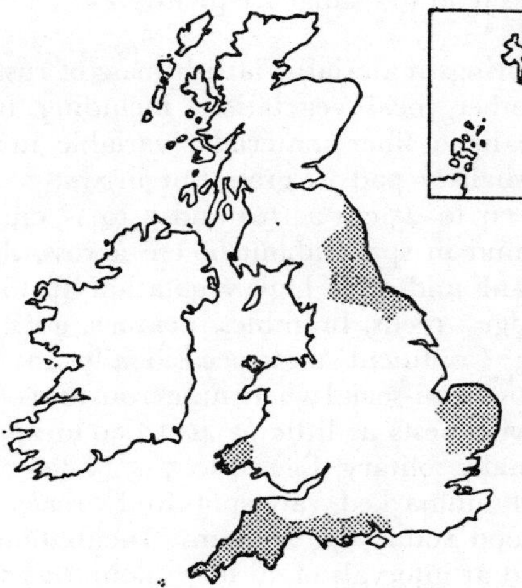

Very scarce (20 to 30 pairs at most); breeds in small and fluctuating numbers in up to a dozen widely separated English and Welsh counties, but annually in only three to six of these; has nested at least once in 20 counties since mid-1950's and in decade before that much more numerous, particularly in south-west England but even nesting as far north as Kirkcudbright and Perth; one or two pairs bred Ireland in at least some years since 1955; no real evidence that it was ever much commoner even in earlier centuries. Overlaps Marsh Harrier in reed beds and marshes, but more commonly on rough ground: moors, heaths and dunes, with especial preference for large areas of young conifers; many habitats, particularly the last, unstable, so breeding sites tend to change frequently.

Nest (♀, ♂ brings material) Flattish mass of rushes, sedges grasses or other local vegetation, including twigs, with shallow cup lined finer materials; variable in size, little more than shallow pad in grass but in wetter sites more substantial, 20 to 25 cm across and 5 to 15 cm deep. On ground or mud in space about 60 cm across, flattened or cleared in rank and often high vegetation up to 2 or even 3 m tall: sedges, reeds, brambles, heather, gorse or young conifers; on Continent and occasionally in Britain in growing crops. Semi-social where numerous and occasionally bigamous, with nests as little as 40 to 50 m apart, but in Britain normally solitary. Eggs 4 to 5 (3 to 10) pale bluish-white, usually unmarked, rare spots and streaks red-brown probably blood stains (42 × 33 m). Incubation (♀) from first egg (laid at intervals of 36 to 72 hours) 27 to 30 days, usually 28 to 29. Fledging (♀, with food provided by ♂) nidicolous, but young leave nest before they can fly, 32 to 42 days, usually 35 to 40. One brood. May repeat if first clutch lost when fresh.

Methods Initial location not difficult as, like other harriers, conspicuous when hunting and soaring. ♂♂ arrive first and have diving display like Hen Harrier, though less energetic: after period of soaring, bird climbs rapidly with body almost vertical, then plunges down with wings half-spread before swooping up and occasionally corkscrew-tilting or even somersaulting before diving again. When ♀ appears some days later, pair soar together for hours on end, ♂ usually uppermost and periodically diving at ♀, even buffeting her, while she turns over on back and shows claws. Many variations to this and, where species common, several ♂♂ may display to one ♀. ♂ brings materials to ♀ at nest, usually in feet. Low swoops continue over nests with incomplete clutches (Connor). In more open sites nest sometimes found by hot searching as ♀ flushes fairly close, but this is not practicable in overgrown areas and prolonged watching normally preferable. Chivvying of crows and other raptors good indication of nest area. During incubation ♂ hardly visits nest, but five or six times a day brings food which ♀ flies up to take in air, either foot to foot or by catching after ♂ drops it; she may then return direct to nest with it or eat it some distance away, usually on ground; if she delays too long, ♂ may drive her back. Risk of desertion with fresh eggs, so best not to visit nest at this stage until ♀ away. She remains at nest for 15 to 20 days after hatch, while ♂ brings food and calls her off for aerial pass; she then returns quickly to nest and this is best time to find it. Later she hunts as well, coming back to shelter young from rain or sun. High-pitched calls uttered in display or near nest.

57 **OSPREY**
Pandion haliaetus

Very scarce; only Inverness, Perth and one or two other Scottish counties but slowly increasing through protection; bred more commonly Scotland 19th century but greatly persecuted and became extinct between 1908 and 1916; increase of summer records in early 1950's heralded first nest in 1954 or 1955; one or two known each year to 1966, then three in 1967, at least 4 in 1969, five in 1970 and six in 1971; additional birds summer without nesting. Usually near lochs or large rivers, particularly with islands, but some nests up to several kilometres from water.

Nest (♀♂) Cupped platform mainly of small branches and sticks often broken off trees in flight, but also incorporating local materials such as heather, grasses, reeds, seaweed, even bones and driftwood, lined finer grasses and moss; very variable in size according to age but often large. In Scotland

and Fenno-Scandia mainly in pines and spruces, particularly with dead branches near top, and usually in crown. Height 15 to 25 m, though sometimes as low as 8 m where no taller trees; former Scottish sites included ruined buildings on two rocky islets and in other parts of cosmopolitan range nests may be on cliff ledges, in bushes or on flat shingle and sand; artificial sites include pylons, oil derricks, telegraph poles and specially provided cartwheels on stakes. Generally solitary in Europe, though two nests recorded as close as 400 m, but in Red Sea area as near as 60 m, and loosely colonial in America, as many as 30 pairs nesting in group of trees or sometimes on ground. Eggs 3 (2 to 4) white boldly blotched chocolate or red-brown and underlying grey (62 × 46 mm). Incubation (♀♂) from first or second egg, 32 to 38 days, usually about 35. Fledging (♀♂) nidicolous, 51 to 59 days, usually 52 or 53. One brood. No repeat if first clutch lost.

Methods Typical nest near top of conifer usually conspicuous and easily located if by loch. Even when well away from water, birds can be watched back: they carry sticks quite conspicuously when building or repairing nest, and stick being broken off tree gives audible crack. During incubation and first half fledging, ♂ catches all fish, regularly hunting same lochs, so may be followed back. ♀ leaves nest only for short periods to feed on fish brought by ♂ or to fetch more sticks, and change-over often accompanied by presentation of fish or stick. ♂ also has characteristic display near nest, flapping wings in exaggerated manner with body surprisingly upright and legs dangling, often carrying fish or stick, and calling repeatedly; but other soaring and plunging displays, though conspicuous, may take place some distance from nest and are even indulged in by non-breeding pairs. Same eyrie may be used for many years. See Brown and Waterston (1962).

58 **HOBBY**

Falco subbuteo

Very scarce (just under 100 pairs); chiefly southern England with three-quarters of population in Hampshire, Sussex, Surrey, Wiltshire, Dorset and Berkshire; one or two pairs breed fairly frequently Devon, Gloucester, Hereford, Oxford, Buckingham, Kent, more irregularly ten or twelve other counties from Huntingdon and Bedford west to Radnor and Cornwall (exceptionally to Glamorgan and Brecon) and north to Cheshire, Derby, York, Northumberland and once even Perth (1887). Heaths, downs and other open country, including agricultural land with isolated clumps of, especially, pines, or old hedgerows with mature oaks and other broadleaves; also wood edges and, particularly on Continent, open woodland.

Nest Like other falcons builds no nest; lays in unoccupied nest (often one built earlier in same rather than in previous season) of Crow, less often Rook, Magpie, Sparrowhawk, Heron or even Jay, Woodpigeon or squirrel. Species of tree and height above ground controlled by available nests, but in southern counties large proportion of chosen sites in Scots pines, the dominant tree on heathland, while farther north majority in hedgerow oaks, but also elms, beeches, birches, larches, spruces and yews; where trees small may be as low as 4 m, but usually 8 to 20 m. Solitary. Eggs 3 (2 to 4) closely speckled all over with reddish-brown which quickly fades to yellowish-brown or pinkish-brown (42 × 33 mm). Incubation (♀♂) from second egg, 28 days. Fledging (♀♂) nidicolous, 28 to 32 days. One brood. Repeats fairly often if first clutch lost when fresh.

Methods Hobbies have precise breeding season in Britain and, although there are early and late nests, most pairs lay mid-June, hatch mid-July and fledge mid-August; thus date can give good clue to stage of breeding cycle. Hobbies catch most of their prey of small birds and large insects in air over open country and, as they settle in breeding areas from mid-May onwards and have pattern of varied aerobatic displays in which they soar, glide (either way up), dive, loop the loop and circle round at great speed, as well as ♂ passing food to ♀ in air, initial location not difficult. Once incubation has started, and particularly when feeding young, general position of nest can often be determined by direction of flight: thus IJF–L once saw Hobby fly in straight line across a Sussex road, returned a week later and found nest without difficulty on that line. Nest can also be located by watching ♂ bring food to incubating or brooding ♀ who may fly up to take it. More usually trees have to be searched for suitable Crow nests: often not difficult in conifers, but can be very hard work in deciduous trees; so good plan to mark down likely nests early in season before Hobbies have returned. Depending on stage of breeding and individual variation, sitting bird may leave nest when observer 50 to 100 m away, when he taps tree or (particularly when incubation well advanced or nest very high) not until he has climbed half way up to it; then bird drops off by swooping low and sometimes up and down again before climbing rapidly away, or occasionally floundering off and wobbling and zigzagging for first few metres (Walpole-Bond); then often stoops at any passing big bird. Usually very noisy with young, particularly well-grown ones, constantly uttering *kew-kew-kew-kew-kew-kew*.

59 **PEREGRINE**
Falco peregrinus

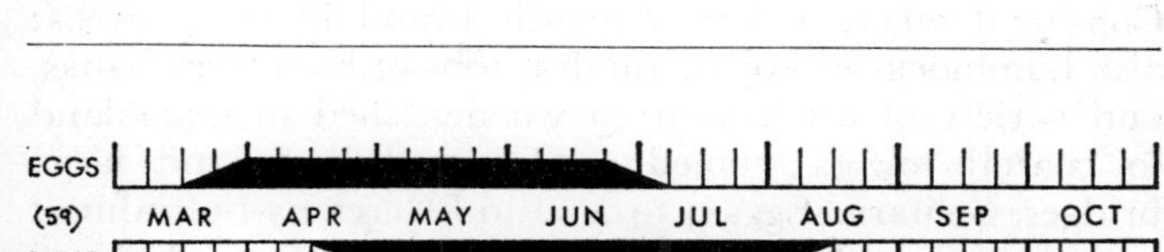

Scarce (350 to 400 sites occupied, some by single birds, and under 200 pairs rearing young); stronghold now Scottish Highlands and islands, including Shetland, Orkney, Outer Hebrides, with smaller numbers south-west Scotland, English Lake District, Irish coasts and mountains; many fewer Wales and south-west England; until 1955 much less scarce, being commoner in Scotland, more widespread north England, Wales and English south coast and more numerous Ireland; then came population crash attributed to effects of organochlorine pesticides and in 1963, probably lowest year, only some 300 sites occupied by birds or single birds out of normal total of 800 and probably under 100 pairs reared young; very gradual recovery since 1966, chiefly from north England northwards. Inland and coastal cliffs, moorland crags, sometimes rocky outcrops in more wooded country, rarely cities; on Continent also regularly in forests (chiefly coniferous) in both lowland and upland areas, in open bogs and treeless tundra, and not infrequently round man-made structures.

Nest Scrape in earth or debris; no material added, though feathers, pellets and prey remains accumulate round eggs and young. On broad ledge (usually in middle of widest part) or, less commonly, in recess of cliff, usually in upper third of face and often within 5 to 20 m of top (occasionally less) but rarely as low as 8 m from foot; sometimes in old cliff nests of Herring Gull, Buzzard, Raven or Crow; has nested on ground (Hampshire), on small offshire islets, and on buildings (at Llanelli and reputedly Salisbury Cathedral), but not in old tree nests of other birds, as on Continent where more frequently found in forest areas; also hummocks in bog or tundra, tops of high river banks, and variety of artefacts from wooden shed in marshland to coastal towers, ruined castles, cathedrals and large bridges. Solitary. Eggs 3 to 4 (2 to 6) creamy-buff almost entirely covered by orange-red, brown-red or even dark red markings; underlying ashy visible only on less thickly blotched eggs (52 × 41 mm). Incubation (♀♂) from second or third egg, 28 to 29 days. Fledging (♀♂) nidicolous, 5 to 6 weeks. One brood. Repeats if eggs lost in earlier stages of incubation.

Methods Unmated ♂ attracts ♀ to breeding cliff by flying from ledge to ledge, alighting momentarily on each, and calling with special creaky note like rusty hinge. Once paired, one or both together spend much time soaring, flying along with switchback flight, diving down with wings half-closed and swooping up again, or diving at each other. ♂ also passes food to ♀ in air. They often scream during displays and are usually very noisy towards intruders, keeping up chattering *kek-kek-kek-kek* with variations, especially when young in eyrie or recently fledged. Thus initial location not difficult. Early in incubation bird may leave eyrie readily, often at clapping from above or below, but is much more difficult to move off well-incubated eggs, especially in recessed site: 'Sometimes, forsooth, a hole-breeder utterly ignores repeated showers of rubble dropped past its haven and even, stranger still, repeated shots from a revolver' (Walpole-Bond). After being disturbed from eggs or young, usually flies back and forth along cliff, or high above, or makes circuit over surrounding sea or land, often diving at and occasionally even striking other birds, but sometimes perches on cliff. Normally returns to nest reasonably quickly if observer not too close, diving straight into site or first making several dives from height past it. Same cliff and sometimes ledge often used for many years and such traditional sites with green stains below may show up kilometres away; in newer sites actual nest ledge may be hard to see. Coastal nests often only accessible by rope, but many inland eyries can be inspected much more easily and it is often possible to get oblique downward view of nest. Large young often visible on ledge from considerable distance below.

60 **MERLIN**
Falco columbarius

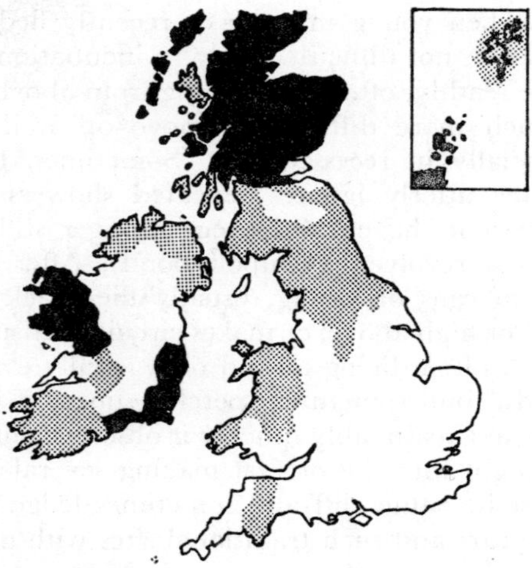

Scarce; widely distributed in upland areas over much of Scotland and northern England south to Derby, in Wales, Shropshire and south-west England (only irregularly in Cornwall) and many parts of Ireland; generally decreasing (except apparently some larger Scottish islands). Typically open moorland and fell country with heather, grass or bracken, but also bogs, rough ground above sea cliffs, coastal dunes and occasionally among trees at forest edge (much more commonly in Fenno-Scandia).

Nest Usually only scrape on bare or nearly bare patch among moderate to thick cover of heather, bracken, grass or marram, either on sloping ground or top of hillock or dune; sometimes a few bits of grass, heather or moss gathered in scrape, presumably by incubating bird: records of quite substantial nests accumulated like this. Sides of small valleys and re-entrants favoured for ground nests; also takes over disused nests of, particularly, Crow on cliffs or in trees at heights of 2 to 20 m (usually 5 to 12 m), though tree-nesting much more common elsewhere in range (e.g. Fenno-Scandia); in one very old Crow's nest scrape hollowed in centre and rimmed with odd stalks like tern's nest. Solitary. Eggs 4 to 5 (3 to 7) light buff almost completely obscured by thick, even stippling of purplish-brown, red-brown or chocolate (40 × 31 mm). Incubation (♀♂) from second, third or fourth egg, 28 to 32 days. Fledging (♀♂) nidicolous, 25 to 27 days. One brood. Repeat clutch likely if first lost when fresh.

Methods Where scarce, initial location hardest part; even when ♂ seen hunting, he can be very unobtrusive and difficult to follow. Does not hunt by spectacular stoops, but by dashing low after larks and pipits, grasping them in air. When ♂ returns to breeding area in spring, he makes distinctive short flights between perches, uttering high-pitched *kee-kee-kee-kee-kee* regularly; this behaviour ceases largely if not entirely after pairing; aerial displays few, though pair will circle high over nest-site and are very aggressive towards other birds of prey and Crows, also demonstrative when people in vicinity. Once breeding area located (same part of moor, though not necessarily same site, used year after year) birds help observer by whitewashing perches and feeding places, by flying off nest at easy range and returning readily when observer hides. ♂ calls ♀ off during incubation or when brooding small young to receive food, either on ground or by aerial pass; but 3 to 6 small birds a day probably enough to feed ♀ and 3 young, so this does not happen very often during watch. Tree nests can be found, and sometimes blundered on, by examining all Crows' nests in moorland area.

61 **KESTREL**
Falco tinnunculus

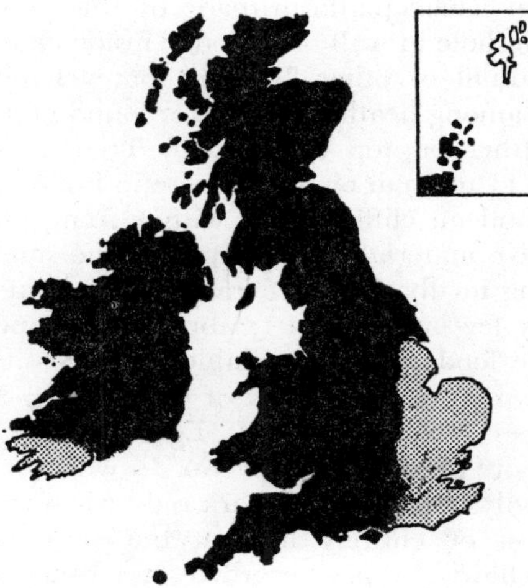

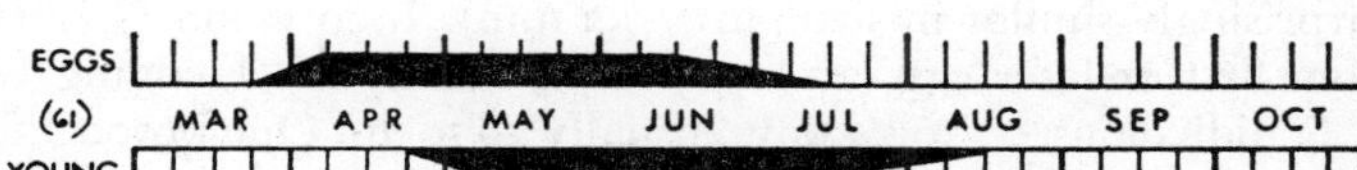

Fairly numerous; breeds in most of Britain and Ireland, but not Shetland since early 20th century; decline in east and south-east England from late 1950's but some recovery since 1964. Habitat very varied from parks and open woods or wood edges and farm land, to rocky hills, sea cliffs, moorland, reed beds and marshes; also traditionally round ruins and other old buildings and since about 1930 increasingly in urban areas, even central London.

Nest Essentially scrape in debris or earth, in old nest of Crow or Magpie (more occasionally Rook, Raven, Woodpigeon, Heron, Sparrowhawk, Buzzard or squirrel), in hollow tree, in depression where several big branches spread out or where platform made by thick ivy or other vegetation, in hole in wall or on ledge inside church tower, disused windmill or other building, or even on ground, particularly among heather; Whitaker found nest in tunnel in long heather on top of sea cliff. Tree nests vary in height from 1½ to 20 m or more, those in buildings seldom below 8 m and on cliffs usually within 10 m, often much less, of top. No material used but pellets and small feathers gather during incubation. Generally solitary but two nests may be only few metres apart; abroad in steppe or semi-desert where food readily available but nest-sites scarce, several pairs may use old nests of Crows (e.g. Rooks) in adjacent trees (*BB* 65: 256–8). Eggs 4 to 5 (3 to 7, while 8 or more probably due to two ♀♀) white or yellowish often so heavily blotched with dark red-brown that ground colour almost or entirely hidden, but pure white and generally yellowish types recorded and other variations include pale yellowish-brown blotches and underlying ashy marks; usually darker than Hobby, closer to Merlin and surprisingly similar in size (40 × 32 mm). Incubation (♀♂) from first or later egg, 27 to 29 days, usually 28. Fledging (♀♂) nidicolous, 27 to 34 days, usually 28 to 30. One brood; repeat laying if first clutch lost.

Methods Being generally more numerous and hovering conspicuously, Kestrel often easier to locate than other falcons, but because of catholic site-choice nest can be harder to find, particularly in extensive woodland or urban areas. Often returns annually to same territory, not necessarily to same site. Aerial displays in early spring indicate general area but, unless observer sees return to nest, hot searching of likely sites then best method, though whitewashing of nest hole or ledge, adjacent twigs and ground below, as well as of feeding places nearby, often good guide. Tree nesters often leave when trunk tapped, regardless of stage of incubation, but some sit much more tightly and are easily overlooked unless tree climbed. When flushed, sitting bird flies off with twisting snipe-like flight. Some then fly right away, others circle with winnowing action or call at intervals a rapid *kee-kee-kee* (though even with young not usually as vociferous as Hobby).

62 **RED GROUSE**
Lagopus lagopus

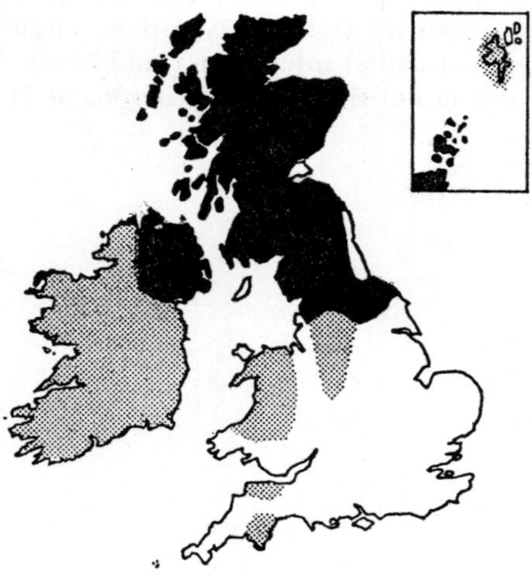

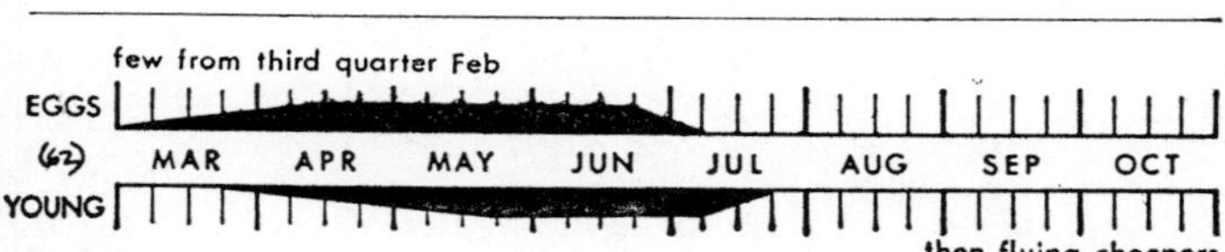

Numerous; widespread on moors of Britain and Ireland, including Orkney, Hebrides, England south to central Stafford and counties bordering Wales; introduced Shetland (Mainland), Exmoor and Dartmoor, and native stock reinforced by aliens or artificially reared birds in many areas (Fitter 1959). Associated everywhere with heather *Calluna* but spills over to moors and heaths dominated by grasses, rushes and crowberry *Empetrum*. Most numerous on drier moors, where heather burnt in rotation to provide cover and food, but also on bogs and mosses; from sea level to 700, even 1,000 m.

Nest (♀) Scrape on ground, sometimes lined grasses, moss, heather; feathers added during incubation. Typically sheltered by heather 30 to 45 cm high, but also in much longer growth, e.g. on mossy hummocks overgrown by long heather in bogs, and often in rushes and long grass; sometimes in short heather and blaeberry *Vaccinium*, or quite open in dead bracken and burnt heather (Whitaker). Solitary, but nests may be close together in areas of dense population. Eggs 6 to 11 (4 to 17) yellowish-white blotched all over with dark chocolate or red-brown which smears during incubation (46 × 32 mm), nest often covered during laying. Incubation (♀) 23 to 26 days. Fledging (♀ broods, ♂ guards) nidifugous, flying about 12 to 13 days, long before full-grown. One brood.

Methods Location by pairs early in season, as ♂♂ establish territories previous autumn. ♀♀ may make scrapes up to fortnight before laying (♂♂ also makes scrapes). ♂ remains near laying ♀. Incubation begins with last egg and ♀ leaves nest several times a day, normally without covering eggs, for periods of ½ to 1½ hours, probably according to weather and state of incubation. She walks off for several metres, then flies accompanied by ♂, who may display at her and remains close while she first drinks, then feeds.

Large droppings often excreted near drinking place; their appearance sure sign that nesting has begun (Black). ♀ flies back towards nest, but walks last few metres, unaccompanied by ♂. When flushed off eggs or young, ♀ may fly for kilometre without stopping, or may show various forms of distraction display: injury-feigning, crouched run, 'heavy flight', or walking in circles (of about 100 m within territory). Circling also used by ♂ early in season, becoming more frequent when laying starts. (Much of above from Watson and Jenkins, *BB* 57: 137–70.) Since ♂ usually perches near sitting ♀, watching him until ♀ leaves nest or searching vicinity to flush her recommended. In snow Whitaker found nests by following footprints to breathing holes under which ♀♀ were sitting.

63 **PTARMIGAN**
Lagopus mutus

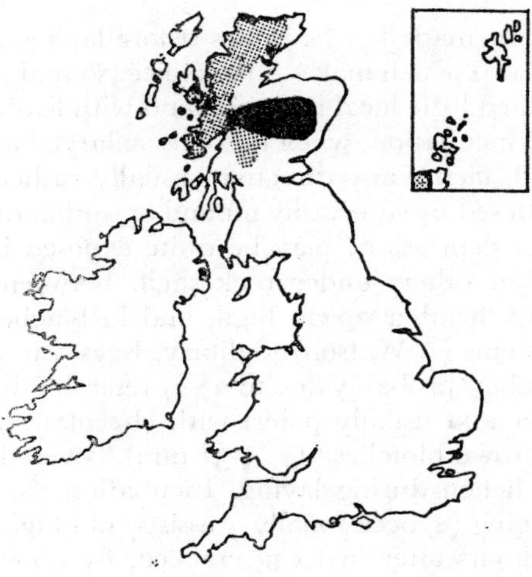

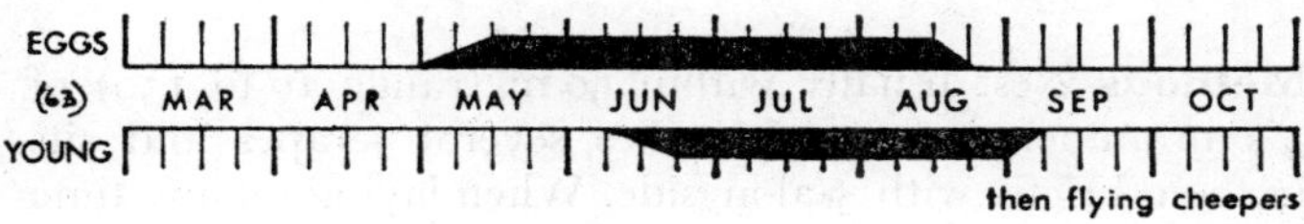

Fairly numerous; breeds Scottish Highlands from Ben Lomond northward, also Mull and Skye; some evidence recent spread into former areas, e.g. 2 coveys Ben Rinnes, Banff, 1970 and birds reported Rum (extinct 19th century) and Outer Hebrides (extinct since 1938); formerly bred Orkney, Arran, Jura, Islay, south-west Scotland and Lake District (extinct 19th century). Alpine zone of hills, either in detritus of stones with patches of lichen-covered earth, or in sparse vegetation: short heather, blaeberry *Vaccinium*, mosses and lichens with areas of pebbles and larger stones; up to 1,300 m but descends westward with alpine zone to under 700 m; brood reported Sutherland 1970 at about 360 m.

Nest Scrapes made by ♂ 14 days before laying, later by ♀, but not known which makes final choice (sometimes natural hollow); lined little local material, and with feathers during laying and incubation, when becomes enlarged and deeper. On ground, facing any direction, usually rather open but partly sheltered by stone, tiny mound or solifluction terrace, or in slight depression; may be quite exposed in moss on bedrock, but others under rock shelf, between boulders, sheltered by heather 25 cm high, and in blaeberry clump on living stems (A Watson). Solitary. Eggs 5 to 9 (3 to 12, larger numbers probably due to 2 ♀♀) resemble Red Grouse but smaller and usually paler, with chocolate more usual than red-brown blotches (44 × 31 mm), covered by ♀ with grass and lichen during laying. Incubation (♀) 21½ to 26 days. Fledging (♀, occasionally ♂ assists) nidifugous, leaving about 24 hours after first egg cracked, fly about 10 days, long before full-grown. One brood; repeat layings rare if eggs lost in later stages of incubation.

Methods Nest usually within 50 m (range 10 to 150) of ♂'s prominent stance. ♀ makes several scrapes and sits in them briefly with ♂ alongside. When laying, at any time of day, she flies to within 10 m of nest, then walks to it but does not sit on incomplete clutch even in frost; may drop fresh eggs away from nest. In good weather ♀ leaves nest 2 to 4 times a day for periods of 25 to 45 minutes, but may sit for 36 hours in snow (C and D Nethersole-Thompson); clutch arranged with pointed ends downwards and towards centre of nest. When leaving to feed, ♀ walks off 5 to 10 m, then flies, often accompanied by ♂; deposits large droppings away from nest except within 2 days of hatch. ♂ may accompany her part way back and, on approach of man or dog, may try to divert them from nest or ♀ (before nesting) by walking or running in circular path; when ♀ disturbed, both may do this. Flushed ♀ often scatters some eggs from nest, rarely feigns injury during first week of incubation, but frequently during second and regularly during third, and for 2 weeks after hatch; ♂ occasionally feigns injury when eggs hardset but in general much less assiduous than ♂ Red Grouse and deserts ♀ and brood after hatch. Alternatively ♀ may crouch and hiss at observer, but usually sits very tight and often allows herself to be stroked on nest, though flushing at 5 m off fresh eggs. Best method therefore thorough search of likely spots in neighbourhood of ♂'s perch, narrowing field where several used by taking cross-bearings, as nest certain to be within his view. Rope useful on fairly level ground. Technique in snow as for Red Grouse. Try watching back if time and weather allow. (Much of above information from A Watson, *BB* 65: 6–26.)

64 **BLACK GROUSE**

Lyrurus tetrix

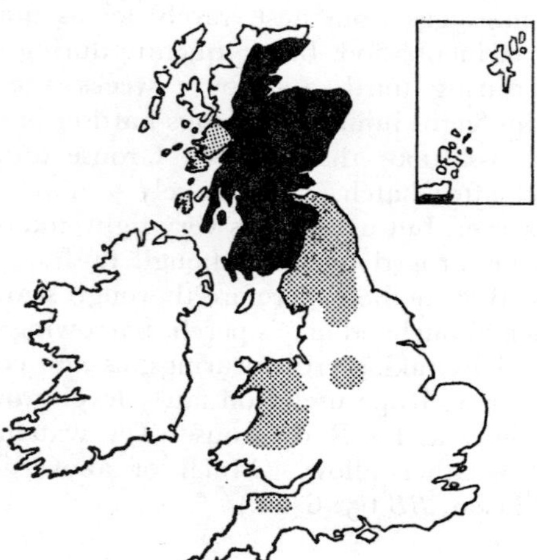

Fairly numerous; breeds much of Scotland (including some Inner Hebrides where partly introduced) south to north Derby, north Stafford and east Cheshire, most Welsh counties (introduced to west), possibly south-west Shropshire, very small numbers Quantocks and Exmoor but possibly extinct Dartmoor; formerly bred much more widely south and east England. Open woodland of conifer or oak-birch scrub, and woodland-moorland edge: bracken and heather banks, rushes and long grass; hence early stages of conifer afforestation particularly suitable; sometimes in open heather and grass moorland, up to 450 m.

Nest (♀) Scrape on ground with little or no lining. Usually in fairly thick vegetation, rushes, bracken, blaeberry *Vaccinium*, heather, grass tussocks, often on slope or near burn (Black); sometimes protected by bush (e.g. juniper), trailing branch (Whitaker) or fallen tree (Black), but also slightly elevated and exceptionally in old nests of other birds up to 6 m (*Handbook*). Solitary, though a number of ♀♀ nest in general vicinity of lek. Eggs 6 to 10 (5 to 13) yellowish-white sparsely marked yellow or red-brown (51 × 37 mm), covered with vegetation during laying. Incubation (♀) 24 to 29 days. Fledging (♀) nidifugous, fly in 15 to 20 days, well before full-grown. One brood.

Methods Hard nest to find unless population dense as there is no firm pairing and ♂♂ therefore usually no guide though Connor has twice put up Blackcocks only 50 m from sitting ♀♀. R Robel (*Ibis* 111: 395–9) found ♀♀ only moved average of 140 m daily during laying period, spending 1½ hours near nest. During incubation normally three feeding sessions: about 54 minutes in morning (longer when cool and foggy) and 37 minutes early afternoon, moving each time in 1.4 ha round nest, and average 111 minutes in evening, flying 250 m from nest and working area of 5 to 6 ha. He located several nests by watching ♀♀ back after evening feed, a preferable method to hard searching.

65 **CAPERCAILLIE**
Tetrao urogallus

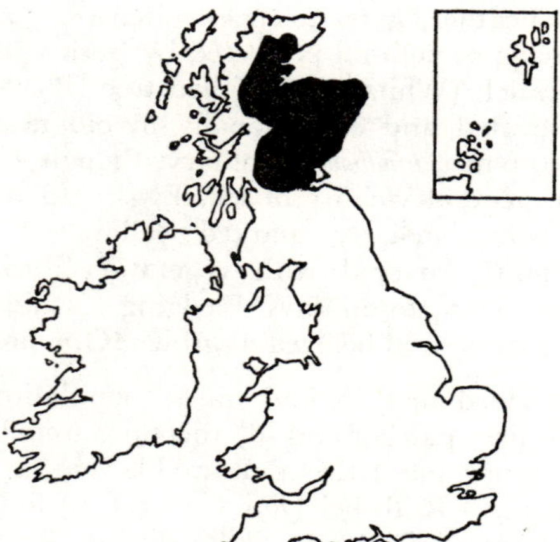

Not scarce; breeds mainly eastern Scotland from Fife and Stirling to south-east Sutherland, following 19th century reintroductions, but many elsewhere in Britain failed. Native stock extinct 17th century in England, 18th in Scotland and Ireland. Coniferous woodland and its edge with preference for 'old open pinewoods on the hillsides with an undergrowth of heather and blaeberries' (I D Pennie, *Scottish Naturalist* 62: 65–87, 157–78; 63: 4–17, 135), but sometimes in younger woods down to 20 or 30 years old and often in mixed stands of pine, spruce, larch and hardwoods; occasionally in birchwoods or open moor with juniper and long heather; up to 500 m.

Nest (♀) Scrape on ground, lined local material during laying, feathers during incubation. Usually in bay between exposed roots of tree, but sometimes away from trees in long heather and blaeberry *Vaccinium*; exceptionally in old nest of other bird up tree (Nethersole-Thompson) and on live ant heap (Whitaker). Solitary, but several ♀♀ may nest near ♂'s display ground. Eggs 5 to 8 (4 to 15 or more, probably due to 2 ♀♀) pale yellow sparsely marked with spots and blotches of yellowish to red-brown (57 × 41 mm), covered with pine needles and other debris during laying. Incubation (♀) 27 to 29 days. Fledging (♀) nidifugous, young flutter in 15 to 20 days, long before full-grown. One brood.

Methods Searching of likely habitat, e.g. where ♂ has been displaying, probably most successful, though no close bond is formed; fondness for tree-base sites helpful. Watching back of ♀ after feeding not economic in time. Provided habitat unchanged, returns to favoured area year after year (Connor).

66 **RED-LEGGED PARTRIDGE**

Alectoris rufa

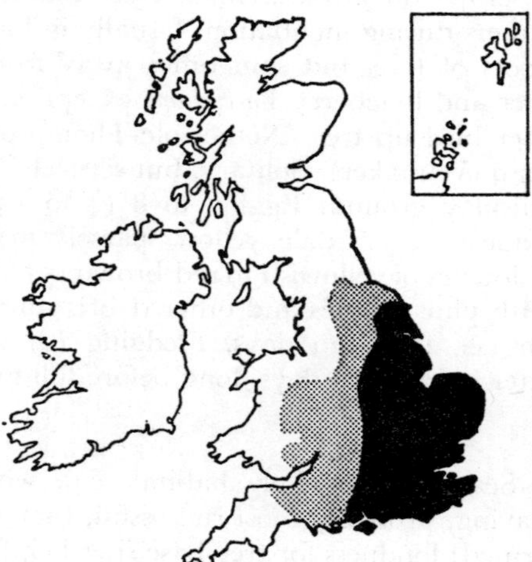

Numerous; breeds much of east and southern England to north York, Shropshire, Monmouth, Somerset, after introductions from late 18th century; these continue and include various parts of mainly east Scotland (e.g. young seen Roxburgh 1970, perhaps from introduction at Floors Castle 1968). Generally on drier soils: chalk downs, brecks, sandy heaths, warrens, dunes, old quarries, even coastal shingle, as well as farmland and very open woodland.

Nest (♀) Scrape on ground lined grass and leaves. Usually well-concealed in hedge base, nettles at foot of wall or other thick cover; in tufts of grass and under bushes in barer habitats, but sometimes quite exposed; on ledge of quarry; exceptionally on stack (*Handbook*). Solitary. Eggs 10 to 16 (7 to 20) pale yellow-brown spotted dull red and ashy (41 × 31 mm). Incubation (♂ and ♀) 23 to 24 days; ♀ frequently, perhaps regularly, lays two clutches, one incubated by ♂, resulting in protracted laying period. Fledging (♂ or ♀, sometimes ♀♂ with combined brood) nidifugous, fly 6 m at 3 weeks, fully grown 16 weeks (C L Coles). One brood.

Methods Presence of pair early in season some indication, but ♀ very unobtrusive during laying and cold searching best method. During incubation it may be possible to watch birds back after feeding and trail leading to nest gives final clue. Same nest-site may be used for several years (Walpole-Bond). Sometimes lays in nests of Pheasant, Partridge, even Mallard.

67 **PARTRIDGE**

Perdix perdix

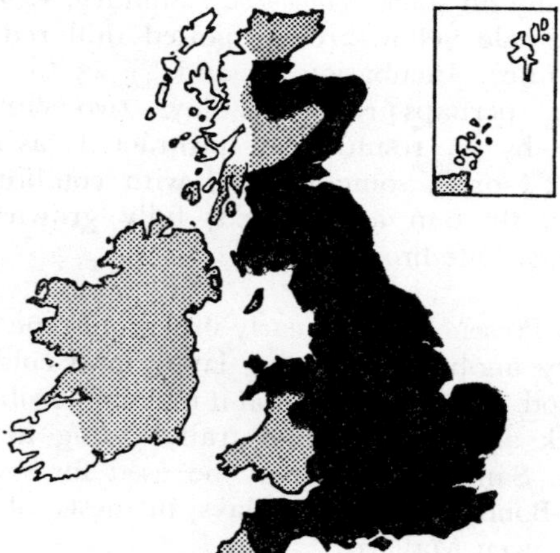

Numerous; breeds most counties of Britain and Ireland, but not (despite attempted introductions) Orkney, Shetland or other Scottish islands except Arran, Bute and Islay; local or absent much of north-west Scotland and south-west Ireland. Well-farmed land on light soils with plenty of hedges and marginal cover; sometimes woodland edge; less commonly moors (up to 500 m), rough pastures, heaths, commons, dunes and brecks.

Nest (♀) Scrape on ground lined grasses and leaves, and feathers during incubation. Usually at hedge base, but also in nettles away from hedges, in grass tufts and verges, to some extent in mowing grass and clover (where frequently destroyed by silage-cutting) and corn crops; avoids wetter sites but found on moorland edge in rushes, grass and heather; occasionally off ground on stacks. Solitary. Eggs 9 to 20 (8 to 23, and larger numbers due to 2 ♀♀) uniform olive-brown and pointed, occasionally whitish or pale blue (36 × 27 mm), covered with grass and leaves during laying. Incubation (♀) may begin after completion of clutch, 23 to 25 days. Fledging (♀♂) nidifugous, flutter from 10 to 11 days, fly at 16. One brood.

Methods Presence of pairs indicates territories early in season and nests found during laying either by looking for tracks into vegetation or by morning watch to see ♀ leave ♂, who mainly stays on guard while she feeds busily; eventually she moves direct to nest if not alarmed. This behaviour continues during incubation, when she will also return if sudden rain shower. Pheasants frequently and Red-legged Partridges sometimes lay in Partridge nests.

68 **QUAIL**
Coturnix coturnix

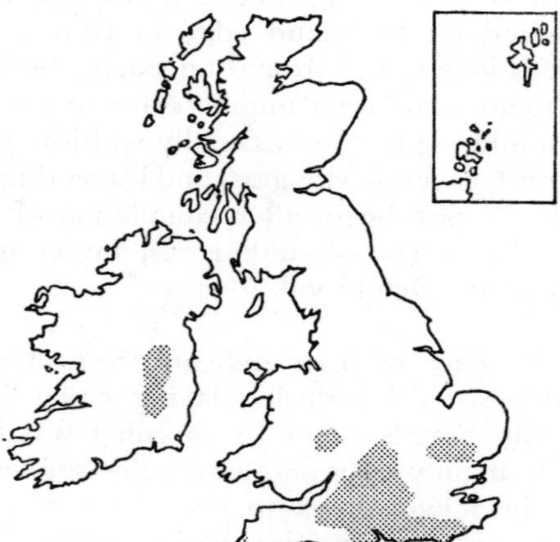

Scarce; breeds more or less regularly Cornwall, Somerset, Gloucester, Hereford, Wiltshire, Oxford, Berkshire, Hampshire, Sussex, Cambridge and Suffolk in England, and Carlow, Offaly and Kildare in Ireland; sporadic elsewhere, but in 1954–66 probably bred at least once in all other English counties except Middlesex, in 13 other Irish counties, six in Wales, seven in south Scotland and in Caithness, Orkney, Shetland and Outer Hebrides; also widespread in 1970. 'Annual herbaceous vegetation' (R E Moreau *BB* 44: 257–76; 49: 161–6); in Britain chiefly corn, grass and leguminous crops in rolling country, less often in rough marginal land.

Nest (♀) Scrape on ground sparsely lined. Well concealed in crops, sometimes in rough grass. Solitary or very loosely social. Eggs 7 to 12 (6 to 18, larger numbers due to 2 ♀♀) yellowish-white heavily blotched or spotted with shades of very dark brown (30 × 23 mm). Incubation (♀) 16 to 21 days. Fledging (♀) nidifugous, flutter at 11 days, fly well at 19 (*Handbook*). Sometimes a second brood.

Methods Initial location by *wet-my-lips* calls, but this also used by migrants and Moreau believed that it might cease after pairing; thus it gives no certain indication that birds are nesting in a particular field. In absence of other clues, thorough search of field where calls heard by dragging rope seems only practical method; watching back almost impossible though one Suffolk nest found in rough ground to which pair seen to fly (L R Flack in *BB* 44: 268); where several pairs descend on area of low cover, as in Northern Isles or Hebrides, searching prospects much better. S Lewis found runs leading from nest to 'dusting-earth' 2 m away. But most of few nests reported are revealed by reaping or mowing.

69 **PHEASANT**
Phasianus colchicus

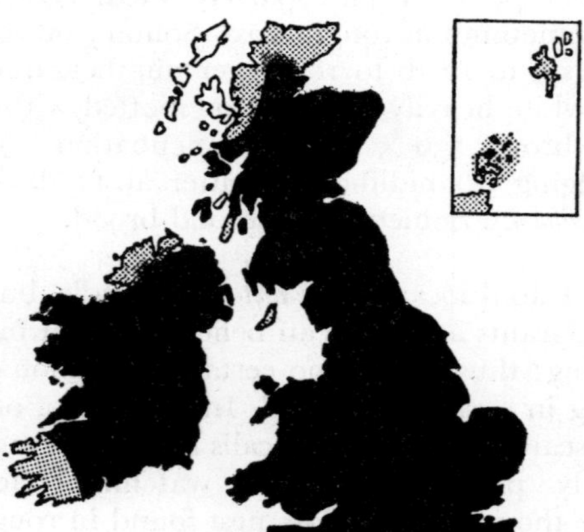

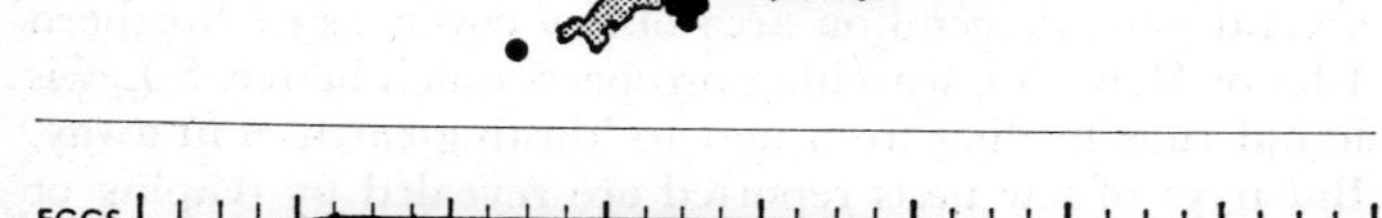

Numerous; introduced England before 1059, Scotland and Ireland 16th century; now breeds all counties, though very local or absent many islands (including Outer Hebrides where doubtfully persistent 1972), north-west Scotland, Cornwall and south-west Ireland, surviving only through constant reinforcement. Originally bird of reed beds, now characteristic of 'settled' English countryside but also found in rushy and sedgy fields and marshes, reed beds, damp thickets, even on bogs in Islay; in large gardens and parks; at other extreme in close hazel and birch scrub of highland and coastal regions, up to 300 m.

Nest (♀) Scrape on ground lined grass and leaves, feathers added during incubation. Under variety of cover in hedge bottoms, copses and wood edges; inside woods with ferns, bracken and bramble cover; on all types of waste ground, hillsides and banks; in nettles at foot of walls or buildings; occasionally off ground on stacks, on top of old walls, even in other birds' nests and dreys up to 10 m (*Handbook*). Solitary or loosely social where many ♀♀ attached to one ♂. Eggs 8 to 15 (6 to 22, large numbers due to 2 ♀♀) uniform olive-brown, occasionally pale blue (46 × 36 mm), covered with grass and leaves during laying. Incubation (♀, exceptionally ♂) 22 to 27 days. Fledging (♀) nidifugous, fly 12 to 14 days, long before full-grown. One brood.

Methods No firm pairing and a hard nest to find where population thin, unless ♀ watched when off nest. Good gamekeepers develop knowledge of likely sites and G Stonebridge believed all nests (perhaps 150 a season) should be found on 400 ha beat of farmland and riverside. Track into nest best clue during laying; incubating ♀ sits very tight and will allow vegetation to be parted over her during search. Often lays in duck and partridge nests, even in those of Moorhen and Woodcock.

70 GOLDEN PHEASANT
Chrysolophus pictus

Scarce; feral population established for 30 or 40 years in many localities of breckland (west Norfolk and west Suffolk) north to Wash, with recent evidence of increase and spread; also in Kirkcudbright (and perhaps elsewhere in Britain). Habitat as Pheasant. Probably monogamous naturally, nesting on ground. Eggs about 8 in wild, smooth, glossy, pale buff to cream (45 × 34 mm). Incubation (♀) 22 to 23 days in captivity (D Goodwin, *Ibis* 90: 280–4; other information from Beebe 1937).

71 LADY AMHERST'S PHEASANT
Chrysolophus amherstiae

Very scarce; small feral population descended from collection at Woburn Park survives on borders Bedford, Buckingham and Hertford; probably also west Norfolk. Habitat as Pheasant, especially rhododendron coverts. Probably monogamous naturally, nesting on ground. Eggs 7 (Szechuan, China) pale creamy-white, richer cream in captivity (45 × 34 mm). Incubation (♀) 22 to 23 days? (Beebe 1937).

72 **CRANE**
Grus grus

Bred East Anglia until about 1600, and in Ireland (where remains in lake dwellings and other sites show it was once common) perhaps until 14th century. Recent occurrences mostly in autumn (500 or more in 1963) and no suggestion of return as breeding species. North European habitats wet mosses, often with scrub, wooded swamps and open marshes; in south by shallow, reedy lagoons, approximating to former condition of Fens. Eggs 2 (1 to 3) pale grey to red-brown with darker spots and blotches (96 × 62 mm); April to June from southern Europe to Scandinavia.

73 **WATER RAIL**
Rallus aquaticus

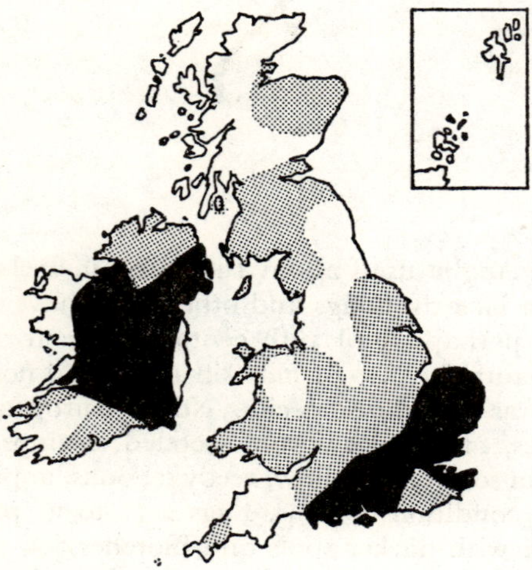

Not scarce; widespread but local in Britain, probably often overlooked: recorded breeding regularly in well over half the counties, commonest East Anglia, but absent several large areas, especially north-west Scotland and islands; breeds every Irish county. All types of thick riparian and aquatic vegetation, from reed beds, osiers and fens to sedge and rush bogs.

Nest (♀♂, 15 cm) Like small Moorhen, of dead reeds and other easily available material, lined with smaller loose fragments. Generally very well hidden in reeds, sedge or grass tussocks, sometimes raised like Moorhen, exceptionally on osier stub (Walpole-Bond) and completely open nest recorded; usually in wet site, though Whitaker described one on dry ground burrowed into soft herbage like gigantic Willow Warbler, also in bedstraw *Galium* by pool, and in rough grass on bank; occasionally in rushes on moor (Black); up to about 250 m in Scotland. Solitary. Eggs 6 to 11 (5 to 16) creamy-white lightly marked with dark red and ashy blue, often concentrated near big end, and occasional blotches (36 × 26 mm). Incubation (♀♂) 19 to 20 days. Fledging (♀♂, one broods, other feeds) nidifugous, 7 to 8 weeks. Two broods.

Methods Medley of grunting, squealing and screaming calls (known as sharming) locates birds; may show themselves when observer near nest (Black) and appear with young if watched from a distance. But hot searching only generally effective method of finding nests with eggs. Sitting bird usually flushes at close range, but even then nest may be difficult to see; some birds creep off and escape notice; eggs may be covered by loose lining when leaving nest. Grunting call of ♂, who becomes 'more alarmed and vociferous' as observer approaches nest, is useful indication (S Sloan Chesser).

74 **SPOTTED CRAKE**
Porzana porzana

Very scarce; probably breeds every year in some part of Britain (only Irish record about 1851). Decrease before mid-19th century owing to drainage of sites, but probably bred in about ten English (4 to 5 pairs Somerset 1940) and Welsh counties 1926–37; in recent years certainly or probably bred Somerset (1963), Suffolk (1963–4), Sutherland (1966–8), perhaps four other southern and two northern counties. Thick riparian and marsh vegetation, from lowland swamps and fens to highland sedge and rush bogs.

Nest (♀♂, 10 cm) Of local material lined finer stems of grasses; Somerset nests in 1940 of 'dead pieces of sedge and rush' and 'dead leaves and sedges' *Carex rostrata* (Lewis 1952; P M Meeson, *BB* 24: 56). Usually well-concealed in tussock or clump of sedges or grasses: 'at bottom of a cone-shaped tuft of peculiar, soft grass' about 45 cm high, surrounded by shallow water and entered by side tunnel (Walpole-Bond about Welsh nest 1928); Connor found Polish nests in tussocks in shallow pool; Somerset nests on 'wet earth' and 'on the ground', possibly after fall in water-level. Solitary. Eggs 8 to 12 (6 to 15) olive-buff marked purple-brown and ashy (34 × 25 mm). Incubation (♀♂) sometimes before clutch complete, 18 to 21 days. Fledging (♀♂) nidifugous (but hatch said to take place over several days), period unknown. Two broods in Netherlands.

Methods Very little known about British breeding habits; the few reported nests have been found by systematic quartering of marsh or bog after bird flushed or explosive whiplash call heard. Meeson had help of marshman, who showed him one nest, and his dog, which killed sitting bird off second nest, after it had been flushed with 'sharp squeak' and remained in vicinity.

75 BAILLON'S CRAKE
Porzana pusilla

Proved to breed three to five times 1858–89 in Cambridge and Norfolk; no recent records. Swamps and fens with thick vegetation. Neat nest of dead reed leaves and grasses. Eggs 6 to 8 (4 to 9) glossy, described by *Handbook* as 'ochreous, finely stippled and spotted with yellow umber' (29 × 21 mm), from late April in southern Europe.

76 **CORNCRAKE**
Crex crex

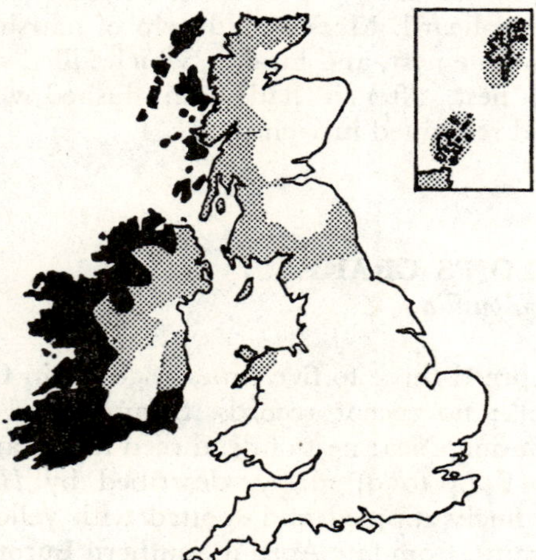

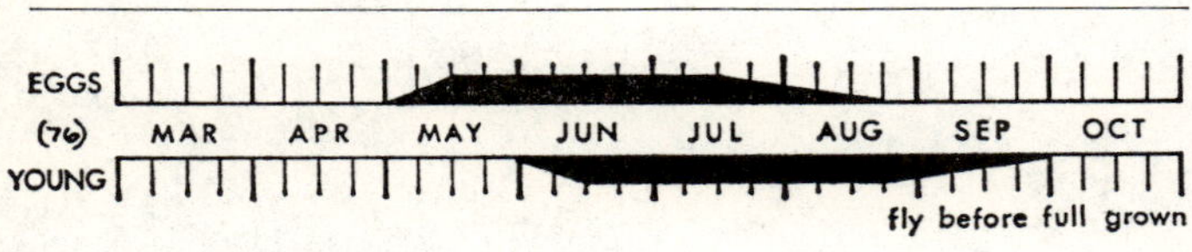

Not scarce; formerly bred all over Britain and Ireland, but now common only in Hebrides and west and south Ireland from Derry to Wexford; small to very small numbers still breed Shetland, Orkney, north, west and south-west Scotland, north England, Man, Anglesey, Caernarvon, most Irish counties; elsewhere only sporadic. Preference for mowing grass, where little chance for eggs or young broods in face of mechanical cutting; also in clover but rare in corn crops and potatoes; in north and west commonly in rough, damp pastures bordering bogs; in nettle beds even of small extent (e.g. on islet); on hill farms up to about 350 m.

Nest (♀) Hollow in ground neatly lined usually with dead grass stems and sometimes a few leaves; often canopy of crossed living stems above (cf Shoveler, Black-tailed Godwit, Redshank). Many nests in conspicuous clumps (e.g. nettles or docks) in hayfields, but others in apparently uniform areas, close to edge or right in middle; marginally in nettles, brambles, tall plants, e.g. umbellifers, grass and sedge tussocks, iris clumps in bogs. Solitary to social. Eggs 8 to 12 (6 to 14, higher numbers probably due to 2 ♀♀) pale greenish-grey to light brown, spotted red-brown and ashy, often one light egg in otherwise brown clutch (37 × 27 mm). Incubation (♀) apparently variable, 14 to 21 days. Fledging (♀, or ♀♂) nidifugous but young fed for first 3 to 4 days, fly under 5 weeks but not fully feathered until 7 or 8 weeks. Sometimes two broods.

Methods Location by crekking of ♂, followed by thorough search (with rope if possible), successful in fairly small fields and their margins; grass canopy over nest catches eye. Crekking may cease when clutch complete but continues where several pairs close together. Occasionally easy to find where habitat restricted, e.g. nettle-covered islet, small overgrown garden. Seldom possible to watch or hear bird (apart from crek) but scream of alarm uttered when nest or brood threatened (C A Norris).

77 **MOORHEN**

Gallinula chloropus

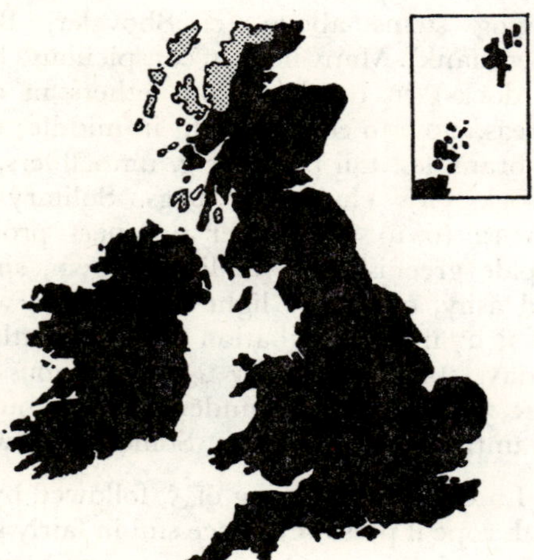

Numerous; breeds all counties of Britain and Ireland, though absent some Inner Hebrides and outlying islands. Neighbourhood of fresh water and riparian vegetation: lakes (including urban parks), meres, lochans, pools down to very small field ponds, farm duckponds, woodland pools and spinneys with only trickle of water through them; along slow and some quite fast-flowing rivers and streams, but not usually moorland burns and becks though found up to 600 m in Scotland; on wet meadows, marshes and bogs, often quite close to sea.

Nest (♀♂, exceptionally juveniles of earlier broods) Well-built platform of dead water plants (but green stems late in season) with rather shallow saucer of same or finer materials, often also lined dead leaves; sometimes stands 50 to 75 cm high and may be added to if water level rises. Typically in shallow water among aquatic plants or supported by trailing branches, brambles or flood debris; also in tussocks of sedges, rushes and grasses in marshes, or hidden under brambles and bushes with trail leading to water; on tiny islets in garden ponds; many nests in bushes and trees, especially hawthorn, blackthorn and willows, up to 8 m, sometimes in old nest of another species, e.g. Woodpigeon, Magpie, even Rook. Solitary or loosely social where population dense. Eggs 5 to 11 (2 to 14, larger numbers due to several ♀♀) whitish or greenish-grey to buff with dark red-brown and ashy spots, sometimes one or more lighter eggs in darker clutch (44 × 34 mm). Incubation (♀♂) from first egg or not until clutch complete, 19 to 22 days. Fledging (♀♂, and juveniles of earlier broods) nidifugous after hatching (which may take up to week) if disturbed; otherwise young stay in nest 2 or 3 days, fly in 6 to 7 weeks. Two or three broods.

Methods Usually easy to see or, where well-hidden, bird may squatter away noisily from vicinity. But in Scottish Highlands extremely secretive and initial location can be difficult.

78 **COOT**

Fulica atra

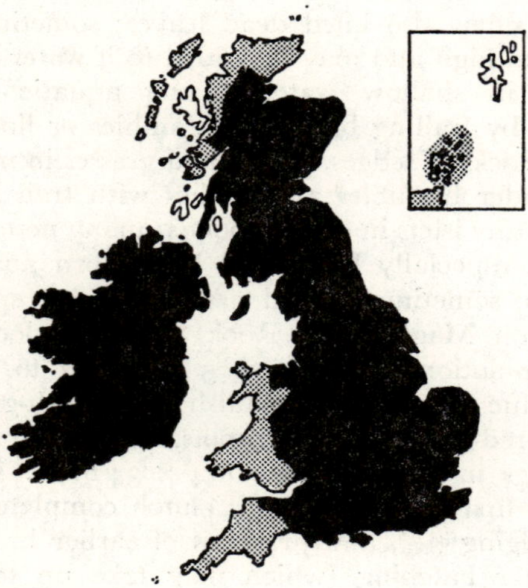

Fairly numerous; breeds all counties Britain and Ireland except Shetland where now only occasional; scarce or absent parts of north-west Scotland, Inner Hebrides, Wales and south-west England. More restricted than Moorhen to larger lakes, ponds and slow-flowing rivers with extensive riparian vegetation; also on very wet meadows near lakes and rivers; occasionally by bare reservoirs; and on brackish tidal waters and marine islands in Ireland; up to about 350 m in Scotland.

Nest (mainly ♀, ♂ brings material and builds platforms for young) Larger than Moorhen with deeper cup, of dead or live aquatic vegetation, often thick-stemmed like *Typha* and *Glyceria maxima*, sometimes mixed with dead sticks and lined finer plants like rushes and waterweed *Elodea* (B L Sage, *BB* 62: 134–43). More aquatic than most Moorhens, often in same sites as Great Crested Grebes, though normally built up from bottom and not floating; usually masked by vegetation but sometimes in open, e.g. on wooden platform in St James's Park lake, London; in wet marshes or bogs usually surrounded by standing water and placed in iris clumps, bogbean, marsh marigold, or well built-up on slight rise. Solitary to social. Eggs 4 to 8 (3 to 15, larger numbers probably due to 2 ♀♀) stone-coloured with small spots or speckles of very dark brown (53 × 36 mm). Incubation (♀♂) sometimes from first egg, 21 to 24 days. Fledging (♀ broods at first, ♂ feeds) semi-nidifugous, young leaving nest after 3 or 4 days (but returning at night to be brooded) and separating on water to be fed by each parent; feed themselves after 4 weeks, independent about 8 weeks. Two, even three broods.

Methods Easy nest to find owing to size and situation, except in dense reed beds; built-up nests in marshes can be seen at a distance, presence of birds giving initial location.

79 **GREAT BUSTARD**
Otis tarda

Bred anciently many parts of England to south-east Scotland (Berwick before 1526); last nests Norfolk 1830, Suffolk 1832, ♀♀ lingering at least to 1838, perhaps 1845 in Norfolk. Attempt to reintroduce to Salisbury Plain began 1971. British habitats open chalk downs, grass heaths and East Anglian brecks; on Continent mainly in crop fields, treeless plains and steppes. Nest a trampled scrape in vegetation with a few feathers. Eggs 2 to 3 (2 to 4) glossy, greenish-olive to olive-brown with darker smears and blotches in lines down shell and ashy marks (79 × 57 mm); from late April to June on Continent.

80 **OYSTERCATCHER**

Haematopus ostralegus

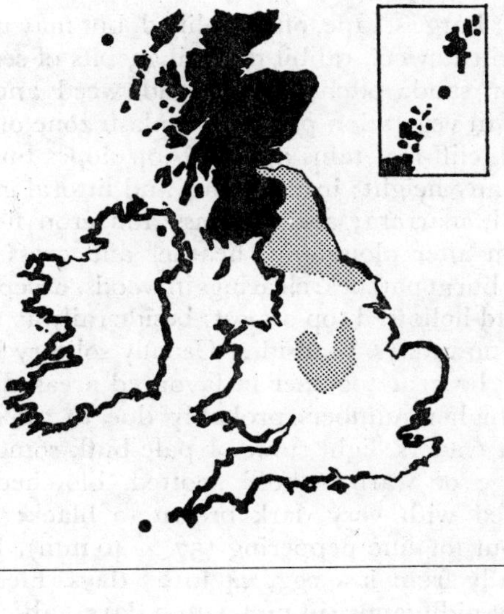

Fairly numerous; breeds almost all round British and Irish coasts and far inland in Scotland, especially along east-flowing river systems of central Highlands, south to north Lancashire and Yorkshire, and for short distances inland in west Ireland and Norfolk; single pairs bred 1969–70 Nottingham, Leicester, Stafford and probably Warwick. Shores of many types: rock, shingle, sand, saltings but less commonly mud; all over some islands, e.g. Skokholm; characteristic of sea lochs, especially headlands and islets, but less so of muddy estuaries; also dunes, links, coastal warrens and inland up rivers, especially with shingle beds, and round larger lochs, spilling over to arable and pasture fields, moorland, even open woodland, up to about 600 m.

Nest (♀♂) Large scrape, often unlined, but may use pebbles, shells, thrift flowers, rabbit droppings, bits of seaweed. On shingle or sand, often where dead weed and drift has collected, in vegetation patches of splash zone or on almost bare rock, cliff-foot talus and cliff-top slopes but rarely on ledges at any height; in thrift turf and littoral growth, e.g. silverweed, marram; also in grass and crop fields, sometimes soon after ploughing; heather and grass moorland, including burnt patches; clearings in woods, exceptionally on stumps and hollowed top of post; beside railway tracks and, less often nowadays, roadsides. Usually solitary but several nests may be near together in favoured areas. Eggs 2 to 4 (2 to 7, higher numbers probably due to 2 ♀♀) rounder than most waders, light stone or pale buff, sometimes pale green tinge or warmer buff, spotted, blotched, streaked or scrawled with very dark brown to black; rarely unmarked but for fine peppering (57 × 40 mm). Incubation (♀♂) usually from last egg, 24 to 27 days. Fledging (♀♂) practically nidifugous (in nest 1 to 2 days), about 5 weeks. One brood.

Methods Pairs proclaim territory before laying and may be watched scrape-forming. Sitting birds often easily seen from car or boat, but some, especially on beaches, may walk off at long range and need watching back; look out for false-brooding. In broken ground can be flushed at short range, and many nests found by searching coastal splash zone. Returns year after year to same vicinity, often using same site or ringing changes on two or three.

81 LAPWING

Vanellus vanellus

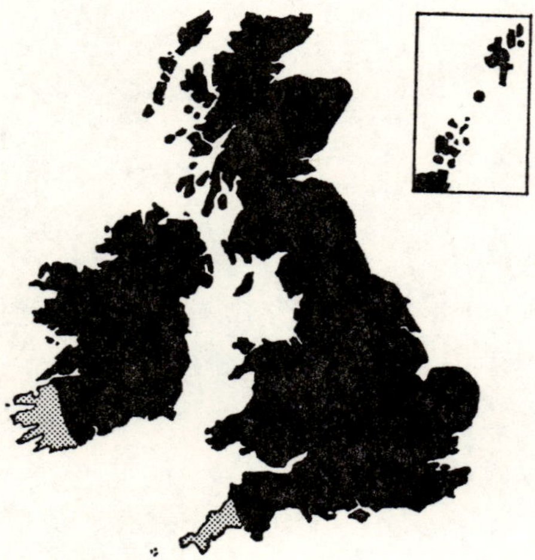

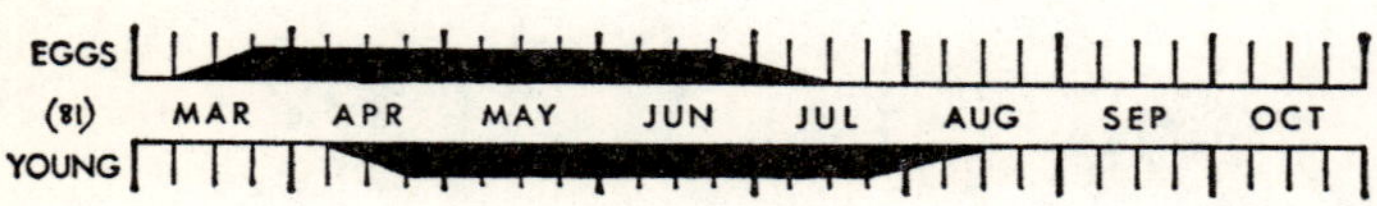

Numerous; breeds every county of Britain and Ireland, though local west Cornwall, south-west Ireland, and parts of north-west Highlands, and generally decreasing southern Britain. All types of open country, flat or rolling, but not steeply contoured, with short, intermittent or negligible plant cover, from sea level to 1,000 m: saltings, dunes, *machair*, links, sometimes shingle and mud flats; rougher pastures, stubbles, fallows, ploughed land, young corn and other crops; damp riparian meadows, upland rushy fields, old sewage farms, exceptionally reed grass *Glyceria* beds; wet grass and grass-heather moors and mosses, overlapping Golden Plover, up to hilltop detritus; breckland, industrial waste land, lake margins, gravel pits in south, where majority probably now nest in uncultivated land.

Nest (♀ selects from ♂'s scrapes) From scantily lined scrape to substantial saucer of grass and straw, especially in wet sites. Usually exposed on slight elevation, e.g. mossy hummock, old ant-hill, ridge between furrows, even cow-pat; may be in flattened tussock but not concealed or protected; normally in drier parts of wet habitats, e.g. in clumps of dead bracken bordering bog, on mound surrounded by water, even built up in water. Solitary to social. Eggs 3 to 4 (2 to 5) pear-shaped, light stone to dark brown, sometimes tinged greenish or olive, spotted and blotched even darker brown or black; pale bluish-grey (with ashy markings and few darker spots), and erythristic varieties occur, also eggs almost covered with black (47 × 34 mm). Incubation (♀♂) 24 to 31 days recorded, varying with altitude, but normally about 27 days. Fledging (mainly ♀, ♂ guards) nidifugous, 4½ to 5 weeks. One brood.

Methods Likely breeding area proclaimed by birds early in season; then scrape-forming can be watched over several days or longer, orange-buff undertail coverts of rotating ♂ conspicuous. Sitting bird can be picked out from cover (e.g. car, wall, hedge or trees) and marked. If observer shows up at several hundred metres, it usually runs some distance from nest (often at right angles to his line of approach) before taking wing, but at shorter distances it flies straight up and can be marked quite easily; exceptionally one sits close. Birds off eggs usually leave silently; mobbing is sign of hardset eggs or young. Monograph: Spencer (1953).

82 RINGED PLOVER

Charadrius hiaticula

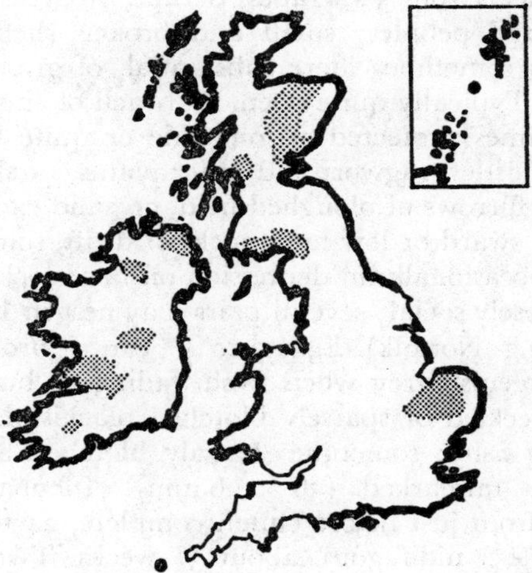

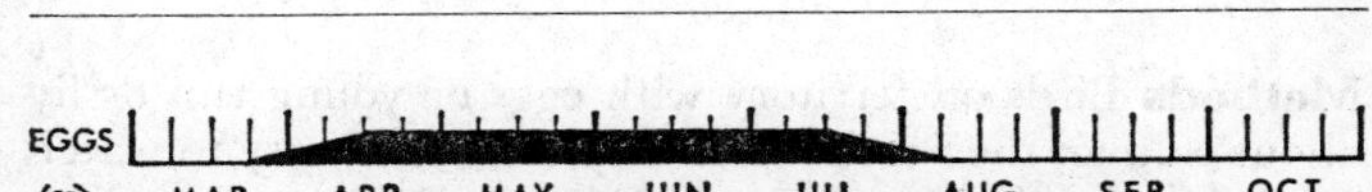

Not scarce; breeds round coasts of Britain and Ireland, but very local or absent some areas (e.g. Devon and mainland Cornwall, South Wales and Cheshire); inland along river valleys of Scotland and north England and by lakes in Ireland; a few pairs nest East Anglian brecks and occasionally London reservoirs. Sand or shingle beaches by sea, lakes or rivers; also on thrift turf and saltings with patches of mud and shingle, occasionally on cliff tops (C M Veysey, *BB* 56: 152); on slabs and promontories of rock; fallow fields and young crops, dried mud flats, old sewage farms, *machair*, warrens, links, sandy heaths and flint-strewn brecks; up to 450 m.

Nest (♀ selects from ♂'s scrapes) Scrape, often bare or lined with selected pebbles, small and broken shells, rabbit-droppings; sometimes more substantial, of grass, marram and litter. Typically quite open, on beach or shingle ridge, but sometimes protected on one side or quite hidden by marram, thistles, ragwort and other plants, or shielded by jetsam; in furrows of ploughed field, on sand excavated by rabbits, in sward or low hummocks of thrift, sometimes on cow-pat, occasionally in depression on bare rocks. Solitary or very loosely social; several pairs may nest in Little Tern colonies (e.g. Norfolk). Eggs 3 to 4 (3 to 5) broadly pear-shaped, greenish-grey when fresh, fading to buff, usually spotted, freckled or sparsely blotched blackish-brown and underlying ashy; sometimes heavily blotched at big end or almost unmarked (36 × 26 mm). Incubation (♀♂) generally from just before clutch complete, 24 to 25 days. Fledging (♀♂) nidifugous, about 3½ weeks. Two, perhaps three broods at times.

Methods Birds on territory with eggs or young run or fly about calling, then retire to shoreline but are easy to watch back where suitable cover, e.g. dunes. Return often with initial flight, then series of runs and pauses until critical point: a longer pause, with anxious movements, after which runs may be resumed in reverse or lateral direction, or bird goes, often with short low flight before final run (Connor), to nest, arranges eggs with bill and settles on them. Sometimes return journey begins along water's edge, until directly opposite nest; observer should therefore avoid placing himself above where he thinks it may be. Undisturbed birds may be watched for frequent changes-over; Whitaker recorded one running 300 m to do this. Look out for false brooding, allow bird several minutes on nest and mark carefully against objects in vicinity. Nests can sometimes be found by seeing birds run off towards water, and on sand footprints are helpful; grey of eggs against sand may show them up, but during laying or light incubation they may become partly buried by drifting. Watch back for dispersed young as for eggs: adults may brood or stand near them.

83 **LITTLE RINGED PLOVER**

Charadrius dubius

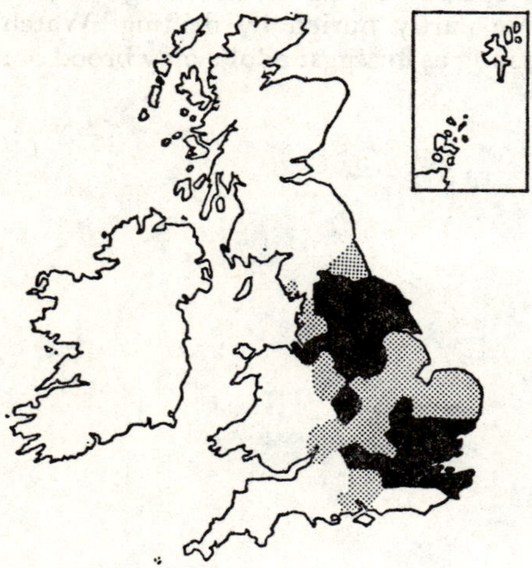

Scarce; first bred Hertford 1938, then Middlesex 1944, regularly since, spreading to all counties in eastern and central England, from Kent and Hampshire (formerly also Sussex) north to Durham and in 1968 reaching Northumberland and even Clyde Valley; established west to Gloucester, Warwick, Stafford, Cheshire and, less regularly, Lancashire. Marked preference for gravel pits with flooded areas, but sometimes up to 1 km from water; also on shingle by sea, rivers (Midlands and north England, as on Continent) or reservoirs; islets where water level has fallen at reservoirs and lakes; black industrial silt and rubbish tips near water; patches of gravel and chalk deposits in ploughed fields or rehabilitated gravel pits (Connor).

Nest (♀ selects from ♂'s scrapes) Scrape normally lined with fine, white stones; failing them, small pieces of chalk, chemical waste or fertiliser and bents added during incubation, sometimes forming substantial layer (Connor). Usually quite exposed on gravel, but sometimes on sand, silt or dried mud; frequently on slight mound or ridge; sometimes with plant (e.g. coltsfoot, ragwort, thistle) or prominent flattish stone, even waste plastic container, at one side; in sparse vegetation but not as hidden as many Ringed Plovers; quite often on tiny islet (down to 1·5 m square) in flooded area; on bare stretches exposed before or during digging. Solitary or very loosely social. Eggs 4 (3 to 5) more oval than Ringed Plover and mat-surfaced, pale green or greenish-grey at first, turning grey-buff, peppered all over (rarely blotched) with very small brown spots and underlying ashy (30 × 22 mm). Incubation (♀♂) from third or fourth egg, 24 to 25 days. Fledging (♀♂) nidifugous, 3 to 3½ weeks. Sometimes two broods (Connor).

Methods According to Connor, who has found well over 100 nests, ♂ makes 7 or 8 scrapes, ♀ choosing that in which coition takes place. ♂ also scrapes frenziedly as distraction display when ♀ disturbed off eggs, thus misleading observer who has not found nest. Birds at change-over frequently add small white chips to nest lining, which tends to stand out in cold searching, particularly after rain has darkened ground; but eggs also stand out when darker than gravel and point-to-point arrangement catches eye (BC). Where nest far from feeding site, watching back may have to be done in stages from different vantage points. Birds sit tight at dusk. Two nests within a few metres when ♂ has more than one mate. Strong inclination to return to same site, even within ½ m of previous year's nest. Proximity to Lapwings suggests these may be used as warning cover, cf Redshank with Lapwings, Ringed Plovers with Little Terns.

84 **KENTISH PLOVER**
Charadrius alexandrinus

Formerly bred in small numbers Sussex (regularly to 1920, then 1923 and 1949 to 1956), Kent (to 1935, and 1943); also Suffolk 1952. Still breeds Channel Islands and may return to Britain, where annual visitor. Small colonies at Dungeness and Rye mainly on shingle with sparse wiry grass, but also on marram-covered dunes; shell-sand on Herm and Continental beaches, dunes, sandy and muddy riversides and estuaries.

Nest (♀♂) Varies from slight scrape in sand, with eggs half or almost wholly buried, points downward, to more obvious nest in pebbles, even dead seaweed, lined vegetable fragments or shells; often on slight rise, sometimes partly sheltered by marram or other shore plants. Loosely social, several pairs nesting near each other. Eggs 3 (2 to 5) rather oval, mat-surfaced, very variable but usually pale buff with scattered black spots and streaks, sometimes zoned and interlaced (33 × 23 mm); early May onwards. Incubation (♀♂) at least 24 days, average 26·3. Fledging (♀♂) nidifugous, about 6 weeks, apparently much longer than other plovers (H Rittinghaus, *Journal für Ornithologie* 97: 117–55). Possibly two broods.

Methods As for Ringed Plover, but accurate marking essential after watching back, as only tops of eggs may show in sand.

85 GOLDEN PLOVER

Pluvialis apricaria

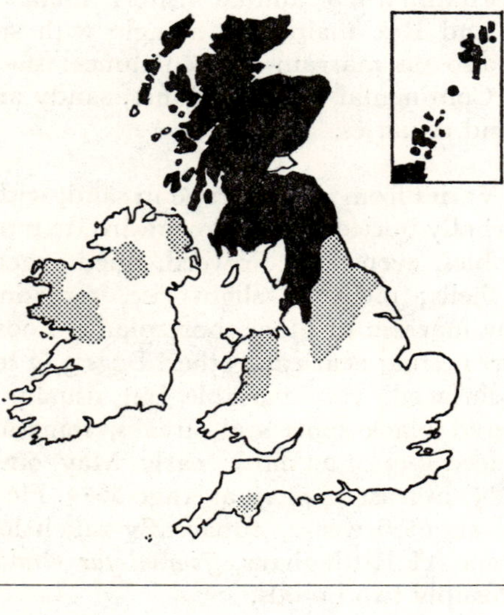

Fairly numerous; breeds throughout Scotland and northern England south to Yorkshire, Derby and northernmost Stafford; locally in mid and North Wales, perhaps Radnor and Pembroke, sporadic Anglesey; in south-west only very small numbers Dartmoor; in Ireland local Antrim, Fermanagh, Cavan, Mayo, Galway, occasional Donegal. Peat moors and mosses, especially disintegrating bogs with hummocks carrying heather, deerhair sedge and grasses among pads of *Rhacomitrium* and *Sphagnum* mosses and bare patches with lichens; also on pure heath and 'white grass' moors, often when recently burnt, and upland pastures; occasionally among scattered pines (Nethersole-Thompson) from sea level in Scotland and Ireland to 1,000, even 1,300 m in Cairngorm Hills.

Nest (♀♂) Scrape usually sparsely, sometimes more substantially lined, with heather, twigs and lichens. Generally on slight elevation of bog hummock, but nests in grass may be partly sheltered by tufts. Solitary to loosely social. Eggs 3 to 4, more oval than Lapwing, usually creamy buff to apricot, occasionally pale green, with bold blotches and spots of dark red-brown to blackish-brown, frequently zoned towards big end (52 × 36 mm). Incubation (♀♂) from third egg, 27 to 28 days. Fledging (♀♂) nidifugous, about 4 weeks. One brood.

Methods Probably hardest of commoner wader nests to find, especially when several pairs nesting close together, unless watching can begin at early stage. First contact usually with off-nest bird which may come towards observer calling, while sitting bird runs a few metres away, then flies to join mate. They dog observer while he stays in area, so one course is retreat and attempt to watch back. But even if concealment is possible, broken nature of typical habitat makes it hard to follow movements of right bird through hummocks and sometimes, when one of pair under observation, mate begins piping behind observer. This behaviour probably more usual when eggs hardset or young hatched, but often used at earlier stage. S Sloan Chesser suggests walking after pair until they quit territory, often with flight of 400 m or more; then he hides until one returns, usually directly to area of nest, sometimes within a few metres. When off-nest bird absent, sitting mate may be marked from nest, which is found by searching (trial scrapes often near occupied site) or watching back. Minority sit tight during day and can be flushed at short range, and more do so during heavy rain or hail, and at dusk. Once bird ran round BC's legs before flying, making him search back in vain; nest was metre in front. Same site may be used for several years.

86 **DOTTEREL**
Eudromias morinellus

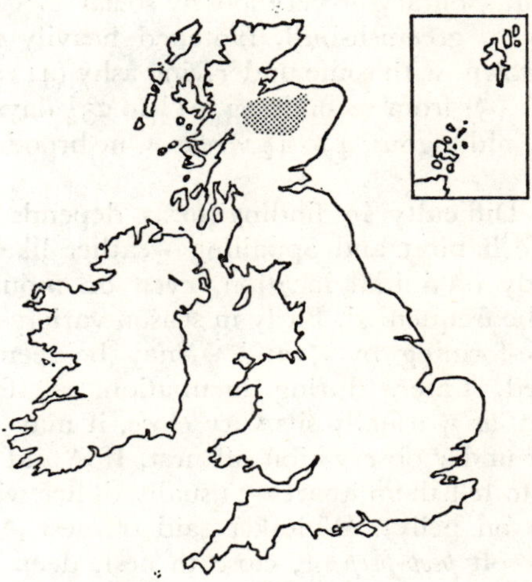

Very scarce; breeds mainly central Scottish Highlands (Perth, Angus, Aberdeen, Banff, Inverness) with scattered pairs Ross and perhaps Sutherland, where has bred; has also nested Galloway and formerly English Lake District where now sporadic. Mountain tops with sparse vegetation of fescue, short heather, *Vaccinium*, mosses and lichens, often with bare stretches of stones, gravel and peat; 800 to 1,300 m, but at sea level both in arctic and on reclaimed ground in Netherlands.

Nest (♂♀) Scrape, bare or lined mainly with lichen or moss. Usually in vegetation patch, often on slight elevation; sometimes among gravel, sometimes partly sheltered by grass tuft. Solitary or very loosely social. Eggs 3 (2 to 4) oval, light to greenish-buff, blotched heavily reddish or blackish-brown, with some underlying ashy (41 × 29 mm). Incubation (♂) from second egg, 21½ to 25½ days. Fledging (mainly ♂) nidifugous, 4 to 4½ weeks. One brood. (Plate 7a)

Methods Difficulty in finding nests depends partly on inaccessible habitat and appalling weather likely even in June, partly on initial location, even on mountain tops known to be frequented. Early in season variety of displays and scrape-forming by ♂ and ♀ may be seen near site finally used. Later, during incubation, ♀♀ form small parties and, as ♂ usually sits very close, it may take hours to get him under observation off nest. If ♂ and ♀ both on move, try to tell them apart (♂ usually duller with smaller black area on belly). Whitaker said off-nest ♂ might be silent, call soft *peep-peep* or, close to nest, deep *trup*, often accompanied by violent bobbing, decreasing in intensity as he approached nest. Sometimes ♂ remains near nest, repeatedly false-brooding. Owing to confiding nature of most Dotterel, watching back not difficult once bird located – one ran on to nest with Whitaker following him – and sudden hailstorm may hasten return. ♂ leaving nest may run or fly towards observer, then circle away, soon returning to watch him, but occasionally one explodes off nest (Nethersole-Thompson) or runs some yards and flies straight away. Do not be put off by this; sit tight and watch for return (I E Hills). On very bare ground sitting ♂ may be picked up by search through binoculars (Hills).

87 **SNIPE**

Gallinago gallinago

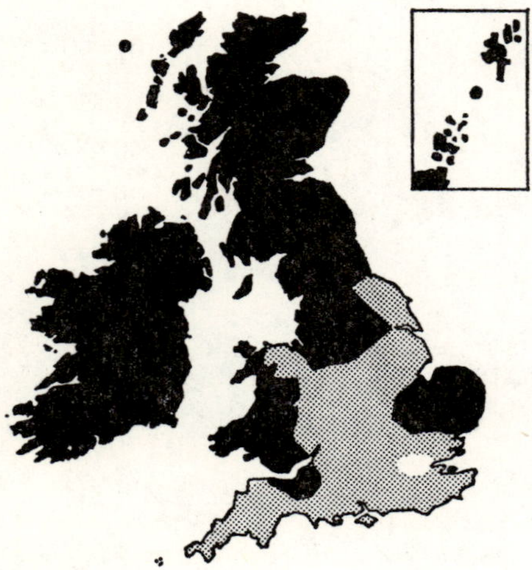

Fairly numerous; breeds all counties of Britain and Ireland except Middlesex, but very local south and central England. Usually wet ground: moorland with damp rushy pockets, mosses and bogs, washes and water meadows; marshy margins, especially with sedges, of lochs, lakes, pools, old sewage farms; occasionally on salt marshes and in wet woodland clearings; sometimes on quite dry heather and grass moors and rough pastures; from sea level to 750 m or higher.

Nest (♀, ?♂) Scrape lined with grass, sedge or moss. In tussock of grass, sedge, rush or other marsh plants, sometimes mixed with heather; tussock may be actually in water, but drier patches usually chosen; occasionally quite exposed by grazing cattle but generally well hidden. Solitary to social. Eggs 4 (3 to 6) pear-shaped, rather glossy, pale grey-brown to olive-brown but also pale blue, buff or umber, usually boldly spotted and blotched, often in zone towards big end, with shades of dark brown and underlying ashy (39 × 29 mm). Incubation (♀) from third or last egg, 19 to 20 days. Fledging (♀♂) nidifugous, may fly from 2 weeks. Sometimes two broods.

Methods Initial location easy from drumming and chippering flights of ♂ and, according to Whitaker, clicking note of ♀ indicates nesting. In thick mist on Suffolk marsh Connor found drumming localised immediately above nests, and was thus guided to them. Nest hard to find except by flushing ♀; watching back usually impossible owing to thick cover, though Gosnell recommended it, but disturbed bird may fly back and land on or near site. Some habitats suitable for dragging with rope, effective as most ♀♀ rise at 10 to 15 m range, though some sit very tight. ♂ may squat close to incubating or brooding ♀, and birds with young will come close to observer. Eggs sometimes partly covered in absence of ♀ (Walpole-Bond).

88 **WOODCOCK**
Scolopax rusticola

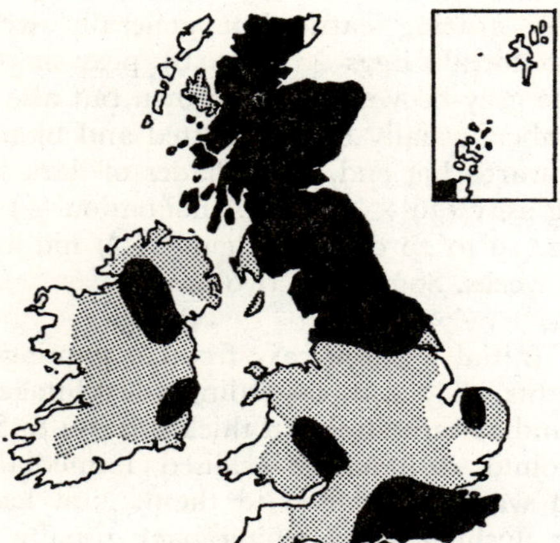

Fairly numerous; breeds most counties of Britain and Ireland, but local or absent south-west England, parts East Anglia, Pembroke, west and south-west Ireland, Outer Hebrides, Orkney and Shetland. Principally woodland with moderate or light ground cover, so most frequently under oak, birch, pine, larch, beech in that order (Alexander 1945–7), also alder, mixed deciduous woods, other conifers (usually young plantations) and shrubberies, even gardens; open bracken and heather ground, less often marshes and grass fields; occasionally warrens (Whitaker). Both dry (nesting) and wet (feeding) ground required in breeding area.

Nest (♀) Hollow lined with dead leaves from vicinity and a few shed feathers. Protected by light cover of dead bracken or close to base of tree; also under brambles, briars, hazels, dead and low branches of trees, in thick drifts of leaves; under *Deschampsia* tussocks and among dog's mercury in ash and similar woods; among rhododendrons, gorse, juniper and other low scrub; in heather and bracken away from trees; also in sedge near pool, among nettles and willowherb (Whitaker), in hedge, osier bed, exceptionally haystack (Alexander) and in hole in sand-bank (J Russell, *BB* 64: 76). Solitary. Eggs 4 (2 to 6, probably product of 2 ♀♀) rounder than most waders, glossy, greyish to brownish-buff or warm brown, spotted and streaked brown, chestnut and underlying ashy, frequently zoned near big end (44 × 34 mm). Incubation (♀) 20 to 21 days. Fledging (♀) nidifugous, fly from about 2½ weeks. No definite evidence of second broods (Alexander).

Methods Initial location by roding flights of ♂ and his pursuit of ♀ (mainly dusk but also dawn), then prolonged searching usually needed (16 hours each for three nests in Argyll scrubwoods) as little chance of watching back this crepuscular species nesting in woodland and usually sitting tight. ♀ recorded leaving nest to meet ♂ with ensuing display, which might be seen by sustained watching in likely area, and J E Griffith saw ♀ return direct to nest after daylight feed. Search narrowed if pair (suggesting incubation not yet begun) or ♂ put up and no nest found; it is likely (but by no means certain) to be within 50 m. Concentrate on thinner patches of bracken and brambles, round fallen trees and on level spaces (sometimes old charcoal-burning platforms); in uniform woods, look near edges, along clearings, rides and streams. Off eggs ♀ rises silently, usually close but sometimes up to 15 m in front or to one side of observer, whereas off young she may be noisy. Hatched eggs with white membranes left in nest show up much better than superbly camouflaged sitting ♀; three such nests found in 45 minutes in Perthshire birch-wood. Nests in same vicinity in successive years.

89 **CURLEW**

Numenius arquata

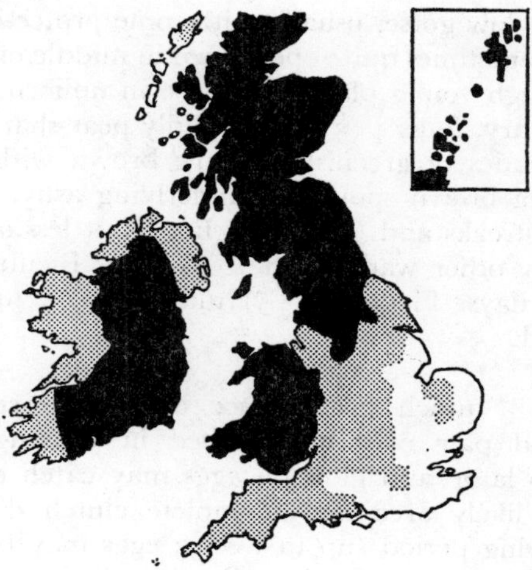

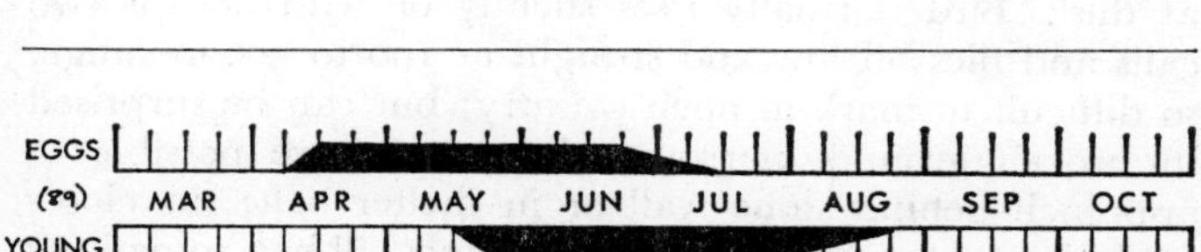

Fairly numerous; breeds throughout north and west Britain and Ireland, having recently colonised Lewis in Outer Hebrides, and has spread into lowland areas, though still absent seven south-eastern English counties (has bred Cambridge). Wetter grass and heather moors or wet pockets in drier moors, but also southern heaths; rushy upland pastures, flats along rivers, lowland valleys with water meadows and lush grass fields; also on burnt areas, clearings in boggy woodland, ploughed fields and young crops; locally on dunes; from sea level to 700 m.

Nest (♀, ?♂) Large basin-like hollow, about 12·5 cm across, unlined or with some dry grass and odd feathers. On hummock of moss or in large tussock of grass, rushes, heather or low gorse, usually with some protection on one side, but sometimes quite open, even in middle of little-used road through young plantation; also in uniform grass and corn. Solitary. Eggs 4 (3 to 6) broadly pear-shaped, glossy, various shades of greenish to dark brown with generous freckling of brown spots and underlying ashy, sometimes blotches, streaks and thin black lines, but less often zoned than many other waders (68 × 48 mm). Incubation (♀♂) 28 to 30 days. Fledging (♀♂) nidifugous, 5 to 6 weeks. One brood.

Methods ♂ much in evidence over territory early in season and pair may be watched in walking displays. As nest so large and gloss on eggs may catch eye, worth searching likely area for incomplete clutch during prolonged laying period (up to week); eggs may be brooded at dusk. Bird normally rises silently or with one or two calls and flies off low and straight at 100 to 500 m range, so difficult to mark in open country; but can be surprised in broken ground, narrow valleys or where possible to approach behind stone wall or in shelter belt; sits closer at dusk or near roads, when head and bill can sometimes be spotted. Bird anxious to return to nest will often false-feed, gradually approaching and moving more quickly until it covers last 40 m or so in low crouching run (J Mulholland), but may take hour or more when eggs fresh (Whitaker). When eggs near hatching, birds fly round calling excitedly as they do with young. Nests hardest to find in cultivated land where watching difficult and searching often impossible owing to crops.

90 **WHIMBREL**

Numenius phaeopus

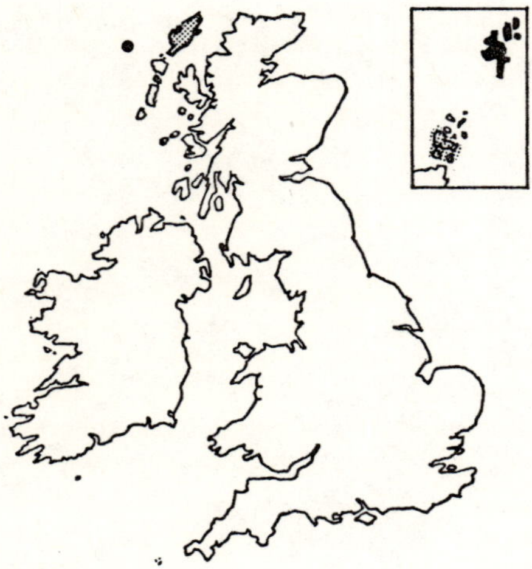

Very scarce; about 150 pairs Shetland 1970 (R J Tulloch) and very small numbers Lewis; breeds sporadically Orkney (1968, 1970), St Kilda (1964), north Scottish mainland (three pairs 1970, possibly bred 1969). Disintegrating bogs with heather, cotton grass and hummocks of *Rhacomitrium* moss, or drier edges of such areas; also occasionally on quite small oceanic islands.

Nest (♀, ?♂) Hollow scantily lined grass, moss and heather. Usually quite open on low hummock among heather and other moor vegetation, or partly sheltered by tuft. Solitary to social. Eggs 4 (3 to 5) broadly pear-shaped like Curlew, pale greenish to olive-brown blotched and spotted dark brown with underlying ashy, usually most heavily at big end; occasional black streaks (58 × 42 mm). Incubation (♀♂) begins before clutch complete, about 24 days. Fledging (♀♂) nidifugous, about 4 weeks. One brood.

Methods As for Curlew in moorland habitats, where fairly easy to watch back after bird has walked off nest and taken wing with one or two calls. After watching pair 'for hours', during which one showed momentary interest in tuft by checking in flight above it, Whitaker walked over to find nest with fresh eggs there, bird going to incubate them as soon as he hid himself again. S Sloan Chesser advocates walking pair off territory, as for Golden Plover; one will return direct to nest after observer has hidden.

91 **BLACK-TAILED GODWIT**
Limosa limosa

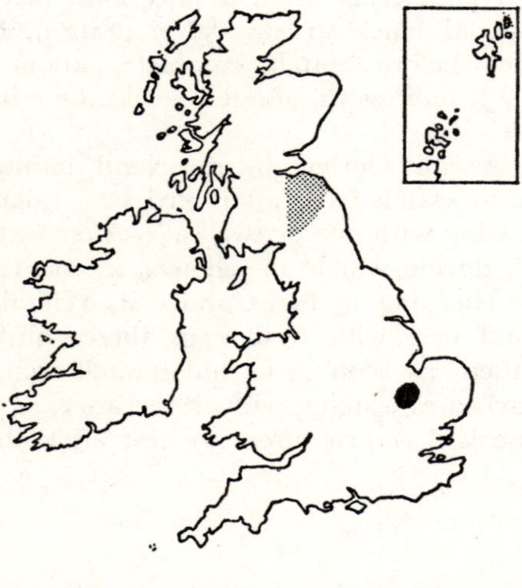

Very scarce; in 1971 over 50 pairs Ouse Washes (Norfolk-Cambridge) where pair first bred in 1952, after occasional breeding East Anglia 1937–49 and more widespread distribution east England (Suffolk to York) in 19th century; since 1940 has nested at least eight other counties west to Somerset and probably Wiltshire, and north from Suffolk to Caithness, Orkney and Shetland, though most regularly south-east Scotland and Unst (probably Iceland race). Main British breeding area flat grazed or mown washes with variety of marsh vegetation, approximating to Dutch polders where so numerous; in Scotland areas of short rushes favoured; also bogs, scrub-covered dunes and moors on Continent.

Nest (♀, ?♂) Usually substantial pad of dead grass and sedge in scrape on ground. In uniform lush grass (*Deschampsia*), sedges, *Phalaris*, rushes and associated vegetation, sometimes canopy of stems formed over nest; one pair accepted built-up site after flooding, others have tolerated fence round nest to keep cattle off. Loosely social. Eggs 4 (3 to 7), little gloss, blue-green through shades of olive-brown to darker brown, variably spotted or blotched with very dark brown and some underlying ashy, usually concentrated at big end (55 × 37 mm). Incubation (♀♂) from third or last egg, 22 to 24 days. Fledging (♀♂) nidifugous, 4 to 5 weeks. One brood.

Methods Initial location by aerial displays, and song of ♂. Sitting bird usually rises at long range like Curlew, but returns with mate and both fly round calling, even when eggs quite fresh, becoming very noisy when near hatching or young about; a few sit tight and others fly off silently. Searching on reasonably close mark may be tried, but nests sometimes well hidden and, if cover available, advisable to retire and watch back, comparatively easy early in season. See Brown and Waterston (1962).

92 **GREEN SANDPIPER**
Tringa ochropus

Apart from pair seen with young Westmorland 1917, breeding recorded only in Inverness in 1959 when young one, estimated 3 or 4 days old, found 30 May with adult in attendance (F R Clafton, *BB* 52: 430–2), but song flights watched same county in several earlier years, especially 1933–9, and more recently birds seen in summer in likely breeding places in Scotland. Habitat in 1959 wet moorland with boggy pools, tall heather and cotton grass and scattered Scots pines; in Fenno-Scandia found in more heavily wooded areas, both broadleaved (e.g. alder) and coniferous, close to streams, ponds and lakes.

Nest (♀?) Usually occupies old nest of another species (especially thrush, crow or pigeon), adding little or no material, at variable heights from 1 to 15 m or more; 'occasionally lays on accumulations of pine-needles among branches, on stumps or among fallen trees; perhaps exceptionally on ground' (*Handbook*). Solitary. Eggs 4 (2 to 4) greenish to buff with rather sparse rich brown and ashy underlying spots, but not certainly identifiable from Wood Sandpiper (39 × 28 mm); from early May. Incubation (♀♂) about 20 to 23 days. Fledging (♀♂, later ♂ alone) nidifugous, about 4 weeks. One brood.

Methods Song flight, circling with alternate rapid rises and steep glides, indicates possible breeding ground, but search for trees with likely old nests exhausting in boggy habitat. Some birds sit close, though others flush at a distance, sometimes with 'cry of protest' (J H McNeile). Also worth looking where off-nest bird put up from cover or ditch (McNeile). Watching back usually very difficult as bird returns by stages through trees. Birds with young become noisily demonstrative, flying round observer from perch to perch.

93 **WOOD SANDPIPER**
Tringa glareola

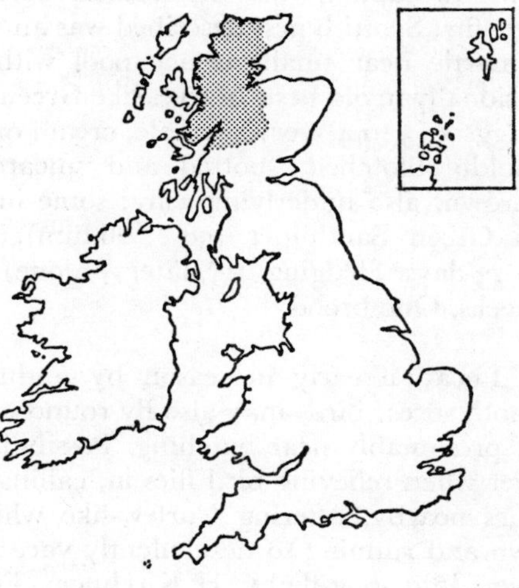

Very scarce; after isolated record Northumberland 1853, has bred at least since 1959 in very small numbers in widely separated parts of Highlands from Sutherland to north Perth and Argyll. Scottish habitat boggy moorland with peat hags and tall heather near lochs; on Continent also on marshes and swamps, even of small extent in forest surroundings.

Nest (♀?) Usually no more than neat scrape in grass, heather or moss, lined grasses and dead leaves, but sometimes substantial (I E Hills). Among open vegetation, e.g. crowberry 30 cm high, or in clearings in pine or birch forest, sometimes on slight hillock and often by birch, alder or willow sapling; also in tussocks surrounded by deep water; first Scottish nest described was among heather and bog myrtle near small surface pool within 50 m of loch; occasionally in old nests in trees like Green Sandpiper. Solitary. Eggs 4 (3 to 4) very variable, cream or pale green to buff boldly blotched, spotted and smeared dark or purplish-brown, also underlying ashy; some indistinguishable from Green Sandpiper (38 × 26 mm). Incubation (♀♂) 22 to 23 days. Fledging (♀♂, later ♂ alone) nidifugous, about 4 weeks. One brood.

Methods Location early in season by undulating song flights of both sexes; birds may also fly round calling when with eggs, presumably near hatching. Possibility of seeing change-over when relieving bird flies in, calling *gip gip* . . . and perches nearby, uttering Curlew-like whistle, before flying down and running to nest, silently vacated by mate which towers into song-flight (H Kirchner). First Scottish nest found by observer appearing suddenly from cover and flushing bird at 20 m range (R Cook, *Scottish Birds* 1: 331–3), but often sits tight, even when hide being put up 2 m away (J B and S Bottomley). Both birds sing, at least during incubation, and alarm note, *tick tick*, usually sounded if observer near nest, according to Hills, who found Danish nest by watching back and hot search, as did Nethersole-Thompson (1971) in Sutherland, where flushed bird '*chipped* and sang and hovered only a few feet above our heads'.

94 COMMON SANDPIPER

Tringa hypoleucos

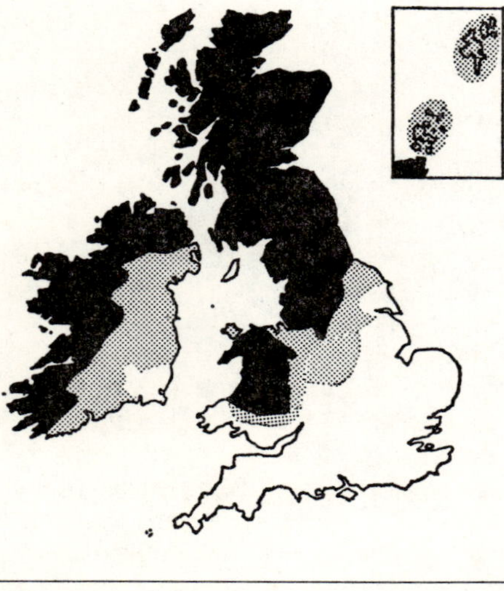

Fairly numerous; typically highland distribution throughout Britain and Ireland, but evidence of decrease in recent years and apparently no longer breeds Dartmoor; has bred many lowland counties, e.g. Berkshire 1955, Hertford 1955–7, Norfolk 1962–3. Associated with clear water in lochs, lakes, sea lochs, rivers or streams at altitudes from sea level to 800 m, often in wooded country but generally avoiding marshes and bogs unless these border open water; sometimes only bird by stony-shored lochans and tarns, but usually absent from peat-hags and reed-fringed meres; occasionally by flooded gravel pits.

Nest (♀♂ make scrapes, ♀ builds) Usually only scrape lined grass, flood wrack, other local materials, but sometimes fairly substantial cup, typically on side (sometimes overhung) or top of slope or bank, often on flat ground, well hidden in vegetation, e.g. grasses, rushes, heather, dwarf willow, bracken, bog myrtle, yellow iris; other sites quite exposed on shingle beds in rivers, young corn crops, ledges of natural rock, roadsides and paths, stone or railway embankments. Odd nests in flower beds, on pollard willow (Walpole-Bond) or pine stump (Whitaker), in Ring Ouzel nest and rabbit hole (*Handbook*). Majority close to water, especially on islets, but sometimes 100 m or more away, right into woodland. Solitary. Eggs 4 (3 to 5) whitish to yellowish brown stippled, spotted, streaked or blotched shades of red-brown: effect rather pink and glossy (36 × 26 mm). Incubation (♀♂) 21 to 23 days. Fledging (♀♂) nidifugous, about 4 weeks. One brood.

Methods Initial location by song flights and chases along shore easy enough, but search may have to extend inland and off-nest bird may be 200 m away. Gosnell found equal division between tight-sitters and those rising up to 100 m off and making for nearest water; some call agitatedly when flushed, but this usually sign of young. Bird tries to return within 5 minutes, after pretending to feed by water; then either disappears into vegetation if nest close by, or flies back to its vicinity, landing perhaps 20 m away. Whitaker recorded one standing by eggs and whistling before settling on them. Sight of bird skimming from place where it would not go to feed almost sure indication of nest, e.g. from opposite side of road to water, but often difficult to get close mark and watching back from hidden position necessary. Gosnell advised working stream sides against wind.

95 **REDSHANK**
Tringa totanus

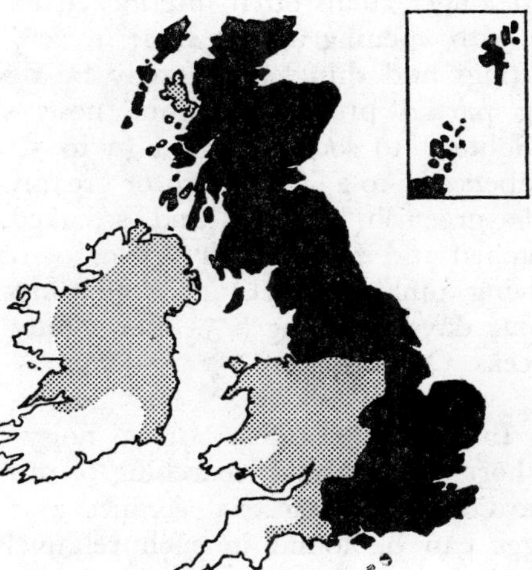

Fairly numerous; breeds nearly all inland and most coastal counties except south-west England, parts of Wales and south and west Ireland, where sporadic or absent. Typically in rather uniform, not too wet marsh, meadow and grass moor, generally avoiding disintegrating bogs and lush lowland marshes; on saltings, shingly areas near water, dunes, pastures, hayfields, water meadows, old style sewage farms, rough rushy fields, grass moors (*Agrostis*, *Nardus*) with admixture of heather, from sea level to 500 m.

Nest (♀ attended by ♂) Hollow in tuft or tussock, scrape in turf or sand lined dead grasses; prominent tufts generally chosen and longer stems often interlocked to make dome or canopy with opening at one side; in very short grass, e.g. on saltings and shingle, nest may be beside isolated tuft giving partial protection; dune nests sheltered by marram. Solitary to social. Eggs 4 (3 to 5, occasionally larger numbers due to 2 ♀♀) whitish or creamy to buff and rarely pale greenish, spotted and streaked, sometimes boldly blotched and zoned with shades of dark reddish-brown, giving pinkish effect (45 × 32 mm). Incubation (♀♂) 23 to 24 days. Fledging (♀♂, later ♂ only) nidifugous, about 4 weeks. One brood.

Methods Initial location easy from noisy presence of birds. In short grass habitats searching of prominent tufts often rewarding, revealing trial scrapes as well as final choice. Eggs can be found in such relatively easy sites before completion of clutch and Whitaker put one bird off empty nest. Although some sit very tight (even allowing themselves to be stroked or lifted), majority rise at 50 to 200 m and in early stages of incubation fly off at once without calling. Many records of nests within a few metres of Lapwings suggest one uses other as warning cover for escape. When eggs near hatching Redshanks often fly round intruder, calling and mobbing. Birds normally rise obliquely from nest without running and can be closely marked. Generally open habitat also assists watching back, particularly if there is handy tree to climb, bank or dune to shelter behind. Young birds can be found in same way, as they stand up on parents' return and run to greet them.

96 **GREENSHANK**
Tringa nebularia

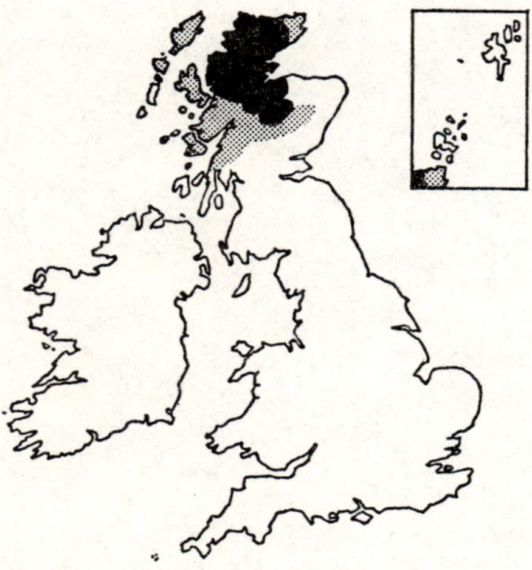

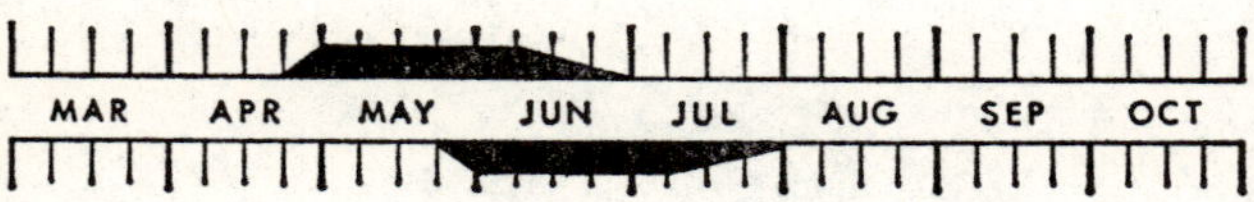

Scarce; main centre north and central Scottish Highlands (south to north Argyll, Perth and Aberdeen) with outliers in Skye and Outer Hebrides; sporadic breeding elsewhere. Typically bare moorland with scattered heather growth on mossy hummocks divided by peat runnels, traversed by long ridges of rock carrying patches of vegetation and dotted with adventitious boulders; also on less rocky moors with scattered pines, even open coniferous forest, and sometimes on flow ground without rocks or boulders; usually within 2 km or less of loch or lochan.

Nest (♀ attended by ♂) Scrape lined small leaves, lichen, pine needles, wood fragments, hare's droppings, according to locality; said to be 'always' touching stone, outcropping rock, or piece of dead, bleached wood, but some nests in mossy hummocks (occasionally surrounded by water) of *Sphagnum* or *Rhacomitrium*. Most sites open or lightly masked with heather or grass; tangential wood may be fallen trunk, log or stump, or, where railway crosses habitat, discarded snow fencing; sometimes against roots of living pine, in recess of big boulder or on patch of recently burnt heather (*Handbook*). Solitary. Eggs 4 (3 to 5, larger numbers due to 2 ♀♀) buff to faintly greenish, streaked and blotched or finely marked all over with reddish-brown, rather glossy (51 × 35 mm). Incubation (♀♂) 24 to 25 days. Fledging (♀♂) nidifugous, about 4 weeks. One brood. (Plate 7b)

Methods This is nest-finder's 'blue riband', normally demanding many hours in field. Variety of calls and distinctive song (by both sexes) enables pair to be located, followed by intensive watching for site-selection routine (very complicated when ♂ bigamous): ♂ and ♀ utter 'broken sobbing cries' and ♂ 'deeper growling note' (Nethersole-Thompson) and number of trial scrapes made. Failing exhaustive watching, usual method is to contact off-nest bird at feeding loch. It becomes excited before flying off direct for 2 km or more and may have to be traced over several days. Near nest it may perch on rock, skyline or tree or walk about, calling repeated *tchook tchook tchook* or *chip chip chip*; sometimes broken sob used. Eventually bird drops quickly to nest. This may have to be observed at very long range so final search of large area of difficult ground often necessary. Bird normally sits very close but sometimes flushes a few metres away; it often rises silently straight off nest, but may scream, even off fresh eggs (Whitaker). Observers stopping to have lunch during search have found Greenshank sitting beside them, and even been able to stroke birds on nest. Behaviour changes when eggs near hatching and parents fly round, mobbing violently. Simson gives detailed account of methods worked out by N Gilroy and developed by himself for Sutherland habitats: nest normally within 350 m of small pool 'with at least one swampy, mossy margin' over which babies can run before being led away to larger lochan or loch; once birds and area located, change over at nest must be awaited every 12 hours (according to Macomb Chance, 6 to 7 a.m. and p.m.). Short-circuiting method successfully used by McNicol brothers involved numbers of artificial sites, provided with tangential wood fragments, on areas frequented by Greenshanks. They maintained that birds always nested near straight line (presumably originally exposed ridge of rock) of old peat road, dyke, fence-line or railway. Monograph: Nethersole-Thompson (1951).

97 **TEMMINCK'S STINT**
Calidris temminckii

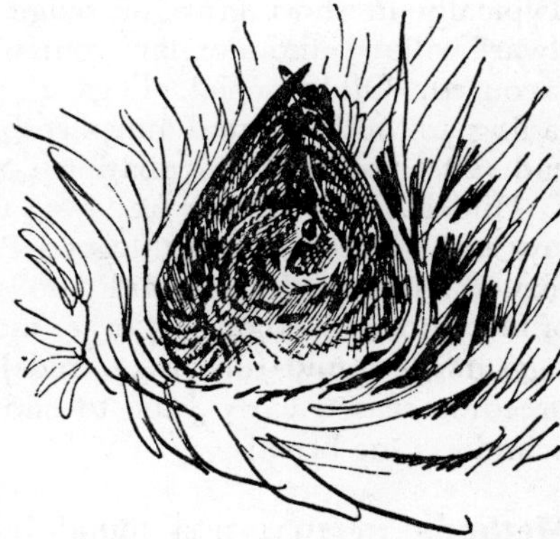

Unsuccessful breeding recorded Inverness 1934, 1936 and 1956 and West Riding 1951; more recently, pairs seen displaying in Easter Ross 1969–71, and in July 1971 two chicks found at one site and evidence of second breeding pair some 200 m away (C G Headlam, *Scottish Birds* 7: 94). Scottish habitats near lochs in wooded country, at 300 m in 1956, but on 'low ground' in 1969–71; Yorkshire nest on industrial waste land near flash; in Fenno-Scandia commonest near sea level but up to 1,000 m, on small islands, fields often near habitations, sedgy ground with low scrub and *Empetrum* heaths.

Nest (♀?) In 1934 'quite a deep, cup-shaped hollow' without added material (G R Edwards, *BB* 28: 97–9); 1936 nest not described (*Naturalist* 1938: 321); in 1956 'small cup sparsely lined with grasses' (D A Bannerman, *Birds of the British Isles* vol. 9: 287–8); Yorkshire scrape about 7 cm diameter (*YNU Ornithological Report* 1951:

85); all nests apparently fairly exposed in short grass, in 1934 only 2·5 m from loch in vicinity of flood debris. Typically in short grass or sedge areas, sometimes with dwarf willow, and not far from water; river islets much favoured. Often social. Eggs 4 (3 to 4) greenish-grey fading to buff, spotted purplish-brown especially at big end (28 × 20 mm). Incubation (♂ and ♀) 21 to 22 days. O Hildén (*Ornis Fennica* 42: 1–5) found that ♀ frequently lays two clutches (cf Red-legged Partridge), ♂ incubating first, ♀ second, which is laid 2 to 4 days after completion of first clutch. Fledging (♂ or ♀) nidifugous, 2 to 2½ weeks. Eggs hard-set mid-June 1934, mid-July 1951 suggest British breeding season early June to end July, much as Fenno-Scandia. One brood.

Methods In 1934 nest found by flushing bird, which fluttered off slowly (Edwards). In 1951 bird returned with 'broken wing display' then walked up to sit on eggs. In 1956 ♂ and ♀ watched making scrapes 18 days before nest found: bird returned with low skimming flight, ran last few yards, froze and disappeared (Nethersole-Thompson). Highly characteristic moth-like display flight with wings half-raised and vibrated, and tail spread, accompanied by continuous trill lasting minute or more, makes up in distinctiveness what it lacks in greater carrying power of aerial displays of other waders; bird may rise and fall like yo-yo, hover, circle round or fly from perch to perch, or glide down to ground; also trills when perched, usually with one or both wings raised, flicked or fanned up and down, flashing light undersides. Actions increase in intensity when observers on breeding ground, clearly indicative of imminent or actual nesting. Change-overs not infrequent and this confiding species is easily watched back.

98 **DUNLIN**
Calidris alpina

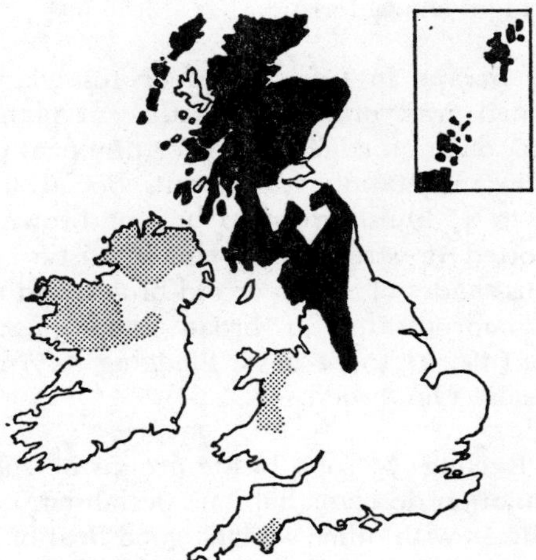

Not scarce; typically highland and coastal from Northern Isles and Outer Hebrides (absent some Inner) south to north Derby; local north and central Wales and north-west Ireland; breeds very small numbers Dartmoor and occasionally Bodmin Moor (Cornwall); sporadically elsewhere (e.g. Norfolk 1938, Cheshire 1955, Lincoln 1956). Range from saltings and Hebridean *machair* to peat caps of hills over 1,200 m in wide variety of boggy and marshy conditions, with extension to quite dry grassland; typical upland habitat wet grass moor of *Scirpus caespitosus* and cotton grass (not rush and *Molinia* bogs), extending to peat moss and flow ground with pools, peat hags and small burns usually close by; in Hebrides boggy pockets divided by rocky ridges characteristic.

Nest (♀?) Scrape in tuft, clump or tussock, or among heather, lined grass or leaves of adjacent plants, usually well hidden, often on edge of ditch or tiny peat pool where tuft of taller vegetation stands out. Social to colonial. Eggs 4 (3 to 4) bluish-green to buff or brown, finely or thickly spotted or streaked in characteristic spiral twist with various shades of brown or red-brown and underlying ashy-grey, concentrated at broad end (35 × 25 mm). Incubation (♂♀) 21 to 22 days. Fledging (♀♂) nidifugous, about 4 weeks. One brood.

Methods Reeling ♂♂ soon locate groups or colonies but, unless population dense or habitat specialised, not an easy nest to find. As with other waders, good deal of individual variation in distance at which sitting birds flush; minority sit very close. Most, however, fly or run off at up to 10 m (their wildness probably increasing on windy days which predominate in many of their habitats) and are very difficult to spot. If incubation not advanced, bird may fly straight away, but when eggs hardset ♂♀ approach observer and play 'hot and cold', continuing this behaviour with guttural *kwot kwot* call after young hatched and at large. Off-nest bird probably warns sitting mate. Searching recommended on calm evenings, with wind and sun behind observer whenever possible. Watching back from pool where off-nest bird feeding may be tried but not very rewarding in broken habitats.

99 **RUFF**
Philomachus pugnax

Formerly bred over much of eastern England and regularly East Anglia until 1871, sporadically Norfolk until 1922, then no records until 1963 when very small numbers started breeding Ouse Washes; has also summered several times at Cley, Norfolk. Apparent preference for winter-flooded lower levels of washes, with variety of vegetation, including many grasses, and heavily grazed in summer; west European habitats similar but extend to tundra marshes in far north.

Nest (♀) Scrape lined fine grasses, usually but not always well hidden in marsh vegetation, e.g. sedge *Carex disticha*, reed grass *Phalaris arundinacea* and rough meadow grass *Poa trivialis*, in general area of display 'hill' or lek, which may be level patch or slight rise, perhaps formed by earth dredged from dyke or ditch. Solitary, though a number of ♀♀ nest in vicinity of lek. Eggs 4 (3 to 4) glossy, pale green to buff, boldly spotted and blotched dark brown with underlying ashy, concentrated at big end rather like Snipe (44 × 31 mm). Incubation (♀) 21 days. Fledging (♀) nidifugous, about 4 weeks. One brood.

Methods Leks or hills indicate general breeding area and, if watched, may suggest number of ♀♀ present and probably nesting within 450 m, but since ♂♂ take no further part after mating, nest hard to find. ♀ usually creeps off silently at long or short range, but sometimes sits tight and may be flushed; even then very well hidden nests not easy to see. Watching back may work where suitable hiding places overlook breeding area, particularly as ♀ flies straight towards nest and pitches close to it (Connor).

100 **AVOCET**

Recurvirostra avosetta

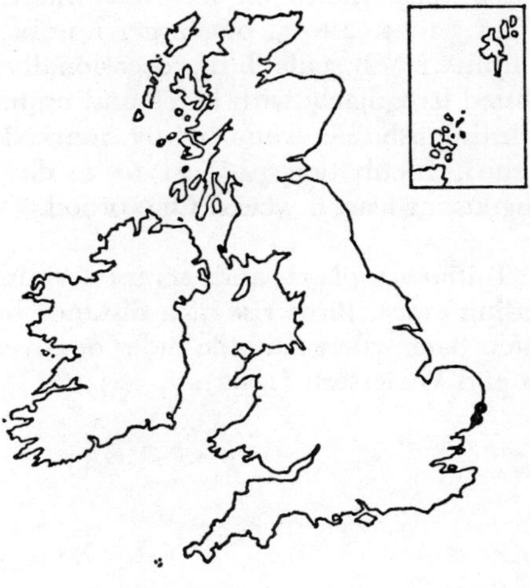

Scarce; bred eastern England (Humber to Sussex) until first half 19th century, then no more records until Wexford 1938 and sporadically Essex and Norfolk 1941–6; recolonised Suffolk 1947 and now confined mainly to Havergate (around 100 pairs) and Minsmere (25 pairs in 1971); odd records north Kent (1958) and probably Essex (1953). Habitat very specialised: shallow brackish 'lagoons' with muddy banks and islets carrying sparse halophytic vegetation.

Nest (♀♂) Scrape, sometimes bare, usually lined and rimmed with dead stalks and drift litter, occasionally built up substantially under threat of flood; sited on low mounds often only metre or so from water. Social to colonial. Eggs 3 to 4 (2 to 5, but larger numbers recorded evidently from 2 ♀♀) pale buff, occasionally yellowish-brown, spotted irregularly with black and underlying ashy marks, indistinguishable from lightly marked Lapwings (51 × 35 mm). Incubation (♀♂) 21 to 22 days. Fledging (♀♂) nidifugous, at least 6 weeks. One brood.

Methods Initial displays and scrape-forming indicate likely breeding areas. Birds rise at a distance but are very easy to watch back where suitable hides or cover available. See Brown and Waterston (1962).

101 BLACK-WINGED STILT

Himantopus himantopus

Two pairs bred successfully and third nest robbed Nottingham 1945, year of exceptional influx (J Staton, *BB* 38: 322–8). Habitat was old type sewage farm, resembling shallow lagoon, with rapidly growing vegetation; on Continent frequently on shallow pools and flooded marshland with tussocks.

Nest (♀♂?) Varies from mud scrape lined with few pieces of grass or dead reed, or simple hollow in tussock, to substantial structure built up from below water with local vegetation and mud; two English nests had few small white stones in hollows in rapidly growing persicaria, mayweed, dock and chickweed. Social to colonial. Eggs 3 to 4 (3 to 5, larger numbers due to 2 ♀♀) pale stone fairly evenly spotted and blotched dark brown with underlying ashy marks, like one type Lapwing but smaller (44 × 31 mm). One English nest hatched 25 June and juvenile flew after 30 to 31 days. Birds rose at long range and both ♂♀ demonstrated over observers, who found nests by searching suspected area.

102 **RED-NECKED PHALAROPE**
Phalaropus lobatus

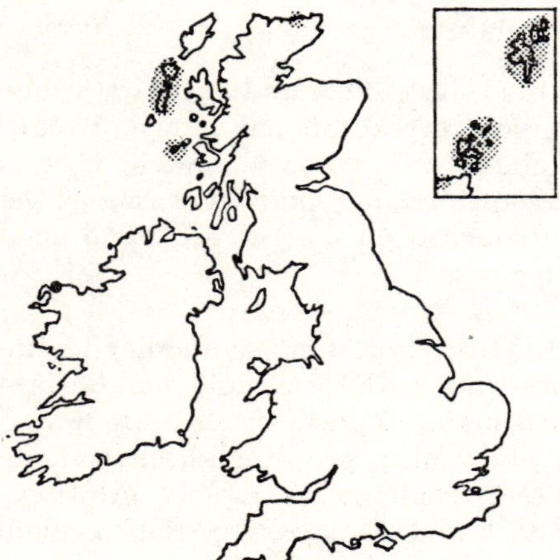

Very scarce (fluctuating between 28 and 65 pairs in 1968–70); main strength now Fetlar, but a few pairs elsewhere Shetland, Orkney, Outer Hebrides, Tiree, and single localities Scottish mainland and north Mayo (M J Everett, *BB* 64: 293–302). Prefers boggy margins of shallow lochans or water-filled peat cuttings, characterised by bogbean, sedges and yellow iris.

Nest (♀♂ make scrapes, ♀ lays in one) Scrape rather large for size of bird, lined grasses, other dry stems and small leaves, usually well hidden in grass tussock, sedges, iris or moss, but one Hebridean nest in tall reeds and *Scirpus lacustris*; in Iceland often under dwarf willow (J H McNeile); sites usually damp but up to 400 m from open water. Social to colonial. Eggs 4 (3 to 7) pale green to buff with heavy sepia blotches and spots (30 × 21 mm). Incubation (♂) 20 days. Fledging (♂) nidifugous, 2½ to 3 weeks. One brood.

Methods Birds, confiding and faithful to particular localities, easily located as they swim about in lochan or pool, and search in vicinity may be successful if suitable area not too extensive: three out of four Hebridean nests found like this with incomplete clutches. ♂♂ on water may also be watched until they visit nests; one, chased by ♀, flew straight to nest with complete clutch; another, watched by Whitaker, flew 1 km and visited nest 'momentarily'. ♂ usually sits very tight (McNeile).

103 **STONE CURLEW**

Burhinus oedicnemus

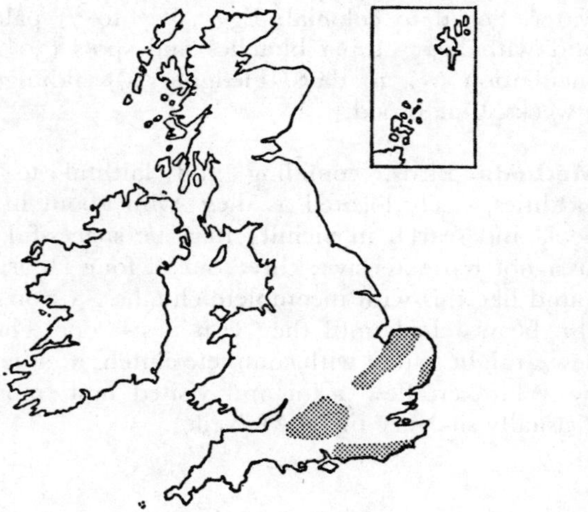

Scarce; restricted to calcareous areas in East Anglia and southern England west to Wiltshire and Dorset. On chalk downs, brecks, sandy heaths and warrens, dunes and shingle beaches; has tried to adapt to arable land and wide fire traces between conifer plantations, as much of old habitat either ploughed up, planted or grown over since decline of rabbit, and majority of decreasing population now on cultivated land with remnants on heaths and sheep-grazed grassland.

Nest (♀♂?) Usually deep and rather obvious scrape lined pebbles and rabbit droppings, but sometimes hardly perceptible; generally on open bare ground from ploughed field to flinty breck, occasionally in turf, sometimes by shrub and nowadays close to plantations; exceptionally in straw stack 3 m up (*Handbook*). Solitary to loosely social. Eggs 2 (1 to 3) rather rounded, pale buff or stone irregularly spotted, streaked or blotched with dark brown and some underlying ashy marks (54 × 38 mm). Incubation (♀♂) 25 to 27 days. Fledging (♀♂) nidifugous, 6 weeks. Occasional second brood (*Handbook*).

Methods Best advice from Walpole-Bond who found many nests in south-east England. Pair in breeding area for some time before laying; often sitting in scrapes. (N W Orr recommends searching with binoculars into sun, when shadows often shows birds up.) When incubation starts, off-nest bird frequently nearby and first to run, then fly away, usually silently, followed by sitter who may run 250 m before rising (in at least one fenced-in nature reserve today birds do not fly at all). Watching back from concealment 100 m or more from suspected site recommended, bird usually returning within 15 minutes, though approach varies: generally low direct flight followed by crouching run-in perhaps for several hundred metres. But may make several short flights or runs, even pausing apparently to feed before reaching nest, beside which it sometimes stands before settling down. Occasionally overshoots nest and retraces steps. Pair may return part of way together, off-nest bird then resuming watch. They can also be watched back to young which keep together after leaving scrape, but beware of birds crouching on tarsi as if brooding.

Ducks not illustrated individually: left from top, pair of Long-tailed Ducks (p. 99) and pair of Goldeneyes (p. 98); right, ♀ Velvet Scoter and young (p. 99) and pair of Red-crested Pochards (p. 92)

104 **GREAT SKUA**
Stercorarius skua

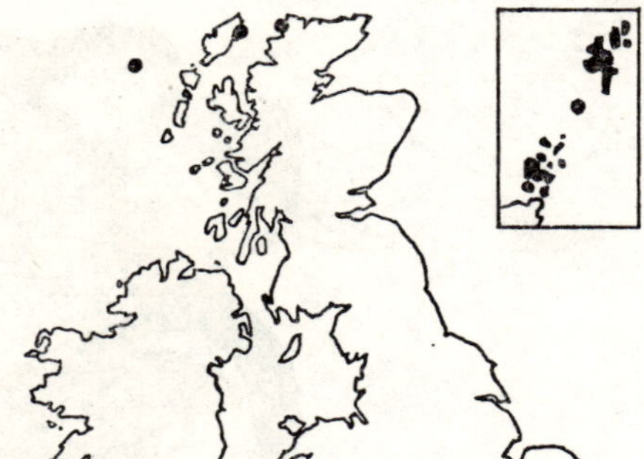

Not scarce; main centres Shetland and Orkney, especially Foula, Fair Isle and Hoy; small numbers Lewis since 1945, spreading to St Kilda 1962, Handa 1964 and recently Eilean nan Roan; reports in breeding season Caithness and mainland Sutherland. Grass or heather moorland near sea: 'flattish stretches of tussocky grass with small waterholes' (Whitaker); also on peat mosses.

Nest (♀♂) Scrape or hollow with some lining of local material, but grass brought to nests in heather; sometimes on tussocks in very wet ground. Solitary to social from few to many pairs, often well scattered. Eggs 2 (1 to 3) variable from light stone to reddish-brown, usually with dark spots and blotches; pale blue varieties occur (71 × 49 mm). Incubation (♀♂) 28 to 30 days. Fledging (♀♂) nidifugous, 6 to 7 weeks. One brood.

Methods Look-out birds on eminences indicate area of nests; pairs circle over and 'buzz' observer as he crosses their territory, but attacks not usually pressed home. Birds may be seen on nests in bare moorland, but rise at long range and need careful marking. Trial scrapes near occupied sites. Grass-lined nests in heather areas much easier to see than those on grass heaths. Nests usually some distance from 'clubs' of birds on traditional patches, characteristically green from years of droppings.

105 **ARCTIC SKUA**
Stercorarius parasiticus

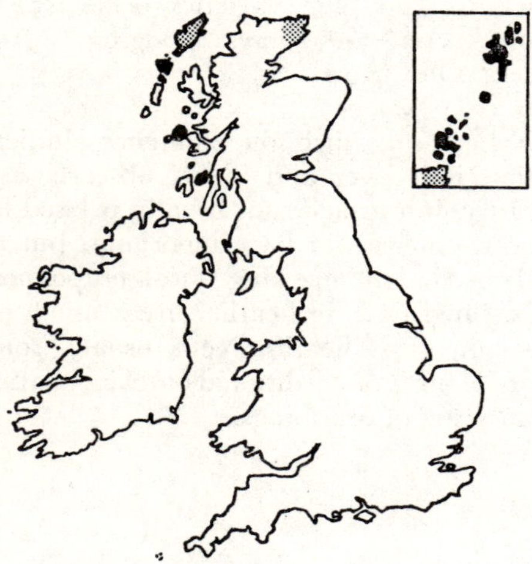

Not scarce; locally common Orkney and Shetland, very local Outer Hebrides, Inner Hebrides (Coll and Jura) and extreme north Scotland. Dry or wet heather or grass moorland, peat mosses and flow ground with small pools; usually near sea but some kilometres inland in Caithness, sometimes among or close to gull colonies.

Nest (♀♂) Shallow scrape or hollow with little or no lining of local material. In tussocky grass and heather or on hummock of moss in flow ground, usually near green perching place. Social, from few to tens of pairs. Eggs 2 (1 to 4) variable green to brown with dark brown spots and a few blotches (57 × 40 mm). Incubation (♀♂) from first egg, 24 to 28 days. Fledging (♀♂) nidifugous, about 4 weeks. One brood.

Methods Before laying, pairs occupy territory, one often sitting as if incubating, without even a scrape. Whitaker described characteristic behaviour with eggs: birds stand or lie on tussocks about 70 m from observer, bobbing upper part of body violently up and down, usually with wings extended; when very excited, flopping and rolling about, with curious call reminiscent of Kittiwake. Bird soon returns to nest if observer can hide 150 to 200 m away, but on rough flow ground may rise 500 m off and nests therefore hard to find by marking and searching. Will also 'buzz' intruders like Great Skua and sometimes, perhaps accidentally, strike them with wing or foot.

106 **GREAT BLACK-BACKED GULL**

Larus marinus

Fairly numerous; along north, west and south coasts of Britain and all coasts of Ireland; breeds Forth islands, otherwise absent Kincardine to Hampshire (though has nested Havergate, Suffolk) and also parts of Wales, but present Man; small numbers breed inland north and west Ireland, parts of Scotland (e.g. Loch Thom, Renfrew, 1970) and Lancashire. Typically on rocky islands and headlands, but not on precipitous cliffs; inland on moors, mosses and islands in lochs; exceptionally on buildings.

Nest (♀♂) Often large pile of grass, woodrush, heather, twigs, seaweed and litter, with a few feathers, but sometimes sparsely lined scrape in peat or among rocks (Connor). Usually sited prominently, either on top of ridge, boulder or eminence, e.g. on very summit of rock 30 m high in Orkney (Whitaker), or along top of cliff face; sometimes just below ridge, sheltered by rock; also on slopes with other gulls, and on moorland and mosses. Sometimes social to colonial, but single pairs common or even usual in some areas. Eggs 2 to 3 (1 to 5) usually pale buff or olive brown, spotted and blotched dark brown, underlying ashy (77 × 54 mm). Incubation (♀♂) before clutch complete, 26 to 28 days. Fledging (♀♂) semi-nidifugous, about 7 or 8 weeks. One brood.

Methods If pair seen on island or headland, look first at highest point in vicinity. Size of nest usually makes watching back unnecessary, but it may sometimes be advisable to clinch identity in this way.

107 **LESSER BLACK-BACKED GULL**

Larus fuscus

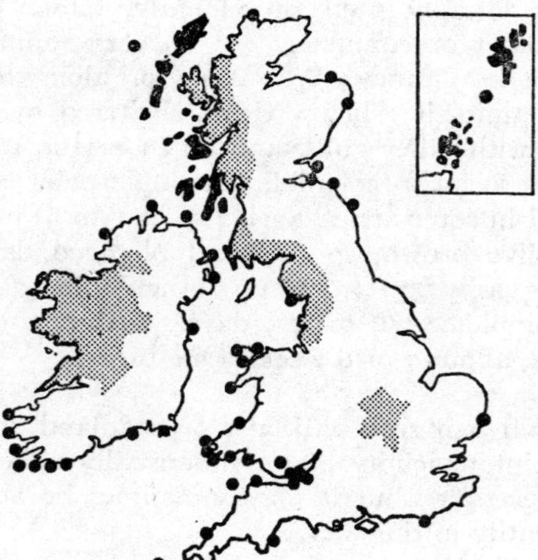

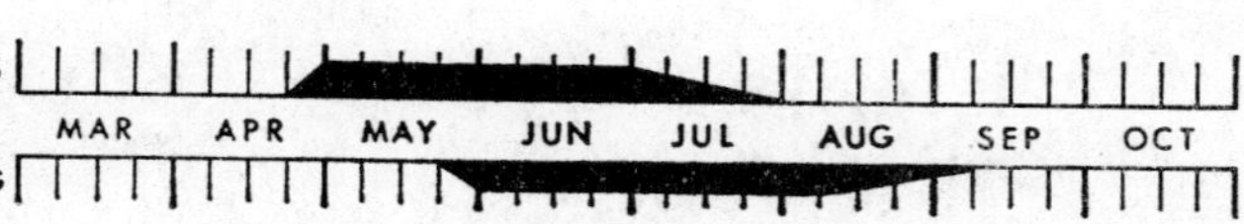

Fairly numerous; widespread but local round coasts, though largely absent east and south England; also inland west Scotland, north-west England, west Ireland, Glamorgan and recently odd pairs in English Midlands. Although overlapping Herring Gull in many coastal (cliff-top and island) colonies, and in great dune 'city' of Walney, Lancashire, also found extensively on moorland and mosses and on islands in lochs; occasionally saltings or shingle, increasingly on buildings (S Cramp, *BB* 64: 476–87).

Nest (♀♂) As Herring Gull on coast, but inland of moss, heather and lichen, as well as grass; rarely only lined scrape. Often in much thicker cover where available: on island with extensive vegetation cap, Herring Gulls found along lower edge more or less on bare rocks, or by large outcrops at higher levels, Lesser Black-backs hidden in heather, bracken or other tall plants (e.g. bluebells on Pembrokeshire islands, alexanders on Puffin Island) though nests often on edge of small bare patch; moorland nests may be widely scattered, but area betrayed by green perching mounds; on buildings almost always with Herring Gulls. Social to colonial, occasional single pairs. Eggs 2 to 3 (1 to 4) varying from pale blue or greenish-blue to dark brown, usually spotted and streaked with blackish-brown, indistinguishable from Herring Gull (68 × 47 mm). Incubation (♀♂) before clutch complete, 26 to 28 days. Fledging (♀♂) semi-nidifugous, 4 to 5 weeks. One brood.

Methods Watching back may be necessary in moorland colonies and certainly to distinguish from Herring Gulls nesting in vicinity, when careful marking essential.

108 **HERRING GULL**

Larus argentatus

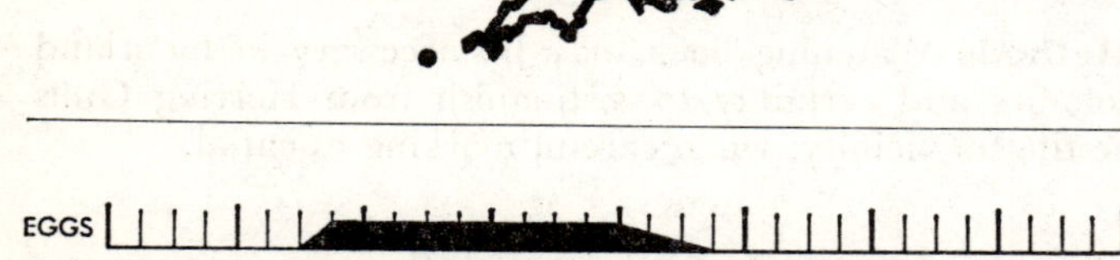

Numerous; general round coasts, except Essex to south Yorkshire (now one colony Suffolk); also inland in western Ireland, Glamorgan, some parts of Scotland and England, even central London. Typical colonies on coastal promontories, on sea cliffs with broad ledges and on broken ground above them, also on steep banks, rocky islands (occasionally in freshwater lochs), sand-dunes (e.g. immense colony Walney, Lancashire) and beaches; recorded on bogs in Ireland and Scotland, by lakes in Merioneth and china clay pits in Cornwall; has colonised buildings in many ports and coastal towns (S Cramp).

Nest (♀♂) Usually substantial mass of grass, seaweed and litter, but sometimes only lined scrape. On cliff ledges, among rocks or littoral vegetation; on dunes or shingle; regularly now on roof tops, against chimney stacks and other supports on buildings; exceptionally in tree or garden bed (C J Stevens). See Lesser Black-back for distinctions between sites. Social to colonial, rarely solitary. Eggs 2 to 3 (1 to 4) vary from pale blue and shades of green to dark brown, spotted and streaked very dark brown, indistinguishable from Lesser Black-back (70 × 48 mm). Incubation (♀♂) begins spasmodically before clutch complete, 28 to 33 days. Fledging (♀♂) semi-nidifugous, about 6 weeks. One brood.

Methods None usually necessary, except when watching back to make census of colony or to distinguish from Lesser Black-backs. Monograph: Tinbergen (1953).

109 **COMMON GULL**
Larus canus

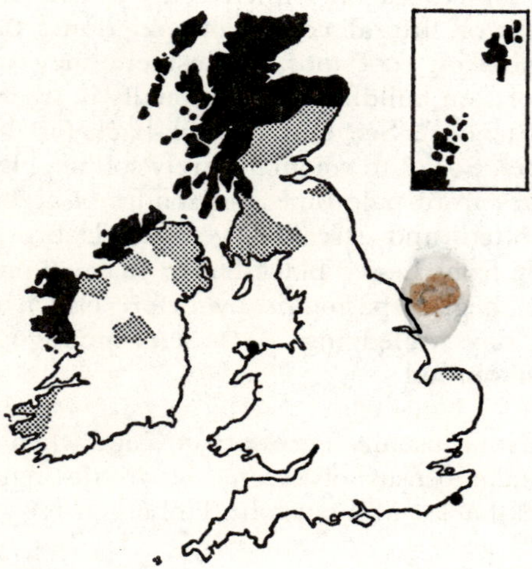

Not scarce; general in Scottish Highlands and islands, Galloway and north and west Ireland; small numbers Berwick, north Norfolk, Anglesey since 1963; long established Dungeness, Kent; sporadically in other Scottish Lowland and English counties (recently Nottingham, York and Durham). The gull of sheltered waters: islets and headlands in sea lochs, hill lochs and moorland tarns; less commonly on islands in sea and coastal slopes; very seldom on or near sea cliffs; also on islands in many large lochs, by shores and shingle rivers, and mosses and moors from sea level to 900 m.

Nest (♀♂) Varies from lined scrape to substantial platform of grass and other vegetable material or seaweed, with odd feathers. On rocky knolls and ledges or among vegetation, sometimes very well hidden; also at water's edge among boulders or rushes. Nests on shingle often well built-up (Whitaker) but on mosses sited like Lapwing or Golden Plover; exceptionally in trees, e.g. islets in Perthshire reservoirs (R N Campbell), also on stonework of dams, tops of posts, even between joining plates of hydro-electric power line (Valerie M Thom) and gantry framework of sliding doors of airfield shed (C J Bridgman). Solitary, social or colonial; sometimes with other gulls or terns. Eggs 2 to 3 (1 to 4) pale blue or green to dark olive, with brown blotches, spots and streaks, often concentrated at big end (58 × 41 mm). Incubation (♀♂) probably before clutch complete, 22 to 25 days. Fledging (♀♂) semi-nidifugous, about 5 weeks. One brood.

Methods Presence of birds usually betrays colony, but those nesting singly or scattered over moors need careful marking after watching back. Sometimes 'buzzes' observers more fiercely than larger gulls when with hardset eggs or young.

110 MEDITERRANEAN GULL
Larus melanocephalus

Several present in huge colony of Black-headed Gulls and some terns on alluvial island covered with *Spartina townsendii* in Hampshire 1968–71. In 1968 one pair reared young and another ♂ mated with ♀ Black headed; presumed hybrid ♂ mated with ♀ Mediterranean or Black-headed in each year (J H Taverner, *BB* 63: 67–79, 380–2; 65: 185–6). Odd individuals have summered elsewhere in England.

Nest (♀♂) In Hampshire bigger and bulkier than Black-headed and decorated with seaweed (nests of mixed pairs not distinguishable from Black-headed); built of *Spartina*, which provided site. Mainly colonial but in recent expansion in north-west Europe usually scattered pairs in Black-headed Gull colonies. Eggs 2 to 3, British clutch very much like paler Herring Gulls, relatively larger and broader than Black-headed (average of three: 54 × 40 mm); from early May. Incubation (♀♂) 22 to 24 days. Fledging (♀♂) semi-nidifugous, about 30 days for 1968 brood. One brood.

Methods Worth examing Black-headed colonies for individuals or pairs. If located, extremely careful watching and marking needed to identify nests.

111 **BLACK-HEADED GULL**
Larus ridibundus

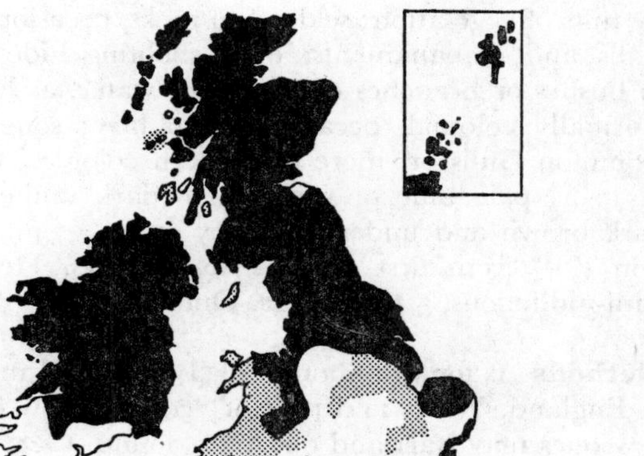

Numerous; local to general throughout highland and coastal Britain and Ireland (except south-west); scattered lowland colonies elsewhere. From moorland pools (up to 750 m) with boggy, often treacherous fringes, to dry dunes and tidal mud flats and saltings; also on or by meres, lakes, flashes, gravel pits, rushy bogs, and formerly old sewage farms; but seldom on rocky coasts or sea islands.

Nest (♀♂) Varies from mere scrape to substantial structure of dead grass and local plants, littered with a few feathers. Often among aquatic plants, e.g. bogbean, bulrushes, reeds, or in tussocks of rushes, sedges, grasses; other sites flat on mud, sand or shingle, sometimes partly sheltered by tufts of vegetation; seldom on rocks, occasionally on low walls and embankments, even shooting hide, sometimes in bushes or branches of trees over water, as high as 7 m. Normally colonial, occasionally solitary; sometimes with Common Gulls or, more often, tern colonies. Eggs 2 to 3 (2 to 4) pale blue or greenish to dark umber, blotched dark brown and underlying grey (52 × 37 mm). Incubation (♀♂) from first egg, 22 to 24 days. Fledging (♀♂) semi-nidifugous, 5 to 6 weeks. One brood.

Methods As for Common Gull. Location of most colonies in England, Wales and part of Scotland now known, but new ones may start and odd pairs found. Overhead attentions of adults do not necessarily mean nest in vicinity.

112 **KITTIWAKE**
Rissa tridactyla

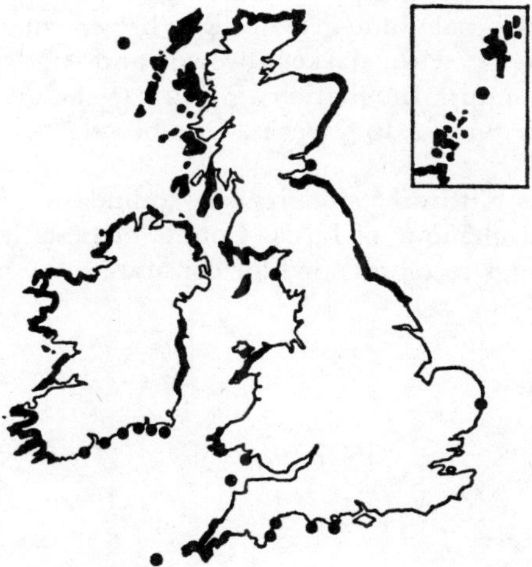

Numerous; local round coasts of Britain (absent most of West Highland mainland, south-east England except Suffolk), Ireland and Man. The gull of sea cliffs, stacks and caves; also colonies in east coast ports, including one 15 km up Tyne (J C Coulson and A Macdonald, *BB* 65: 171–7; S Cramp); exceptionally on shingle beaches (Norfolk 1946, 1958).

Nest (♀♂) Neat construction of seaweed and sometimes grass and moss, with deeper cup than other gulls, becoming very white and compacted after young hatch. On small ledge or bracket of cliff or wall of sea cave, often somewhat overhung and usually inaccessible; on window ledges of buildings, walls and piers; on shingle in Norfolk. Colonial. Eggs 1 to 3, pale blue-grey to light brown, marked, chiefly at big end, with darker brown and underlying ashy (55 × 40 mm). Incubation (♀♂) 21 to 24 days. Fledging (♀♂) nidicolous, 4 to 5 weeks. One brood.

Methods Kittiwake colonies easy to find and identify from continual clamour of birds. Counts of nests large enough to hold eggs recommended for censuses.

113 **BLACK TERN**
Chlidonias niger

Very scarce; bred several east English counties to mid 19th century; several pairs nested Ouse Washes 1966 and 1969, one pair Ireland 1967. On flooded marshland and lakes with floating vegetation; Irish nest on rocky island in freshwater lough; on Continent also on large lakes with much floating vegetation and on old river courses (Connor).

Nest (♀♂) Floating heap of local vegetation, lined finer stems, in wet marshes or resting on aquatic plants; also thinly lined scrape on firmer ground. Solitary, social or colonial. Eggs 3 (2 to 4) brownish or greenish heavily streaked or blotched with dark or blackish-brown and underlying ashy (35 × 25 mm); late May to early June. Incubation (♀♂) 14 to 17 days. Fledging (♀♂) semi-nidifugous, 3 to 4 weeks. One brood.

Methods Presence of birds reveals likely locality and colonies easily found, though single nests may need watching back. Disturbance of site should be kept to minimum.

114 **GULL-BILLED TERN**
Gelochelidon nilotica

Bred on island in Abberton reservoir, Essex, 1950 and probably 1949 (G A Pyman and C B Wainwright, *BB* 45: 337–9). Birds still recorded annually on south-eastern and south coasts and breeding could take place again on saltings, sandy coasts or inland lakes. Nest a shallow scrape, scantily lined grass or other local materials, on island, shore or beach. Solitary to colonial. Eggs 3 (2 to 5) creamy white or yellowish to brownish, sparingly spotted dark brown (49 × 35 mm); May to early June.

115 **COMMON TERN**
Sterna hirundo

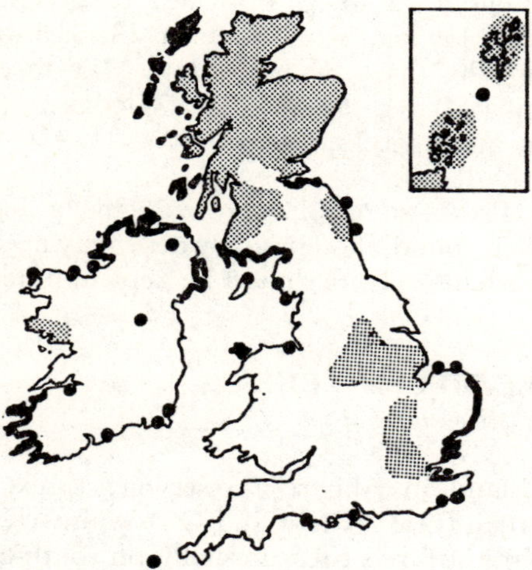

Fairly numerous; colonies local round British and Irish coasts, except much of west England and Wales; also inland in many north Scottish and some north and west Irish counties, and recently in about twelve English counties from Kent to Stafford and York. Coastally on low-lying sandy, shingly or thrift-turf shores, low rocky islets and skerries, sand banks, dunes and links; inland on islets in lochs, shingle beds, mosses and moorland by rivers (up to 400 m in Scotland) and on gravel pits and old sewage farms in England.

Nest (♀♂) Scrape or hollow lined or framed with varying amounts of local materials, especially thrift or marram stalks. Usually open, even on slightly raised areas; sometimes in line of dead seaweed or drift on shore, in old gull nests or partly protected by marram clump; in vegetation patches of splash zone on rocky islets; occasional floating nests (regular on Continent); also on wooden artefacts, e.g. sunken boats, old piers and specially built rafts (Norfolk). Social to colonial, occasionally solitary; sometimes with other terns, Black-headed or Common Gulls. Eggs 2 to 4, varying from cream to dark brown, also pale green and blue, with spots and blotches of dark brown and underlying ashy (41 × 30 mm). Incubation (♀♂) from first egg, 22 to 26 days. Fledging (♀♂) semi-nidifugous, about 4 weeks. One brood.

Methods Watching back in mixed colonies necessary to determine species, and greatest care should be taken when attempting to separate Arctic and Common Terns. Isolated or scattered nests need very accurate marking, especially on moorland.

116 **ARCTIC TERN**
Sterna paradisaea

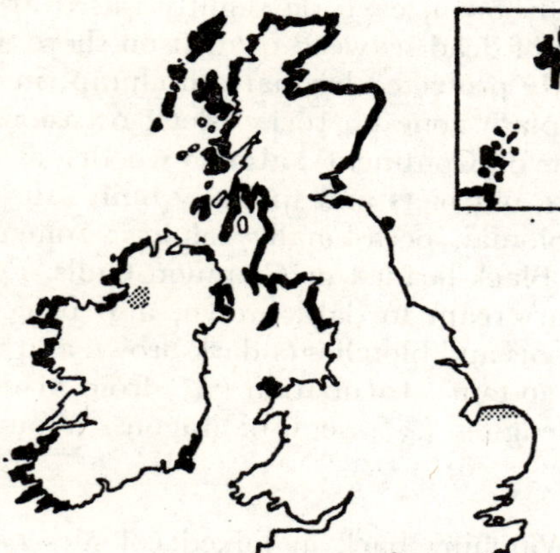

Fairly numerous; widespread Scottish and some Irish coasts but inland now in only one Irish locality, though kilometre or more from sea in Shetland, Caithness; more northerly than Common Tern, but odd colonies Man, north and east England and North Wales; sporadic farther south, including Scilly where formerly regular. Habitat similar to Common Tern on coasts; Sutherland colony in dry gravel pit near rivermouth.

Nest (♀♂) Scrape or hollow lined with local material in similar sites to Common Tern; occasionally surrounded by ring of stones (Mayer-Gross). Social to colonial, sometimes solitary, also with other terns and smaller gulls. Eggs 1 to 3 (1 to 4) not certainly distinguishable from Common Tern though usually more boldly marked (40 × 29 mm). Incubation (♀♂) sometimes from first egg, 21 to 22 days. Fledging (♀♂) semi-nidifugous, 3 to 4 weeks. One brood.

Methods As for Common Tern, but attacks intruders with greater determination when close to nest, often striking head and even drawing blood. Isolated pairs may nest among Common Terns in south; where both species in strength, they generally keep slightly apart.

117 ROSEATE TERN
Sterna dougallii

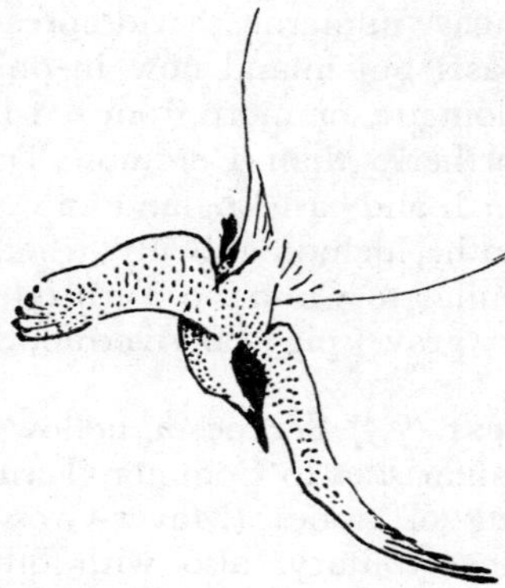

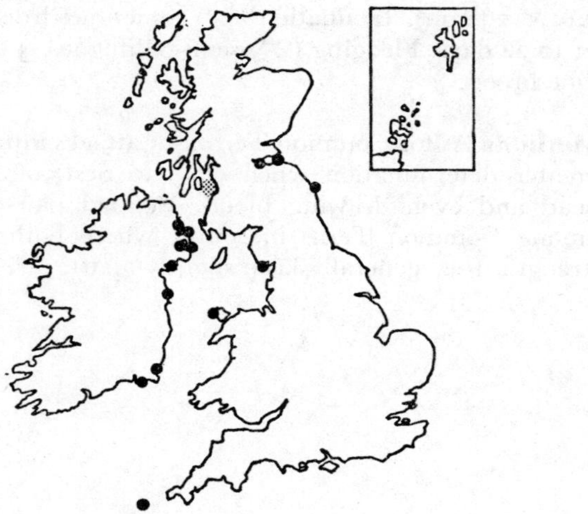

Not scarce; centre of distribution now Irish east coast, also colonies west Ireland (localities suppressed), north Lancashire, Anglesey, Scilly, Northumberland and Forth islands; formerly and now sporadically Clyde; three pairs Orkney 1969. Maritime, on low rocky, sandy or grassy islets and sand-shingle beaches.

Nest (♀♂) Scrape or hollow with practically no lining. Preference for recessed, even concealed sites in hollows between fescue tufts (Forth), under tree mallow (Dublin) or buried in bluebells and grasses (R J Connor); Whitaker found Welsh nests exposed on rocky knolls; evidence of both sites from other colonies; overlaps Common Tern in large, mixed aggregations. Social to colonial. Eggs 1 to 2 (1 to 3) cream or buff with tendency to freckles and thin streaks of light or reddish-brown with underlying ashy, often in spiral and sometimes in zone near big end; usually longer and more pointed than Common or Arctic but no absolute determination advisable without seeing birds (44 × 30 mm). Incubation (♀♂) from first egg, 21 to 26 days. Fledging (♀♂) semi-nidifugous, 3 to 4 weeks. One brood.

Methods Watching back necessary for specific identification where Roseates nest with Common and Arctic. Deeply hidden nests require accurate marking. 'Spiky', pale-downed nestling quite distinctive.

118 **LITTLE TERN**

Sterna albifrons

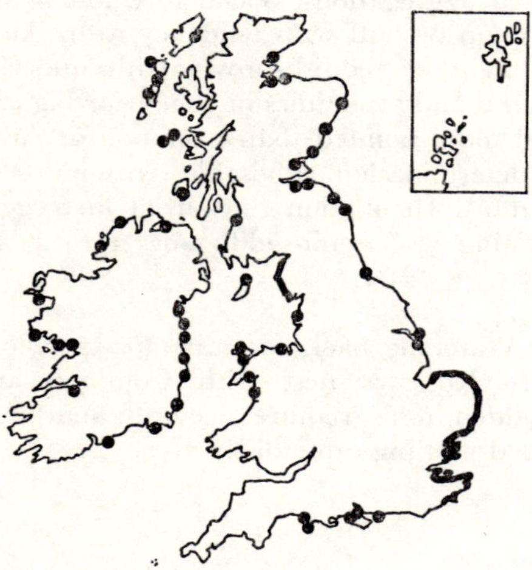

Not scarce (1,600 pairs in 1967); over a hundred colonies locally distributed round low-lying coasts of Britain (especially Norfolk to Dorset), except south-west peninsula, South Wales and West Highland mainland; over forty Irish colonies, mainly very small (R K Norman and D R Saunders, *BB* 62: 4–13). More restricted than Common, Arctic or Roseate to shores or islets of sand, fine shingle, broken shells or occasionally mud; British and Irish colonies normally maritime or in estuaries close to sea, but rarely near fresh water a little way inland (e.g. Minsmere Scrape, Suffolk; formerly island in Essex reservoir); also on crumbled foundations of hangar on Scottish airfield.

Nest (♀♂) Scrape or hollow, usually unadorned, though sometimes small pebbles selected to form lining. Exposed on sandy, shingly or muddy shores with tendency for several nests along same contour line. Social to colonial but usually several metres between nests; Ringed Plovers often associated with Norfolk colonies. Eggs 2 to 3 (1 to 4) pale stone, green or blue with blotches and rather fine spots of light brown and prominent underlying ashy (33 × 24 mm). Incubation (♀♂) from first or second egg, 19 to 22 days. Fledging (♀♂) almost nidifugous, chicks leaving nest within day of hatching, flying at about 4 weeks. One brood.

Methods Requires careful watching back and marking owing to absence of nest material and excellent blending of mat-surfaced eggs with surroundings; also lack of obvious landmarks near many sites. Birds flutter over nests, then drop vertically on to eggs. Cold searching not recommended owing to danger of treading on eggs.

A.F.G.T.B.N.—K

119 **SANDWICH TERN**
Sterna sandvicensis

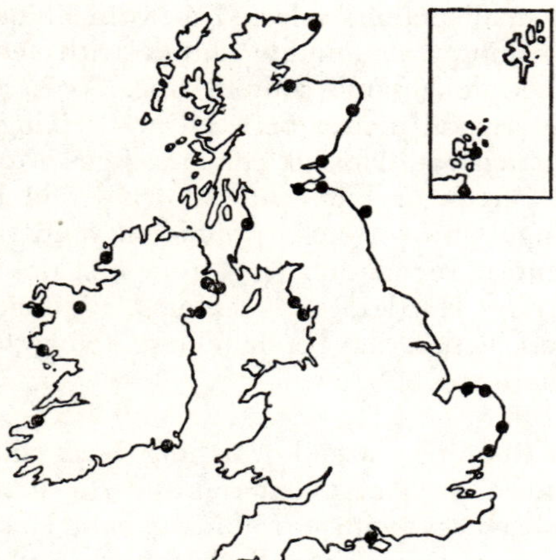

Not scarce (about 6,000 pairs); about forty colonies (though some rather temporary) round British and Irish coasts as far north as Orkney (has bred Shetland), but not from Essex round south coast (except Hampshire), on west coast north to Anglesey (where only occasional) or in West Highlands. Most colonies on dunes, shingle beaches, lagoons, flat mosses near sea, low rocky and sandy islands and shores, and, in west Ireland, grassy islets in freshwater loughs.

Nest (♀♂) Scrape or hollow, sometimes lined with a little local material. Closer together than any other tern; sometimes hidden by marram or other grasses but, as season advances, whole area often shows up as white patch. Strongly colonial, frequently near Black-headed Gulls and Common Terns. Eggs 1 to 2 (1 to 3) white, cream or brown with streaks, spots, blotches or reddish-brown smears and prominent underlying ashy; size and colour distinguish from all other British terns and gulls (52 × 36 mm). Incubation (♀♂) from first egg, 21 to 24 days. Fledging (♀♂) semi-nidifugous, about 5 weeks. One brood.

Methods Penetrating calls and dense white cloud of birds advertise colonies; outlying nests identified by watching back. But more susceptible to disturbance than relatives, perhaps owing to dense aggregations, and visits should be kept to minimum.

120 **RAZORBILL**
Alca torda

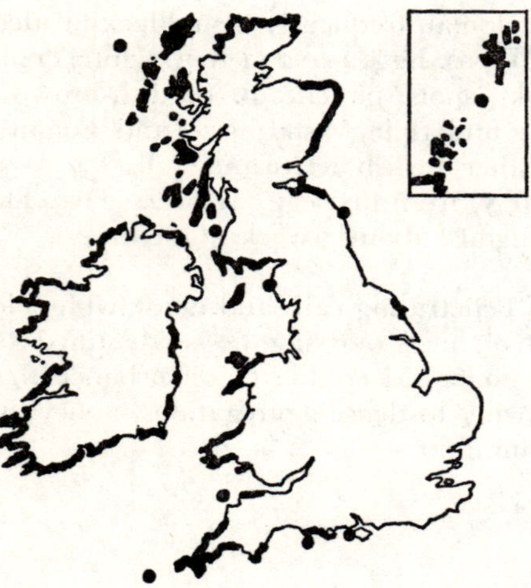

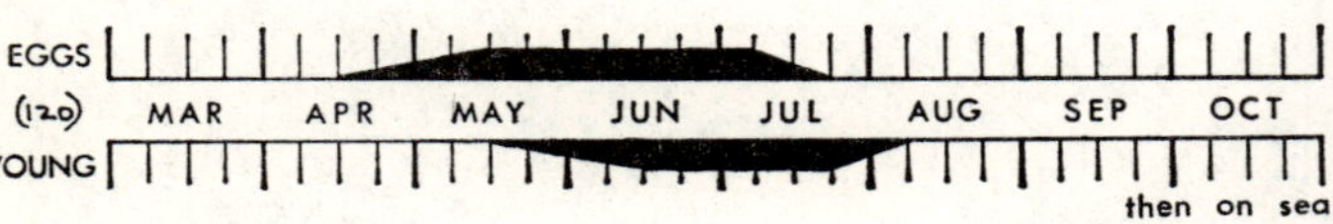

Numerous; colonies widely separated, and absent nearly all English east and south coasts from Humber to Wight, also Cheshire-Lancashire, most of West Highland mainland and part of east coast Ireland. Sea cliffs and precipitous islands with cracks, fissures and loose boulders.

Nest None made. Usually in some recess: hole or crack in rock, under boulder or on sheltered ledge; but sometimes in open, so overlaps with Guillemots and Shags. Colonial, but sometimes scattered among Guillemots. Eggs 1 (1 to 2) less pear-shaped than Guillemot, with rougher surface but less variable: white, greenish to light brown with blotches, spots, speckles or zone markings of dark brown or black (73 × 47 mm). Incubation (♀♂) 26 to 30 days. Fledging (♀♂) nidicolous for first 2 weeks, then descends to sea where continues to be fed. One brood.

Methods None really necessary once colony located unless attempting complete census which, owing to nature of sites, is not normally feasible (more difficult than for Guillemot) and should only be carried out with great care. Birds leave eggs at variable range.

121 GREAT AUK
Pinguinus impennis

Extinct; almost certainly bred St Kilda (last British specimen there 1840), probably Orkney, where last pair killed 1813, possibly elsewhere. Laid single egg on sites generally more accessible than Razorbill.

122 **GUILLEMOT**
Uria aalge

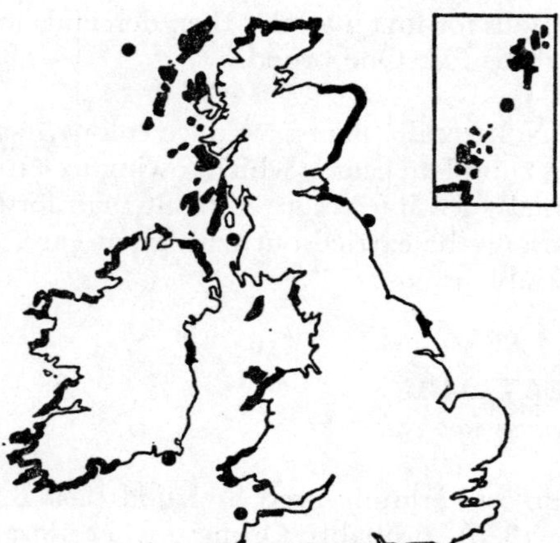

Numerous; distribution much as Razorbill, but usually in far greater numbers, especially in Orkney and Shetland. Sea cliffs with defined ledges, or pinnacles and stacks with flat or terraced tops; occasionally on low rocky islands.

Nest None made. Ledges on cliffs and stacks. Usually strongly colonial in tightly packed ranks or groups, but may nest scattered among larger species, e.g. Cormorants on Farne Islands, Gannets on Grassholm. Single egg extremely variable from creamy white through pale or deep blue-green to shades of buff, even red, with light brown to black spots, blotches, or 'intricate pattern of interlacing lines' (*Handbook*) sometimes zoned, sometimes absent (81 × 50 mm). Incubation (♀♂) 28 to 30 days. Fledging (♀♂) as Razorbill, nidicolous for first 2 weeks, then descends to sea where continues to be fed. One brood.

Methods None needed once colony located, but accurate counts not easy to make. Incubating birds face cliff, half crouching. When counting bridled variety, desirable to make sketch maps of sub-colonies, which should be counted separately, as bridled percentage may vary. Do not count bridled birds unless they can be recognized instantly through binoculars.

123 BLACK GUILLEMOT

Cepphus grylle

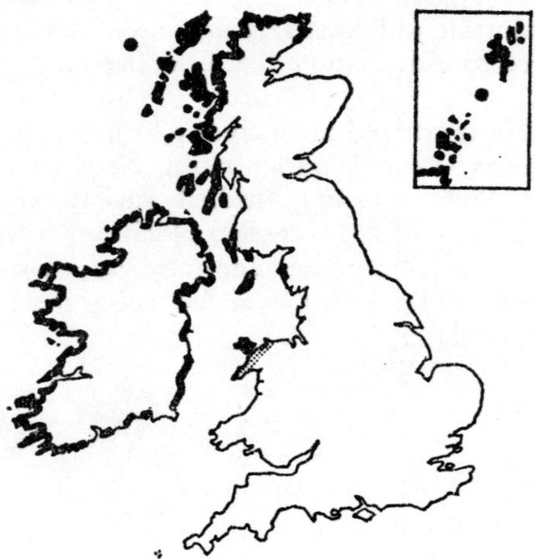

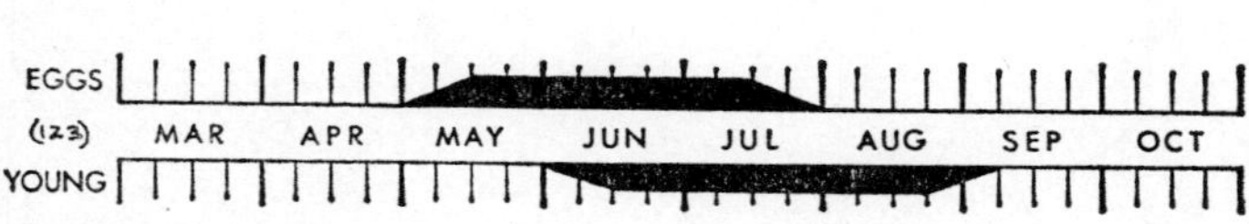

Fairly numerous; widespread Shetland, Orkney, Caithness, then Scottish north and west coasts and islands south to Kintyre, Galloway, Man, Cumberland (St Bees Head), a few pairs Anglesey, perhaps Caernarvon; all Irish coast and islands except for stretches in east; occasionally elsewhere. Rocky but not necessarily cliff-bound or exposed coasts and islands; well up sea lochs in West Highlands, also harbours in Galloway and Ireland.

Nest Apparently none. Typically in holes, crevices and under boulders; under flat slabs of rock in projecting shelves of low cliffs or in talus slopes below big cliffs, holes in masonry (e.g. quay at Bangor, Down), rabbit burrows and exceptionally moored boat and barrel of old cannon. Artificial sites successful in Shetland (R J Tulloch). Sometimes up to 2 m from entrance but eggs can often be seen and may even be reached by sunlight. Solitary to loosely colonial. Eggs 1 to 2 (1 to 3) whitish to pale blue-green and buff, spotted or blotched dark reddish-brown or black with underlying ashy (58 × 39 mm). Incubation (♀♂) from first egg, 21 to 24 days. Fledging (♀♂) nidicolous, about 5 weeks. One brood.

Methods Pairs present near sites before laying; during incubation off-nest birds often in vicinity on rocks or water where joined by mates leaving nests as observer approaches, on foot or by boat. Others sit tight but eventually number on water gives some idea of pairs in colony. On small accessible islands most nests can be found by searching – look out for smoothed entrances and use nose – but accurate counts of large colonies not practicable. Successful nests may be estimated by watching birds fly in with food for young, but good concealment necessary. Same sites used year after year.

124 **PUFFIN**
Fratercula arctica

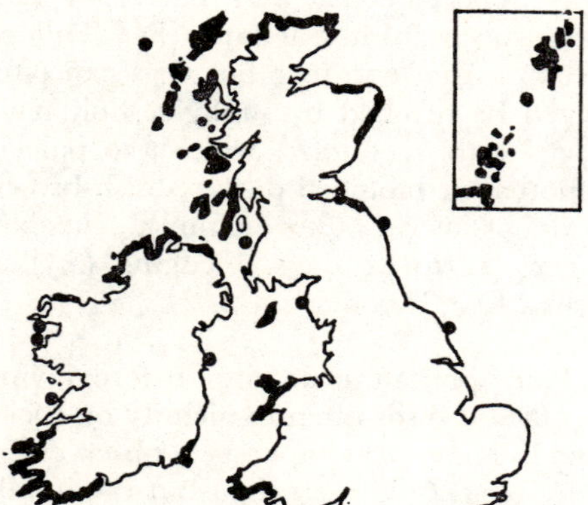

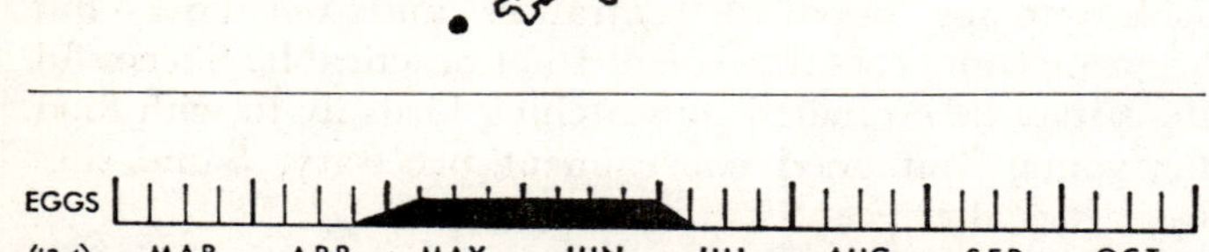

Numerous (until recently classified as abundant but now considerable evidence of decrease); main concentrations round Irish and west British coasts from Scilly north to Shetland; local on east coast south to Yorkshire, then absent Lincoln to Hampshire, very local and decreasing Wight to Cornwall. Turf-clad tops and slopes of cliffs and small islands; also on cliff faces and talus slopes.

Nest (♀♂) Scrape in burrow or hole anything from 50 cm to 2 m from entrance, sometimes lined with dry grass and feathers. Burrows excavated or taken over from Manx Shearwaters and rabbits; also cracks and holes in cliffs and under boulders. On St Kilda and occasionally elsewhere nests in scree up to 1,000 m from sea. Colonial. Eggs 1 (1 to 2) white with traces of markings below surface, but sometimes well-marked with lilac brown, often in zone round big end (61 × 42 mm). Incubation (♀♂) 40 to 43 days. Fledging (♀♂) nidicolous, chick deserted by parents after about 40 days, flies in about 7 weeks. One brood.

Methods More confiding than Black Guillemots and many nests can be found simply by sitting down and watching comings and goings of birds, especially when feeding young. But estimates, let alone accurate censuses, even of small colonies, very difficult to make.

125 **PALLAS'S SANDGROUSE**

Syrrhaptes paradoxus

Bred on sand dunes in Yorkshire in 1888 and in Morayshire in 1888 and 1889 following one of several invasions of Europe by this Asiatic bird of steppe and desert (see *Ibis* 32: 207–14; H A Macpherson, *The Visitation of Pallas's Sand-Grouse to Scotland:* 19–27; T H Nelson, *Birds of Yorkshire:* 502). Westward movements became almost unknown after 1908, but one or two birds reached Britain in 1964 and 1969.

Nest A shallow scrape, often unlined but sometimes with a few bits of grass, either out in open or sheltered by tuft of vegetation. Eggs 3 (2 to 4) markedly elliptical and blunt-ended, stone or buff to yellowish-brown, spotted and blotched with purplish-brown and underlying ashy marks (42 × 30 mm); May to July.

126 STOCK DOVE
Columba oenas

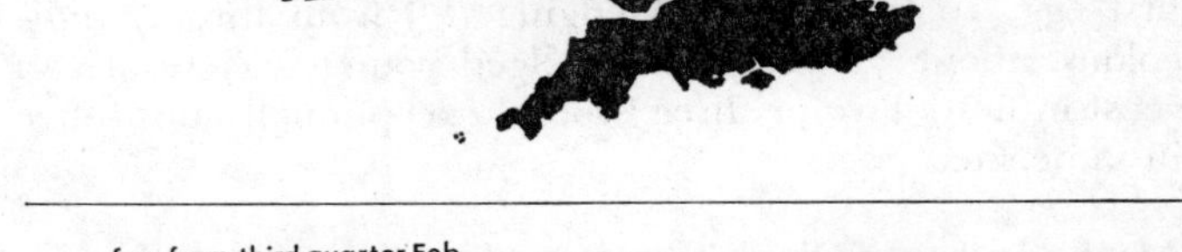

Numerous; general in Britain (except much of north Scotland and islands) and in most Irish counties, though absent parts of Fermanagh, Leitrim, Sligo, Roscommon, Galway; breeds Man. Marked decrease in England, especially south-east, from 1957 to 1965, but appreciable recovery since. Habitat typically with big old trees, e.g. parks, riversides in lowlands, tree-lined hedges; but also quite commonly on inland and sea cliffs, steep banks, old buildings, sand dunes where there are rabbit warrens; and other open country with suitable nest-sites. Penetrates into some towns and up highland valleys.

Nest (♀, material collected by ♂) Small platform of sticks, rootlets, straws, leaves, but in soft debris of tree-hole or cavity in thatch bird may add nothing to scrape; feathers at times, probably mainly or only during moult. Nest-site typically in cavity of some sort, even a metre or more down, in tree, building, dug-out, thatch or rabbit hole; also on sheltered ledges of cliffs, recesses in steep banks, dreys, old nests of other birds, especially Magpie and Woodpigeon (D Goodwin), nestboxes, epicormic shoots (e.g. of lime), almost open sites on flat branches, and on ground under bushes; sometimes in derelict army tanks and other artefacts; exceptional nests in hedges like Woodpigeon. Solitary, social and colonial. Eggs 2 (1 to 3) pure white, but may become dirty, often more pointed and with less gloss than Woodpigeon (38 × 29 mm). Incubation (♀♂) from first egg, 16 to 18 days. Fledging (♀♂ from throat) nidicolous, about 3½ weeks, but fledged young may return to roost in nest. Two or three broods, exceptionally up to five in same site.

Methods Especially where several pairs are breeding together, Stock Doves make enough fuss near nest-sites to give away general location. But to find individual nests may not be so easy, as some sites are well hidden and some birds sit very close, or whip away so quickly that it may be difficult, e.g. in ruinous wall, to see from which hole they have come. So several visits and thorough searching may be necessary; but some sites may be used again and again. Birds may also be watched back where possible sites can be kept in view.

127 **ROCK DOVE/ FERAL PIGEON**
Columba livia

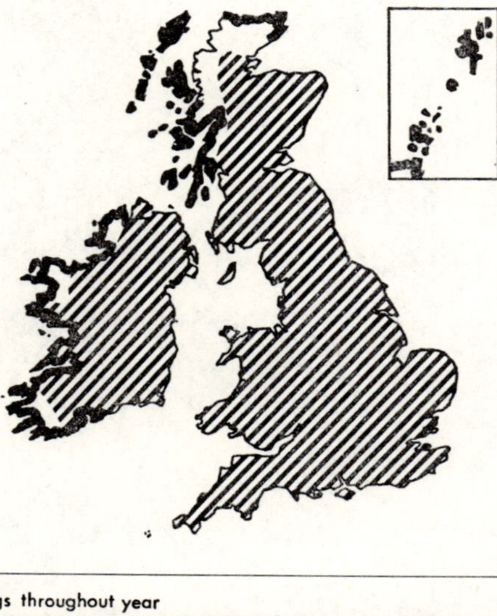

Fairly numerous describes more or less 'pure' stock confined to north and west Scottish and Irish coasts and islands, but coastal populations of feral origin elsewhere, e.g. Flamborough Head, Yorkshire, are now perfectly wild. Habitat of pure stock is sea cliffs, especially with caves, rocky shores and their vicinities, close to feeding areas in fields. Feral stock, showing assorted plumages, including many of original Rock Dove type, and of varying degrees of wildness, now occupy urban habitats in large numbers; other groups are found in rural areas based on old or ruined buildings and on sea cliffs; distribution striped on map.

Nest (♀, material collected by ♂) Sometimes quite substantial, of heather stems, seaweed, grass and roots, but often vestigial; usually in sea cave, which may or may not be accessible at low tide, and placed on ledge or in crevice at varying heights; occasionally on sheltered cliff ledges, under boulders like Black Guillemot (Eynhallow, Orkney) or in ruined buildings and other artefacts like Stock Dove. Urban feral stock nest on occupied buildings, on ledges and in ornamentations and other crevice-like sites. Social. Eggs 2 (1 to 2) pure white and rather glossy (39 × 29 mm). Incubation (♀♂) 17 to 19 days. Fledging (♀♂ from throat) nidicolous, about 4 weeks. Three or four broods from five clutches (see R K Murton and S P Clarke, *BB* 61 : 429–48, for study of Yorkshire population).

Methods Breeding areas of wild stock usually easy to locate by watching birds fly in and out, and accessible sites can be found with aid of torch. Sites of other nests revealed by droppings where cave floor is dry.

128 **WOODPIGEON**

Columba palumbus

Abundant; breeds all counties of Britain and Ireland, but local in north-west Scotland, Outer Hebrides, Orkney and Shetland. Habitat woodland and wooded country everywhere, especially small belts and conifer plantations, but local or scarce in highland scrub-woods. Penetrates to tree limit in upland valleys, to osier-beds and bushes in fens, marshes, saltings and bogs, and well into towns, especially London; also on some tree-less heathery islands, e.g. Orkney, Shetland and Hebrides, and on rocky hillsides.

Nest (♀, material brought by ♂, who sometimes builds) Well described in *Handbook* as 'lattice of small twigs', but some much more solid, and most have definite lining of rootlets, grass or straw; often built on previous nest or other platform, occasionally in old nest of other species or nest-box, but ground nests consist only of lining. Sited variously from ground level through bushes to mature trees at 25 m. Preference for evergreens and ivied trees early in season, with density highest in sitka spruce stands about 25 years old. Later in deciduous cover, especially shrub layer: hawthorn, hazel, blackthorn, elder, honeysuckle. Probably flat boughs on which flimsy nest can be laid are important, e.g. spreading branches of hawthorn, apple and horse chestnut; sometimes overlaps Stock Dove at base of boughs, also on old nests and dreys. Nests on ground in heather (Scottish islands), hedge bottoms, nettle beds, even growing crops and marram-covered dunes. Exceptionally on lighthouse ledges 800 m offshore (M R Williams *BB* 64: 194–5). Apparently social in very suitable habitats. Eggs 2 (1 to 4), pure white and glossy (41 × 30 mm). Incubation (♀♂) from first egg, 16 to 17 days. Fledging (♀♂ from throat) nidicolous, about 4 weeks. Usually tries to rear two broods, exceptionally three.

Methods Anyone can find a few Woodpigeons' nests every season by walking along thick hedges or under spreading trees and looking up, but it is much harder to find large numbers of nests for census or ringing purposes. This is partly due to thick cover favoured at all times in conifer areas, and partly to late breeding peak when deciduous cover is densest. If birds can be watched, it will be found that pairs perch near chosen site and that cooing is a good clue; where there is not time to do this, thorough searching must be relied on. Since parents cover eggs and small young at all times, it is not worth climbing to nests unless there is a sitting bird or large young, normally visible from ground. Monograph: Murton (1965).

129 TURTLE DOVE

Streptopelia turtur

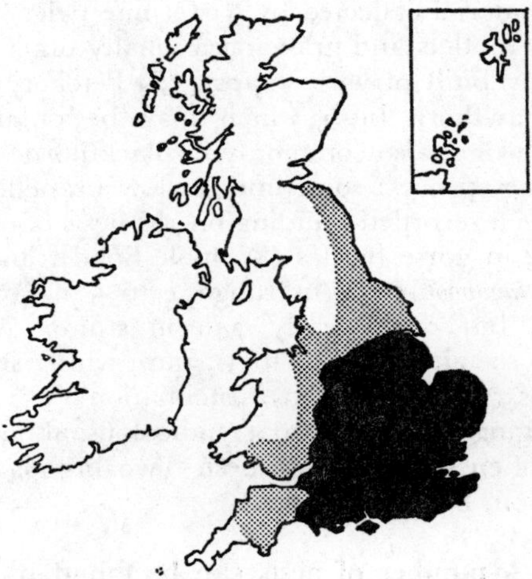

Fairly numerous; general in southern England to Devon and through Midlands north to south Lancashire in west and to Scottish Lowlands in east, but very local north of Yorkshire. Some decrease recently in Wales and does not nest western and north-western counties. Summers east Irish coast from Dublin to Cork, occasionally proved to breed. Distribution closely related to that of principal food plant, fumitory (see R K Murton *et al.*, *Ibis* 106: 174–88). Habitats typically bush-height: thorn-clad downs and commons, overgrown hedges, thickets, copses and woodland edge; also in young conifers, parks and large gardens and orchards.

Nest (♀, material collected by ♂) Of fine twigs, stiff stalks, lined with rootlets and grass, occasionally other materials, e.g. entirely built of wire scraps (J L Petcher). Typically sited in hawthorn bush which may be isolated, or in clump or hedge; also commonly in blackthorn, elder, fruit trees, young spruces; sometimes in low branches of trees, and has been recorded building on old nests of other birds, and dreys; in gorse bushes (Walpole-Bond), and even on ground (*Handbook*); height range 1 to 5 m, average less than 2 m, but once nearly 7 m in stump (Whitaker). Solitary to social. Eggs 2 (1 to 3), pure white, smooth and rather glossy (31 × 23 mm). Incubation (♀♂) about 14 days. Fledging (♀♂ from throat) nidicolous, about 3 weeks; last days often spent outside nest. Two broods usual (see R K Murton, *BB* 61: 193–212).

Methods A number of nests can be found by searching likely habitats where pairs have been seen; sitting bird often flushes noisily, sometimes with mate beside it; others sit very closely. Location by watching, especially during building which may spread over several days. Purring song does not seem to be good guide to site. Same bush may be used for several years (Walpole-Bond).

130 COLLARED DOVE

Streptopelia decaocto

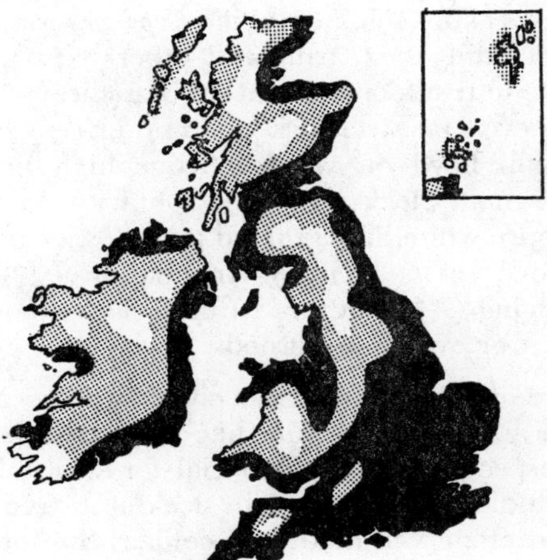

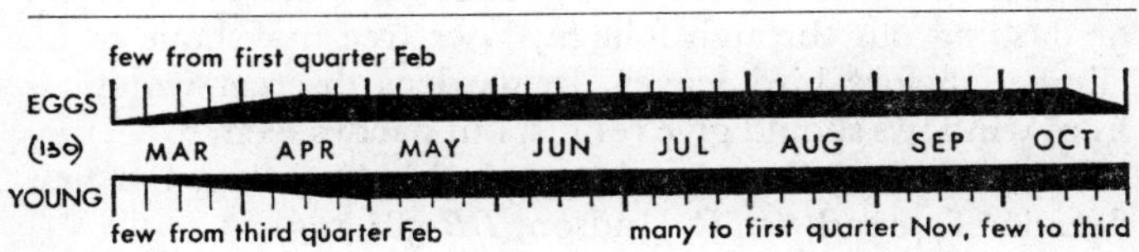

Fairly numerous; rapid spread since first nesting Norfolk 1955 and now breeds throughout Britain, except higher uplands, and in most Irish counties. Associated everywhere with habitations and gardens, especially where poultry and conifers coincide, in suburbia, villages and isolated farms; also penetrates town parks but perhaps not so generally in British cities as on the Continent.

Nest (♀, material collected by ♂) Usually very slight, flat structure of stems lined finer grasses, normally distinct from nest of Turtle Dove except when sticks used; occasional nests entirely of wire scraps; nest sometimes added to during incubation and used for successive broods or in successive years, becoming quite bulky (Simson). Site preference for conifers, especially thick ones like *Cupressus macrocarpa*, also bushes, including box, fruit and other trees up to 20 m, either close to trunk or well out on branches; sometimes on buildings, even on steelwork of crane in centre of Bristol, and in bulb bowl on window ledge high up on Leeds University main block (Simson). Solitary to social. Eggs 2 (1 to 3), pure white, fine grained and glossier than those of Turtle Dove (31 × 24 mm). Incubation (♀♂) about 14 days. Fledging (♀♂ from throat) nidicolous, about 3 weeks. Two, three, or even more broods.

Methods General location by cooing and repeated alighting call of ♂ not difficult but, like other noisy species, can be circumspect near nest, material for which is collected close at hand. Nest easy to see in deciduous tree when bird sitting, but often well hidden in conifer. Simson finds bird leaves nest readily in early stages of incubation if tree tapped, either diving towards ground, and fluttering away, or dashing out through foliage; later tree may have to be climbed before bird leaves. In gardens discreet watching from windows should give results, but parties seem to occupy suitable habitats for several years before breeding. For first decade of spread, see R Hudson, *BB* 58: 105–39.

131 **CUCKOO**
Cuculus canorus

Fairly numerous; breeds all counties of Britain and Ireland, but scarce Orkney and irregular Shetland. General decrease reported since about 1950, except perhaps in Scotland. Habitat very varied, covering those of main fosterers.

Nest Parasitic on other species. British fosterers in probable order of popularity are: Meadow Pipit, Dunnock, Reed Warbler, Pied Wagtail, Robin, Tree Pipit, and Sedge Warbler. Other species also successfully victimised at times, and eggs laid in nests of many more (total for Britain and Ireland over 50). Eggs probably 6 to 18 (P Davis)* laid in different nests, usually of one species; less variable in Britain and Ireland than on Continent, usually off-white through bluish and greenish to brownish and reddish, speckled with grey, brown and greenish-yellow, often with black spots; blue eggs, common on Continent, exceptional in Britain (23 × 17 mm). Incubation (foster-parents) 12½ days. Fledging (foster-parents) nidicolous, about 3 weeks.

Methods One method is to find nests of popular fosterers in area full of Cuckoos; subtler to watch ♀ finding nests herself or preparing to lay in one (normally afternoon). Full account by E P Chance (*The Cuckoo's Secret*, 1922; *The Truth about the Cuckoo*, 1940). Gosnell located breeding Cuckoos by *wha-wha* call of both sexes and bubbling of ♀, and believed that each laid only 8 to 10 eggs against Chance's maximum of 25 obtained by 'farming' Meadow

* P Davis remarks that ♀ will lay at every opportunity within her territory at 48 hour intervals. Clutch-size governed by (1) pairs of host species present, (2) predators, weather and accidents, including human interference, leading to repeat layings by host, (3) desertion: some pipits will not accept Cuckoo's egg; one pair deserted three nests in 14 days. In 53 nests of known contents, Cuckoo laid twice in empty nests, 12 times each to first and second egg of host, 17 times to third egg, 7 to 4th, 2 to 5th and once after one day's incubation.

Pipit nests. P Davis distinguishes three methods and has kindly given us detailed accounts of these. First, watch ♀ searching for nests, usually soon after dawn; repeated glides are made to particular spot, whence Cuckoo makes thorough search of likely sites, often staying on ground for up to an hour. On locating nest she normally keeps still for about a minute before flying away; in hedgerows she finds nests much more easily. Second, watch ♀ make glide to nest before laying; may be very difficult to see against dull background and essential to spot initial flap, since she presents very thin line when wings outstretched. Should she fail at first attempt, she regains perch with laborious flaps, but second and subsequent glides may follow immediately, so do not relax vigilance. Third, look in vicinity of feathers frequently lost by Cuckoo when attacked during her searches. Davis has often found Meadow Pipits' nests by spotting small feathers caught in gorse clumps; many of these eventually contained a Cuckoo's egg. Cuckoo seen to leap into air from ground has almost certainly just laid; normal take-off is rather shallow. If ♀ seen with egg in bill and pursued by pipits, watch them: after breaking off chase they usually return to nest and one flutters over it. Young Cuckoo's loud food-begging from about 12 days old gives it away in otherwise well-hidden nest.

132 **BARN OWL**
Tyto alba

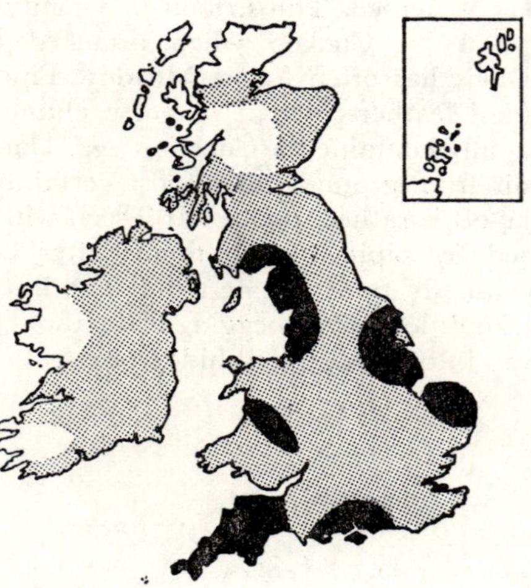

Not scarce; breeds throughout Britain to central Scotland, then very locally to Sutherland; local in Ireland and absent much of Mayo, Galway and south-west. Decrease more or less general since 1947 and very thinly distributed in many areas. Truly found in barns as well as ruins, and overlaps Tawny Owl in old timber of parks and hedgerows. Distinct habitat in rocks, quarries, sea cliffs and islands of remote districts.

Nest Makes scrape in debris. Preference for large cavity whether in tree or building, though will compete with Tawny Owl; so found in really big old trees and stumps, in lofts and spaces under roofs, sometimes in big holes in thatch, in dovecotes and towers; also in crevices of rock; occasionally in old Jackdaw nests; may be encouraged to use special boxes in barns. Solitary. Eggs 4 to 7 (3 to 11) white, more pointed than those of other owls, with mat surface (40 × 31·5 mm). Incubation (♀) often from first egg (laying usually at 2-day intervals), 32 to 34 days. Fledging (♀♂) nidicolous, 9 to 12 weeks. 'Two broods in many cases' (*Handbook*).

Methods Should be fairly easy to locate in accessible sites as pairs roost in them or nearby early in season and fly out readily; so does sitting bird, except in large lofts. But can be very unobtrusive when incubating; BC had nest in chimney of his house several times, unnoticed until young hatched; then parents seen hunting and taking food to brood, whose peculiar snoring note (like waves on distant shingle beach) gives them away.

133 **SNOWY OWL**

Nyctea scandiaca

Bred Fetlar, Shetland, 1967–71, after appearing for several summers on this and other islands; has also occurred in central and north-eastern Highlands in recent years. Tundra or high fells of Scandinavian habitat closely paralleled on Fetlar by bare moorland of rough grass and heather with rocky outcrops and boulders at 150 m above sea level.

Nest Bare scrape on open ground: on Fetlar in patch of short grass close to exposed slabs of rock. Solitary. Eggs 4 to 10 (4 to 14); on Fetlar 7, 6, 6, 6, 5 in successive years; white, rounded (57 × 45 mm); early May onwards. Incubation (♀) from first egg (laying on Fetlar at irregular intervals), about 33 days. Fledging (♀♂) nidicolous for first $2\frac{1}{2}$ to $3\frac{1}{2}$ weeks, flying from 5 to 6 weeks. One brood.

Methods ♀ not conspicuous after incubation begins. ♂ sits sentinel about 150 m away; ♀ leaves nest briefly four to six times in 24 hours. (See R J Tulloch, *BB* 61: 119–32; *Scottish Birds* 5: 244–57.)

More birds not illustrated individually: upper, pair of Lady Amherst's Pheasants (p. 178) and Goshawk (pp. 129–30); lower, Savi's Warbler (p. 428) and ♂ Bluethroat (p. 421) with Baillon's Crake (p. 183) at foot

134 LITTLE OWL

Athene noctua

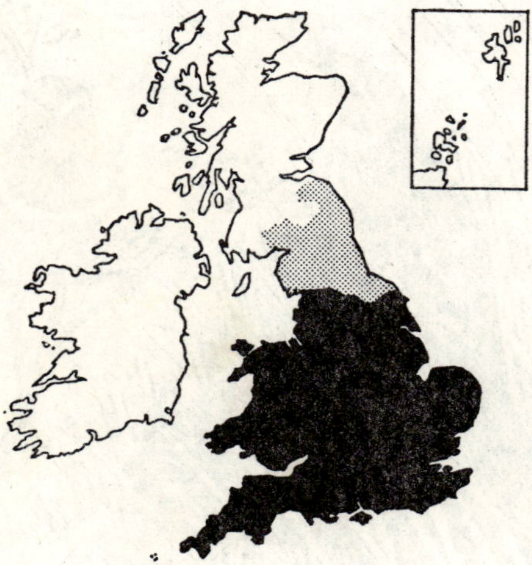

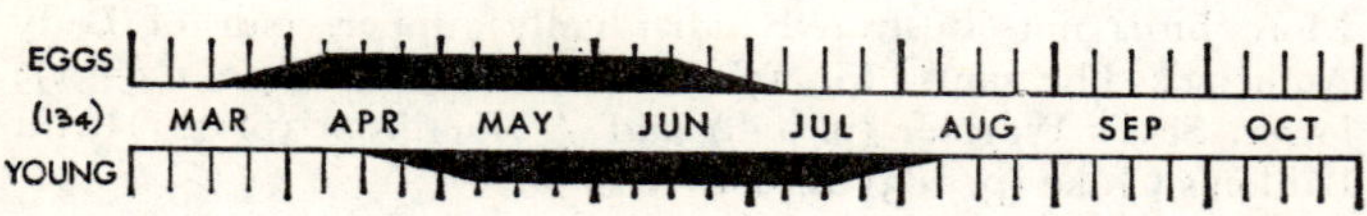

Not scarce; introduced 19th century and now breeds all counties of England and Wales (except perhaps Radnor); but rare northern England and much decreased in south-east. Breeds Berwickshire and occasionally neighbouring counties (Midlothian 1968–70); not Ireland or Man. Habitat typically agricultural land with plenty of old timber and farm buildings, spreading from this to industrial waste-land, sand-dunes, moorland edge, quarries and screes, sea cliffs and islands, villages and suburbia; characteristic of old orchards in south.

Nest No nest made – only scrape in debris. Typically in old hedgerow tree or stump at heights from 50 cm to 8 m, but also frequently in buildings, especially under eaves at the corners of old barns, often with second escape exit (Mayer-Gross); also in rabbit holes and other cavities in banks, in holes in quarries and low cliffs, in hay and corn ricks; occasionally in piles of wood, on floor in centre of small Somerset peat stack (Lewis); in nest-holes of Jackdaw, Starling, Stock Dove; rarely in nestbox (A W Boyd). Solitary. Eggs 3 to 5 (2 to 8) mat white, rather elliptical (36 × 30 mm). Incubation (♀) often from first egg, 24 to 25 days. Fledging (♀♂) nidicolous, about 3½ weeks. One brood.

Methods May often be seen sitting near or actually outside future nest-site early in season, a good guide for subsequent search. Sometimes bird flies off nest at a distance and can be seen, but others sit close and can be handled carefully. Even when pair located, some nests extremely hard to find, particularly in buildings. Little chance to watch back as ♀ only feeds off nest early morning and evening. Same site used year after year, though sometimes there is competition with other owls. Young sometimes hiss rather like young Barn Owls.

135 **TAWNY OWL**

Strix aluco

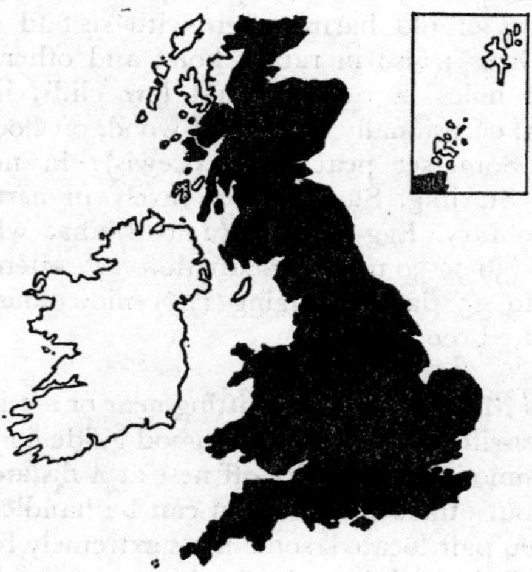

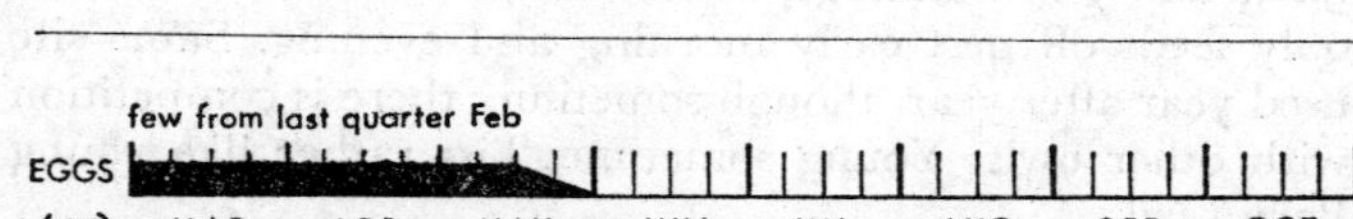

Numerous; breeds throughout British mainland, except north-west Highlands; absent Orkney, Shetland, many Hebrides, Man and Ireland. The owl of deciduous woodland (though not uncommon in conifers), parks, churchyards, large gardens, even town squares; occasionally in quite open country near rocks and buildings.

Nest Makes scrape in debris, usually in hole of tree, rock or building (especially down chimney), but in some districts often uses old nest, e.g. Whitaker found 43 in Magpie's nests, one in Sparrowhawk and one in drey, against 32 in tree-holes, 19 in boxes and 4 on ground; nests of other corvids, Heron, and Buzzard on cliff also recorded; old nests up to 25 m high occupied, but sites in cavities usually up to 12 m; ground sites include space between roots of trees and in blind burrows; preference seems to be for flight downward into nest-hole, which may be quite small, and this has been exploited to produce highly acceptable chimney-type nest-boxes (H N Southern); other large boxes also taken. Solitary. Eggs 2 to 5 (1 to 7), white, slightly glossy, sometimes with irregular surface, nearly round (47 × 39 mm). Incubation (♀) from first egg, 28 to 30 days. Fledging (♂ brings food) nidicolous, about 5 weeks, but may leave nest earlier. One brood.

Methods Location of pair by calls at night fairly easy, but actual sites, especially in large woods, may be very difficult to find, and some birds sit very close. Short of full-time attention, searching best method. Site, once found, saves future trouble, as it is usually used again, or changes rung on two or three. Care needed when visiting nests owing to danger of desertion when eggs fresh, or of their chilling during absence of ♀. Hunger-calls of young begin after they leave nest (Mayer-Gross). In years when food is scarce some to many pairs do not breed (H N Southern). The occasional individual attacks intruder at nest. See Southern (1970).

136 LONG-EARED OWL
Asio otus

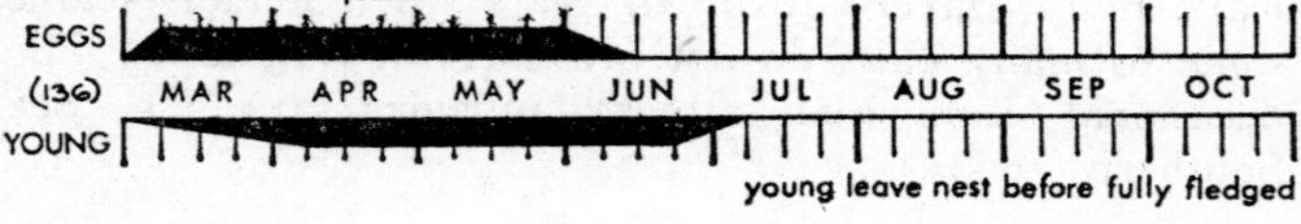

Not scarce; generally distributed in small numbers over much of Scotland, northern England, Ireland and Man, but very local in rest of England and Wales, and absent South Wales and south-west. Typically in Britain the conifer owl and found in plantations, even in small shelter belts and clumps of pine, spruce and larch, in farmland or moorland; also in deciduous woods, especially with ivied trees, down to low bushes in marshes, dunes and moorland, even on islands in lochs.

Nest Makes none but generally takes old nests of other species, e.g. from Whitaker's records: Magpie (70 cases), Sparrowhawk (12), Woodpigeon (2), Jay (1), squirrel's drey (1); also Crow, Rook and Heron; height up to 17 m. Sometimes on wide platforms on boles of trees; in barer habitats often on ground under bushes, brambles and bracken; occupies nesting baskets put up for Mallards in Netherlands and has used artificial platforms in Britain. Solitary. Eggs 3 to 6 (3 to 8), white, elliptical, less glossy than Woodpigeon which are much the same size (41 × 33 mm). Incubation (♀♂?) from first egg, about 27 to 28 days. Fledging (♀♂) nidicolous, leaving nest in 3½ weeks. One brood.

Methods Obscure status in many areas due to difficulty of locating odd pairs; but this may be done by listening for calls or looking for roosts, betrayed by neat circle of pellets and excrement below. Once pair located, search all possible old nests and find occupied one, which is not always easy; birds usually sit very closely. Roosting mate often within 40 m of nest (Whitaker). Young can be located by 'un-oiled gate' hunger call. Long-eared Owls are faithful to a locality, returning year after year to breed in same wood or clump, but rarely to same nest; may be displaced by Tawny Owls in some areas.

137 **SHORT-EARED OWL**
Asio flammeus

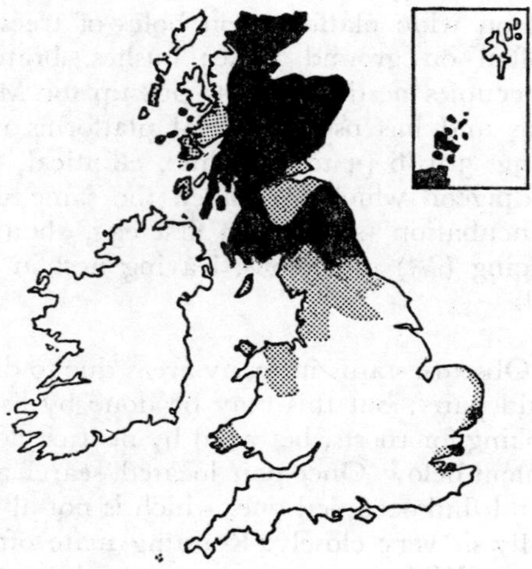

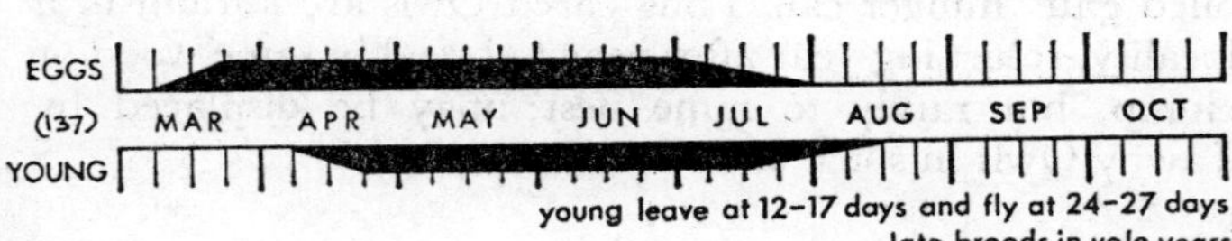

Not scarce; irregular or absent most of England; very local Kent, East Anglia and Wales; more regular northward from Lancashire and Yorkshire to Orkney, but scarce or absent West Highlands and very local Hebrides; has bred Ireland. Liable to short-term fluctuations with food supply. The owl of open habitats: moorland and heathland (especially soon after afforestation), marsh, bog and fen, sand-dunes.

Nest Makes scrape in variety of ground cover: heather, tall grass, gorse and brambles; rushes, sedges and dead reeds; marram-grass; sometimes fairly well sheltered and even concealed. Solitary. Eggs 4 to 7 (3 to 14), mat white, elliptical (40 × 32 mm). Incubation (♀) from first egg, 24 to 28 days. Fledging (♂ via ♀) nidicolous, for 2 weeks or less, but do not fly before 3½ weeks. Two broods in years of vole plagues.

Methods Diurnal, so can be located rather more easily than Long-eared but, as ♀ sits tight, almost impossible to find nest by searching. S Sloan Chesser once watched pair fly into suspected nest area and alight a few yards apart: ♂ departed after about a minute, leaving ♀ on unfinished clutch of 3 eggs. Best chance is to find ♂'s hunting territory and watch for him to bring prey to sitting ♀, when he usually alights beside her. She may rise 1 to 2 m in air or just flop off nest towards him (Chesser). Visits to nest happen punctually, ♂ flying in low and needing careful watching (Whitaker). When young in or near nest, parents mob intruder with 'quacking' (Whitaker) or barking *kwowk* calls (*Handbook*).

138 **NIGHTJAR**

Caprimulgus europaeus

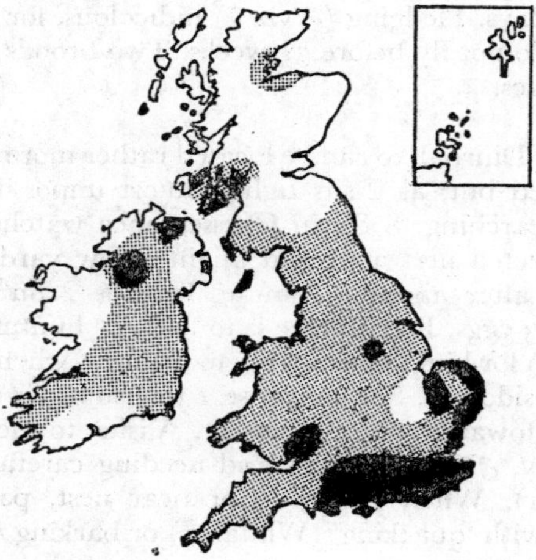

Not scarce; widespread though local in England, Wales, much of Ireland, and south-west Scotland; but irregular or absent farther north and west. Subject to general decrease, perhaps through loss of habitat, essentially open ground, though often in vicinity of rocks or trees; so found on dry heaths and moors, commons, bracken-clad banks and talus slopes, clearings and felled woodlands, very young plantations, industrial waste land and tips, flinty downland, brecks, sand dunes and even beaches. Sometimes in thick cover, e.g. young sweet chestnut stand in Kent (H J Hoffman).

Nest None built; only slight scrape in bare patch, often quite small, particularly among growing bracken or long heather but may be surrounded by boulders, stony outcrops (S Lewis), stumps, bushes or young trees. Solitary. Eggs 2 (1 to 3) usually elongated and elliptical, off-white marbled and spotted with grey, yellowish-brown and darker tints (32 × 22 mm). Incubation (♀ relieved by ♂) from first egg, 18 days. Fledging (♀♂) about 2½ weeks, independent 6 to 7 weeks. Two broods regular.

Methods Location by loud reeling of ♂ usually at dusk or in night, followed by careful search until one or both birds are flushed; where bracken patches occur among other cover, they should be searched first (D Humphrey). If ♂ only is put up, continue search for sitting ♀. If she rises, but there are no eggs, mark spot carefully and revisit. Eggs may show up against normal background of bare earth. When with young, parents will approach and reel boldly at observer; and if young are found they soon move or are moved a short distance. Birds usually sit close, rising in full view of observer (Humphrey).

139 **SWIFT**
Apus apus

Numerous; breeds all counties England, Wales, Ireland and in Scotland north to Argyll in west, Sutherland and Caithness (Thurso) in east. Large villages, towns and cities, but still found on inland crags and sea cliffs in North Wales and elsewhere; seldom at solitary houses and farms.

Nest (♀♂) Of aerially collected material, chiefly grass and other vegetable fragments and feathers, cemented together with saliva; building continues during incubation and same nest may be used for several years, becoming quite substantial; also takes over used Starling nests. Preference for holes and crevices, especially under eaves of large buildings, rather than for big cavities, though may congregate on floors of lofts and church towers; height very variable, down to 3 m in thatch on low cottages and in stone walls; can be persuaded into well devised nestboxes; exceptionally in old House Martin nests and Sand Martin burrows, and in House Sparrow nests on Wells Cathedral (Lewis); uses holes in trees on Continent. Social and colonial, though individual sites may be scattered along a street. Eggs 2 to 3 (2 to 4) elongated, dull white (25 × 16 mm). Incubation (♀♂) at night from first egg, average 19½ days. Fledging (♀♂) nidicolous, from 5 to 8 weeks according to weather. One brood.

Methods Prolonged watching may be necessary to locate all nests in a street colony, but sooner or later birds will be seen to enter sites at all stages of cycle until young very well grown. Nest-cracks high in cliffs may be very difficult to pinpoint even with birds as guides and remarkably little information exists on such sites in Britain. Monograph: Lack (1956).

140 **KINGFISHER**
Alcedo atthis

Not scarce; widespread in England, Wales and Ireland (especially east) but local south Scotland, and absent from islands and most of Highlands, though young hatched Easter Ross 1970. Typically along slower-flowing rivers, streams and canals, with steep excavable banks, but overlaps Dipper along Welsh Border and in Scotland and Ireland.

Nest (♀♂) In hole, usually circular in section and 50 cm to 1·5 m deep; tunnel rises slightly to circular nest-chamber where eggs laid in bare scrape or on a few fish bones, added to during incubation; entrance may be less than 1 m above water and liable to flood in spring spates, but is often higher. Typically in sand or earth bank of river or canal and regularly now in sides of gravel pits and sand pits, occasionally chalk pits and other suitable faces well away from water; also 'among roots of trees', in hole of wall (*Handbook*), and in rotten post (C R Tubbs). Solitary. Eggs 5 to 7 (4 to 10) translucent white, round and very glossy (23 × 19 mm). Incubation (♀♂) 19 to 20 days. Fledging (♀♂) nidicolous, 23 to 27 days. Two broods.

Methods Location of birds on territory followed by search generally successful, as holes usually easy to see (but sometimes well hidden, e.g. behind trailing ivy) and circular appearance distinguishes them from holes of rats and Sand Martins. During excavation pile of fresh sand or earth below is indication; young vociferous and dark slime begins to trickle from hole, followed by droppings; look also for droppings on or below perches near hole. Holes may be used twice in same season or in successive years and same locality favoured for many years. Sitting bird can be seen if torch flashed up tunnel, or may be flushed by noises overhead. Monograph: Eastman (1969).

141 **BEE-EATER**
Merops apiaster

Attempted to nest Midlothian 1920; three pairs nested, two successfully, Sussex 1955 (and one pair Alderney 1956). Generally open country with trees near river or lake.

Nest (♀♂) Chamber at end of excavated hole, 50 cm to 3 m long, with characteristic claw-marks at bottom corners. Usual site low sandy or mud cliffs and faces of pits, also in open flat ground; Sussex birds and colony of Sand Martins shared large sand pit with standing water (K E I Barham, P J Conder and I J Ferguson-Lees, *Bird Notes* 27: 34–43; Simson). Social to colonial. Eggs 4 to 7 (4 to 8) glossy white and almost round (26 × 22 mm); May onwards. Incubation (♀♂) from first egg, 20 days. Fledging (♀♂) nidicolous, 20 to 25 days, brood leaving at one to 2 day intervals (J J Swift, *Alauda* 27: 7–143). One brood.

Methods Location of birds easy as they perch conspicuously on wires and bare branches; then watching at suitable faces for excavation, but possibility of nesting in flat ground must be taken into account.

142 **HOOPOE**
Upupa epops

Has bred sporadically southern half England as far north as Herefordshire. Only about four nests reported in each of two recent decades but probably many more attempts have been made. Open wooded country, often near water and close to habitation: several English nests have been in large gardens.

Nest Rough chamber in cavity, usually unlined, though material may remain from previous occupant. Holes may be in trees from ground level upwards, e.g. 2 m in partly decayed apple, Somerset 1931 (Lewis); also in walls and buildings, e.g. Hampshire 1956; and in piles of stones, drains and nestboxes. Solitary. Eggs 5 to 8 (5 to 12), off-white or yellowish-olive, soon stained (26 × 18 mm), from early May into June in England. Incubation (♀) begins before clutch complete, even with first or second egg, 16 to 19 days. Fledging (♀♂) nidicolous, 20 to 27 days. Two broods recorded on Continent.

Methods Like other hole-nesting species becomes unobtrusive when incubating and, as it does not excavate or normally line hole, may be difficult to locate. But ♂ calls repeatedly near nest at dawn (Connor). He feeds sitting ♀, who may not leave nest for long periods, so always worth watching and following Hoopoe that seems to be collecting food; this becomes much easier when both parents feeding young. Hole has characteristic musky odour which increases as brood develops.

143 GREEN WOODPECKER
Picus viridis

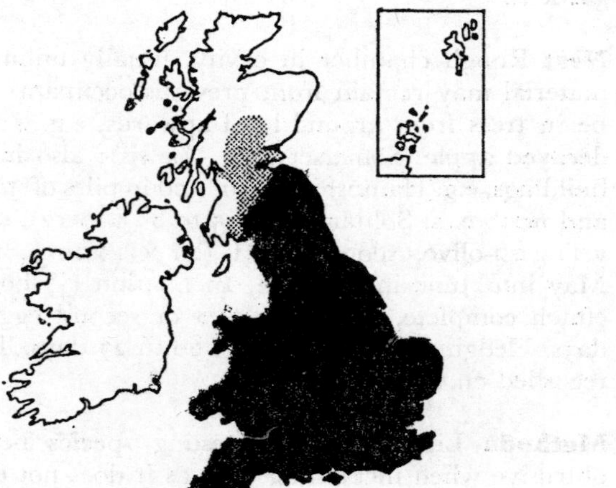

Not scarce; general in Wales and England to Border counties where becomes local, but increasing and has spread north into Scotland as far as Perthshire. Found in wooded country rather than woodland: parks, orchards and large gardens, timbered hedgerows, copses, roadside and riparian trees, heaths and commons; generally avoids conifers.

Nest (♀♂) Bare scrape or wood chips at bottom of excavated shaft, entered by short horizontal, almost circular tunnel about 7 cm in diameter; shaft may be about 75 cm deep (Whitaker), but often much shorter. Generally in tree externally sound, but with rotten centre; sometimes in quite dead trees; heights 2 to 15 m (Whitaker), occasionally even lower (J C Robson), usually in main trunk, but sometimes in large sloping bough; tree species probably unimportant, though Whitaker found ash, oak, elm and apple popular; also birch, alder and both chestnuts in different regions. Solitary. Eggs 5 to 7 (4 to 9), translucent white (32 × 23 mm). Incubation (♀♂) 18 to 19 days. Fledging (♀♂ from throat) nidicolous, 18 to 21 days. One brood.

Methods Excavation gives best opportunity, when pecking may be heard and fresh chips seen below tree; sometimes trial borings. Incubating birds can be flushed if hole found by searching, but usually require heavy blows on tree or actual climbing; H Sielmann advocates scraping trunk like mammalian predator below this and other woodpecker nests. As young grow they become noisy and latterly poke heads out of hole; parents also become very demonstrative. Holes may be used more than once, or fresh hole bored in same tree, normally below old one.

144 GREAT SPOTTED WOODPECKER

Dendrocopos major

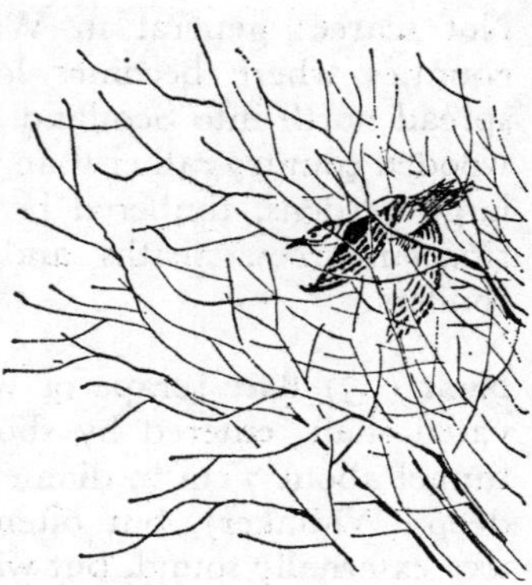

Fairly numerous; breeds all mainland counties of Britain, now including Caithness, and Isle of Wight, Anglesey, some Inner Hebrides; not Ireland or Man. More a bird of continuous woodland and of conifers than previous species, but in conifers requires suitable old trees or adventitious birches as nest-sites; also in parks, orchards, gardens if well wooded, but not often in hedgerow timber or scattered trees.

Nest (♀♂) Of same type as previous species, but entrance diameter slightly less and 30 cm shaft relatively wider at base; more often in obviously dying or dead trees than Green Woodpecker, but also in apparently sound trunks and limbs; *Handbook* suggests holes seldom bored below 3 m but Whitaker recorded 1 m in rowan and upper limit about 14 m; birch and pine in north very popular, but elsewhere oak, alder, sycamore and many others used; deep nest-boxes with chips on floor sometimes taken; holes seldom if ever face direct sunlight (J C Robson); may begin boring very early in season (Walpole-Bond). Solitary. Eggs 4 to 7 (3 to 8) translucent white and rather glossy (26 × 19 mm). Incubation (♀♂) about 16 days. Fledging (♀♂) nidicolous, 18 to 21 days. One brood.

Methods Much as for Green Woodpecker. Searching not profitable for high sites in continuous woodland. Incubating birds may be impossible to flush when holes located. Changeover of sexes may be seen and young reveal site by loud calling. Same hole may be used again or new hole bored, usually lower down, in same tree.

145 LESSER SPOTTED WOODPECKER

Dendrocopos minor

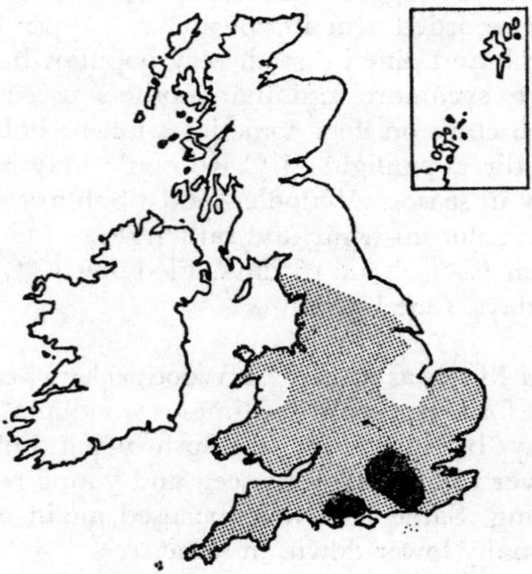

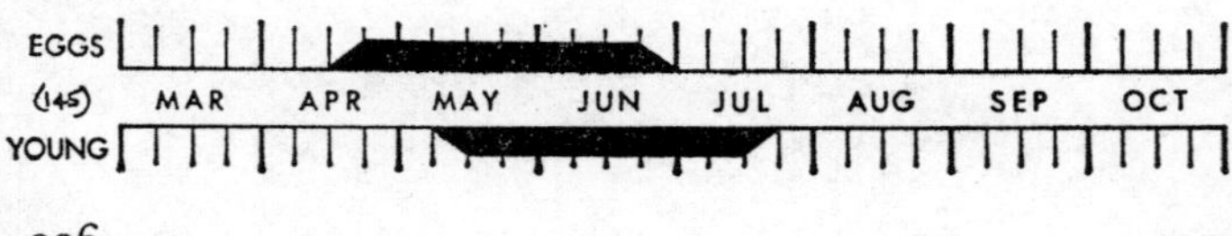

Not scarce; widespread England and Wales north to Lake District and north York, though not regularly Wight and parts of Fens; identified central Scotland 1968, 1970–1, though no nest recorded. Habitat much as previous species, though tends to be absent from scrub-woods as from highland districts generally; sometimes in quiet urban parks and avenues, hedgerows with trees, and particularly associated in south and west of England with decaying orchards.

Nest (♀♂) Of woodpecker type already described with entrance hole only about 4 cm diameter and relatively broad, short shaft (20 to 25 cm) in dead wood, chips of which may cover eggs (Lewis). Often on underside of sloping branch or short snag, but also in main trunk of small tree; hole tends to be squarer in very soft wood; sometimes difficult to distinguish from Willow Tit holes, though these usually in limbs or trunks of smaller diameter (J C Robson). Whitaker recorded hole in branch only 15 cm in diameter; height enormously variable, almost from ground level to 20 or 25 m; many trees used, but beeches, sycamores and fruit trees among most popular; used polystyrene-filled nestbox Hertford 1971 (Colin Brown). Solitary. Eggs 4 to 6 (3 to 8) translucent white and glossy ($19 \times 14 \cdot 5$ mm). Incubation (♀♂) 14 days. Fledging (♀♂) nidicolous, 21 days. One brood.

Methods One of hardest species to locate in its more natural habitats, though occasional low site in garden or orchard easy to find, and same tree or vicinity may be used in successive years (Robson). Calling or drumming ♂ only a general guide, but he sometimes flies to nest after drumming. Close watching of birds in excavating stage seems best chance, though Whitaker saw ♂ apparently call ♀ off nest. Calling of young not so loud as previous species, but nests found like this, or by following full-beaked adults.

146 **WRYNECK**

Jynx torquilla

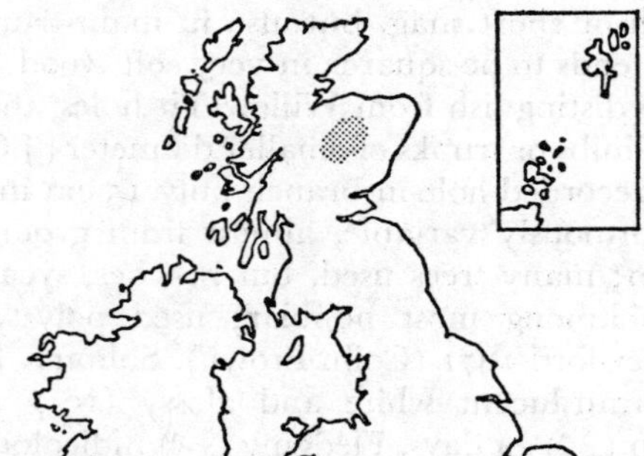

Very scarce; now apparently confined in south to Kent, with perhaps one or two pairs elsewhere; but three pairs bred Inverness 1969 after increasing spring records since 1950. Habitat in south much as for Green Woodpecker, with decided preference for orchards and gardens in some districts. Scottish habitat, open pine and birch woodland, resembles that favoured in Scandinavia.

Nest In all types and sizes of tree-holes, not excavated and with no material added; also recorded in banks, walls, thatch, posts and Sand Martin burrows, and nestboxes readily taken; may dispossess other species, even Lesser Spotted Woodpeckers (J C Robson); height varies, usually 1·5 to 4 m, occasionally much higher; nest chamber in low sites may be just below entrance hole (Robson). Solitary. Eggs 7 to 10 (5 to 14 and more due to two ♀♀), dull white (21 × 15 mm). Incubation (♀♂) 12 to 14 days. Fledging (♀♂) nidicolous, 19 to 21 days. Two broods occasionally.

Methods Location of birds, which are noisy enough when first present, followed by watching likely to be most profitable, though, like other hole nesters, they become hard to find when incubation begins. But sexes may be seen changing over. Young call loudly and nests can be found most easily at this stage.

147 WOODLARK

Lullula arborea

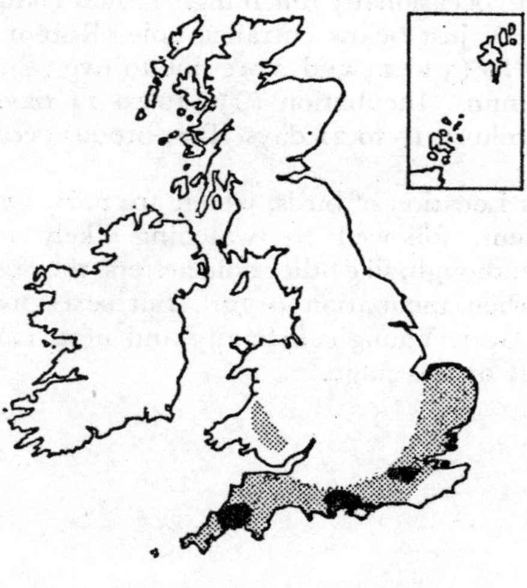

Scarce; since decrease in 1963 restricted to arc from Norfolk through south coast counties to Cornwall and South Wales. Open ground with trees, posts, or other high perches and with or without low bushes; hence in felled woodland, sometimes with light bramble cover, bracken and grass banks, heaths, breckland warrens, derelict pastures, even old industrial tips with no more cover than grass tufts, thistles and ragwort; exceptionally in growing corn (T G Gordon, *BB* 40: 116).

Nest (♀♂, 7 cm) Of grass with moss foundation in scrape on ground, lined finer grasses and some hair. Sometimes half-hidden by low cover, e.g. against young conifers in new plantations (Whitaker), in Somerset strawberry beds (Lewis); elsewhere quite open with small tuft or plant at one side; often near track and below pylon line 'launching pad' for ♂ (N W Orr). Solitary. Eggs 3 to 4 (1 to 6) whitish with variable brown freckling, usually of reddish tinge, and underlying violet-grey marks, sometimes zoned at big end; less heavily marked and rounder than Skylark (22 × 16 mm). Incubation (♀) about 14 days. Fledging (♀♂) nidicolous, young often leave nest before they can fly and fledge in 11 to 13 days. Usually two broods.

Methods Generally agreed to be one of harder ground nests to find with eggs, but location at beginning of season by singing ♂ or flushing pair fairly easy. According to Gosnell they may continue to 'hang about' when building or laying. He and Walpole-Bond recommended watching singing ♂, who may fly over nest and call ♀ off. But according to Simson, who gives detailed advice, ♂ sings very little during incubation period; technique based on ♀'s regular routine, during first nine days, of about 45 minutes on nest and eight minutes off to feed. She runs off nest and ♂ joins her in flight to feeding area, both 'calling cheerfully'. Feeding may take place up to 800 m from nest, average 400 m.

♂ does not feed but watches 'ravenous' ♀ from 'small prominence'. On return, ♂ lets ♀ fly on for about 50 m, when she pitches and runs last 15 m to nest. If birds located in feeding area, flight line must be traced, which may take a long time, and watch shifted to presumed nest area. Final hot search to flush ♀, who may sit very tight. When parents feeding young, comparatively easy to watch back. Same few square metres may be used as nest-site for several years, a useful guide once a nest has been found.

 SKYLARK

Alauda arvensis

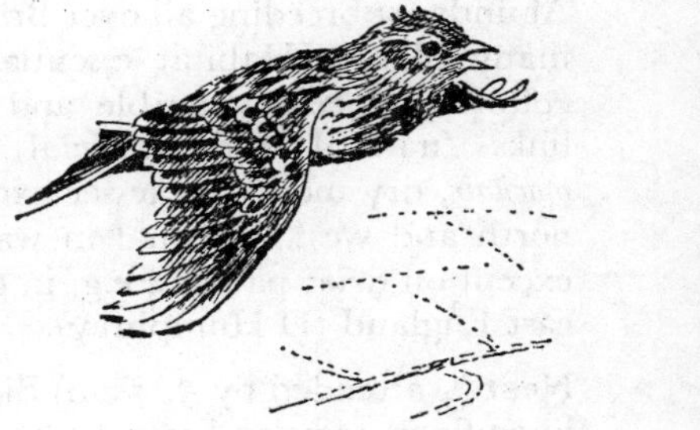

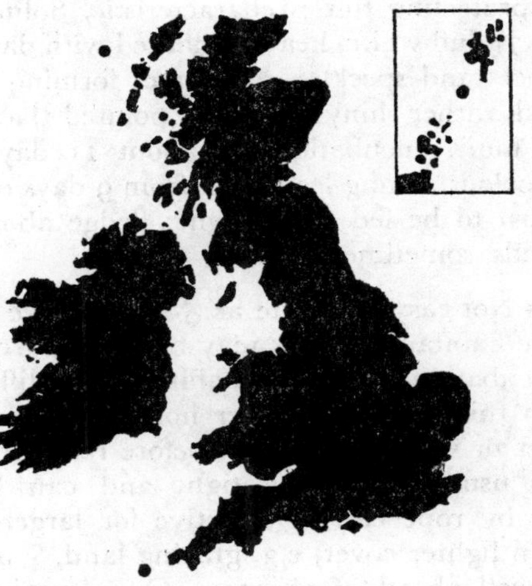

Abundant; breeding all over Britain and Ireland, including many islands. Habitat essentially open, treeless types of country, especially arable and large grass fields, downs, links (natural and artificial), dunes, saltings, heaths, *machair*, dry moors; to lesser extent bogs and wet moors of north and west. Unusual in water meadows and marshes except on drier patches, e.g. in grazings in south and south-east England (D Humphrey).

Nest (♀ attended by ♂, 7 cm) Simple grass cup on ground, lined finer stems and sometimes a little hair; normally open with shelter of tuft on one side, but late nests may be completely hidden in crops such as corn and clover; occasionally in side of low bank. Track leading to nest on side opposite protecting tuft is characteristic. Solitary. Eggs 3 to 5 (2 to 7) dull white, heavily marked with dark and light brown spots and speckles, sometimes forming dense zone at big end, rather shiny and more pointed than Woodlark (24 × 17 mm). Incubation (♀) about 11 days. Fledging (♀♂) nidicolous, young leave nest from 9 days onwards but may return to be fed or at night; fledge about 20 days. Two broods, sometimes three.

Methods Not easy to locate as ♂ sings above large areas of suitable habitat, but pair may be flushed from territory before incubation begins. Watching back difficult but ♀ nesting in thick, uniform cover normally hovers momentarily over or very near to nest before returning; in these situations usually sits very tight and can be flushed. Dragging by rope can be effective for larger-scale nest-finding. In lighter cover, e.g. grazing land, ♀ usually runs off nest well ahead of observer. On returning, ♀ lands closer to nest than when leaving it, a good point when watching back (Humphrey). ♂ sometimes drives ♀ back to eggs. Cold searching effective only where many nests in open area, and sites limited to tussocks or small patches. Parents with food easier to watch back, but may run to nest.

149 **SWALLOW**
Hirundo rustica

Numerous and widely distributed, though scarce or absent north-west and north Scotland and islands; associated with domestic animals, but also where there is abundant insect life, e.g. along rivers. Typically around farms and smallholdings, penetrating suburban areas, but not town centres. Doubtful if any still breed in caves or other natural sites in Britain, but in some highland districts found round bothies and old buildings far from occupied houses; presence of sheep perhaps relevant factor.

Nest (♀♂, 7 cm) Bracket-like structure of mud held together by straws and grass stems, lined first fine grass, then feathers which may curl over the cup; occasionally in dry summers in old nests of other species (Blackbird, House Sparrow) without mud foundation. Side support against vertical surface as important as support underneath, so often against rough wall, side of roof or inside wide chimney as well as resting on beam, rafter or ledge; favourite site probably where beam joins roof. Steel and other metal buildings (e.g. modern cowsheds, large garages) frequented as well as stone and wooden sheds and byres; majority in buildings where animals kept, but quite often in empty sheds, ruins, boathouses, under bridges (sometimes very small ones), in attics or even bedrooms of houses, and public lavatories; nests on outside of buildings not unknown and has taken over House Martins'; height generally not more than 10 m. In south of England pill-boxes and gun sites remaining from 1939–45 war much favoured even when flooded and wholly or partly below ground (Connor); also occasionally in wells, sluices and mine-shafts; chimneys far less used than formerly and, though *Handbook* gives caves and branches of trees as exceptional sites, Swallow may be claimed as the one British species of which to all intents whole population nests on human artefacts. Solitary to social, but no large colonies. Eggs 4 to 6 (3 to 8) white and pointed, with small or large dull red spots and underlying grey marks, sometimes zoned at big end; occasionally without markings (20 × 14 mm). Incubation (♀) 14 to 16 days. Fledging (♂♀ from throat) nidicolous, 17 to 24 days, but young sometimes return to roost in nest. Two, occasionally three broods.

Methods Swallows soon advertise their presence, return year after year to same site if successful and build nests which are usually easy to see except in high, dark barns. Look on floor for droppings and building material—mud, grass stems, feathers. Not all nests seen in one place should be dismissed as those of one pair; two or three pairs often nest close together. Worth examining buildings or under bridges where Swallows seen to fly.

150 **HOUSE MARTIN**
Delichon urbica

Numerous; breeds throughout Britain and Ireland; but very irregular Orkney and absent Shetland and Outer Hebrides. At once more urban and more rural than Swallow, reaching centres of cities, even London (especially again since anti-smoke legislation) and Edinburgh, yet also on a number of coastal and inland cliffs, and at least one quarry in Cornwall (Mayer-Gross); common round farms, in villages and small towns, with some large colonies on river bridges.

Nest (♀♂) Like half inverted beehive with small entrance hole or slit near or at junction with 'roof'; made of locally available mud or peat, held with grass and lined with litter collected in air, e.g. vegetable down, fine bents, and feathers; normally both inner and top edges stuck to supporting structure, but nests often jammed against each other and shape varies. Originally in cracks and crannies of rock faces, as can still be seen along coast, but most British nests now under eaves of houses or other buildings (sometimes inside) at varying heights; bridge nests under mouldings, ribs and other features providing right-angled support; new houses with broad eaves sometimes colonised at once, and artificial nests adopted. Colonial from several to several hundred pairs. Eggs 4 to 5 (2 to 6) pointed, glossy white, rarely with well-defined pale red markings (19 × 13 mm); sometimes soiled by droppings from flies or parasites (Connor). Incubation (♀♂) about 14 days. Fledging (♀♂ sometimes assisted by older young) nidicolous, 10 to 22 days. Two, even three broods.

Methods No great skill required to find colonies of this highly social species, but individual nests on cliff face may be hard to spot. Often mud used differs slightly from colour of rock; otherwise few minutes careful watching usually reveals any occupied nest. Nests with protruding material have usually been taken over by sparrows.

151 **SAND MARTIN**
Riparia riparia

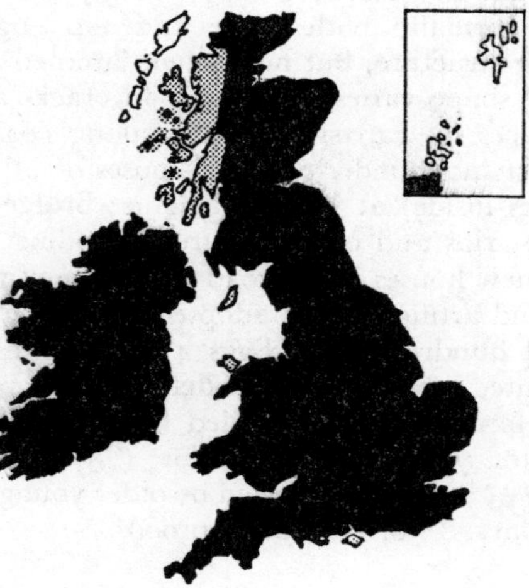

Numerous; widespread but local, nesting all mainland counties of Britain and Ireland, but scarce Isle of Wight and West Highlands and absent Shetland, Orkney and Outer Hebrides. Colonies by lakes and along rivers with steep sandy, peaty or gravel banks; sand and gravel pits, railway cuttings; sand-dunes; usually near or over water.

Nest (♀♂) Hole with flattish top and bottom excavated for distances up to 1 m in bank or face; nest at end of burrow in round chamber about 6 cm across, loosely made of aerially gathered vegetable downs, stems and feathers. Sometimes holes only 1 m above water and get flooded, but in sand pits may be 7 m up in suitable layer; sometimes in drain pipes and other man-made holes, e.g. colony under platform of Ballinluig station, Perthshire (T H Evanson, *Scottish Birds* 5: 175); occasionally in heap of sawdust, and peat cutting (S Lewis); exceptionally in Dipper's nest (G C Hamer, *BB* 56: 419). Colonial, up to several hundred pairs. Eggs 4 to 5 (3 to 7) white and thin shelled without gloss and variable in shape (18 × 13 mm). Incubation (♀♂) about 14 days. Fledging (♀♂) nidicolous, 19 days. Usually two broods.

Methods Not needed to find colonial nest holes, but geological drift maps may be useful to narrow search for population study. Presence of birds not always a help as they may hunt a long way from colony and be difficult to follow. Look out for isolated pairs occupying drainage holes and other unusual sites.

152 GOLDEN ORIOLE

Oriolus oriolus

Bred in last century in about 10 southern and eastern English counties, especially Kent; breeding proved in last twenty years in Suffolk, Shropshire and north Lancashire, and strongly suspected in five other English and two Welsh counties; pair displayed Kinross 1968. Deciduous or mixed woodland, often near water or even in damp areas, e.g. alder carr (Connor).

Nest (mainly ♀) Unmistakable hammock-like structure bound in fork or between branches of tree at various heights; made of grass or other vegetable fibres, often with wool, strips of bark and paper, lined grass-heads. Lancashire nest in 1958 was 1·5 m up at end of branch of fallen larch, an unusual site (J A G Barnes, *BB* 53: 88). Solitary. Eggs 3 to 5 (3 to 6), glossy white with black spots concentrated near big end (31 × 23 mm); from second half May into June. Incubation (♀♂), 14 to 15 days. Fledging (♀♂) nidicolous, 14 to 15 days. Usually one brood.

Methods Location by song of ♂; both birds very hard to see and watch, though this seems most promising method, except for systematic search of branch-ends in likely area.

153 **RAVEN**

Corvus corax

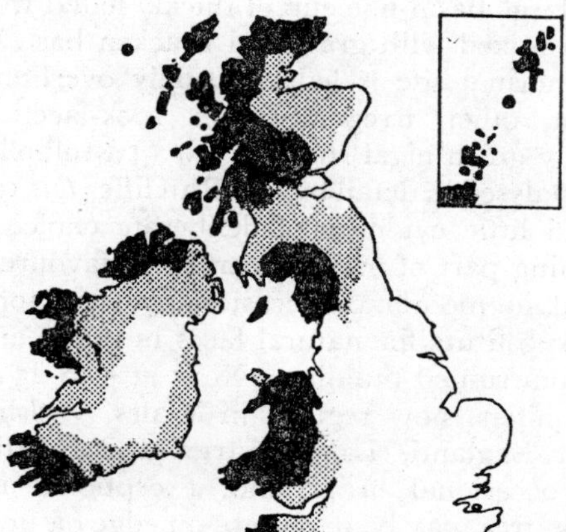

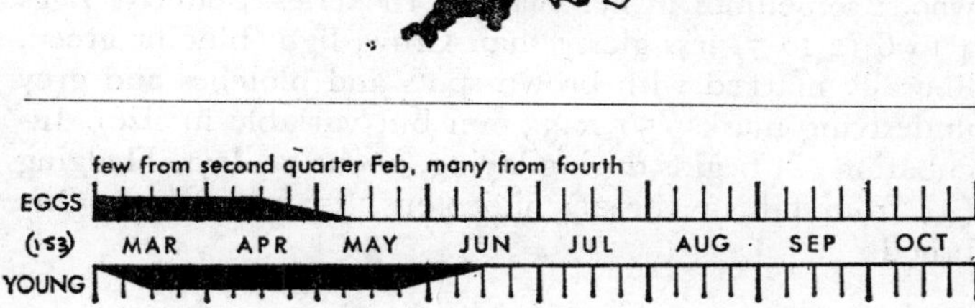

Not scarce; breeds throughout highland Britain and Ireland, along rocky coasts and on larger islands. Apparent preference for wilder areas may be due both to persecution and to dependence on sheep carrion and placentae (to feed young). Attempts since about 1940 to recolonise semi-lowland valleys and wooded country, but typical breeding habitat still coastal and inland cliffs, crags and wooded glens, ranging almost from sea level to 700 m, though seldom higher owing to prevalence of snow in February and March.

Nest (♀♂) Substantial structure of sticks, heather stems, and on coast seaweed, solidified with grass or lumps of moss and with large basin-like cup of thickly felted wool or hair, sometimes mixed with grass and bracken bast. Over most of range normal site is ledge (usually overhung), recess, crevice or other irregularity in rock-face, sometimes revealed by green algal stains below (J Mulholland); preferences analysed in detail by D A Ratcliffe (*Ibis* 104: 13–39), who found little evidence of deliberate choice of aspect; faces forming part of major escarpment favoured, but low crags used in moorland, occasionally even top of bank. Quarries substitute for natural faces in many areas; a few records from ruined buildings. Nests at 5 to 25 m in trees, usually conifers, now regular in Wales, Welsh Marches, south-west England, Lake District and Scottish Border counties, occasional in Ireland, exceptional in Scottish Highlands; tree may be in clump, on edge of, or well inside wood: sometimes in heronries or rookeries. Solitary. Eggs 4 to 6 (2 to 7) less glossy than Crow, light blue or green, liberally marked with brown spots and blotches and grey underlying marks (50 × 33 mm but variable in size). Incubation (♀) begins during laying, about 21 days. Fledging (♀♂ from bill or throat) nidicolous, 35 to 40 days. One brood.

Methods Building usually conspicuous process and birds may be followed back to site; watching back also possible at long range throughout breeding cycle, but Ravens notoriously shy and only occasional ♀ will return when observers near, unless on road (car 'hide' especially useful). During incubation, inspection of likely sites, accompanied by clapping, often flushes bird, which leaves nest with characteristic rocketing action. When eggs near hatching or young in nest, parents usually demonstrate and nest can be found by searching cliff with glasses; it often shows brown against grey rock-face but becomes whitened during fledging period. New nests told by freshly broken ends of twigs. Sites often used again and again, or changes rung on two or three close together. Nests in conifers quite hard to find if bird flies away at long range.

154 **CARRION/HOODED CROW**

Corvus corone

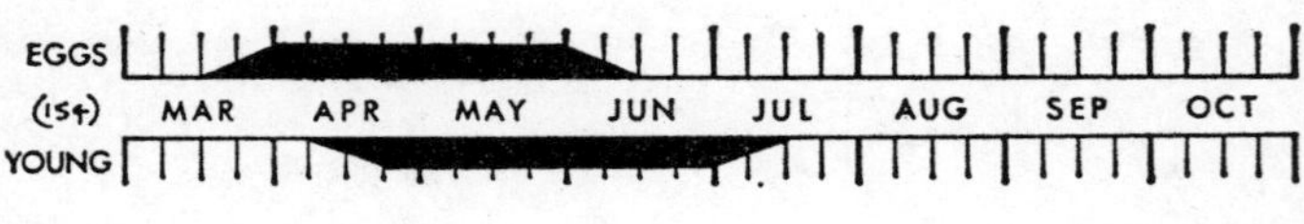

Numerous; the two races cover all Britain and Ireland except some remote islands. 'Hoodie' is crow of Ireland and Scottish isles, also predominating in Man and Scottish Highlands, where there is wide hybrid zone (striped on map); elsewhere Carrion Crow is breeding race. Habitat choice catholic, from squares of central London to wildest sea-cliffs; on edge of large forest areas but scarce on well-keepered estates; up to 350 or 500 m.

Nest (♀♂) Crow's to Raven's nest is as cup to basin; constituents often the same, though smaller, and rim of cup often made of thin birch or other twigs; lining of wool and hair may include grass and/or feathers; seaweed as foundation on sea cliffs and bones sometimes used; 'coarse reed-stems' in Somerset (H B Elton). Most nests in trees, from a few to nearly 30 m up, but usual sites on rocky coasts and islands and treeless country are cliffs, steep banks, among long heather; sometimes on buildings and telegraph poles, e.g. in Shetland, and rarely on ground in dunes; tree nests often on edge of small wood, in clumps and hedgelines, frequently in isolated trees, even bushes on hillsides and windswept islands; in moorland, trees lining stream or below outcrop favoured; tree preference probably reflects most abundant species in habitat, but possible favourites, from highland to lowland, are birch, pine, sycamore, ash, wych elm, English elm and willow; unlike Rooks, Crows seldom build at top of tree, generally in fairly stout fork on main trunk or well out on limb; some nests well hidden on ivied trees; cliff sites similar to those of Raven, though can find lodgement in smaller cracks. Crows' nests afterwards used by many other birds, especially birds of prey. Solitary. Eggs 4 to 6 (3 to 7) like small Raven's but rounder and much glossier (43 × 30 mm). Incubation (♀) starts with first egg, about 19 days. Fledging (♀♂) nidicolous, 26 to 35 days. One brood.

Methods Some nests hard to see but, on approaching wood, watch for ♂ on tree-top look-out and for ♀ slipping off nest. Where several structures to choose from, freshly broken ends of twigs, as in Ravens' nests, are some guide to new nest. Some Crows sit very tight and must be flushed by knocking and scraping the trunk. Several sites may be used over the years in same area of about 60 ha (J Mulholland).

155 **ROOK**

Corvus frugilegus

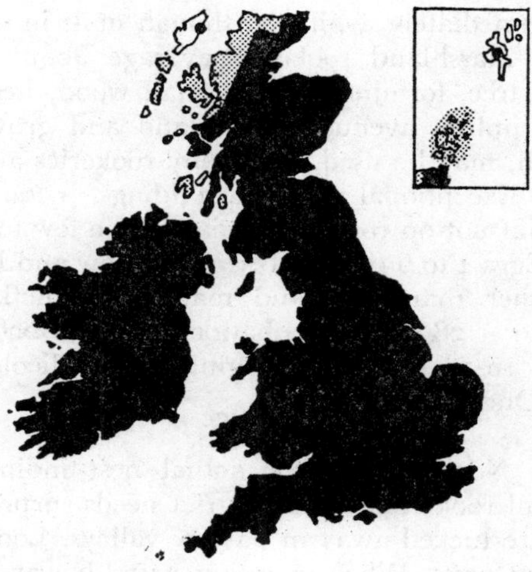

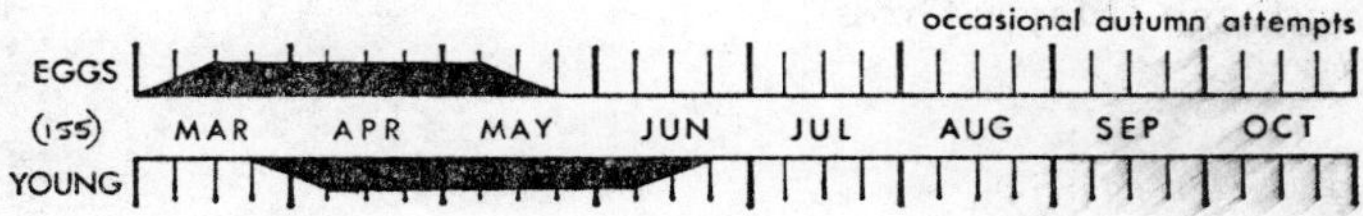

Abundant; nesting all counties of Britain and Ireland, though very local Orkney and parts north Scotland, with single colonies Shetland and Outer Hebrides. Essentially bird of tree-clad arable land, but penetrates suburbia to centres of towns; avoids large woods and forest areas; often in grounds of large houses.

Nest (♀ assisted by ♂) Can be discriminated from Crow with experience: rather less neat in appearance (ends of twigs stick out more) and more taper at bottom; general construction much the same, but lining usually of grass, leaves, moss and various vegetable materials, with only odd lumps of wool, feathers copious near free-range chickens (J Mulholland). Vast majority of nests in trees, usually highest immediately available, though nests in some highland and marshland rookeries average about 7 m; any species of tree, forming part of small wood, hedgerow or riverside timber, avenue or parkland and growing sufficiently tall, may be used, but many rookeries are in pines and oaks. Exceptional nests on buildings, pylons, even on ground, but not on rocks. Colonial from a few to hundreds of pairs. Eggs 4 to 6 (3 to 9) resemble Crow and Raven but green rather than blue and markings sometimes more intense (40 × 28 mm). Incubation (♀) starts before clutch complete, 16 to 19 days. Fledging (♀♂) nidicolous, 29 to 30 days. One brood.

Methods None needed for actual nest-finding, but to discover all rookeries in one district needs surprising care, as some are tucked away in narrow valleys. Look out also for isolated nests. When counting nests, beware of agglomerations of old ones; some become 'miniature cornfields' with age (Mayer-Gross).

156 **JACKDAW**

Corvus monedula

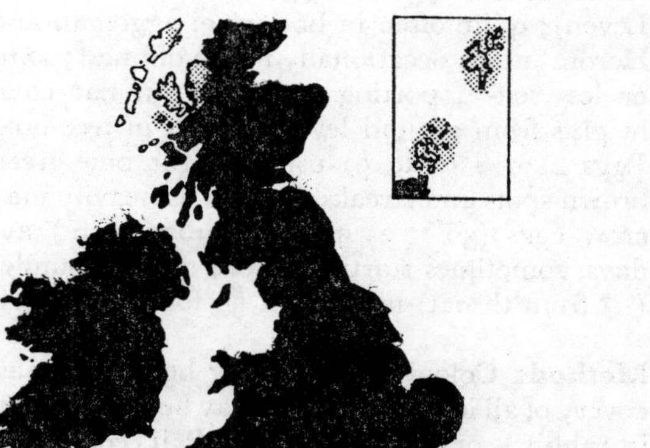

Abundant; widely distributed, breeding in all counties Britain and Ireland, but local north-west Scotland and islands. Habitat from centres of towns, but not large cities, to sea-cliffs, vicinity of rocks, steep banks, quarries, buildings or old trees; less tied than Rook to arable land.

Nest (♀♂) Normally in cavity of some kind and enormously variable in size, from mere lining to over 2 cu m of material, generally foundation of sticks and all kinds of rubbish, with lining mainly of wool, but including hair, fur, paper, grass and other oddments. Sites include cracks and crevices in rocks; holes, chimneys and lofts in buildings, thatched roofs; holes in trees and among dense shoots (as on limes); rabbit holes even on flat ground (e.g. St Serf's Island, Loch Leven); quite often in bottom of aggregation of Rooks' or Herons' nests, occasionally inside old nest; sometimes more or less self-supporting in ivy or on flat conifer branch; heights from ground level to 15 m in tree-holes. Colonial. Eggs 4 to 6 (2 to 9) usually light blue-green with dark brown spots and streaks, but not as heavily marked as most crow eggs (36 × 25 mm). Incubation (♀) averages 18·5 days, sometimes starting before clutch complete. Fledging (♀♂ from throat) nidicolous, 30 to 35 days. One brood.

Methods Colonies can usually be located easily, but discovery of all individual nests may be very difficult, especially in rabbit warrens and quarries. Pairs constantly perch near chosen site before building (E T Lees). Many birds flush from nest at clap, while some fly away at long range and others sit close. But sustained watching should be successful as this species less shy than Raven and Crow. Young can be heard in nest in early part of nestling period.

157 **MAGPIE**
Pica pica

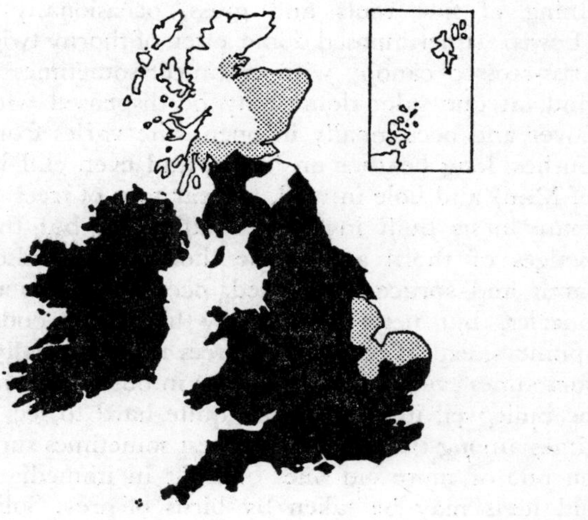

Numerous; breeds throughout Britain and Ireland (where probably introduced 17th century) to Forth-Clyde line, except south-east Scotland; local in eastern Highlands to Ross and absent most of West Highlands and islands north of Bute; also scarce parts of eastern England. In all types of habitat within flight of tree or bush cover, but perhaps preference for poorly kept farmland, e.g. on outskirts of towns and along edge of moorland, where hedges tall and bushes frequent, and cattle or sheep present. Penetrates town parks, e.g. in Dublin, also low scrub above sea cliffs and on other coastal areas such as Dungeness.

Nest (♀♂) Of twigs, strongly lined mud, and with inner lining of fine roots and grass, occasionally some hair (Lewis); superimposed dome, often of thorny twigs, is really criss-crossed canopy with entrance, sometimes difficult to find, at one side; dome may be dispensed with in thick cover and occasionally in open. Site varies from bramble bushes, long heather on banks, and even cliff ledges (Isle of Man) and hole in wall, to near tops of trees 25 m high; many nests built in isolated tall trees, but thickets and hedges of thorn and single thorn bushes also popular; larch and spruce often used, occasionally even monkey-puzzles, but nests not usually built in woods or large spinneys, except on edge; in trees nests normally near top, sometimes even at top (Connor); in bushes and hedges may be built well into cover and quite hard to see, but sometimes among thin twigs. New nest sometimes superimposed on one or more old ones or built in immediate vicinity; old nests may be taken by birds of prey. Solitary. Eggs 5 to 7 (5 to 10) greenish or yellowish densely mottled brown and grey, often concentrated at big end and very variable (34 × 24 mm). Incubation (♀) often begins with first egg, 17 to 18 days. Fledging (♀♂) nidicolous, 22 to 27 days. One brood.

Methods Most nests rely on difficult situations rather than on concealment, and are usually found by cold searching, beginning in winter as there is strong compulsion to return to previous year's site. Birds can be watched back most easily when building, which may begin in February, the nest remaining virtually complete but empty for up to two months before laying. When ♀ is sitting (sometimes from first egg) chattering of ♂ a good indicator; if clutch incomplete, both ♀ and ♂ chatter (Connor).

158 **JAY**
Garrulus glandarius

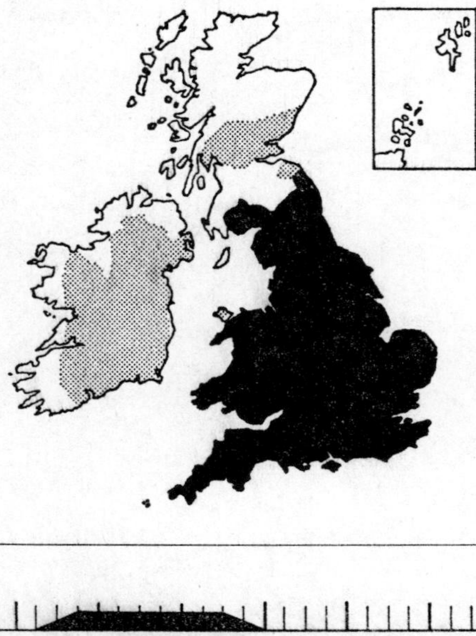

Fairly numerous; breeds throughout England and Wales, though local in western extremities, and in southern Scotland; locally in central Scottish counties and Argyll; Irish race widespread except in parts of north and west; absent Man and Scottish islands. Typical of oakwood, especially coppice-with-standards, but common in thickets and young plantations both deciduous and conifer, and extending into parks (as in central London), orchards, overgrown gardens and shrubberies.

Nest (♀♂, 12·5 cm) Of small, usually dead twigs with lining of rootlets, sometimes of hair, but lacking mud or other stiffening – more like large Bullfinch's than small Crow's nest. In fork, near top of sapling, young conifer or bush, or in epicormic shoots of oak and sweet chestnut and in well-established ivy (E T Lees); often where leaning tree meets upright one, or out on horizontal bough; but near trunk on bigger conifers (Mayer-Gross); favourite trees include pines, spruces and larches, holly, oak, birch, hazel, sycamore, rowan, hawthorn, blackthorn, elder, apple and pear; height range 1 to 10 m, but up to 20 m recorded (*Handbook*); exceptionally in tall heather (*Handbook*) or tree cavities (H R Tutt, D Goodwin *BB* 46: 98, 113). Solitary. Eggs 5 to 6 (3 to 8) greenish-buff with close darker mottling and usually black hair-line at big end (32 × 23 mm). Incubation (♀♂) begins with first egg, about 16 days. Fledging (♀♂) nidicolous, about 20 days. One brood.

Methods Easily hardest of crow family to find, owing to secretive behaviour and thick cover frequented; many nests simply found by searching in woods where Jays seen or heard; high nests look very like Woodpigeons' (Mayer-Gross). Jays can, however, be watched building. Incubating birds sit very close, usually only flying off as tree is climbed. Risk of desertion in early stages.

159 CHOUGH

Pyrrhocorax pyrrhocorax

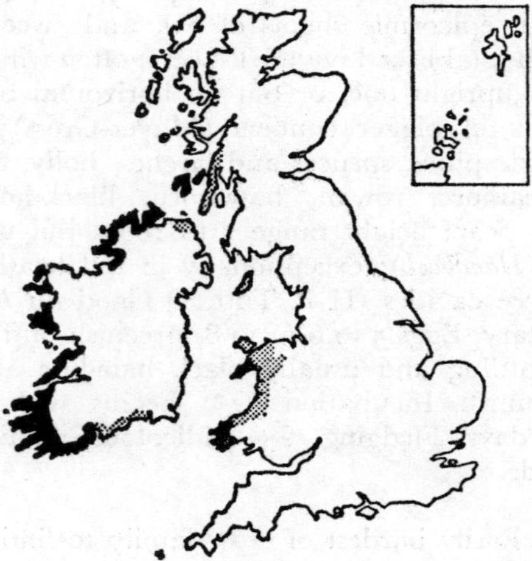

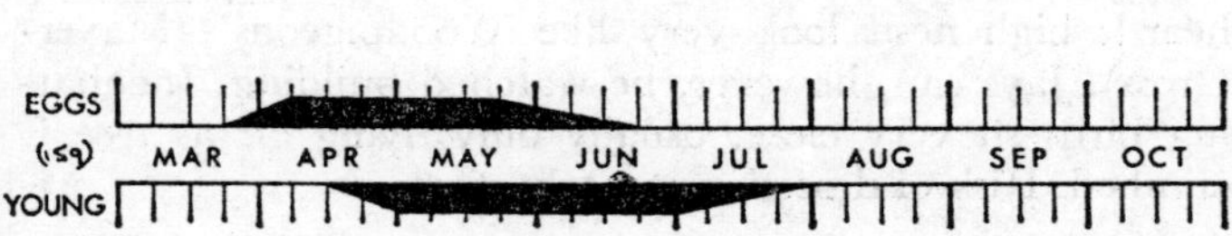

Scarce; breeds locally seven Welsh counties (commonest Pembroke and Caernarvon), Isle of Man, two or three localities south-west Scotland and Inner Hebrides where some evidence for increase; locally common western Ireland (Donegal to Cork), also Antrim and Waterford; now extinct England (last bred Cornwall 1952). Along cliff-bound coasts and islands, often with caves and deep crevices; also inland rock-faces and quarries up to 700 m; sometimes round old mine buildings, chimneys and shafts.

Nest (♀♂) Usually in cavity, substantial but much neater than Jackdaw; heather twigs, sticks, gorse and various plants may form foundation, material grading down in size to frame inner cup of wool or hair, with some grass and feathers. Typically in crevice of cliff or sea-cave at varying heights above sea; inland in similar sites in rock-faces and quarries, thus overlapping Jackdaws in some areas; sometimes on quite accessible ledges, especially in ruined buildings, where Choughs relatively common. Solitary to social. Eggs 3 to 5 (2 to 7) pale yellowish-white, mottled in shades of brown with grey under-lying (39 × 28 mm). Incubation (♀) starts with first egg, 17 to 18 days. Fledging (♀♂ from throat) nidicolous, 38 days. One brood.

Methods Watching recommended as Choughs far less shy than other crows and will soon reveal nest-site at all stages though most easily during building when pairs visit site together (N W Orr). Whitaker recorded ♂ feeding ♀, which then returned to nest. Type of site usually frequented makes searching out of question and, in any case, birds do not flush easily. Many sites 'traditional' and, especially in Ireland, have been occupied for a hundred years (Connor).

160 **GREAT TIT**

Parus major

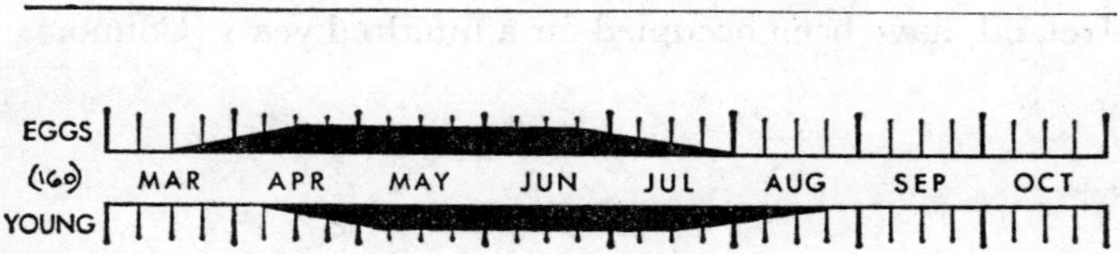

Abundant; nests all counties of Britain and Ireland except Orkney and Shetland; has bred Stornoway, Outer Hebrides, since 1966; absent treeless isles. In woodland of all types, but scarce to absent in pure conifers unless sites available; also in gardens, parks, orchards, tree-lined hedges and even in low scrub.

Nest (♀♂) In cavity; normally of moss and a little grass, lined thick felted hair, sometimes with wool and other soft ingredients which cover eggs during laying; like many other hole-nesters, nest asymmetric, cup being placed against side of cavity farthest from entrance. Typically in hole of tree or stump from ground-level to 5 m, but often higher, up to 15 m (E Cohen); also sometimes in rock crevices, behind bark, among or inside large birds' nests and dreys; rarely in Sand Martin's and Kingfisher's burrows (Walpole-Bond); open nests in hedges or debris recorded (*Handbook*); will take to nestboxes readily; many other artificial sites deliberately or accidentally provided by man recorded, of which inverted flower pots, vertical hollow pipes and tubes perhaps most interesting; exceptionally in thatch and under tiles (Lewis). Appears to prefer a minimum entrance diameter of about 4 cm, but some very small holes used in nature where choice limited. Solitary. Eggs 5 to 12 (5 to 18) white with variable red-brown spotting and blotching; sometimes unspotted (18 × 14 mm). Incubation (♀) 12 to 16 days. Fledging (♀♂) nidicolous, about 19 days, but period variable. Normally one brood, but a few second layings in early seasons or where food abundant.

Methods Generally agreed to be shyer than other tits, but nest can be found fairly easily by watching during building and fledging periods. More patience needed during incubation, but ease with which this and next species can be studied in nestboxes tends to short-circuit problem. Simson points out that all *Parus* tits behave similarly at this period, ♀ leaving nest to feed every 40–50 minutes, ♂ usually calling her off and accompanying her during absence of about 8 minutes. Pair can readily be kept under observation as ♀ calls continuously with begging note and quivering wings and is often fed by ♂. Calls usually cease as ♀ flies to nest, and direction can be noted and followed; next time observer should be able to see ♂ call ♀ off. ♂ may also feed ♀ on nest, usually silently, so this is only a chance method. During long laying period ♀ will occasionally give begging note and be fed by ♂. Some nests can be found in the course of general search, because of relatively large entrance holes. This and other *Parus* tits, except Willow Tit, may add lining during incubation (Simson).

161 BLUE TIT
Parus caeruleus

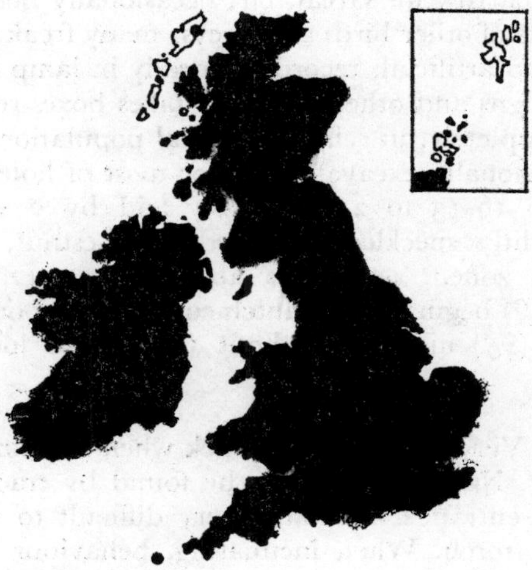

Abundant; nests all counties of Britain and Ireland except Orkney and Shetland; in Outer Hebrides only at Stornoway (since 1963). Typically the tit of oakwoods, but found in woodlands of all types, except uniform young conifers; extends farther into urban areas than Great Tit, nesting even in very small gardens.

Nest (♀♂) In cavity; of moss with bast and grass; asymmetrically placed cup lined with hair, wool, feathers (sometimes added after laying begins and covering eggs). Usually takes smaller holes than Great Tit, but otherwise types of site much the same, though more commonly found nesting in walls, probably because holes between stones often too narrow for Great Tit; occasionally behind bark, in old nests of other birds and dreys; many freak sites, both natural and artificial, recorded; locally in lamp standards, bus stop signs and other artefacts; takes boxes readily, but not so completely, in relation to total population, as Great Tit. Occasionally excavates part or most of hole. Solitary. Eggs 7 to 16 (3 to 24, probably laid by 2 ♀♀) white, rather lightly speckled with red or chestnut, markings sometimes zoned, sometimes absent (15×12 mm). Incubation (♀) begins before clutch completed, about 14 days. Fledging (♀♂) nidicolous, about 19 days or longer. One brood.

Methods Very easy to watch back when building or feeding young. Nests in walls can be found by traces of hair caught at entrance, but often very difficult to see inside, even with torch. When incubating, behaviour similar to Great Tit and same methods will be successful (Simson).

162 **COAL TIT**
Parus ater

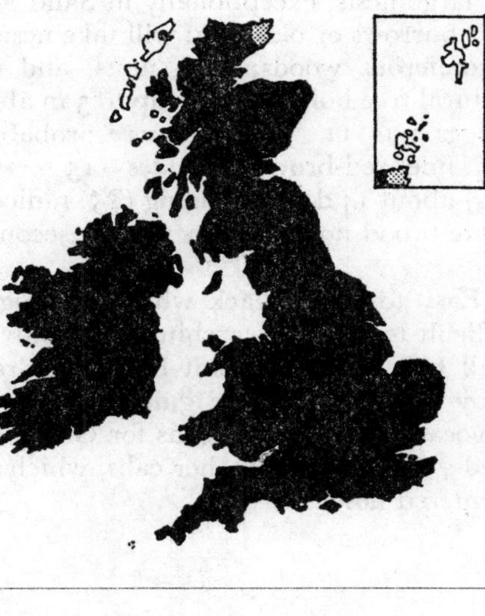

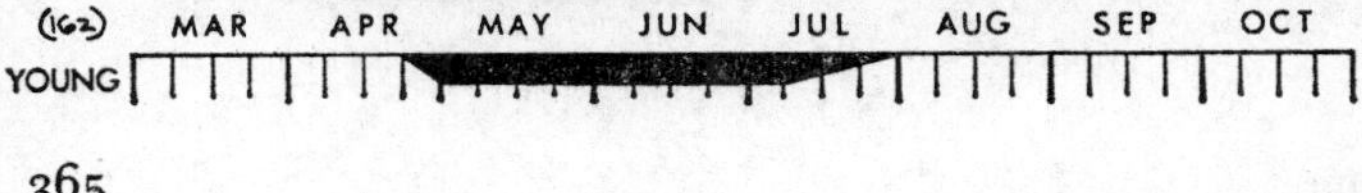

Numerous; breeds all counties of Britain and Ireland except Orkney and Shetland; only at Stornoway in Outer Hebrides (since 1966). The tit of coniferous and highland scrub woods, even in young plantations where ground-nesting habit gives advantage; widespread but not numerous in woodlands of all types, and in parks and large gardens where there are conifers.

Nest (♀♂) In cavity usually in or near ground; foundation of moss and thick felted lining of hair, fur and other soft materials; sometimes feathers as well. Frequently in mouse hole, stump, among tree-roots, in low rock-face or wall, especially a breastwork; sometimes recorded from the bottoms of large nests, exceptionally in Sand Martin's and Kingfisher's burrows or old drey; will take nestboxes, quite freely in coniferous woods; such nests, and occasionally those in natural tree holes, may be up to 5 m above ground. Solitary. Eggs 7 to 11 (5 to 14, more probably by 2 ♀♀) white with fine red-brown speckles (15 × 12 mm). Incubation (♀) about 14 days. Fledging (♀♂) nidicolous, about 16 days. One brood normal, sometimes a second.

Methods Easy to watch back when building or feeding young. Difficult to find by searching, especially when nesting in small holes in banks, but hairs and 'rabbit-flecks' (Gosnell) by entrance may be guide. During incubation Simson advocates same methods as for Great Tit. But BC has followed ♀ back to nest by her calls, which only ceased when she entered hole.

163 **CRESTED TIT**
Parus cristatus

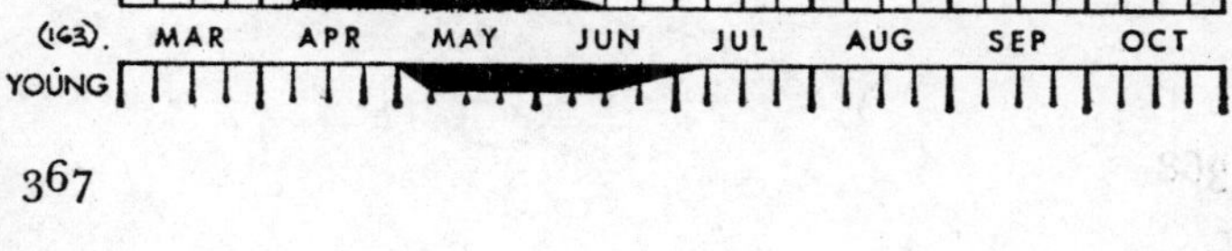

Scarce; breeds five Scottish counties bordering Moray Firth with stronghold in Strathspey; may be spreading to south-east Sutherland, north Aberdeen and west in Inverness. Typical of mature pine forest and open heather areas with stumps; also in mixed woodland of pine, birch and alder, and in conifer plantations where nest-sites provided.

Nest (mainly ♀) In cavity partly or wholly excavated by ♀ in rotten wood usually of old pines; a pad of moss with lining of fur, wool, hair and feathers; 90% below 3 m down to ground level, even hole in ground, but occasionally up to 15 m; also in birch, alder, fence posts, even inside iron post and exceptionally in old nests or dreys; in young plantations has used nestboxes. Solitary. Eggs 5 to 7 (5 to 8) but larger clutches abroad; white with dark red spots, often zoned (16 × 13 mm). Incubation (♀) 13 to 15 days. Fledging (mainly ♀) nidicolous, 16 to 20 days. One brood, exceptionally a second.

Methods Excavation by ♀ for several days gives additional chance to find nest at building stage. ♂ attends, occasionally with materials, and may enter hole, also to feed sitting ♀. Location in uniform areas may be hardest task and familiarity with calls essential, when methods as advocated for Great Tit should be successful. Holes may be found by searching (Nethersole-Thompson).

164 **MARSH TIT**
Parus palustris

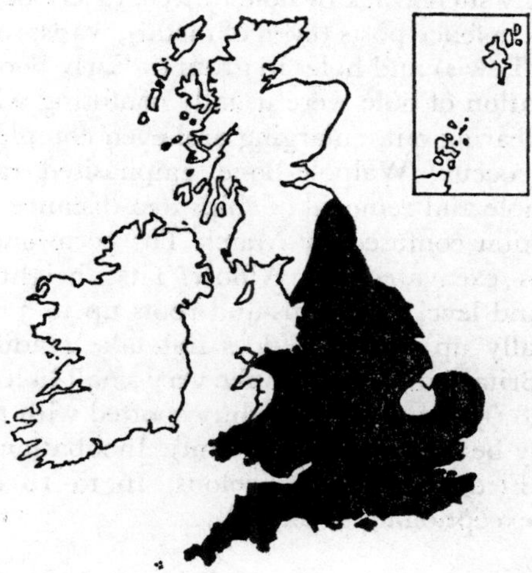

Not scarce; generally distributed in England (except Fens) and Wales (except Anglesey and parts of north-west); breeds Roxburgh, Berwick (and East Lothian 1966); absent Ireland and Man. 'Marsh' a misnomer: found in all types of deciduous woodland with preference perhaps for ash, birch, alder and oak; also woodland edge and wooded country, including gardens with trees and orchards; and elder brakes in chalk and limestone country; but low density in mature forest and absent pure conifers.

Nest (mainly ♀) In cavity, of moss foundation varying in size, with felted cup of hair, fur or vegetable down; in small cavities may be much slighter, resembling Willow Tit. Usually sited crack or hole in tree, rarely behind bark; sometimes in fence posts (even of metal), walls, rock-faces at Cheddar (Lewis) and holes in ground. Early books describing excavation of hole were usually confusing with Willow Tit, but clearing out, enlarging and even complete excavation does occur; Walpole-Bond emphasised ragged, less rounded hole and removal of chips to a distance (cf Willow Tit); position confused by Marsh Tits occasionally taking over holes excavated by Willow Tits; height normally from ground level in stumps and roots up to 3 m in trees; exceptionally up to 15 m; does not take readily to nest-boxes in Britain and may prefer very small holes. Solitary. Eggs 6 to 8 (5 to 11) white, lightly spotted with red-brown, which may be zoned (16 × 12 mm). Incubation (♀) about 13 days. Fledging (♀♂) nidicolous, 16 to 18 days. One brood (? exceptionally a second).

Methods As for other tits. Whitaker added that, when building, ♂ calls and shivers wings near nest before ♀ goes in. She sits very closely but may be called off by ♂ when observer near nest.

165 WILLOW TIT
Parus montanus

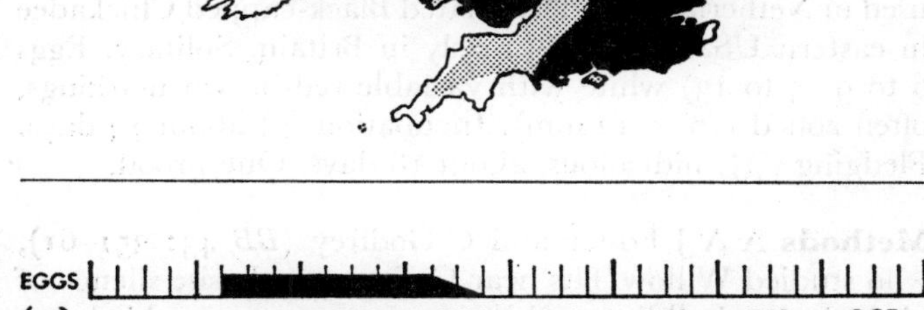

Not scarce; detailed distribution not yet fully worked out owing to confusion with Marsh Tit. Probably breeds most English and Welsh counties, except Anglesey, north to south and west Scottish Lowlands (formerly farther north); absent Ireland, Man. Habitat difficult to classify, but probably depends on presence of small rotten boughs or stumps in which nest hole can be excavated; so generally in birch and alder swamps, but locally in south of England and Midlands in dry spinneys and belts with elder bush storey. Probably more usually near water than Marsh Tit, but where both species occur no clear habitat distinction emerges.

Nest (mainly ♀) In cavity excavated by ♀; slighter and with less moss and more grass, fibres and bark strips than most tits' nests, even fur, hair and feathers of cup being mixed with vegetable fibres and wood chips. Excavation usually in rotten wood of birch, willow, elder or alder, but also in lilac, ash, apple, rowan and especially hazel (L Ballard), even in fence post (BC) or in earth in bank (W H Mullens); entrance usually round or oval (if bough not vertical); several trial borings may be made. Cavity of variable size and shape, according to site; generally from a few cm to not more than 2 m but rarely up to 8 m above ground, with no evidence of preferred aspect; nestboxes, filled with sawdust or shavings to satisfy excavating drive, used in Netherlands and by related Black-capped Chickadee in eastern USA, but only rarely in Britain. Solitary. Eggs 6 to 9 (5 to 13) white with variable red-brown markings, often zoned (16 × 12 mm). Incubation (♀) about 13 days. Fledging (♀♂) nidicolous, about 18 days. One brood.

Methods A A J Foster and C Godfrey (*BB* 43: 351–61), who studied Willow Tits near Oxford, emphasise silence of birds during building and laying, but excavating birds are noisy and can easily be tracked, when chips below hole proclaim site. ♀ leaves nest more easily than Marsh Tit and famous *chay* call will then be heard, as also when feeding young. ♂ feeds sitting ♀ usually on nest in early stages, away from it later. Same vicinity, even same stump may be used in successive years, but fresh hole excavated. L Ballard points out that trial and unused complete borings often indicate vicinity of nest; he believes ♂ may excavate some of these while ♀ is incubating. Beware of Marsh Tits taking over old or even new holes.

166 **LONG-TAILED TIT**
Aegithalos caudatus

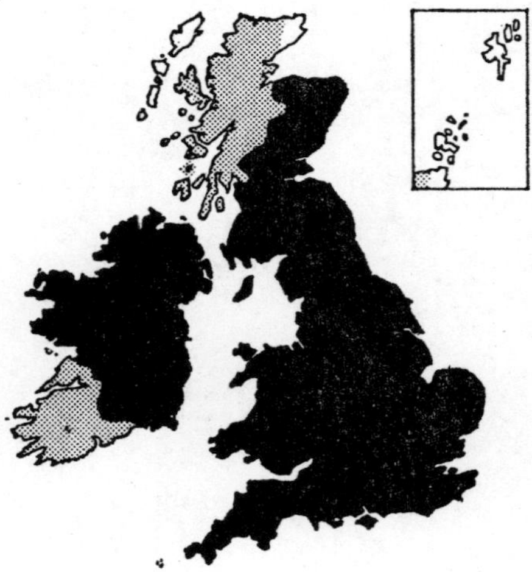

Fairly numerous; now breeds all mainland counties of Britain and Ireland, but not Orkney and Shetland; also absent many islands, including Outer Hebrides (bred 1939); liable to crashes in hard winters, but recovers in three or four years. Woodland and wood edges, thick hedgerows, bushy commons and marginal land, gardens, riparian copses; woods either have bush storey or narrowly forking trees, e.g. oak, birch; hence birch and conifers in younger stages may be avoided. Uncommon in suburban habitats which support other widespread tit species.

Nest (♀♂) Celebrated oval ball of moss, cobwebs and hair, covered with grey lichen and lined with enormous number of feathers (often over 2,000); entrance usually in side near top, sometimes on top. Sites of two distinct types, either high (8 to 20 m or more) in forks or branch ends of deciduous and coniferous trees, or at bush height (1 to 5 m) in great variety of shrubs and creepers, of which brambles, honeysuckle, ivy, clematis, holly, hawthorn, blackthorn, gorse are favourites; Whitaker recorded barberry, and thorn-bearing species seem definitely favoured; exceptionally near ground level (Mayer-Gross) and in reeds 80 cm above water (C Frelin, France); evergreens of many kinds used, including near ends of lower branches of conifers, and Whitaker noted nest woven laterally into ivy. Solitary. Eggs 7 to 12 (5 to 20, probably by 2 ♀♀) white with zone or cap of very fine reddish speckles, but almost or totally spotless types quite usual (14×11 mm). Incubation (mainly ♀) 14 to 18 days. Fledging (♀ served by ♂) nidicolous, 15 to 16 days. One brood.

Methods One of easiest nests to find when building owing to length of time and distances birds carry feathers, often for week or more and over several hundred metres. Watching necessary for tree-nesting pairs as lichen exterior beautifully blended to bark and nest looks like thickening of fork. But many low nests very conspicuous, especially against light. Birds' calls often give away neighbourhood.

167 NUTHATCH

Sitta europaea

Not scarce; breeds all counties of England and Wales to Mersey-Wash line but becoming local north of this to Westmorland and south Northumberland; absent Scotland, Ireland and Man; not yet proved to breed Wight. Broad-leaved and mixed woods, with possible preference for oak and beech, of all types except low scrub, but not in pure conifers; parks and well-wooded gardens and hedgerow country with tall trees. Up to 350 m and over in Wales.

Nest (♀♂) In cavity; unique among British birds in reducing size of entrance with mud and in using nothing but flakes of pine or larch bark where available; elsewhere birch bark or dead oak and beech leaves; once, near timber-yard, entirely of wood shavings (Simson); no division into foundation and lining; eggs hidden by bark or leaves when no bird on nest, hence no fixed cup or general dimensions. Usually in knot hole of trunk or branch, often old wood-pecker boring; sometimes in wall, including masonry of railway bridge 1 m from rail (Lewis); height range 1 to 20 m, mainly 2 to 6 m; exceptional sites in old Magpie nests, Sand Martin holes and haystacks (*Handbook*). Nest-boxes taken and there is strong tendency to return to same site year after year. Solitary. Eggs 6 to 9 (4 to 13) white usually heavily marked with dark red-brown and under-lying grey marks (19 × 14 mm). Incubation (♀) 14 to 15 days. Fledging (♀♂) nidicolous, 23 to 25 days. One brood.

Methods Easy to find when both birds building – ♂ may call from nest tree (Mayer-Gross) – or feeding young. ♂ also feeds incubating ♀. Unnaturally rounded hole some-times catches eye while searching. But birds often become silent at height of breeding cycle, so location advisable in April when they are very noisy.

168 **TREECREEPER**
Certhia familiaris

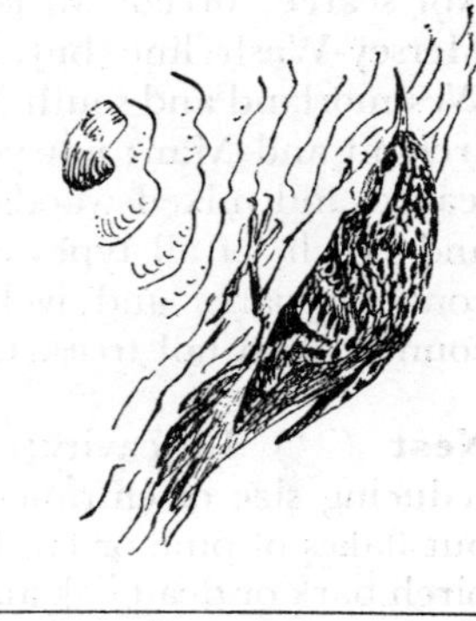

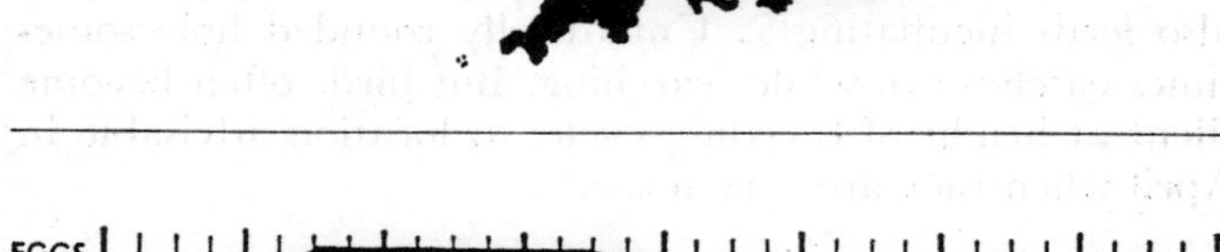

Fairly numerous; breeds all counties except Orkney and Shetland, at Stornoway in Outer Hebrides and on most wooded Inner Hebrides. Mainly conifers abroad, but prefers broadleaved woods in Britain and Ireland; also in wooded parks, gardens, riversides with pollard willows, and hedgerow country with frequent tall trees.

Nest (♀♂, about 3·5 cm across narrow diameter) Squeezed into narrow cracks, where cup becomes flattened oval or even crescent; often, however, surprisingly bulky foundation of twigs, dead ivy stems (Lewis) and wood chips below cup of rootlets, grass, moss, and bark strips, with lining of more bark, feathers, hair, wool. Typically behind dead bark or ivy against trunk of tree, from ground to 10 m but mainly between 1 and 4 m; also in cracks or split trunks, sometimes in cavities and crevices in trees or buildings and walls. Occasionally in nestboxes and will nest behind bark put up artificially; also behind noticeboards fixed to trees and similar artefacts. Solitary. Eggs 5 to 6 (3 to 9) white with zone of red-brown markings at big end, usually dense; paler underlying marks distinguish from most tit eggs (16 × 12 mm). Incubation (mainly ♀) 14 to 15 days. Fledging (♀♂) nidicolous, 14 to 15 days. Sometimes two broods, occasionally in same nest.

Methods Not as easy as tits to find by watching, except when feeding young, and location of right tree does not mean nest is found if there is much dead bark or ivy. But foundation of twigs and white chips can often be seen sticking out of cracks in bark; nests behind ivy are often better concealed. Location of adults followed by search of likely trees often successful. Birds flushed from eggs or young often return readily, even when observer present. Great care must be taken when examining nests behind dead bark, which may easily be detached.

169 **SHORT-TOED TREECREEPER**
Certhia brachydactyla

Very scarce; until recently unknown in Britain though resident Channel Islands, but several birds identified south and east England, 1969 and subsequently and breeding proved 1971 at least in Dorset; clearly worth observing closely treecreepers in south coast counties as species either spreading or previously overlooked. On Continent, where Treecreeper often limited to coniferous forests, Short-toed confined mainly to edges of broadleaved and mixed woods, though occurs in conifers where other absent; also orchards, parks, large gardens, spinneys in cultivated land and rows of trees beside rivers and roads; steep wooded valleys in Channel Islands; surroundings of first British nest 'mainly scattered mixed woodland and grassland' (T J and S E Christmas).

Nest (♀, ♂ accompanies, sometimes helps) Foundation of small twigs, 1 to 2 mm diameter, often birch, with moss, roots and grass, lined feathers, hair, fur and wool; materials on Continent include bark, dry leaves and silk of cocoons.

Typically as Treecreeper behind loose bark on dead or dying trees, usually with two entrances, 2 to 5 m up (extremes 30 cm to 20 m); also in cracks and crevices of dead trunks (first British nest in crevice of 'medium-sized Scots pine, 1 m up'), rarely in woodpecker holes; sometimes in artefacts: wooden sheds, between shute and wall of empty house (G F B de Gruchy), under slate, behind noticeboard, in hole or crevice in fence or wall. Solitary. Eggs 5 to 6, white with zone of rich red-brown spots towards big end and underlying reddish-violet; addled British egg 'white, strongly speckled with magenta, particularly at the blunt end' (17 × 12 mm). Incubation (♀♂) 14 to 15 days. Fledging (♂♀) nidicolous, 15 to 16 days. Eggs laid first week May in Channel Islands, earlier on Continent where second brood regular, June to July; 4 young left first British nest 26 May. (R Dobson, *The Birds of the Channel Islands:* 38–9; P Géroudet, *La Vie des Oiseaux, Les Passereaux II:* 80–5).

Methods Song best means of locating and identifying birds (louder and fuller than Treecreeper without thin, high-pitched notes); also, like Treecreeper, spiral chases round tree with calls Identity can be confirmed in close view of typical birds by longer, almost bent bill, shorter and indistinct supercilium, less white underparts becoming brownish on flanks and vent, and less rufous upperparts. Methods of finding nest as for Treecreeper.

170 **WREN**
Troglodytes troglodytes

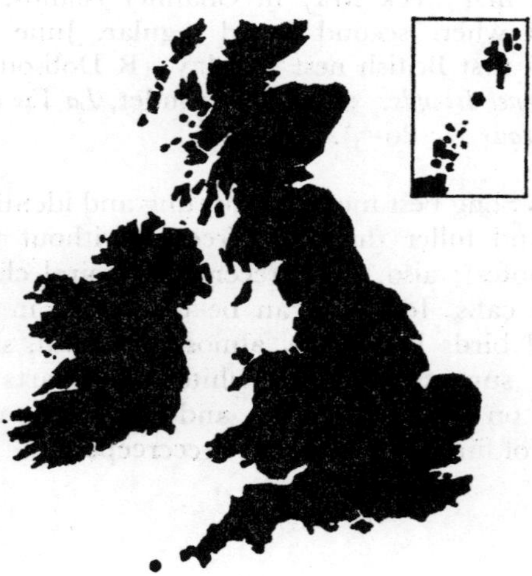

Abundant; breeds all over Britain and Ireland to remotest islands where represented by local races, e.g. Shetland, Fair Isle, St Kilda. Habitat about most varied of any British breeding bird but avoids centres and perhaps inner suburbs of large towns; absent also on flat, featureless moorland and heaths, but occurs wherever there are steep banks, rock-faces, walls, bushes and trees, and is a typical farmyard bird (E T Lees); up to 1,000 m in hills.

Nest (♂, lined ♀) Ball of very variable size and shape, according to situation; exterior of dead leaves, bracken and fern fronds, moss, grasses, vegetable fibres, straw and any other locally available material; entrance at side less than 2·5 cm diameter, usually somewhat overhung; lining of feathers; moss, leaf or fern nests often have entrance outlined in firmer material, e.g. stalks or fibres; typical free nest really egg-shaped with narrower end at bottom, but in holes and crevices whole top or dome may be dispensed with. Site shows great variation, from free nests in forks of bushes to nests completely hidden in small crannies and crevices, or in other birds' nests, e.g. House Sparrow, Swallow, Heron, House Martin, Dipper; majority of early nests probably in banks, especially just under fringe of vegetation at top, in upturned tree roots, or in ivy and creepers on walls and trees; later nests, when cover thicker, tend to be out in bramble clumps, thorn hedges and bushes; other favourite sites clumps of dead bracken and tangle of dead leaves and sticks, e.g. in drift left after flood along banks of streams, in epicormic shoots of many trees, also in eaves of thatch, wooden sheds and holes in walls of buildings; St Kilda race fond of nesting inside the peculiar buildings called *cleitean*, found round old village, as well as on cliffs; few nests, except those in cliffs, above a man's reach but Mayer-Gross has records up to about 5 m on trees; will sometimes take nestboxes with large entrances. Solitary. Eggs 5 to 6 (3 to 16, presumably due to more than one ♀) white with brownish-red frecklings, often as zone at big end, sometimes sparse or absent (17 × 13 mm). Incubation (♀) 14 to 15 days. Fledging (♀, sometimes ♂) nidicolous, 16 to 17 days. Two broods.

Methods When building or feeding young is careless of all beholders, but many nests can also be found by careful searching. Main structure built by ♂, who makes several 'cock's nests', one lined by ♀ and laid in; another may be used for second clutch. Same one sometimes used again next season, or cock's nest of previous year may be lined. Several nests have therefore usually to be found before right one; some risk of desertion if site investigated before eggs laid. Beware of false 'nest records' due to use of nest as roost (Mayer-Gross). Monograph: Armstrong (1955).

171 **DIPPER**
Cinclus cinclus

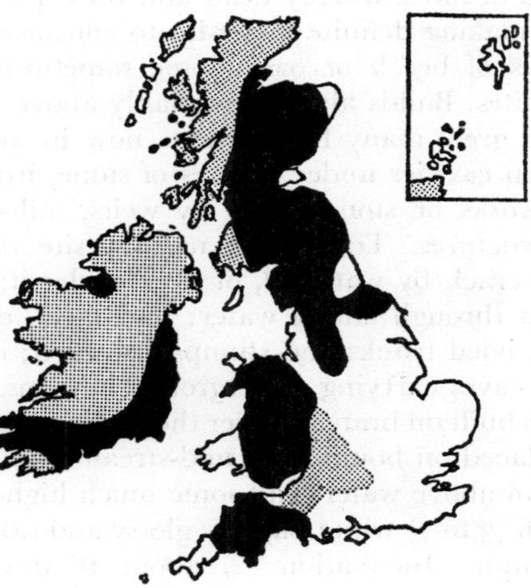

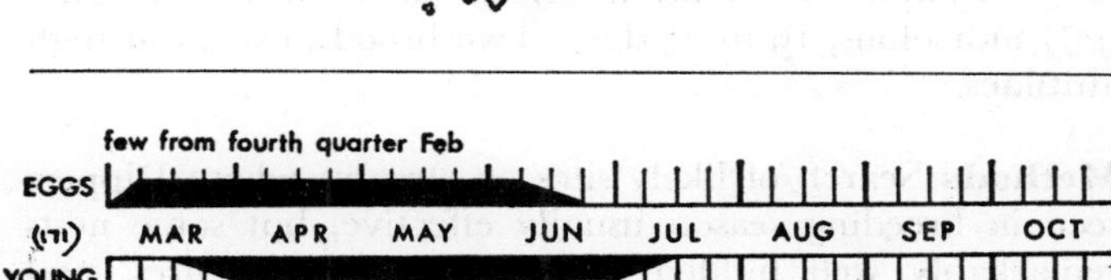

Not scarce; essentially of highland distribution in north and west Britain and Ireland; nest found Hoy (Orkney) 1970 but absent Shetland and also Man; exceptional to east of line running from Dorset through Cotswold counties to Staffordshire and south Yorkshire (but nested Hampshire 1938–50); local or absent many coastal areas in west and north. Typically found along fast-running rivers, burns and brooks; but on edge of range along slow-running rivers where these are broken by weirs and other artificial falls; up to 800 m or more.

Nest (♀♂) Size variable with site, externally like large Wren's nest, with entrance even more overhung; dome and foundation of moss, usually dead and brown looking, with grass cup making definite lower lip to entrance; cup lined with leaves of beech or oak; dome sometimes absent in sheltered sites. Builds almost invariably above fast-moving water, and great many British nests now in artefacts: on ledges or in cavities under bridges of stone, iron or wood, in breastworks or stone walls, by weirs, mill-lashers and similar structures. Traditional natural site on ledge or stuffed in crack by waterfall, or even under it, bird flying in and out through falling water; rock-faces, overhanging tree roots, ivied trunks and stumps also used; occasionally in roof of caves carrying underground streams, and sometimes nests built on branches over the water, on earth banks, or even placed on boulders in mid-stream; but most nests at least 1 m above water, and some much higher. Solitary. Eggs 4 to 6 (3 to 7) white, slightly glossy and rather pointed (26 × 19 mm). Incubation (♀) about 16 days. Fledging (♀♂) nidicolous, 19 to 25 days. Two broods, except at high altitudes.

Methods Search of likely sites on streams where Dippers seen in breeding season usually effective, but some nests remarkably well hidden for such bulky structures, and usually blend well with surroundings. Watching should be successful when building or feeding young if birds can be followed easily up and down stream, but more difficult during incubation because many ♀♀ sit very close, only leaving nest briefly to feed. Traditional locality used year after year and same nest may be occupied twice in one season or rebuilt and relined in a following year; but often changes rung on several sites.

172 **BEARDED TIT**
Panurus biarmicus

Scarce; very local Norfolk and Suffolk, with recent small colonies in Essex and Kent and breeding recorded in one more eastern and two southern English counties, also in Anglesey (1967). Confined to reedbeds, usually large, but recent English record from a small one.

Nest (♀♂, lined ♂) Foundation of dead leaves of reeds and sedges with lining of flowering reedtops and occasional feather. Low down in thick sedge, soft dry grasses overgrown with bindweed or dead reeds; generally near edge of reedbed; usually in swampy ground but some sites quite dry (Whitaker). Solitary, but several to many pairs in same reedbed. Eggs 5 to 7 (5 to 12) white with many streaks, scrawls and spots of grey-brown (17 × 14 mm). Incubation (♀♂) 12 to 13 days. Fledging (♀♂) nidicolous, young leave nest 9 to 12 days, often before they can fly. Two broods, sometimes three.

Methods Easy to watch when building or feeding young if suitable observation point found. Whitaker watched ♀ back to nest as she flew from stem to stem through reedbed before dropping on to well-incubated eggs; another ♀ returned to eggs while observer stood by nest. Simson points out that change-overs take place every 20 to 30 minutes, relieving bird calling on way to nest, then pitching into reeds close by. Relieved bird, however, usually appears several metres away, having climbed through reeds before flying. So incoming bird must be watched and carefully marked (and equal care taken to obliterate traces of visit).

173 **MISTLE THRUSH**

Turdus viscivorus

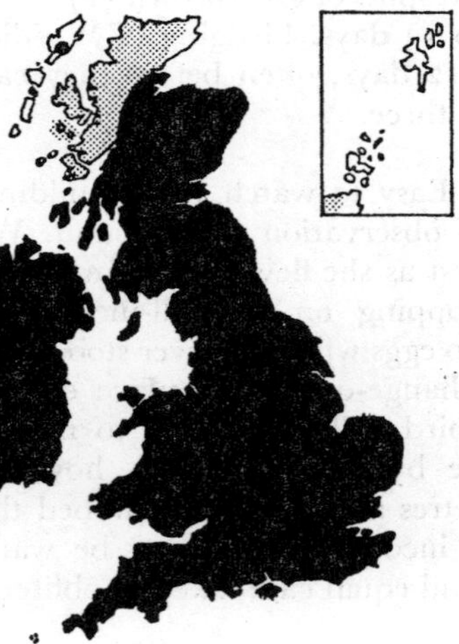

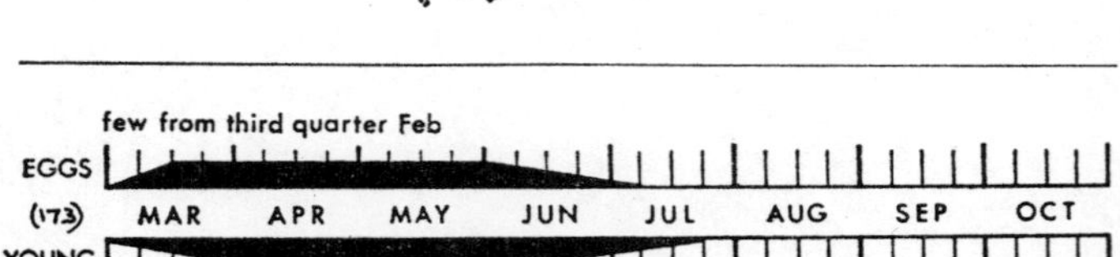

Numerous; breeds all counties of Britain and Ireland except Shetland and Orkney (irregular); absent or scarce in Hebrides and parts of north-west and north Scottish mainland. Typically bird of wood edges and open wooded country (parks, tree-lined hedges, large gardens and orchards) rather than continuous woodland; frequent in conifer areas, upper limit of scrub in highland valleys and occurs in bare areas (e.g. Llanddwyn Island, Anglesey), also right into cities, including London; often in churchyards with yews and along avenues.

Nest (♀, 10 cm) Substantial structure of grasses (sometimes green) and other vegetation, often dead or green moss and lichen, wool and paper, feathers and string (A W Boyd) strengthened with earth and lined with fine grasses; rim frequently ornamented with various oddments: wool, feathers, rags, paper, ivy seeds, flower petals and green leaves. Most thrush species use readily accessible material, particularly true of Mistle, and this has bearing on nest-finding, for moss and lichen nests in highland districts blend much better with boughs and rocks than grassy nests of the south, often trailing wisps below. Typically in trees, either close to trunk on base of branch, or well out on fork of horizontal bough; tree depends on species available, e.g. of 193 tree nests recorded by Whitaker, only two in yews, whereas of 60 nests found in Hampshire in 1926–30, 27 in yews; definite preference for yews in areas where they occur reasonably commonly, and perhaps for apple trees; otherwise, locally abundant species chosen, provided they have suitable sites; many conifers used, even monkey-puzzles. Some evidence that first nests in conifers are followed by second nests in deciduous trees which have come into leaf, e.g. yew followed by elder on Hampshire downs; height range 1 to 17 m, but normally 3 to 10 m; also on ledges and in recesses on or even inside buildings, (especially ruins), stone walls and pergolas, rock-faces down to rocky banks, sometimes even where trees also available. Solitary. Eggs 3 to 5 (3 to 6) creamy-buff or greenish-blue with red-brown spots and blotches, sometimes zoned, and underlying grey or violet marks (31 × 22 mm). Incubation (♀) 13 to 14 days. Fledging (♀♂) nidicolous, 14 to 16 days. Two broods, very occasionally in same nest.

Methods Watch for site selection routine in early spring (sometimes in autumn), when ♀ squats in forks in trees. Actual building may be done unobtrusively early in morning; nests at this stage often disclosed by ♀ rocketing off as observer passes; during incubation usually sits tight, but when with young will scold boldly. With practice, nests easily found by cold searching and often recognised by trail of material below. Frequently returns to same site, even after many years (Whitaker).

174 FIELDFARE
Turdus pilaris

In recent years has bred Orkney, Shetland (more than one pair), east Inverness and one English county, so may well become regular nesting species. On Continent found in deciduous, mixed and coniferous woods, particularly birch, alder, pine and spruce, often by marshes or water; also wood edges, parks, orchards, and other cultivated country with trees.

Nest (♀, 10 cm) Resembles Mistle Thrush, sometimes with foundation of twigs; main structure of grasses and other local material, with thin cup of mud and inner lining of fine bents. First Orkney nest (1967) 1·5 m in elder in little valley; in 1969 in heather; Shetland nests under overhang in bank and in trees; Inverness nest in oak. On Continent buildings, rocks, even on ground. Social to colonial. Eggs 4 to 6 (3 to 8) usually resemble Blackbird, but others bright blue with red-brown blotches (29 × 21 mm); from early or mid-May through to July. Incubation (chiefly ♀) 13 to 14 days. Fledging (♀♂) nidicolous, about 14 days. Possibly two broods.

Methods Colonial habit on Continent usually makes finding easy, and searching where pair located should be successful in Britain, with resort to watching back if necessary. Birds very demonstrative when with young.

175 **SONG THRUSH**
Turdus philomelos

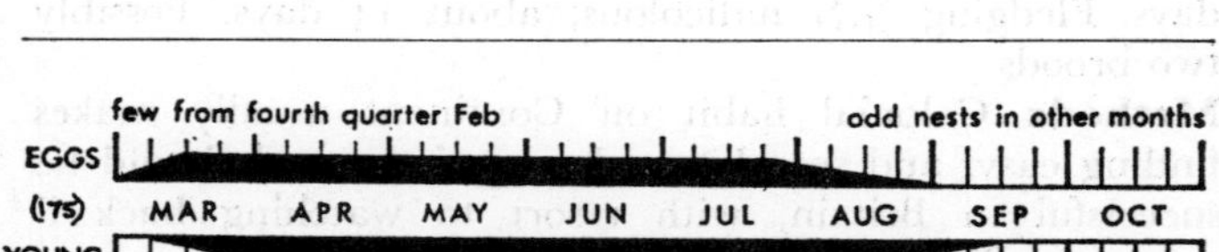

Abundant; breeds all counties of Britain and Ireland, except Shetland, where only occasional, and some remote islands. Found in all types of woodland and wooded country, especially gardens and shrubberies, copses and thick hedges, but scarcer where bush-storey deficient or absent, e.g. medium-aged conifers, some scrubwoods; also bushy commons and uncultivated rough ground, extending to moorland edge, rocky hillsides and islands in lochs.

Nest (♀, 9 cm) Normally of grass in open habitat and of moss in woodland with small twigs as foundation, mud-strengthened and hard lining – unique amongst British birds – of mud, wet rotten wood, dung or peat cemented with saliva and moulded by ♀'s breast; in Hebrides (J W Campbell) and elsewhere in dry weather this sometimes replaced by grass lining; rim often ornamented, especially with ivy seeds. Enormous range of recorded sites, but vast majority in hedge-stock or ivy; bush or tree from 1 to 4 m up, occasionally higher, to 17 m; quite often in trailing creepers; early preference for evergreen cover; also in banks, small cliffs and on ledges or in recesses of buildings; occasionally on ground in crops, bracken or grass tussocks; even without a nest (F Birley, Whitaker); rarely in old nests of other species; Hebridean nests in long heather. Solitary, but sometimes occupied nests may be close together, three within 3 m triangle (Mayer-Gross). Eggs 3 to 5 (2 to 7) blue, tinged green and sparsely spotted or blotched with black; spotless clutches and some with red-brown markings occur (28 × 21 mm). Incubation (♀) 12 to 14 days. Fledging (♀♂) nidicolous, 12 to 15 days. Two or three broods, sometimes in same nest.

Methods Early nests usually easy to find by hot or cold searching, but later in season may be very well hidden; for census work location by singing ♂♂, then watching for building should be undertaken; most pairs return readily to nest when feeding young.

176 **REDWING**
Turdus iliacus

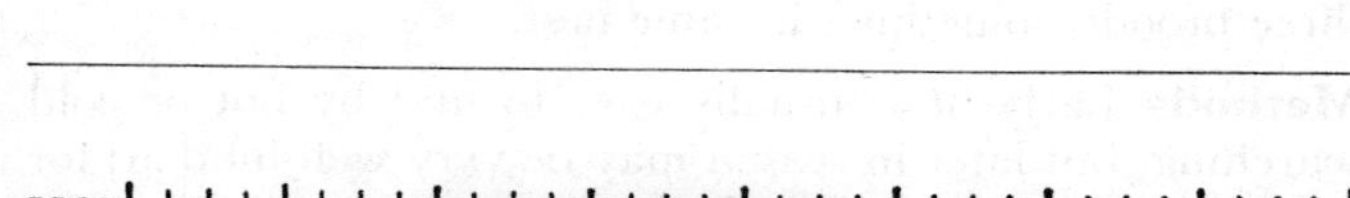

Scarce; now breeds in increasing numbers north Scotland as far south as north Perth and sporadically Shetland; attempted to nest Kerry 1951. Policies (mixed amenity woodland often with rhododendron shrub layer) seem favourite habitat, even close to houses, but also found in scrub (alder, birch, gorse) woodland near water up to 250 m; one record of young from treeless Fair Isle.

Nest (♀, ♂ may accompany, 9 cm) Scottish examples usually of grass, with birch twigs, moss and wool, thin but strong mud cup and inner lining of fine grass. Scottish sites from 25 cm to 7 m, several in forks of rhododendron bushes, but also in beech hedge, beech, birch, oak, willow, rowan, sycamore, conifer, gorse, red currant bush and creeper (relined Song Thrush nest) against house, in dead stumps and tree roots, and steep peaty bank. Single pairs or loose groups up to 15 pairs reported. Eggs 5 to 6 (2 to 7) very like small Blackbird, greenish with fine brown markings, but sometimes boldly blotched and showing much ground colour (Connor) (26 × 19 mm). Incubation (♀♂) about 13 days. Fledging (♀♂) nidicolous, 12 to 14 days. Two broods. (Plate 8a)

Methods Location of singing ♂♂ should be followed by watching and searching of likely areas. I D Pennie found birds in one Ross group shy and unobtrusive, but other pairs reported to be demonstrative near nest, even with eggs; alarm call like subdued Mistle Thrush (Mayer-Gross).

177 **RING OUZEL**
Turdus torquatus

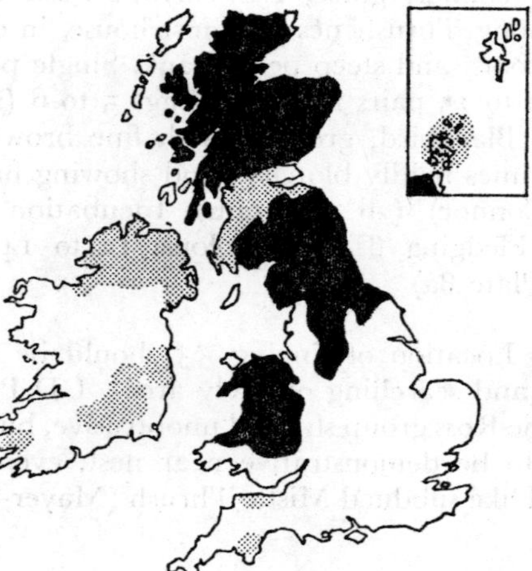

Not scarce; breeds throughout highland Britain from Devon to Caithness (less regularly Orkney) but not extreme South Wales, Anglesey, Man, Outer or most Inner Hebrides or Shetland; local on hill ranges in about 12 counties of Ireland. Usually found in steeply contoured moorland, with rocky outcrops and ledges covered by heather or blaeberry; hence characteristically along glens and open-sided gorges, but sometimes on smoother slopes among bracken and bushes; on Exmoor also in roadside banks of heather and small heather-covered quarries (P Davis). Altitude not important where sites suitable, but mainly from 300 to over 800 m, and locally to sea level.

Nest (♀♂, 9 cm) Of moorland grasses, some heather and bracken, with strengthening of peaty earth; thick lining of finer grasses, which give distinctive crosswise effect, quite different from lining of Blackbird's nest (Whitaker); may be decorated with moss (P Davis). Typically in bulge of vegetation (heather, blaeberry, grass, woodrush) overhanging small rock-face or peat-bank, but also often among heather, bracken or ferns on steep banks and even flat ground; in north of England quite often in small stone buildings or walls; exeptionally in bush or small tree; sometimes on sea-cliffs and in old mines (Walpole-Bond). Solitary. Eggs 4 to 5 (3 to 6) like well-marked Blackbirds, bluish green with dark red-brown blotches (30 × 21 mm). Incubation (♀♂) about 14 days. Fledging (♀♂) nidicolous, 14 days. Usually two broods.

Methods Difficult to find where large area of suitable habitat makes searching unrewarding. One pair took two hours to go back to nest (Whitaker), and others record similar experiences, but such delays probably due to observer being too close. A long view of suspected nesting places should be possible in many habitats and, when building or feeding young in progress, watching certainly effective. When searching, look out for bird leaving nest some way ahead; others sit very close but may flush to clap of hands; more subtly, P Davis imitates ♂'s whistle which often brings ♀ off nest to investigate. Song of ♂ may be little guide to location, but parents sometimes scold in vicinity of nest. Some nests easy to see, but others well hidden. Same site or neighbourhood often used for several years.

178 **BLACKBIRD**
Turdus merula

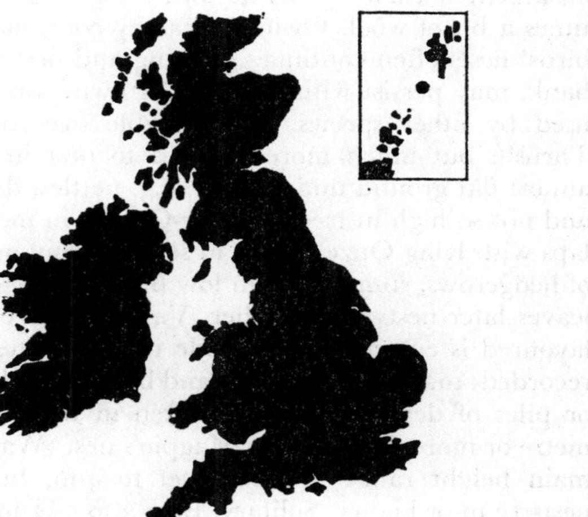

Abundant; breeds all counties and most islands. Habitat hard to separate from Song Thrush, difference showing chiefly in relative numbers, but more tolerant of bare areas and penetrates well into moorland regions up valleys and glens and to sea coasts where there is cover; more successful than Song Thrush in urban areas, reaching city centres in numbers.

Nest (♀, ♂ occasionally assists, 9 cm) Generally rather bulkier and darker than Song Thrush (A W Boyd) and more cylindrical than Mistle Thrush; for differences from Ring Ouzel see that species; foundation of moss, main structure of grasses, with mud cup, lined finer grasses; rim less often ornamented than by Mistle and Song Thrush, but sometimes a bit of wool. Owing to earthy core, moss on Blackbirds' nests often continues growing and nest, especially in bank, may persist with a life of its own, sometimes being used by other species. Considerable overlap with Song Thrush, but much more inclined to nest in banks or on almost flat ground under cover, e.g. nettles, dead bracken; and not so high in trees (Mayer-Gross); in moorland overlaps with Ring Ouzel; early in season many nests on stocks of hedgerows, stumps and in low brambles; with flushing of leaves later nests often higher. Variety of trees and bushes favoured is enormous, and wide range of sites in artefacts recorded: many in or on walls and buildings, also in bundles or piles of dead sticks; quite often in tree cavities up to metre or more deep, also in Magpie's nest (Walpole-Bond); main height range ground level to 4 m, but some tree nests 12 m or higher. Solitary. Eggs 3 to 5 (2 to 7) greenish-blue with underlying grey marks and more or less freckling with brown or red-brown, often zoned at big end; spotless blue clutches occur (29 × 21 mm). Incubation (♀) 12 to 15 days. Fledging (♀♂) nidicolous, 12 to 15 days. Two, even three, broods quite regular and five recorded; may use same nest two or more times.

Methods See under Song Thrush. Usually easy to watch back when building or feeding young, but individuals vary. Late nests, especially on or near ground among nettles and other thick cover, likely to escape discovery. Building material, especially grass stalks, often dropped and abandoned close to nest (E T Lees). Monograph: Snow (1958).

179 **WHEATEAR**

Oenanthe oenanthe

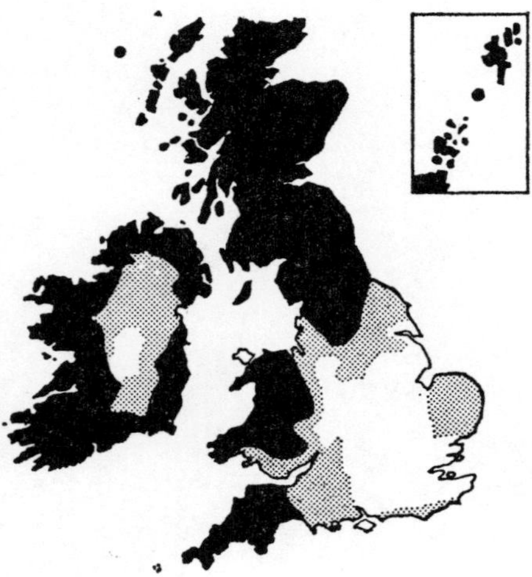

Fairly numerous; breeds generally in highland Britain and Ireland, but now very local lowland Britain and absent many south-eastern English counties; breeds many islands but not now Scilly. Essentially bare types of country with loose boulders and scree, rabbit warrens or stone walls; so on rocky moorland, along roads in highland regions, on chalk downs, sandy commons and dunes, brecks and stony shores; common on many rocky islands.

Nest (mainly ♀) In cavity or recess, of grass, roots and some moss, paper wrappings at Cheddar (Lewis), lined rabbit's fur, hair, feathers and wool. Usually either under boulder, stone or slab, with small entrance, in rabbit or other hole in ground, or in stone wall, but traditionally at Dungeness and elsewhere under tins, corrugated iron and other objects left on beach; artefact sites using three bricks made over 40 years ago in Sussex (P W Harvey), and nestboxes sunk in shingle have been developed since 1950's. Average depth of 13 nests about 50 cm (Whitaker), but under small slabs or in blind burrows may be much nearer entrance and occasionally almost in open under tufts of grass. Solitary. Eggs 5 to 6 (3 to 8) pale blue, occasionally with small red-brown spots (21 × 16 mm). Incubation (mainly ♀) about 14 days. Fledging (♀♂) nidicolous, about 15 days. One brood, sometimes two, especially in south.

Methods Chats are group for which watching back almost essential; they sit tight and very few nests can be found by flushing birds, though occasionally one flies out close to observer and ♂ Wheatear once flew into hole when BC was only a few metres away. Usually ♂, having seen observer, flies away to call ♀ off nest, after which only good vantage point and patient watching needed. Final dive to nest sometimes difficult to see, since for quick results vantage point should be as far as feasible from suspected area. ♂ usually accompanies ♀ back, even driving her at times; good sign when they turn backs to observer and begin series of purposeful 'hops' from perch to perch (fortunately normally exposed), though final flight to nest may be at least 10 m. Sometimes both birds slip observer and disappear; immediate second attempt to find nest inadvisable, as ♂ seldom calls ♀ off again once she has returned like this. Nests easier to find when building (but risk of desertion if site examined) or with young. As use proceeds, smoothed appearance of entrance good guide where choice of several holes has to be made.

180 STONECHAT

Saxicola torquata

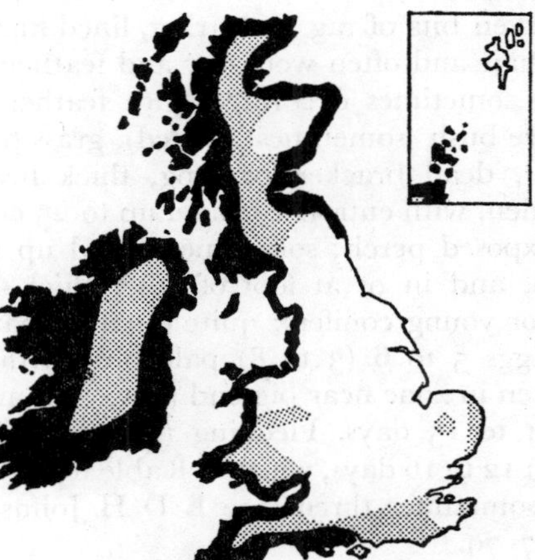

Not scarce; breeds almost all littoral and insular counties of Britain (sporadic Shetland) and Ireland, but irregular English east coast except Northumberland and East Anglia; breeds some Scottish and all Irish inland counties but in England and Wales regularly only in Montgomery, Shropshire and Surrey. Typically gorse and heather country with exposed perches and observation points: commons, moorland, heaths, coastal waste ground, young conifer plantations; in long heather without gorse in Scottish Highlands and islands; rarely now in marginal land round fields, which appears to be second choice habitat.

Nest (♀, 7 cm) Of grass and sometimes moss, with odd bits of other plants, pine needles, bracken, heather, gorse, wool and even bits of rag and string, lined fine grass, moss filaments, hair and often wool, fur and feathers (cf. Whinchat); rim sometimes decorated with feathers. Favoured sites in gorse bush (sometimes isolated), grass tuft (marram near coast), dead bracken or long, thick heather, often deeply hidden, with entrance tunnel up to 25 cm long, and adjacent exposed perch; sometimes raised up to 60 cm in gorse bush, and in or at foot of other thick bushes, low brambles, or young conifers; quite often on bank or slope. Solitary. Eggs 5 to 6 (3 to 8) pale blue with red-brown speckles often in zone near big end (19 × 14 mm). Incubation (♀) 14 to 15 days. Fledging (♀♂) nidicolous, young leaving nest 12 to 16 days, when well able to fly. Two broods regularly, sometimes three. See E D H Johnson, *BB* 64: 201–13, 267–79.

Methods See under Wheatear, but sometimes very difficult to watch back owing to thick cover. Unless actual spot where ♀ disappears is marked, may be almost impossible to flush her again. Nests occasionally found by searching after locating pair, e.g. in heather country, or by seeing ♀ leave nest. Whitaker described technique of watching roadside pairs from car: ♂ (often located on telegraph wires) followed till ♀ appears. She works back to nest in short flights, after initial long flight (100 to 200 m) away. Gosnell advocated similar technique, but if ♀ does not come off nest, ♂ may be approached and play 'hot and cold', even fluttering overhead when near nest, often near path. P G Davis has had remarkable success by marking approximate sites when birds building, then returning when young ringable and watching parents back with food, though it may take half hour to make certain of spot and avoid trampling vegetation; in two seasons he ringed six consecutive broods of two pairs by this method.

181 **WHINCHAT**
Saxicola rubetra

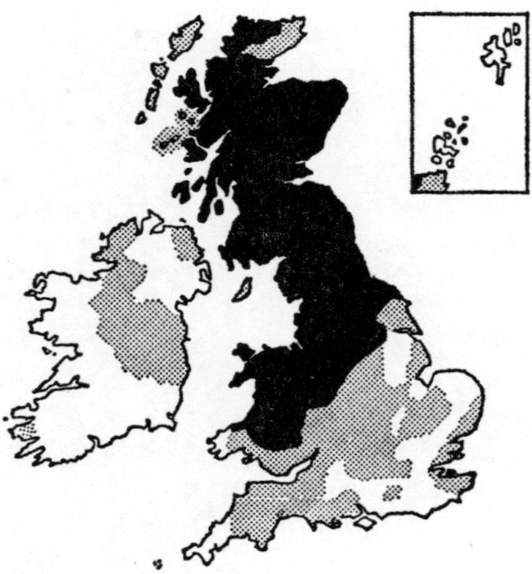

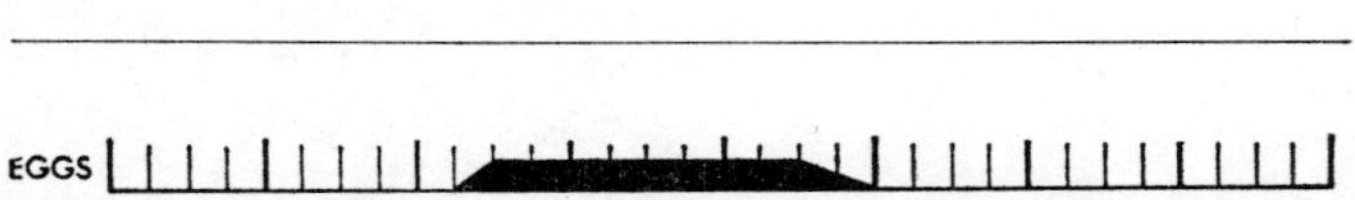

Fairly numerous; breeds all over highland Britain (erratic Orkney and absent Shetland), but local in lowland Britain and in Ireland where has bred recently in about half the 32 counties, though numerous only in Kildare and Westmeath. Habitat rather diverse, with rough grass and exposed perches as common denominator: in south England water meadows, heathy commons, chalk downs, along railway lines, on coastal warrens; in Wales typical of bracken-clad hillsides; in moorland regions in *Molinia* bogs with heather, bog-myrtle and sallow bushes; everywhere young conifer plantations provide ideal conditions.

Nest (♀ attended by ♂, 5·5 cm) Of dry grass on foundation of coarser grass and moss, lined fine bents, rootlets and often hair but no wool, fur or feathers (cf Stonechat). Usually well hidden in grass tuft, under dead bracken or where grass grows into small bush, e.g. gorse; often on bank or side of ditch, or near wire fence, but also in open field with exposed perches close by (considerable overlap with Tree Pipit); occasionally at end of tunnel up to 30 cm long, and smoothed way-in, sometimes dog-legged, leads to all sites; Whitaker recorded nests under various plants (e.g. crosswort, knapweed) and Lewis under clod of earth. Solitary. Eggs 5 to 6 (4 to 7) deep greenish-blue with or without fine red-brown speckles near big end (19 × 14 mm). Incubation (♀) 13 days. Fledging (♀♂) nidicolous, leaving nest about 13 days, usually before full-grown. Sometimes two broods.

Methods See under Wheatear. Searching usually hopeless and watching must be tried. G O Stephens suggests moving round ♂'s apparent territory until ♀ appears, then back away, keeping her in view; she returns by stages without ♂. Gosnell found three nests in one field, two within 5 minutes, by this method, also advocated by Walpole-Bond; normally time must be no object. BC watched ♂ fly out from perch about 15 m and return without alighting; hot search where ♂ had turned revealed ♀ on very well hidden nest. Birds with young will sometimes hover over nest without going down; at all stages they often run or flutter last metre or two (Mayer-Gross).

182 REDSTART

Phoenicurus phoenicurus

Fairly numerous; British distribution predominantly highland, but breeds all mainland counties except Cornwall (where irregular), though local Caithness; absent Man, Outer Hebrides, Orkney and Shetland, occasional and erratic in Ireland. Wooded country of all types frequented in different parts of range and sometimes rocky and stone-walled zones just above tree-line; so may be found from moorland edge through hanging woods down river valleys and glens to parks, lowland woods, orchards, gardens, commons, along slow-flowing rivers lined with pollard willows, as well as round ruins and quarries; ancestral habitat considered by John Buxton to be Scots pine forest and still found there in Scottish Highlands, but not normally in young conifer plantations.

Nest (♀, 5·5 cm) In cavity or recess or on ledge, of dry grass, bark and vegetable fibres, rootlets and moss, lined fibres, hair and especially feathers. All sorts of holes may be taken, in trees, buildings, walls, rocks and quarries, even in cast-lead statue (Whitaker), and Martello Tower on beach at Crumbles, Sussex (E W Leach); takes nest-boxes readily, but prefers entrance holes of larger diameters (about 5 cm) resembling old woodpecker holes, commonly used in nature; also in crevices and under bark. In some districts, e.g. Sheffield (Whitaker and G Broadhead), nest is placed under dead bracken or grasses and entered by tunnel; quite often Robin-like nests on ledges in buildings and occasionally in old nests of other birds, e.g. Swallow (*Handbook*) and Song Thrush, and in other freak sites, e.g. in rusty tin under brambles and in drey up pine tree on Surrey common (Mayer-Gross); height usually less than 8 m, but exceptionally up to 18 m in Cheshire elm (C G Bennett). Solitary. Eggs 5 to 7 (5 to 11) blue sometimes with greenish tinge, occasionally with small red-brown spots (19 × 14 mm). Incubation (♀) 13 to 14 days. Fledging (♀♂) nidicolous, 14 to 16 days. Occasional second broods.

Methods Many nests found by searching suitable holes, but ♀ can be watched back, often uttering a disyllabic off-nest call—the first syllable like a Chaffinch's alarm, the second a sharp clicking sound. Many ♀♀ very wary and Whitaker considered tunnel nests near Sheffield among the most difficult to find. Watching becomes much easier when eggs hatch and both parents feed young. ♀♀ can sometimes be flushed by tapping trees, but some leave nest many metres away, perhaps warned by ♂. Tends to return to same site or immediate neighbourhood and second clutches often in same nest as first brood, although ♂ may have fresh mate. Monograph: Buxton (1950).

183 BLACK REDSTART

Phoenicurus ochruros

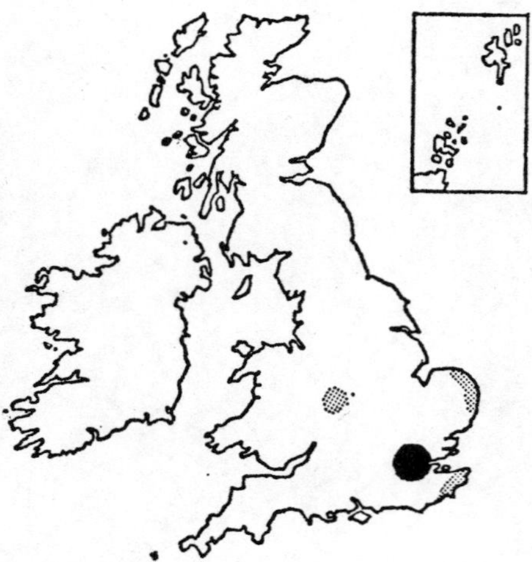

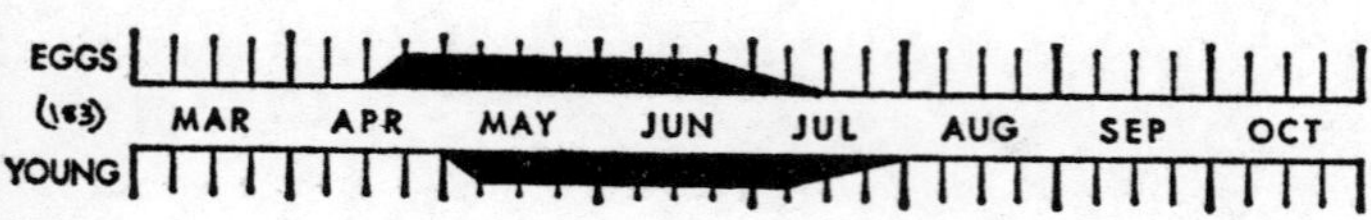

Very scarce; now breeds regularly London and some surrounding counties, Kent, East Anglia and West Midlands, less often coastal Sussex; has bred much more widely to Cornwall, Shropshire, Lancashire and Northumberland. Abroad associated with towns, villages and farms, and with rock-faces in mountains and hills. Early colonists in Britain (1923 onwards) mainly on south coastal cliffs, but in 1940's took readily to bombed sites in London and other towns; clung tenaciously to decreasing areas of these in 1950's; and in 1960–70, while still scattered in built-up areas and rather less on coastal cliffs, characteristic site became large modern power stations in coastal and rural settings.

Nest (♀) In cavity, recess or on ledge, of grass, moss, vegetable fibres, lined hair and feathers. All sorts of fairly open holes and ledges in buildings may be taken, also cracks and cavities in rocks; height very variable. Solitary. Eggs 4 to 6 glossy white, occasionally with bluish tinge or small red-brown spots (19 × 14 mm). Incubation (♀) 12 to 13 days. Fledging (♀♂) nidicolous, 16 to 18 days. Two broods.

Methods Far-carrying song attracts attention to ♂, though actual location in urban setting may be difficult. But proximity of humanity has its advantage and ♀ can with patience be watched back to some sites. Definite tendency to return to same site or neighbourhood of it.

184 NIGHTINGALE

Luscinia megarhynchos

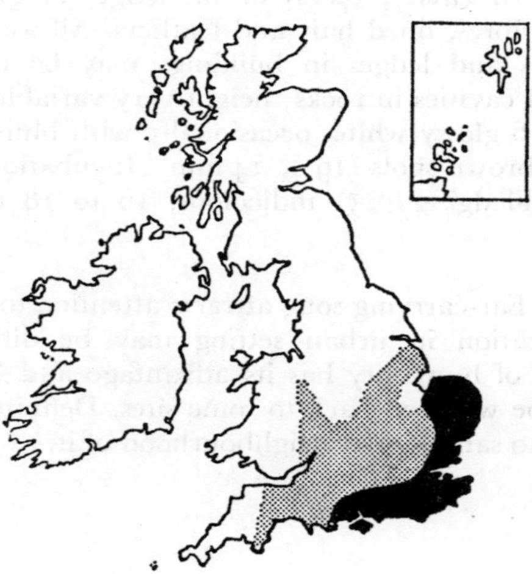

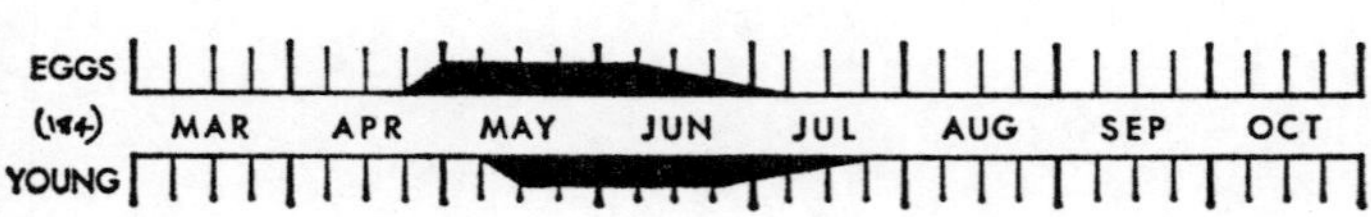

Not scarce; typically lowland distribution in England and Welsh Border with main strength south and east of Dorset-Wash line and outlying areas in Devon, west Gloucester, Monmouth, Hereford, south-east Shropshire, Warwick, Lincoln; formerly south-east Wales, Derby, south Yorkshire. Essentially bird of thickets in England, whether as bush-storey in deciduous woods (e.g. hazel coppice with oak standards), along wood edges and deep lanes, or as stage in botanic succession on their own. Accepted tendency to avoid higher ground, e.g. Cotswolds, Forest of Dean, may therefore really be avoidance of unsuitable habitat not necessarily connected with altitude.

Nest (♀, 6 cm) Foundation of dead leaves especially oak, arranged loosely like outer leaves of cabbage—and sometimes also grass or sedge, moss or bracken—with finer leaves towards 'heart,' lined grasses, leaf fibres and often some hair; exceptional nests domed (H E Woods), or made of reeds (P Clarke). Although usually on or near ground, nest may be 1 m or more in matted brambles, or coppiced stock; some nests quite open, but many very well hidden in or even under low brambles, blackthorn, nettles, long grass, dog's mercury, ivy or general 'tangle'; Whitaker recorded nests 70 cm in butcher's broom and sheltered by burdock plant, Gosnell in gorse bush and against telegraph pole; IJF-L found Suffolk nest in hedge, common Continental site. GO Stephens distinguishes two site types: 'sketchy cover of occasional brambles, a few tufts of grass or perhaps bluebells in flower, usually beneath or near mature oaks' and hedge-bottom in dense tangle of ground foliage. Solitary. Eggs 4 to 5 (3 to 7) blue ground normally completely covered by dense speckling gives olive-green or brown appearance, but markings may be concentrated or occasionally absent (21 × 16 mm). Incubation (♀) 13 to 14 days. Fledging (♀♂) nidicolous, 11 to 12 days. One brood.

Methods Singing ♂ may be misleading guide, though sometimes close to nest. According to Gosnell he sings in thicket whereas nest often in open, close to road, track or ride. Hot searching in likely areas exhausting but fairly successful; ♀ may go off nest openly, even feigning injury, but sometimes 'crawls' away. Stephens says ♀ sits close, but usually returns to nest from inside thicket and it may be possible to watch her. When with young, warning croak of parent alerts P G Davis, who puts down stool and sits on it with hide over head: 26 young ringed on four early morning expeditions using this method between 5 and 8 June.

185 **BLUETHROAT**
Luscinia svecica

Attempted to breed Strathspey, June 1968. Only ♀ seen (J J D Greenwood, *BB* 61: 524–5; *Scottish Birds* 5: 220–2). Habitat was 'acid marsh in which *Carex* and *Phragmites* were dominant, a mat of dead vegetation overlaying most of area', but current year's growth was pushing through. On Continent breeds from sea level to mountains, in far north in swamps with birch and willow scrub, farther south in bushy and shrubby areas (particularly sallows and alders mixed with reeds) on damp ground or near water.

Nest (♀) Scottish example had cup 5 to 6 cm across and was made of dead stems lined with finer grass stems; it was beneath dead branch lying partly in marsh. Continental nests of dry grasses, moss and rootlets, lined fine grasses, vegetable down and hair well-hidden in banks, under tussocks or in dead reeds. Solitary. Eggs 4 to 7 (4 to 9); Scottish nest had 6, slightly smaller than Robin, 'olive-blue with reddish-brown markings (especially towards blunter end)'. Continental eggs usually greenish, but very variable from reddish-cream to greenish-blue, with red-brown spots often zoned (19 × 14 mm), from mid-June in Scandinavia. Incubation (♀) 13 to 14 days. Fledging (♀♂) nidicolous, leave nest after about 14 days before fully fledged. Usually one brood.

Methods Scottish nest found on 13th June when ♀ still laying. When approached by photographer, her *tseep* and *chat-chat* calls became more frequent and she flew towards him giving 'impression of agitation', which led observers to think she might have nest. An hour later she was flushed off three eggs at close range in same area. Later watched incubating, then eggs apparently eaten by small rodent.

186 **ROBIN**
Erithacus rubecula

Abundant; breeds all counties of Britain and Ireland and major islands except Shetland; absent some islands in Hebrides. Found in all types of woodland and wooded country, though not usually bushy commons, or open hedgerows; common along deep lanes and scrubby valleys of small streams, as well as near houses and farms.

Nest (♀, 7 cm) Foundation of dead leaves in many cases, but sometimes only main cup of moss and a little dry grass; lining of rootlets, sometimes moss flowers (Whitaker), and long hairs. Probably more freak and unusual sites recorded than for any other British species, but majority of nests undoubtedly in banks (e.g. 211 out of 315 sites described by Whitaker), though proportion of sites on walls and buildings probably increases to south and east away from deep lanes and sloping woods of west and north. Holes in walls, especially if ivied, perhaps next most popular site; others frequently used include holes in trees, in thick ivy on trees, tree stumps and among tree roots, small rock-faces, especially under trailing ferns, and quarries, discarded tins and utensils, ledges in buildings, haystacks, rockeries and quite often under grass tussocks or in small holes on flat ground; in woodland often very well concealed under dead bracken (cf Tree Pipit); in bog myrtle and cotton grass on Somerset peat moor (Lewis). Bank sites may be rather open or hidden under ferns, ivy and many other plants; with growth of vegetation, late nests become completely hidden; will readily take nestboxes and other provided sites with large entrances. Height of nests in tree-holes, e.g. pollard willows, sometimes up to 3 m, seldom more. Solitary. Eggs 5 to 7 (3 to 9) white or bluish-white with fine freckling of light red, usually zoned at big end, sometimes extending all over; but sparsely blotched and unmarked clutches occur (20 × 16 mm). Incubation (♀) 12 to 14 days. Fledging (♀♂) nidicolous, 12 to 15 days. Two broods, sometimes three.

Methods 'Just about the most cunning and secretive of our common birds' (Simson); but J H Owen, who found over 200 nests in 1951, relied very largely on searching, cycling along country lanes and examining banks. In time smoothed appearance of entrance and arranged frontage of dead leaves below nests can be picked out quite easily in such habitats, but other popular sites give no outward indication. ♀ can be flushed at close range, but she spends much time off nest. Wariness of birds makes watching difficult, though easiest at building stage, and D Lack recommends portable hide to mask human outline. During incubation or when young are small, ♀ leaves nest to be fed by ♂, uttering begging wheeze as well as characteristic *zit* call. This gives valuable clue; if not alarmed, she returns at once to nest after feed, though ♂ does not accompany her. Sometimes ♀ keeps approaching one spot without daring to go on to nest, and this may be sufficient help to find it by searching. Often, especially in early stages, Robins seen to leave a place furtively and pause with eye on observer; this is worth following up. But they have habit of 'false visiting', leading observer to believe they must be doing it on purpose; and if birds see nest examined when building or with incomplete clutch, very likely to desert unless well accustomed to humans—and sometimes even then. Same site often used again, but not usually in same season. Monograph: Lack (1943).

187 **GRASSHOPPER WARBLER**
Locustella naevia

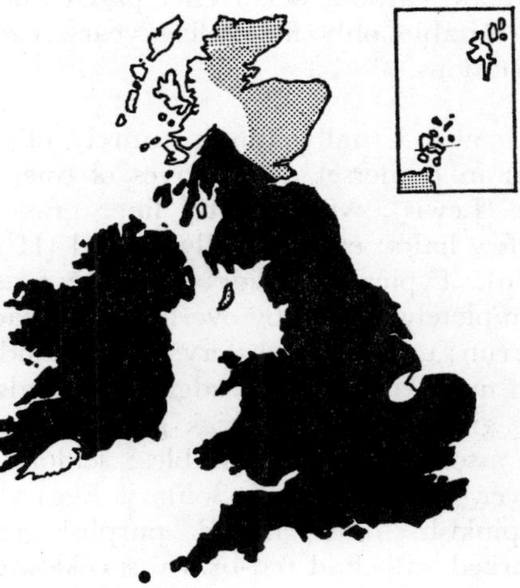

Not scarce; breeds most of mainland Britain and Ireland to north Scottish Highlands where appears to be spreading; breeds at least occasionally Man; singing ♂♂ some Inner and Outer Hebrides. Needs thick ground cover, supplied by sedges (especially *Carex paniculata* tussocks), rushes and grasses in marshes, water meadows and bogs, or by dry gorse and heather commons, moors, and plantations in early stages; and by rough ground with brambles. *Handbook* adds osier beds, neglected hedges (with overgrown ditches), *Salix* patches on dunes, felled or open woods (and wood edges with thick ground cover), even hay and corn crops, though some of these may be only passage habitats where song heard. Presence of bushes seems desirable, presumably as song perches; variable occurrence partly due to habitats remaining suitable only for a few years, e.g. especially young plantations.

Nest (♀♂, 5 cm) Usually almost entirely of coarse dead grasses, but in Somerset dead leaves of osier, birch and bog-myrtle (Lewis), with slightly finer grass lining and perhaps a few hairs; exceptionally domed (H J Hoffman, *BB* 43: 119). Typical site side of coarse grass or sedge tussock, completely hidden by overhanging dead stems and entered by run; usually on or very near ground, sometimes 15 to 30 cm up on top of large sedge tussock; also in rushes, low bushes growing among thick grass (e.g. gorse), and very often associated with brambles; seldom in isolated patch of cover (Walpole-Bond). Solitary. Eggs 5 to 6 (3 to 7) typically pinkish, often tinged purplish-grey, usually densely marked with find red-brown speckles, often zoned at big end and with black-brown hair lines (18 × 14 mm). Incubation (♀♂) 13 to 15 days. Fledging (♀♂) nidicolous, 10 to 12 days. Usually two broods in south.

Methods Hard nest to find because of amount of cover usually available and elusive voice of ♂ which, all the same, is best indication. During incubation Whitaker recommended chasing reeling ♂ until he called ♀ off; and he once saw ♂ feed ♀ off nest. Another suggestion is to search thoroughly but rapidly in area of ♂'s song; said to give best chance of seeing ♀ as she comes off (but ♂♂ singing continually may not have mates). Otherwise ♀ will run off like mouse, getting up behind observer; but when surprised may fly up to 80 m (Whitaker). Song may delude and Whitaker found one nest 90 m from position of ♂. BC once saw bird building, but this was in exposed patch of rushes, and may have been cock's nest (Lewis). Watching not usually effective unless change-over at nest can be intercepted (♂ takes some share of incubation); both sexes sit very tight. Walpole-Bond, who found over 200 nests, including seven in one day, said off-nest bird shows itself and moves by stages, often dipping momentarily to ground, and making final diagonal dive to nest. Relieved bird may appear half a minute later and fly away some distance. Mayer-Gross agrees with Walpole-Bond and suggests moving about presumed territory until alarm call heard or bird seen with food; then watch, though several changes of position may be necessary. Hot searching most successful with one observer in rear of others, able to spot bird slipping off at their heels. If nest not found at once, retire and watch because of risk of treading on it. Easier to find after hatching and from car Stephens watched parents feeding large young openly. Several pairs may nest close together and there is tendency to return to same area, as long as it remains suitable.

188 SAVI'S WARBLER
Locustella luscinioides

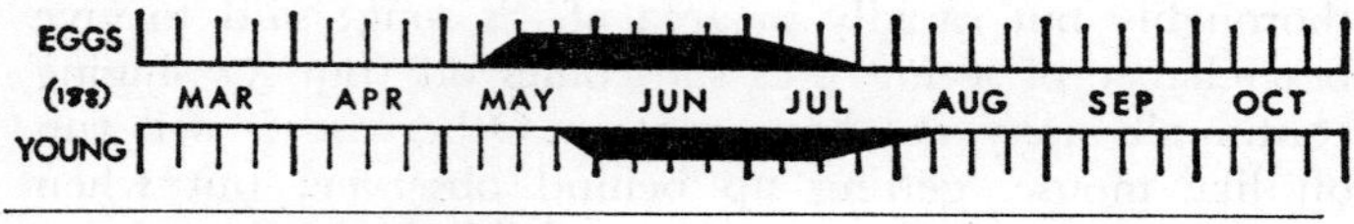

Very scarce; bred Fens of East Anglia until mid 19th century; then extinct for 100 years until small population established Kent from 1960 (perhaps several years earlier) and Suffolk from 1970 (probably also 1969); seems liable to colonise other areas now. In both Kent and Suffolk occupies extensive reed beds where preference for *Phragmites* with undergrowth of sedges, interspersed clear patches of sedge with some sorrel or marsh dock; some territories associated with *Glyceria maxima*; falling water level may also be favourable factor (R G Pitt, *BB* 60: 354).

Nest (♀) Not found in English localities; on Continent, of *Glyceria* or sedge leaves lined with finer leaves and stems. Usually well hidden among dead reeds and sedges and impossible to see from above. Solitary. Eggs 4 to 6 (3 to 6) grey-white densely marked with grey-brown spots and underlying violet; sometimes zoned (20 × 15 mm). Incubation (♀♂?) 12 days (?minimum). Fledging (♀, then ♀♂) nidicolous, about 12 days. Two broods on Continent.

Methods No attempt has been made to find nests in Kent or Suffolk. Techniques as for Grasshopper Warbler most suitable in open sedge areas. In Polish habitat of mud bank 'giving way to quaking blanket of tightly packed *Carex* and light growth of reeds on softer ground', Connor found it relatively easy to locate territory by singing ♂, but nests 'in collapsed and tangled masses of dried *Carex*' only found by systematic searching thereafter.

189 MOUSTACHED WARBLER

Acrocephalus melanopogon

Pair bred Cambridge 1946; birds watched feeding young early August in or near brambles on edge of reed bed (R A Hinde and A S Thom, *BB* 40: 98–104).

Nest Of reeds *Phragmites*, sedges or grasses, lined reed flowers, bents and sometimes feathers; less compact and rather untidier than nest of Reed Warbler. Built over water at heights of up to at least 2 m in reeds and sometimes small bushes; at bases of reed clumps in Sicily and under 'knots made by fishermen tying reeds together in Hungary' (*Handbook*). Solitary. Eggs 3 to 4 (3 to 6) like Sedge Warbler but lighter under olive-brown speckling; from May to July.

190 **REED WARBLER**

Acrocephalus scirpaceus

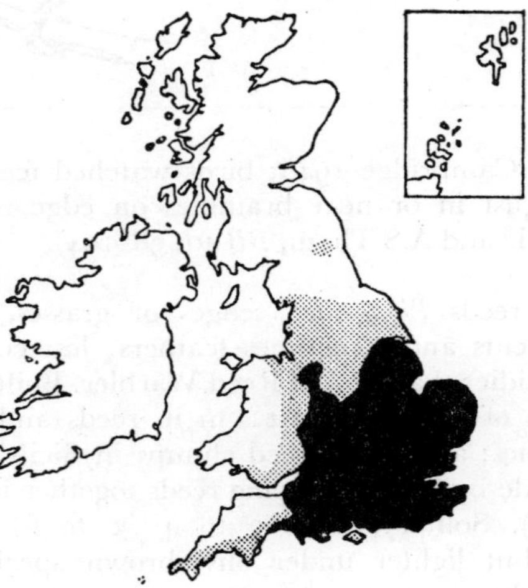

Fairly numerous; predominantly lowland distribution but breeds every English county except Durham, though not regularly Cumberland; in Wales breeds Glamorgan, Brecon, Denbigh, Flint and probably Anglesey (breeding proved 1968); nested Down 1935. Habitat primarily reed beds but also many other types of marsh or riparian vegetation: sallows and willows, willowherb and associated plants, *Glyceria maxima*. Generally over or near water but also away from it in dry reed beds and hedges, exceptionally gardens and cornfields.

Nest (mainly ♀, 5·5 cm) Unique in Britain, a cylinder of variable depth (6 to 20 cm) woven round several reeds or other supports; of grasses, reed-flowers, and sometimes fragments of moss, lined with finer parts of reed-flowers, grass, and occasional feathers, wool or hair; cup deep and overhung. Typically woven into mixture of old and new reed stems from 20 cm to 2·5 m above water (average about 1 m) but also in forks of willows, briars and other shrubs up to about 5 m, in willowherb, loosestrifes, mugwort, nettles and *Glyceria maxima*; even among dead conifer branches forming wall of duck-shooting hide. Social. Eggs 3 to 5 (3 to 6) greenish-white varyingly marked with dark olive-brown and ash-grey blotches, sometimes covering most of egg, sometimes almost absent (18 × 14 mm). Incubation (♀♂) 11 to 12 days. Fledging (♀♂) nidicolous but often leave nest before fledging in 10 to 14 days. Two broods usual in southern England.

Methods Reed bed nests can be found by searching in areas where birds are singing; but success inversely proportional to size of bed, and in other types of vegetation only sample can be found unless search so thorough that habitat is dangerously disturbed. P E Brown and M G Davies describe use of small pieces of coloured wool, apparently irresistible as nest material to building ♀, as means of tracking her to site; nests incorporating coloured wool also easy to see (J F Burton). Watching from high perch also recommended. Sometimes, chiefly in first month of breeding season, ♀ dismantles her incomplete nest and rebuilds it from a few centimetres to 20 m or more away. Monograph: Brown and Davies (1949).

191 **MARSH WARBLER**

Acrocephalus palustris

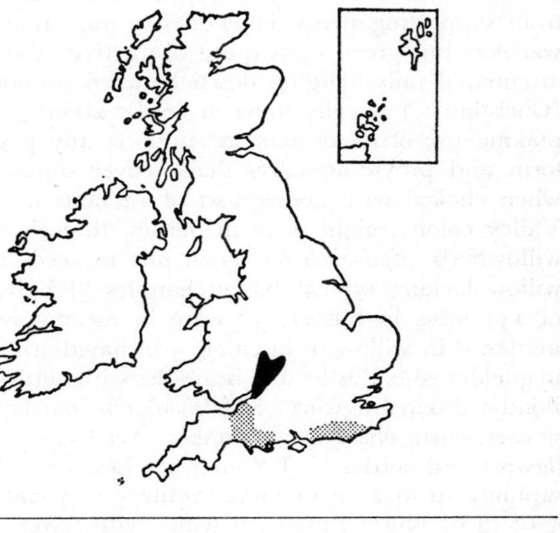

Very scarce; breeds very locally Gloucester and Worcester (valleys of Severn and Avon), south Somerset and perhaps Dorset; occasionally Sussex and Kent, exceptionally elsewhere. Typically in rather dry osier beds near rivers with nettles or meadowsweet, occasionally in dense beds of reed grass (*Phalaris*) associated with willows (R J B Christian), and so possibly in all types of low-lying waste ground of similar facies; also, though rarely in England, in cultivated crops.

Nest (♀ attended by ♂, 5 cm) Of dry or green grasses, varying considerably in bulk, with first nests usually much larger than second attempts (Christian), lined with fine grass, rootlets, hair and usually suspended by basket handles from supporting stems; nests of dry grass resemble *Sylvia* warblers but green nests quite distinctive, also those with attenuated tails hanging down between supporting stems (Christian). Typically slung in nettles about 75 cm up and making use of dead stem as support; any plant of erect form and providing fairly dense cover suitable, but not when choked with goosegrass; of 13 nests in one Severn Valley colony, eight were in nettles, three in great hairy willowherb (*Epilobium hirsutum*), one in reeds and one in willow lacking typical basket handles (J F Burton); but of 144 nests in Sussex, 51 were in meadowsweet, 12 in nettles, 8 in willow, 6 in elder, 5 in hawthorn and 4 each in guelder rose, thistles and brambles with nettles (Walpole-Bond); also in mugwort (*Artemisium*), cow parsley, hogweed, grasses, corn, charlock (Whitaker), reed grass (Christian), figwort and nettles (C J Young per Lewis); in bushes and saplings up to 2 cm or more. Solitary to social. Eggs 4 to 5 (3 to 6) blue or greenish white with fewer and bolder markings than Reed Warbler, sometimes unmarked (19 × 14 mm). Incubation (♀♂) about 12 days. Fledging (♀♂) nidicolous, 10 to 14 days. One brood.

Methods Location by song of ♂, very prolific up to start of incubation (Christian). Only ♀ builds, taking 5 or 6 days in sudden bursts of activity; Burton found nests at this stage by concentrated watching: ♂ perches above ♀ at site and wings fluttering in display make him easy to see even in dense herbage; site should only be inspected between visits by birds. During incubation very careful searching recommended, using long stick and watching for tremor in vegetation made by flushed bird, which often returns to vicinity of nest (Walpole-Bond). Safer but more painful method is to crawl through cover, thus getting view through stems and below foliage.

192 **SEDGE WARBLER**
Acrocephalus schoenobaenus

Numerous; breeds all counties of Britain and Ireland except Shetland. Found in all types of riparian vegetation, marshes and bogs, wherever there is thick cover and, usually, low bushes; sometimes away from water in habitats of similar facies, e.g. commons and bushy, wide-verged hedgerows.

Nest (♀, 5 cm) Rather solid for a warbler, with foundation of moss and grasses and lining of various finer materials, including willow-down, feathers (often curling over cup) and hair; supported by or occasionally suspended from thick vegetation: nettles, sedges, grasses, willowherb, reeds, rushes (Scotland), campion, bittersweet tangle, mugwort, docks and iris, as well as brambles, briars, blackthorn, hawthorn, sallow and willows, on osier stumps; generally. low (30 to 75 cm), but bush sites up to 4 m. Solitary. Eggs 5 to 6 (3 to 8) pale ground almost hidden by dense yellow-brown markings, usually with black hair-lines; sparsely or unmarked types occur (18 × 13 mm). Incubation (mainly ♀) 13 to 14 days. Fledging (♀♂) nidicolous, 10 to 14 days. Two broods in south.

Methods A difficult nest to find owing to variety of possible situations in most habitats. J H Owen advocated searching where ♂ first heard singing, but song not sustained after mating. Whitaker found his nests by hot searching, certainly effective in well populated sedge beds at incubation time. Watching back when building or with young also successful and less exhausting.

193 ICTERINE WARBLER
Hippolais icterina

Eggs of this species or Melodious Warbler *H. polyglotta* taken Sussex and Surrey late 19th century; nest with 3 eggs Wiltshire, May 1907, identified with 'hardly any doubt' (G Pye-Smith, *BB* 19: 311); has been seen recently in south-east England in June. In nearest European habitats often a garden bird, also in woods with thick undergrowth, hedgerows and scrub.

Nest (♀♂) Intermediate in appearance between Chaffinch and *Sylvia* warbler: of down, grasses, birch bark, wool, rootlets, sometimes decorated outside with spiders' webs and lined with finer stems, hair, feathers. Usually built into low fork, similar to some Blackcap and Garden Warbler sites. Solitary. Eggs 4 to 5 (4 to 6) rose pink with rather sparse black spots and streaks (18 × 13 mm); from end May to early June.

194 **BLACKCAP**
Sylvia atricapilla

Numerous; breeds all counties England and Wales, but more local in north; in Scotland extends to Forth-Clyde line, more sparsely to Inverness and irregularly in north-east; scarce Man; in Ireland breeds locally in eastern and southern counties. Habitat difficult to differentiate from Garden Warbler; both species found in woodland (but not pure conifers or beechwood without undergrowth) and wooded country: spinneys and copses, tree-lined hedges, especially along lanes, orchards, shrubby gardens, and riparian growth.

Nest (mainly ♀, 6 cm) Neat structure of dry stems, including *Galium* (Lewis), with cobwebs and wool on well-defined rim; lined finer grass, rootlets and hair; suspension by basket handles. Sites overlap considerably with Garden Warbler, but fonder of hedges and bushes, e.g. snowberry (*Symphoricarpa*), elder, holly and other evergreens, including ivy branching from walls; also honeysuckle and *Clematis*; often less concealed than Garden Warbler in open brambles, but some very well hidden; height 30 cm to 3 m. Solitary. Eggs 4 to 5 (3 to 6) light brown blotched and marbled with darker brown and underlying ashy; a few dark spots superimposed; almost unmarked reddish types occur (20 × 15 mm). Incubation (♀♂) 10 to 12 days, may begin before clutch complete. Fledging (♀♂) nidicolous, 10 to 13 days. Often two broods in south.

Methods ♂♂ of *Sylvia* warblers sing for spells close to nests at all stages and hence give good pointers, but habit of building vestigial platforms not very helpful, as these often long way from chosen site and may be work of unmated ♂ (L Stewart-Brown). Where cover not too extensive, hot or cold searching in area of song is effective. Birds can be watched back when building or feeding young. They scold with staccato *tacc* calls when observer near nest or fledglings; but ♂ may also demonstrate at a distance.

195 **GARDEN WARBLER**

Sylvia borin

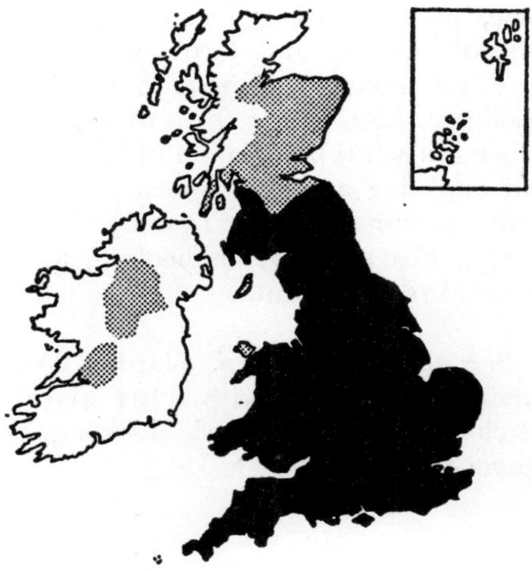

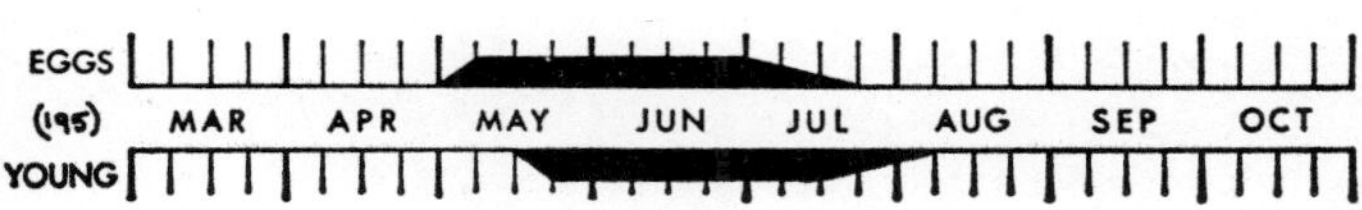

Numerous; breeds all counties England and Wales and spreading north in Scotland, where has bred Easter Ross, Sutherland and Orkney; scarce Man; local in Ireland, mainly Westmeath, Roscommon, Cavan and Fermanagh. Habitat overlaps Blackcap but also found in low scrub away from trees and quite commonly in young conifer plantations.

Nest (♀♂, 6 cm) Of dry grass stems, including *Galium* (Lewis), with occasional leaves or bits of moss; lining of fine grass, very small roots, some hair, untidier than Blackcap or Lesser Whitethroat, rather flatter looking than typical Whitethroat. Favourite site where stems of low brambles cross, or nettles grow through them; also in briars, gorse, base of young conifers, evergreen shrubs, bilberry, dead bracken and ferns, from practically on ground up to one metre; odd nests to 2 m in syringa and bamboo. Solitary. Eggs 4 to 5 (3 to 6) overlap Blackcap's in appearance but whitish or pale buff less densely covered with brown marbling and dark spots; yellowish and grey markings quite common (20 × 15 mm). Incubation (♀♂) about 12 days. Fledging (♀♂) nidicolous, about 10 days. Sometimes two broods in south.

Methods See under Blackcap. Garden Warbler more unobtrusive than Blackcap, with softer alarm call; both may breed close together with risk of wrong identification of nest (Mayer-Gross).

196 **WHITETHROAT**
Sylvia communis

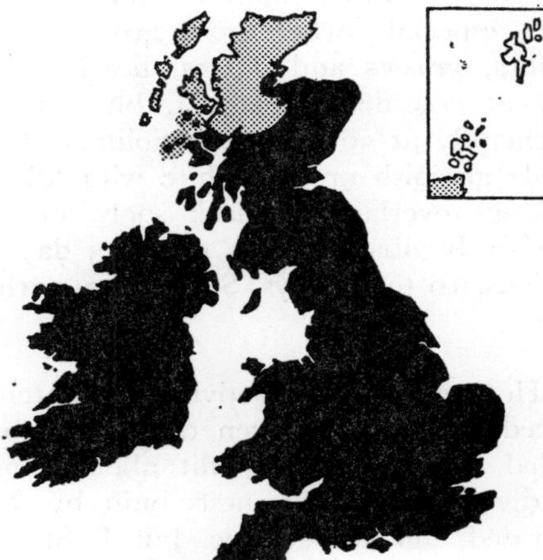

Abundant; breeds all counties of Britain and Ireland except Orkney and Shetland, and very local Hebrides. Habitat typically hedgerows, commons and bushy country, also woodland edges and clearings, young plantations, marginal land with thick low vegetation, moorland edge in highland districts, gardens, riparian vegetation and osier beds.

Nest (♀♂, 5.5 cm) Very similar to Garden Warbler, but materials perhaps finer; cup rather deeper, rim frequently adorned with flecks of white vegetable down; often dark hair in lining. Generally well hidden in thick, low brambles, briars, blackthorn, gorse, nettles (but probably always where dead sticks or other supports available), and many small bushes, especially where grass grows up into them, also in rushes, grasses and sedges, heather and osiers; occasionally at considerable height, but unusual above 2 m and generally at 30 to 60 cm. Solitary. Eggs 4 to 5 (3 to 7) pale greenish or buff-white with 'dirty' yellow-green markings overlaid by dark spots, often in zone (19 × 14 mm). Incubation (♀♂) 11 to 13 days. Fledging (♀♂) nidicolous, 10 to 12 days. Sometimes, perhaps often, two broods.

Methods Hot searching effective; but watching when building, feeding young or even during incubation also recommended as birds usually flit about conspicuously until final dive. Early cock's nests built by ♂ are often much decorated and easy to see, but L Stewart-Brown has never known one to be used for eggs. Location by song and presence of both birds which scold close to nest. Even after flushing or other clear indication, some well-hidden nests extremely difficult to find; insinuation among nettles, as with Marsh Warbler, may be necessary (Mayer-Gross).

197 **LESSER WHITETHROAT**
Sylvia curruca

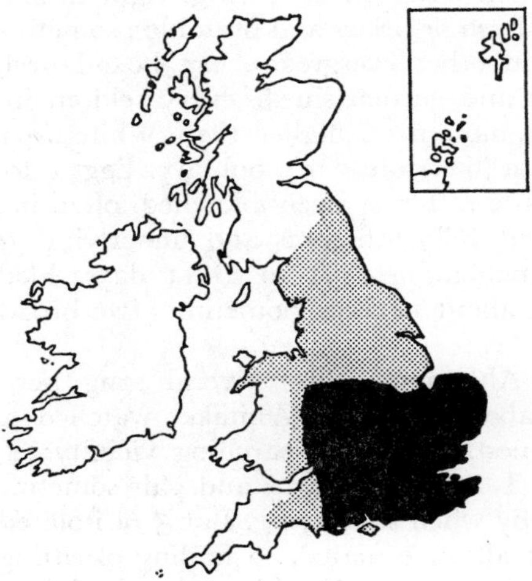

Fairly numerous; breeds southern and Midland counties of England, thinning out north to Scottish Border, west to east Devon and Welsh Border counties; has bred Scotland, Man, Cornwall and recently Scilly; absent Ireland. Habitat typically thick bushy hedgerows with trailing brambles and other creepers; distribution of these probably main factor influencing British range; also in scattered scrub, though usually near trees, and shrubby gardens; in young conifers in north England (Black), typical Scandinavian habitat.

Nest (♀♂, 5 cm) Smaller and more rounded than Blackcap with similar ornamentation of rim and occasional leaves in foundation. Often in dead twigs right inside canopy of hedgerow, bush or briars and brambles, sometimes in small conifers and other evergreens, e.g. box, laurel, in elder, elm shoots and garden shrubs, very seldom in nettles or low cover; most nests higher than Whitethroat, average about 1·5 m (60 cm to 3 m). Solitary. Eggs 4 to 6 (3 to 7) creamy white rather sparsely blotched, often in zone, with dark-centred yellowish spots and underlying grey (17 × 13 mm). Incubation (♀♂) 10 to 11 days. Fledging (♀♂) nidicolous, about 11 days. Sometimes two broods.

Methods Although ♂ has several song perches, often sings just above nest and Whitaker watched one singing in empty nest, so worth searching vicinity; ♀ may join him there (L Stewart-Brown) and pair sometimes demonstrate nearby when still laying. But ♂ of isolated pair may not sing at all once mated, so finding of sitting bird first indication of presence. Watching when building or feeding young feasible. Reacts strongly to stuffed Cuckoo but this should only be used when adults seen with food, as there is strong risk of desertion at earlier stages. The alarm call, *tic*, subdued and infrequent at first, is louder and rapidly repeated when young larger (Mayer-Gross).

198 **DARTFORD WARBLER**

Sylvia undata

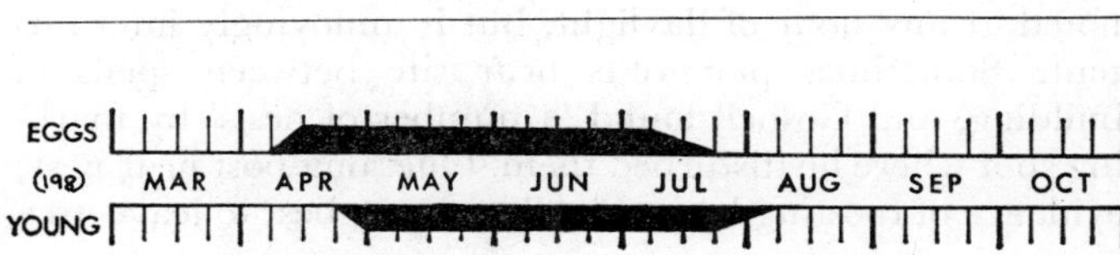

Very scarce; largely confined to a few areas of Dorset and Hampshire with local extensions after series of mild winters into Sussex, Surrey, Isle of Wight and Devon. Heaths and old commons with long heather and gorse clumps, sometimes with scattered pine trees; in recent years also in young conifers with heavy undergrowth of heather and gorse (N W Orr).

Nest (♀♂, 5 cm) More compact and substantial than other *Sylvia* warblers, principally of dead grass but may use heather, dead gorse, moss, thistledown, wool, paper, with fine lining of down, hair, rootlets, occasional feathers; rim adorned with spider cocoons. Built in long heather, usually where it grows into gorse, or inside gorse bush, at heights from 30 cm to over 1 m; occasionally in other vegetation on commons; quite often near a track (Walpole-Bond). Solitary. Eggs 4 (3 to 5) off-white, sometimes with greenish tinge, finely spotted with brown and grey, frequently in zone (17·5 × 3 mm). Incubation (mainly ♀) 12 to 13 days. Fledging (♀♂) nidicolous, 13 to 15 days. Two broods normally.

Methods Walpole-Bond, with much experience, considered nest easiest to find at building stage, though birds may drop material in wrong place. Gosnell, going into great detail with this species, agreed with Walpole-Bond that nest harder to find in gorse than in heather. Birds building may fly direct to vicinity of nest, but complete 'last lap' by creeping through thick cover; also may overshoot nest and go back to it unseen; therefore much better to mark where ♀ reappears after disposing of load. Building may be noted at any hour of daylight, but is annoyingly intermittent. Sometimes pair rests near site between spells of building, and Gosnell found 'a number of nests' by marking spot where he disturbed them. One song post near nest; evidence of roosting by it. If ♂ flies away, best to leave area for about 20 minutes and try afresh to contact him. When birds off feeding together, ♂ may bring ♀ back 'quite openly right to nest'. When incubating himself, he may also fly straight to nest. Whitaker was scolded by ♂ and saw ♀ fly off nest, but this is exceptional. N W Orr believes in watching on calm days and sometimes from a hide as large an area of suitable habitat as possible; this enables him to judge state of breeding; time can be wasted if parents are feeding fledged young. Hot searching effective on windy days when bird cannot hear observer's approach. Nests in heather almost always in clump standing higher than general level. If undisturbed, birds remain in same locality for several years.

199 **WILLOW WARBLER**

Phylloscopus trochilus

Abundant; breeds all counties of Britain and Ireland except Shetland where occasional; local on some other Scottish islands. Habitat limited by song perches rather than nesting cover, for which grass or dead bracken is sufficient, but will sing from much lower heights than Chiffchaff; hence found much more widely over whole range of bushy habitats, copses, open woodland, scrubby heaths, young plantations and orchards, large gardens and lanes, but not usually along uniform hedgerows, and absent from fenny, marshy and boggy land, except on drier 'islands'.

Nest (♀) Domed with underhung entrance; moss, grasses, bracken in main structure with fine grass cup and lining (not invariably) of feathers; occasionally lightly or not domed, but many nests so compact and merged with ground vegetation that only oval entrance (about 4 cm wide) visible, and this often obscured by grass-stems, trailing sprays or nettles. Nests on ground often hidden by grass tufts, dead bracken or tangle, but some near paths are quite obvious when built in bank; in highland districts characteristic site is grass or heather fringe above low rocky outcrop in scrub-wood, elsewhere commonly where grass grows up into young conifers, gorse, thorn or other bushes; in bog myrtle and grass tufts on Somerset peat moors (Lewis). Nests above ground usually sunk in platform of some kind, e.g. matted dead bracken, branch of yew tree or thick ivy on wall; in hole in well and haystack (Lewis). Whitaker found none above 1·5 m (one 1 m on old Song Thrush nest), but *Handbook* records up to about 5 m. Generally avoids continuous bramble or similar cover and thus does not overlap typical Chiffchaff and *Sylvia* sites; also absent under closed tree canopies where Wood Warbler nests, but wide overlap occurs and Whitaker once found nests of both species almost touching. Solitary. Eggs 6 to 7 (3 to 9) pale pink when fresh, usually with small light-red markings, but sometimes heavily spotted or blotched with darker shades like some Chiffchaffs (15 × 12 mm). Incubation (♀) about 13 days. Fledging (♀♂) nidicolous, 13 to 14 days. Usually one brood.

Methods Initial location by song of ♂, then by call-note. Watching back at all stages recommended; when incubating, disturbed ♀ flits about with repeated and characteristic *hooeet* and may be absurdly confiding. T R Waddell points out that *hooeet* does not start until ♀ has been off nest several minutes, and suggests that it is 'genuine alarm note', but see under Chiffchaff, to which he attributes 'compulsive off-nest call'. In any case note often sustained until final drop to nest. But beware of rather similar note from Chaffinch. Shy individuals may take a lot of watching, and may have to be flushed several times if nest well hidden, for some are extraordinarily concealed, with entrance like mouse hole. Whitaker was successful with hot searching and once found seven nests in a day. Gosnell advocated watching for building in morning after rain. Use of stuffed Cuckoo may be effective in drawing birds, one of which will then return to nest.

200 **CHIFFCHAFF**
Phylloscopus collybita

Numerous; breeds all counties of England, Wales, south Scotland and Ireland, including Man, but local north of Yorkshire; spreading in Highlands and Inner Hebrides, singing all counties and breeding in most. Habitat typically woodland and small copses, often with conifers, but also more in open where trees or substantial bushes give song-perches and there is thick low cover for nesting; thus found along wooded cliffs in south-west England and South Wales, and in scrub woods of western Ireland and Lake District, as well as on bushy commons and along tree-lined lanes in southern England. Close association with rhododendrons from Lancashire northwards to Sutherland.

Nest (♀) Externally like rather flattened and untidy Wren, of coarser material than other leaf warblers, normally with foundation or outer casing of dead leaves, inside which are grasses, bark strips, fibres and moss, with lining of feathers, sometimes a little fur and hair. Entrance much larger than to Wren's nest and usually somewhat underhung; whole measures about 10 to 12·5 cm across and, unlike other British leaf warblers, is regularly 15 cm to 1 m above ground, occasionally 2·5 m; even if lower, only touches ground like heap of debris (Walpole-Bond). Majority built in tangle where herb and shrub meet; many associated with low brambles, e.g. in woodland clearings where overlap with Blackcap, also butcher's broom, holly, box, gorse, elm shoots, and similar bushy growths where sometimes quite conspicuous; low bamboos, sweeping branches of trees, dead sticks among nettles, and in creepers on walls (Walpole-Bond) are other variations; sometimes in riparian vegetation well away from trees (once in duck-shooting hide) where Willow Warbler does not penetrate. Whitaker recorded extremely well-hidden nests in thick bushes with entrances facing inwards, but Gosnell often found them along edges of tracks. In spite of close northern association with rhododendrons, absence of records of nests in them.

Solitary. Eggs 6 (4 to 7) white evenly spotted with purplish brown, or sometimes red-brown like Willow Warbler's (15 × 12 mm). Incubation (♀) about 13 days. Fledging (mainly ♀) nidicolous, about 14 days. Often two broods in south.

Methods ♂ establishes several song perches, one near nest site where ♀ can be located and watched building. Feathers may be supplied as for Long-tailed Tit, but risk of desertion at this stage. Some early nests easy to see but many well-concealed and ♀ flushes unobtrusively (sometimes at several metres when eggs fresh). Off-nest note, distinguished from Willow Warbler with practice, is given different prominence by different observers. Both Whitaker and Walpole-Bond regarded this as hard nest to find and latter emphasised that ♀ off eggs 'calls very little', whereas T R Waddell considers that note is 'uttered incessantly', thus assisting watching back. Our experience somewhere between these extremes, and perhaps there is regional variation. Some success by searching likely sites to which there is propensity to return year after year.

201 **WOOD WARBLER**

Phylloscopus sibilatrix

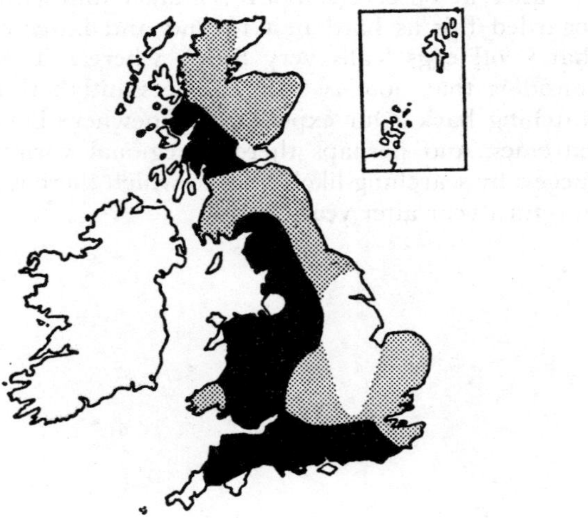

Fairly numerous; widely distributed over British mainland but predominantly highland and very local or absent in eastern counties; also absent many islands, probably including Man, and very few pairs in Ireland (localities suppressed). Much more confined to woodlands than relatives, though low scrub of steep Welsh hillsides ('darrens') sufficient for it; found under closed canopy of oak, ash, birch and, in south east, sweet chestnut and beech, also under Japanese larch in Mid-Wales (T R Waddell) – all habitats where undergrowth scanty or absent; also avoids dense bush storey.

Nest (♀) Domed, in slight scrape on ground, of grass with bracken fibres, moss and a few leaves, lined fine grass, occasional hairs, but not feathers; entrance appears larger than Willow Warbler's; occasionally without dome. Whitaker recorded great variety of settings: dead leaves, bracken, grasses, brambles, bluebells (wild hyacinth), blaeberry (*Vaccinium*), dog's mercury, wood anemones, birch seedlings and hazel-stock; Black added heather and root of a tree; in Wales often in tussocks of the grass *Deschampsia caespitosa*, common in damp and open scrub woods; in Forest of Dean nests sometimes in creeping honeysuckle; in other districts, e.g. Galloway, many in fern-stocks. Common denominator of all these sites is their comparative openness: thick bracken-clumps, brambles and tangle are avoided. A slope is popular, bank-top site described for Willow Warbler also favoured, but many nests on perfectly flat areas; generally nests easier to see than Willow Warbler's, but some well hidden, and rapidly growing cover conceals others after they are built; often trailing branch or seedling tree provides 'stepping stones' to nest (Mayer-Gross). Nests off the ground almost unknown (Walpole-Bond found one at 15 cm). Solitary. Eggs 5 to 7 (4 to 8) white thickly speckled with purplish brown and a few grey underlying marks, sometimes zoned

(16 × 13 mm). Incubation (♀) about 13 days. Fledging (♀♂) nidicolous, 11 to 12 days. One brood normal.

Methods Pre-eminently found by watching and listening. Off-nest call, plaintive *pee* slightly different from Bullfinch's, easier to pick up than similar notes of other leaf warblers, and used at all stages of nesting cycle – but also at other times and by ♂, so that false scents occur. Incubating ♀ usually returns quite readily after feeding (♂ neither sits nor feeds her on nest), but reluctant sometimes to cover last metre. ♂ may drive ♀ back with fierce burst of song; one song area usually close to nest but others may be at considerable distance. Final return from low perch usually very sudden and marked by cessation of call; but birds with young sometimes flutter over nest if afraid to return to it. Nests also found by hot or cold searching, though some ♀♀ very hard to flush. Grassy dome and entrance hole often catch searcher's eye (especially during laying). Nests may be found for several successive years in almost same spot. Gosnell, who once found 13 nests in 24 hours, warned that persistently singing ♂♂ might be unmated.

202 GOLDCREST

Regulus regulus

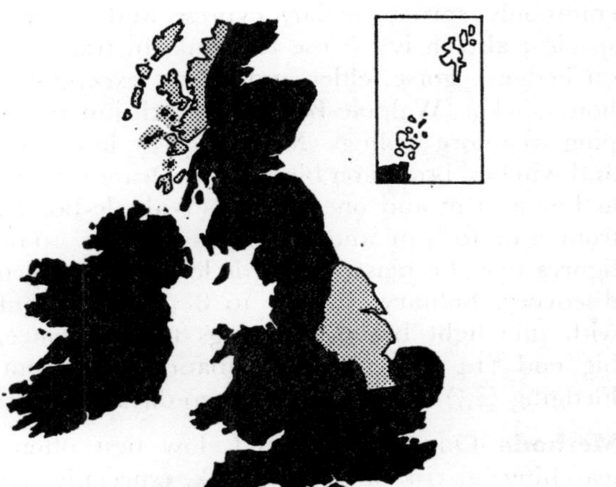

Numerous; breeds all counties Britain and Ireland except Orkney (irregular) and Shetland; less common parts of eastern England and local or absent some Scottish islands and north-west Highlands. Typically in conifers and successful colonist of new plantations, but also in isolated trees, e.g. churchyard yews, and in deciduous woodland where there is ivy; sometimes in bushy country, gorse heaths and thickets.

Nest (♀♂, about 4 cm) Basket of moss suspended by several handles from branch; held together with spiders' webs and lined small dark feathers. Sited typically under tip of horizontal branch of conifer (rarely on upper side): yew, sometimes Scots pine, juniper (e.g. in Strathspey), commonly spruce, cedar, cypress and other introduced species; also in ivy (close to trunk, in trailing creepers or on hedges), gorse, elder and thorn; exceptionally in box, honeysuckle (Walpole-Bond), beneath junction of overlapping sycamore saplings (Mayer-Gross), in larch (Whitaker) and witches' broom on birch (C D Deane). Some in bushes as low as 1 m and once 60 cm (Walpole-Bond), but most from 2 m to 4 m and others as high as 10 m to 12 m; figures may be biased towards lower nests by their easier discovery. Solitary. Eggs 7 to 8 (5 to 13) buffish white with fine light brown markings usually concentrated at big end (14 × 10 mm). Incubation (♀) about 16 days. Fledging (♀♂) nidicolous, 18 to 20 days. Two broods.

Methods Once pair located, low nest often found by searching, at risk of cricked neck, especially where choice of tree restricted. But in clumps of tall conifers watching successful when building or feeding young; Whitaker found birds ignored him when building and took suitable feathers put out for them. During incubation much harder to find nest unless ♀ can be seen returning from feeding. Pairs with young sometimes mob observer, thus drawing attention to site.

203 **FIRECREST**
Regulus ignicapillus

Small breeding population discovered New Forest, Hampshire, 1961 (M C Adams, *BB* 59: 240–6); numbers have subsequently increased and in 1971 at least two pairs nested Buckingham (L A Batten, *BB* 64: 473–5); worth searching for elsewhere in southern England. New Forest habitat mature mixed woodland where conifers, perhaps particularly spruces, dominant, but conifers almost absent from some parts; may have bred in one area dominated by oak and beech with some holly; Goldcrests also present 'at almost all sites except in mainly deciduous areas'. In Buckingham along rides of conifer plantation of larch and Norway spruce 10 to 15 m high, with scatter of deciduous trees. In some parts of Europe commonly in non-coniferous areas, particularly oaks and alders.

Nest (mainly ♀, about 4 cm) Very similar to Goldcrest but perhaps slightly more compact and smaller (*Handbook*); English examples of green moss interwoven with skeletal leaves, conifer needles, sometimes framework of twigs, all held together with spiders' webs and lined freely or even copiously with feathers (chiefly Woodpigeon in one Bucks nest). Mainly along lateral branches of Douglas fir and Norway spruce at heights of 10 to 20 m, but one in Bucks in field maple at only 2·5 m. Continental sites similar to Goldcrest but also in creepers on trunks of alders in Spain (*Handbook*). Solitary. Eggs 7 to 12, distinguished from Goldcrest by pinker ground (13 × 10 mm). Incubation (♀) 14 to 15 days. Fledging (♀♂) nidicolous, at least 19 days. Probably two broods in England as on Continent.

Methods Similar to Goldcrest. Location by ♂ singing frequently and moving round territory of about half hectare. At one Bucks site ♀, carrying feathers to nest already containing one egg, was mounted by ♂. After failure of nest ♂ still sang and accompanied ♀, who took feathers from this nest to new site high in spruce, but ♂ did not himself assist. Evidence from one New Forest nest that ♂ sang from nearby tree and slipped 'quickly and directly to nest'; ♀ approached from dense canopy, and both left together after half minute. Song intensity at Bucks site subsided in July and birds became difficult to locate.

204 **SPOTTED FLYCATCHER**
Muscicapa striata

Fairly numerous; breeds all counties of Britain and Ireland except Shetland, but scarce and local north Scotland and islands. Natural habitat woodland edge; thus in Scottish and Welsh highland regions along glens of burns and streams where canopy broken, also by tree-lined roadsides and in small copses. But very generally round habitations, in gardens, orchards, parks and churchyards, and along avenues and tree-lined streets almost to town-centres; also quarries and ruins.

Nest (mainly ♀, 5 cm) Superficially resembles Chaffinch but much looser and often flimsier in construction, generally of moss, bark fibres, oak catkins (Whitaker) and other vegetable matter, sometimes wool, adorned cobwebs, lichens, even string, rags and paper; lined with rootlets, hair, wool, few or many feathers, which may curl over cup. Typically on small ledges or in open cavities: naturally in tree-forks and at decayed bases of branches, on ivied trunks and low rock faces, at heights from 50 cm to 10 m or more. But ledges, recesses and projections on walls much used, also supports provided by fruit trees and many creepers, especially ivy and Virginia creeper; in several districts recesses behind hinges of farm doors popular. Ledges made when branches sawn off, and rock faces in quarries or road and rail cuttings are other developments from natural sites. Less usually on ends of leafy branches like Goldfinch, sides of hay or corn ricks, decayed lopped tops of conifers, cavities behind bark, epicormic shoots and open nest in twigs on top of *Cornus* bush (last three from Whitaker). Will use open nestboxes but R M Garnett pointed out that bird likes to look out when sitting so front edge should not be too high; also in old nests of other species, particularly thrushes, but even in Greenfinch in bamboo clump (John Buxton). Solitary. Eggs 4 to 5 (3 to 6) greenish or blue-grey with rich chestnut spots and streaks often forming cap; unmarked pale blue eggs occur

(19 × 14 mm). Incubation (♀♂) 12 to 14 days. Fledging (♀♂) nidicolous, 12 to 15 days. Not infrequently two broods.

Methods ♂ on arrival usually seen and heard easily, but pair unobtrusive when building and incubating and require careful watching. Nests away from one's own house easily missed until parents use loud dissyllabic alarm in later stages of fledging. Searching likely sites may be successful, and same ledge or immediate neighbourhood often used again and again (Whitaker recorded one in same crevice after 46 years); same nest may be used twice in one season. D Humphrey locates feeding pair, especially in evening, then searches suitable trees; later watches ♂ fly to feed incubating ♀.

205 **PIED FLYCATCHER**
Ficedula hypoleuca

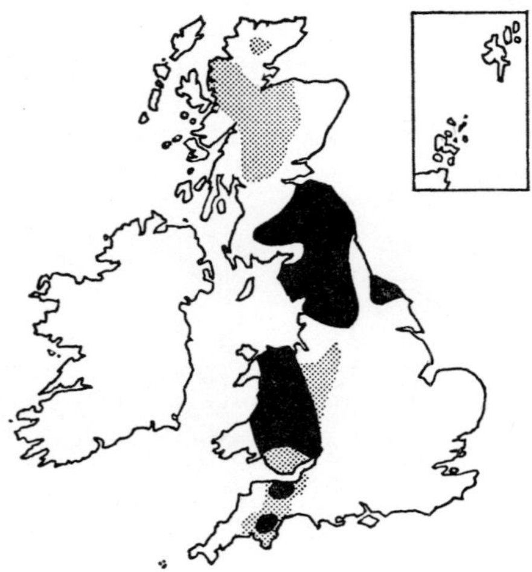

Not scarce; breeds with varying status in English and Welsh counties from Devon north-east to York; strong populations Mid and North Wales, Lake District, Pennines and North York Moors; extends into southern Scottish counties, especially Dumfries, then very locally and in small numbers as far north as Wester Ross, and even Sutherland 1970–1; not Anglesey, Man, Bute, or Ireland. Rather narrowly confined in Britain to open woodland, especially where oaks dominant, with plenty of tree cavities and dead boughs, and sparse ground and bush flora; so in continuous woods, hangers and copses, in riparian tree belts, gardens and orchards, from near sea level to tree limit.

Nest (♀ usually accompanied by ♂, 5 cm). Material appears to vary: nests in Wales and Gloucester normally of oak leaves (occasionally from other trees, and pine bark), honeysuckle bast and bracken fibres, lined with finer fibres, grass, and odd pieces of wool (moss seldom and hair never conspicuous ingredients); elsewhere grasses (e.g. *Molinia*), moss and rootlets in foundation and hair, even feathers in lining; cup usually against wall of cavity farthest from entrance hole. Favourite natural site is old woodpecker hole, but all sorts of holes from ground level to 15 m used, with entrances from about 2·5 cm in diameter; also holes in walls and buildings, and – with extraordinary freedom – nestboxes of usual titmouse type, even prospecting them the moment they have been put up. Where population not dense, open situations probably preferred, e.g. on slope above stream, but in crowded nestbox areas even shaded sites taken. Solitary to social. Eggs 5 to 8 (4 to 10) pale blue (18 × 13 mm). Incubation (♀) 12 to 13 days. Fledging (♀, usually ♂) nidicolous, about 16 days. One brood, exceptionally two.

Methods Visits of conspicuous ♂ to suitable holes do not necessarily indicate nest, but he will – if mated – usually give away site when watched persistently, and sometimes pursues building ♀ to hole with loud chatter; exceptionally unmated ♂ builds foundation of nest. But normally ♀ alone builds and incubates, and ♂ may be watched to nest when feeding her, or she may leave it herself and can be watched on return; as with many small passerines spells on nest quite short, up to half an hour. Once young hatched, repeated visits by (normally) both parents make finding easy, but small proportion of ♂♂ successively bigamous, leaving first mate to rear brood alone. Same sites used in succeeding years, though almost always by different ♀♀. ♂'s invitation display and ♀'s acceptance of site at beginning of season easiest way of all to find nest. T R Waddell has found stuffed Cuckoo 'useful' but BC had little response except of fear when Cuckoo placed near occupied nestbox.

206 **DUNNOCK**
Prunella modularis

Abundant; breeds all counties and most large islands of Britain and Ireland except Shetland. Found in all types of low, thick cover: woodland edge and hedgerows, gardens, shrubberies, open and felled woodlands, commons with clumps of brambles, gorse and long heather, and heather on moorlands, headlands and small islands; penetrates well into large towns.

Nest (♀ often accompanied by ♂, 6 cm) Resembles Greenfinch, but flatter and more felted, with smaller cup; foundation of twigs, main structure of moss with leaves, rootlets and some grass, neatly lined with moss, wool, hair and feathers, sometimes curling over cup. Great variety of nest sites: bushes, such as brambles, briars, gorse, holly, box, rhododendrons, privet, elder, hawthorn, blackthorn; stocks of trees, hedge-stocks; trailers, such as ivy, *Clematis*, honeysuckle, hops; young conifers and epicormic tree-shoots; heather and dead bracken; ricks, steep banks and walls, especially with trailing plants or creepers; in low tangle generally, especially of nettles and dead sticks; in bundles of pea-sticks and sometimes in bush-fruit and even in large vegetables; exceptionally in old nest of thrush and Swallow. Height range normally 15 cm to 1·5 m but occasionally on ground or up to 4 m. Solitary or sometimes in loose groups. Eggs 4 to 5 (3 to 6) deep blue and rather pointed (20 × 15 mm). Incubation (♀) about 12 days. Fledging (♀♂) nidicolous, about 12 days. Two broods, sometimes three.

Methods Nests become harder to find as season advances and cover thickens; not an easy species to watch back, as it slips into thick bushes and hedges without giving exact marks. Many nests can be found by searching, but ♀, fed by ♂, calls from nest and young shrilling for food often give away site that would never be discovered. Highly sedentary, building in same area in successive years, and in same season repeat may be within a metre of failed nest (Mayer-Gross).

207 **MEADOW PIPIT**
Anthus pratensis

Abundant; breeds every county of Britain and Ireland, though local and scarce parts of south-central and eastern England; does not now breed Scilly, though present on most other island groups. Typical small bird of open ground from mountain-tops through hillsides (covered with heather, rushes, grasses, bracken, gorse), bogs and marshes to rough pasture, commons and heaths, waste patches, dunes and sea-shores; particularly common where moorland marches with pastures for feeding (P Davis); rarely on arable land or well-managed grassland; overlaps Rock Pipit in some coastal areas.

Nest (♀ accompanied by ♂, 5 cm) Main structure of dead grass stems and sometimes moss, lined with finer bents and some hair and usually well concealed in tussock of grass, heather and grass, or rushes. Often in low-grazed bushes of gorse with grass growing among them; sometimes under dead bracken like Tree Pipit; in rocky districts in steep banks, even in patches of vegetation on rock faces; in blind rabbit holes; 20 cm down hole in cart track (Lewis); on shore in various maritime plants, even in *Orache* below spring-tide level. On rocky coasts site competition with Rock Pipit may occur. Solitary. Eggs 4 to 5 (3 to 7) off-white with heavy freckling in brown or grey concentrated at big end, often with hair-streaks (20 × 15 mm). Incubation (♀) 13 to 14 days; but may roost on incomplete clutch (Mayer-Gross). Fledging (♀♂) nidicolous, 13 to 14 days. Two broods normal.

Methods Nests of all pipits difficult to find; birds cannot easily be watched back, many are very shy, liable to desert if disturbed when building, while even with young (especially when large) remain suspicious of observers several hundred metres away. Pairs nesting near roads and habitations tend to be less wary, and car may be used effectively as hide. E P Chance in his study of Meadow Pipit as fosterer of

Cuckoo did not explicitly describe method of finding nests, but mentioned hard searching following location of pairs, and watching back while building, incubating and feeding young. As this is a common species of which it is possible to find four or five nests quite casually in an hour's search, there has been less incentive to develop techniques than for Tree Pipit. A rope may be dragged in uniform habitat, especially in evening. Anxious calls of parents betray presence of young, but these may be fledged. ♂ accompanies ♀ back to nest after feeding (Gosnell) and according to P Davis often flutters over incubating ♀ after feeding by himself. During first week of incubation ♀ leaves nest to feed about every 40 minutes, but less frequently in second week, when often fed by ♂. If trying to return to nest but aware of observer, ♀ 'will sometimes effect wild, darting flight as high as 30 m, then suddenly streaks for home and may be lost against dark background' (Davis).

208 **TREE PIPIT**
Anthus trivialis

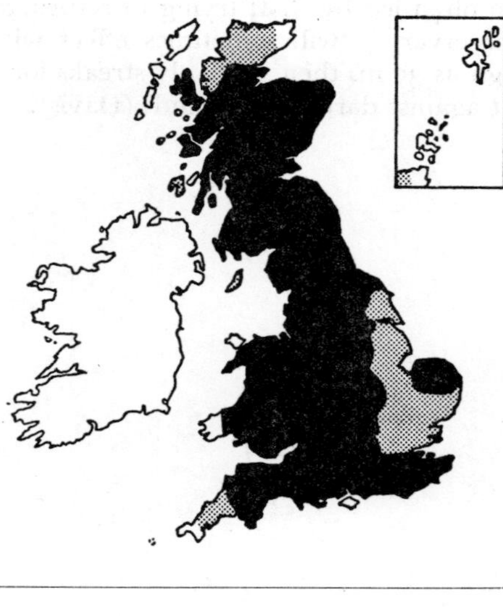

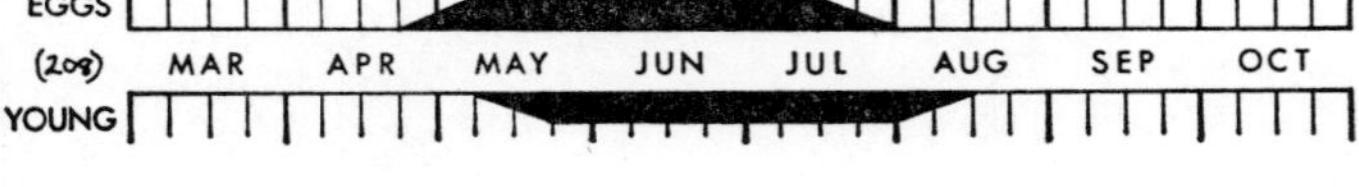

Numerous; breeds all British counties except Shetland, Orkney, Caithness and Anglesey; also absent Outer Hebrides, west Pembroke, west Cornwall, Wight and Ireland, but breeds Man; now local in some south-eastern English counties with decreases west to Welsh Border. Many types of ground frequented provided trees, bushes, wires or even pylons available as song-perches: tussocky grassland and *Molinia* bogs, often in clearings of woodland; heaths with scattered pines; bracken slopes (very popular in Wales); marshy fields in southern England; grassy banks, hence roadsides, railway cuttings and embankments; orchards and open woodland, especially oak and birch, and even quite thick woodland where rides break canopy; also in young conifer plantations and edges of older ones.

Nest (♀ accompanied by ♂, 6 cm) Foundation of moss, main structure of fine dead grasses, often very white fescue and hair-grass stems; lining of even finer grass and some hair. Typically in recess in bank, usually well hidden by vegetation and sometimes entrance no bigger than mouse hole; at times fairly open: often in side of or underneath tussock of *Molinia, Deschampsia* and other grasses, under dead bracken, brambles, nettles, ivy, blaeberry and other low-growing plants, even strawberries at Cheddar (Lewis); sometimes on level ground. Solitary. Eggs 4 to 6 (4 to 8) remarkably variable, pale blue to greenish, pinkish, brown or grey; some freckled all over like other pipits in brown, grey or red; others blotched and spotted like Reed Bunting or Blackcap, but more richly (21 × 15·5 mm). Incubation (♀) 13 to 14 days. Fledging (♀♂) nidicolous, 12 to 13 days. One brood, sometimes or perhaps often two in south (Mayer-Gross).

Methods (with special acknowledgements to D Humphrey) Gosnell devoted much space to methods but Simson was first to devise workable system. Locality with open aspect easiest to cover. Presence of singing ♂ indicates limits of territory and, during site selection and building, observing him can give good indication of nesting area, particularly when he sings on low perch in likely surroundings. Before incubation starts pair feed together near nest, which may then be found later on by hot searching or watching. Where cover near nest too thick for feeding, birds make frequent visits to site from feeding area. First contact often by sound, so important to learn metallic *pip* alarm and hoarse *zeep-zeep* call or contact note. Returning ♀ often calls as she enters area of nest, and both birds utter call when she leaves or approaches nest. The *pip* alarm often indicates ♀ off nest, when she should be located and watched. She may fly off and settle in tree before dropping to nest; if she shows reluctance to move, observer should back away slowly, keeping eyes on her. ♀ will normally return to eggs while being watched, but not so readily to young. If bird giving alarm is on ground, observer should try to watch from 50 to 100 m away, but cessation of alarm without bird being seen indicates that ♀ has run on to nest after feeding close by. Early morning and evening best time to contact off-nest ♀, as she comes off irregularly during day. Nests located when building (mainly in early morning) should not be approached for about a week, owing to strong risk of desertion. Behaviour of ♀ leaving nest very variable: may fly direct to excrete and preen on tree or bush, thence up to 1,000 m away to feed; if ♂ sees ♀, he may chase or accompany her. Alternatively she may run off to feed and return without taking flight; or run off to feed, then preen on tree before going back to nest. ♂ occasionally feeds ♀ on nest, and one singing with loaded bill should indicate incubating ♀. Activity near nest during incubation can be confusing when ♀ is off, as third bird, generally ♂, may intrude and ♀ disappears during ensuing chase and fighting. ♀ tight sitter in thick cover; ♂ may visit her on nest without bringing food.

209 ROCK PIPIT
Anthus spinoletta

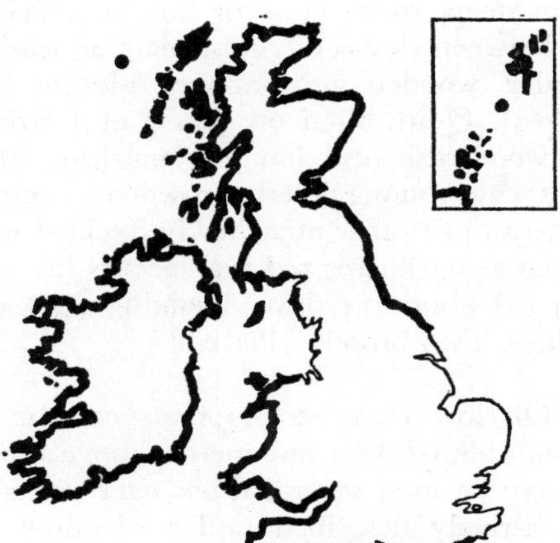

Fairly numerous; breeds most British and Irish coasts, except Dumfries, Lancashire, and east coast from South Yorkshire to Kent; very local Cumberland, Cheshire, Hampshire, but breeds Wight. Usually found from metre or so above tide-line to cliff-top, but on some islands, e.g. St Kilda, Scilly, on moorland some distance from sea; rocky coasts, whether islets, low headlands or cliffs normal, but in south breeds in chalk and in Northern Isles, Hebrides and parts of Ireland on quite smooth shores with grassy banks.

Nest (♀, sometimes accompanied by ♂, 6 cm) Similar to Meadow Pipit, but sometimes adorned with white feathers. Typically in steep, rocky bank or hole or crevice in cliff; sometimes between stones of ruins, piers or seaside breastworks; under wooden box above tide-line on Fetlar (Mayer-Gross). Quite often on grassy or heathery banks or among wood-rush and hanging maritime plants, e.g. scurvy-grass; even among nests in crowded ternery. Solitary. Eggs 4 to 5 (2 to 6) off-white, thickly freckled with brown or grey, often as dark cap; red type occurs (21 × 16 mm). Incubation (♀) about 14 days. Fledging (♀♂) nidicolous, about 16 days. Two broods. (Plate 8b).

Methods On low rocky coasts nests can be found by searching suitable banks a few metres above tide-line, and same site may be used several times over period of years. Difficulties already described under Meadow Pipit, but entrances to Rock Pipit nests often fairly obvious, particularly from below, owing to smoothed appearance of vegetation and their rather prominent position on cliff-face or bank (though others, especially in rock crevices with no vegetation, very hard to see). Incubating ♀ sits tight, but can be flushed. Not easy to watch back, even when feeding young, because of difficulty of finding suitable observation point.

210 **PIED/WHITE WAGTAIL**
Motacilla alba

Abundant; breeds all counties of Britain and Ireland, though scarce or absent Outer Hebrides and irregular Shetland; almost all Pied but exceptionally White and usually this race in Shetland. Habitat very varied but often near water: occupied buildings, churches, ruins, quarries, small crags, Grey Wagtail streams, rocky islets and sea cliffs; along roads in stone wall districts.

Nest (♀ accompanied by ♂, 7 cm) Asymmetrical and substantial with cup noticeably larger than Grey Wagtail, of moss, dead grass stems, twigs and rootlets, lined with wool, hair and feathers. Generally in some recess, often with narrow entrance and much farther in than Grey Wagtail: in stone wall or breastwork, rock face, ivy, creepers on house; in thatch or side of stack; among epicormic shoots or upturned tree roots; in tree cavity or pollard willow, tunnel in bank, heap of wood or at arm's length in pile of pit props (Whitaker); in 'ruckle' of peat and 4 m up in 'roof' of peat stack (Lewis); on ledge in shed or greenhouse, on or in old nest of thrush or other bird, in nestbox of open type and on ground under stone, clod or plant (e.g. coltsfoot) or in rabbit scrape; even in box on floor of empty hut (Whitaker) or under bucket on shingle (R Morris). Solitary. Eggs 5 to 6 (3 to 7) off-white speckled or spotted in shades of grey, occasionally blotched or spotless (21 × 15 mm). Incubation (mainly or all ♀) 13 to 14 days. Fledging (♀♂) nidicolous, 14 to 16 days. Two broods, perhaps three occasionally.

Methods Can be surprisingly hard to find, even on side of house, and concealment (e.g. in car) or long range watching may be necessary. Some birds return quite readily, even perching by nest, and cheeping of young may reveal it. Searching suitable ruins or walls often successful, and in banks smoothed look of entrance may betray nest in later stages; but it may also be hidden by quick-growing vegetation. Sometimes nests year after year in same or adjacent site.

211 **GREY WAGTAIL**
Motacilla cinerea

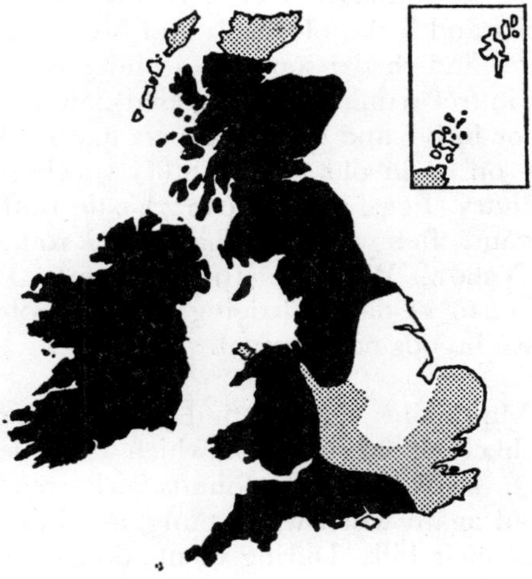

Not scarce; breeds regularly most of Britain and Ireland, except Shetland, Orkney, some Outer Hebrides, Wight and large area of eastern lowland England; also local and scarce in central and south-east England. Typically rocky or gravelly fast-flowing streams in highland districts, though occurs where conditions counterfeited by locks and mill-races; sometimes by lakes or sluggish rivers, and quite often in quarries and ruins near standing water.

Nest (♀ accompanied by ♂, 6 cm) Asymmetrical and solid, mainly of moss with dead grass, leaves, twigs and rootlets, thickly lined with hair, and occasional feathers. Traditional site on ledge over running water, but often occupies artefacts such as drainage holes or recesses in culverts and bridges, weirs and locks, old walls and breastworks, ledges in boathouses and sheds; sometimes under large stones in scree, niche in tree trunk (Walpole-Bond), among tree roots over water or in ivy and other creepers like Pied Wagtail; occasionally on or in old nest of other species, especially Dipper. Solitary. Eggs 4 to 6 (3 to 7) pale buff, marbled grey-brown and often with black hair-streak round big end, very like Yellow Wagtail (19 × 14 mm). Incubation (mainly ♀) 13 to 14 days. Fledging (♀♂) nidicolous, about 12 days. Two broods not unusual.

Methods Many sites easy to find by following streams, looking in likely spots, some of which may be used for many years. Nests may be found fairly readily when building, and again when with young, as birds fly calling with food in their bills. During incubation they are more elusive, and may need careful watching.

212 YELLOW/BLUE-HEADED WAGTAIL

Motacilla flava

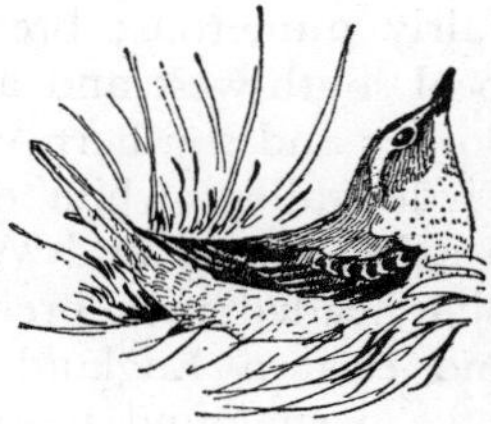

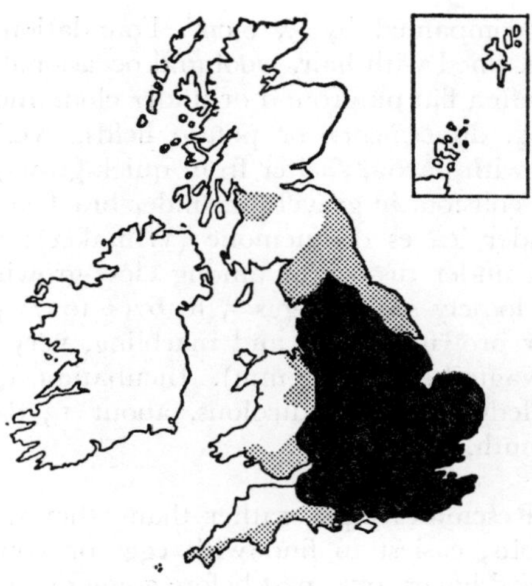

Fairly numerous; breeds most of England, though very local south-west and absent Wight; in Wales confined to Border and southern counties and in Scotland to parts of Clyde valley, while only irregular in Ireland (recently Antrim, Down and Wicklow) and absent Man. Pairs of Blue-headed race breed occasionally, chiefly in southern and eastern England and birds resembling other races have been found nesting. Ranges from moorland (up to 700 m in northern England), through commons, heaths, sand-dunes, gravel pits, industrial waste land, arable and hay fields, bulb farms and market gardens to lush water-meadows and wet, rushy pastures; but water usually fairly accessible.

Nest (♀ accompanied by ♂, 6 cm) Foundation of grass and rootlets, lined with hair, wool and occasional feathers. In hollow, often flat on ground or under clod, and in some habitats, e.g. dunes, corn or potato fields, even shingle, fairly open with partial shelter from quick-growing plant; nests under coltsfoot in gravel pit, under bracken on shale-tip and under leaves of anemone (Whitaker); but often well-hidden under tussock or among close-growing stems. Solitary to loosely social. Eggs 5 to 6 (4 to 7) pale buff with darker brown speckles and marbling, very like eggs of Grey Wagtail (19×14 mm). Incubation (♀) 12 to 13 days. Fledging (♀♂) nidicolous, about 13 days. Two broods in south.

Methods Resembles pipits rather than other wagtails in nesting habits, easiest to find with eggs or young when returning bird hovers over nest before going down; in open habitats may land some metres away and run to nest. May hover elsewhere first, so patience necessary. ♂ also calls ♀ off when observer 80 to 100 m away (Gosnell, Walpole-Bond); she may fly or run towards observer, or slip off quietly. This gives opportunity to hide and watch back.

Some ♀♀ sit closely but others rise at long range and in dense habitats usually advisable to await their return. Nests may also be found by watching when building and desertion risk at this stage is less than with pipits. Birds visiting nest with young may pause only momentarily by it. Monograph: Smith (1950).

213 **RED-BACKED SHRIKE**
Lanius collurio

Very scarce: still declining and now confined to south-east England, mainly Hampshire and East Anglia. Now chiefly on bushy, gorse-clad heaths, but formerly in other scrub country: commons and waste ground, railway cuttings and embankments, old overgrown quarries, unkempt hedgerows, young plantations and thickets.

Nest (mainly ♂, 7·5 cm) Rather large and superficially like small Blackbird, of moss, grass, stalks, small bits of wool and feathers, lined fine grass, rootlets, hair and down (for long list of materials, including threaded needle, see Lewis). In Hampshire area studied by J S Ash (*BB* 63: 185–205, 225–39) 90% nests in thorny growth, including 53% in gorse, 15% in holly, 14% in bramble (or in combinations of these species with others); elsewhere often in brambles or briars trailing over hedgerow thorns; sometimes in elder, sallow, privet, quite often in young conifers or other small trees, occasionally low in tangle; height range 25 cm to 2·5 m, mean about 1 m (Ash); extremes from 'a few inches' up to nearly 5 m (Walpole-Bond). Nest usually well into cover, but sometimes almost exposed on lateral branch or near top of bush. Loosely colonial. Eggs 3 to 6 (1 to 8) very variable (23 × 17 mm). Ash summarised 50 clutches as: 'pale pink, pink, reddish-pink, greenish, yellowish-green, dark green, greyish-green, olive, pale buff, buff, buffish, pinkish-buff, greyish-buff, greyish-white, dirty white, cream, creamy white, white, buffish-white, or stone. Spotted blobbed, speckled or zoned (usually just above the widest part) with reddish, pale reddish, pale reddish-brown, greyish, grey, buffish-grey, olive, pale olive-brown, greyish-olive, brownish, or pale brown'. Incubation (♀) before completion of clutch begins 13 to 16 days. Fledging (♀♂) nidicolous, about 14 days. One brood.

Methods At times ♂ seems to go out of way to show nest: BC located one from moving train, by seeing him dive into bush. But where bushes numerous or in young plantations, may be difficult to follow ♂, or ♀ when she appears. Gosnell advocated watching where ♂ reappears as he may enter cover far from nest. During laying and incubation Ash found many pairs became very inconspicuous, and visits when feeding young were sometimes 'extremely infrequent'. If possible sites restricted, searching effective as nest usually easy to see, but becomes less rewarding when choice is wide; for watching back in thick cover high vantage desirable. Shrikes may return for many years to same small area, or may disappear after one or two seasons, turning up again some distance away in separate area of suitable habitat. Walpole-Bond pointed out that bird sometimes 'shows up of its own accord, even for a few moments seeking the ground', nearly always picking up 'something in the edible line', evidently a displacement activity. He also found birds near nests of young very demonstrative.

214 STARLING
Sturnus vulgaris

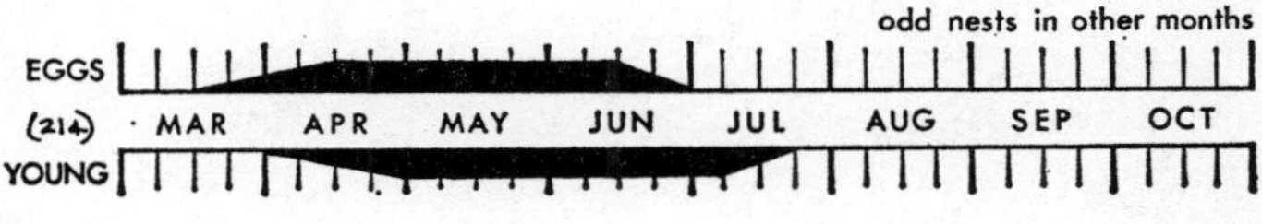

Abundant; breeds all counties of Britain and Ireland, though still local in some western Irish coastal areas. Typically in vicinity of habitations or sea cliffs, and on treeless islands colonises moorland; also considerable penetration of woods, copses, large towns and very commonly in suburbia, villages and farms, even round isolated houses.

Nest (foundation ♂, lining ♀) In cavity, of straw and grasses with various lining materials, often feathers; Whitaker recorded some excavation by birds exceptionally. Holes of all kinds used, in walls and roofs (including thatch) of occupied and empty buildings, especially under eaves; also holes and cracks in sea cliffs; natural holes and those excavated by woodpeckers in trees; in treeless areas, drystone walls, holes in the ground, peat-stacks and piles of stones; long list of occasional and exceptional sites includes metal pipes, Sand Martin holes, foundations of large nests, cup of Magpie's nest (Connor), haystacks; more or less open nests sometimes built in thick ivy and occasionally in dense evergreens; will take nestboxes readily, especially if previous site blocked and box placed near (R Carrick). Height range ground level to 15 m or more. Solitary to social, even colonial. Eggs 4 to 7 (4 to 9) pale blue, sometimes white, and rather glossy (30 × 21 mm). Incubation (♀♂) 12 to 13 days. Fledging (♀♂) nidicolous, 20 to 22 days. One brood, sometimes two in favourable early seasons.

Methods Building best time to find nests, when ♂ goes readily to site with foundation material; changes-over can be looked for during incubation, and any nests not previously found will be revealed when young start their clamour.

215 HAWFINCH

Coccothraustes coccothraustes

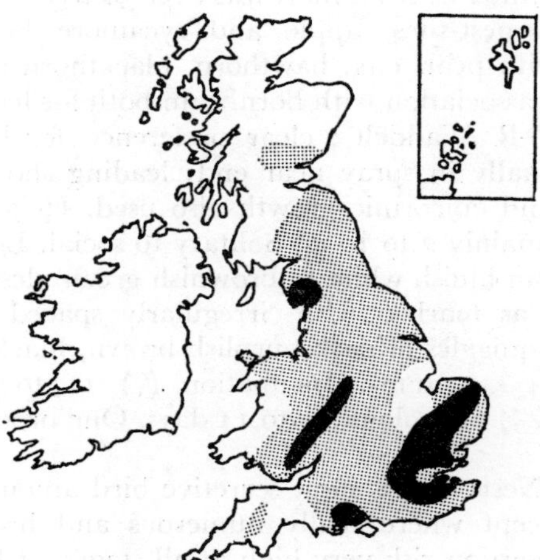

Not scarce; breeds locally all over England except Cornwall, very locally north and east Wales, and Scotland north to Perth and Angus; not Ireland (bred 1902), Man or other islands. Mature wooded habitats from open copses through orchards and gardens to continuous woodland, deciduous or mixed with conifers. Absent from highland scrub and pure conifers; seldom in hedgerows.

Nest (♀ accompanied by ♂, 7·5 cm) Foundation of small twigs, evenly placed on supporting branch or in small fork and very often of birch, strengthened with stouter twigs, e.g. of oak, and interwoven with bark or climbing stems; shallow cup of rootlets, with grass, hair, moss and lichen as other main constitutents. Mountfort lists over 30 trees and shrubs as English nest-sites, apple and sycamore being most popular, with pear, oak, hawthorn, blackthorn and birch next; close association with hornbeam both for feeding and nesting (T R Waddell); clear preference for horizontal branch, usually in spray near end; leading shoots, rising branches and epicormic growth also used. Height 1·5 to 25 m, but mainly 2 to 10 m. Solitary to social. Eggs 3 to 6 (3 to 7) from bluish white to brownish green, described by Mountfort as marked with 'irregularly spaced blotches, spots and squiggles of dark purplish-brown, black or grey-brown' (24 × 17 mm). Incubation (♀) 11 to 13 days. Fledging (♀♂) nidicolous, 10 to 14 days. One brood.

Methods Nests of this most secretive bird among hardest to find except where really numerous and breeding in groups. Desertion risk very high at all stages, at least until after hatching. Whitaker advised moving about until woodpecker-like *tzik* call heard, then waiting until bird is seen. ♂ may feed ♀ off nest every half-hour and with much calling (Mayer-Gross), after which she may be watched back, more easily when with young. Searching in likely localities can be quite rewarding; orchards lend themselves to this method. Nest very slight and not easily visible, but even in evergreens thickening effect and circular shape can be recognised against light. May return to same tree or even branch for several years (Mountfort). 'One to three partially-constructed nests are frequently found near the completed one' (Walpole-Bond). Monograph: Mountfort (1957).

216 **GREENFINCH**
Carduelis chloris

Numerous; breeds all counties Britain and Ireland except Shetland, having now colonised many islands and western districts. Main habitat now hedgerows, gardens, parks and wood edges, seldom far from habitations or roadsides or in dense woodland, but probably originally in open coniferous forest; still found in old pine areas in Strathspey.

Nest (♀ accompanied by ♂, 6·5 cm) Solidly built of moss with some wool and grass interwoven round twigs which form foundation; lined with rootlets and hair, sometimes feathers, often wool on edge of cup. Great variety of sites; height 1·5 to 5 m (average 2 to 2·5 m), but some times much higher, e.g. 15 m on top of cedar (Lewis). Hence found in most common hedgerow bushes or small trees: brambles, elder, holly, hawthorn, bird cherry, elm, but rarely hazel; in gardens and parks builds in ornamental shrubs, evergreens (yew, box), bamboo clumps; also on horizontal branches or against trunks of timber trees, especially if ivied or with epicormic shoots, and in creepers against walls; sometimes in old nests of other species. Late in season often higher in trees or in hedgerow trailers, e.g. hops, *Clematis;* usually just inside leaf canopy, but sometimes much deeper in bush. Solitary or small groups. Eggs 4 to 6 (3 to 7) off-white to pale blue, rather sparsely streaked and spotted with red-brown and underlying pale violet, sometimes zoned (21 × 15 mm). Incubation (♀) may begin before completion of clutch, 13 to 14 days. Fledging (♀♂ from throat) nidicolous, 13 to 16 days. Two broods, occasionally three.

Methods Easy to find during building or with young, when parents visit freely. Rather bulky nest shows up better than most against light in hedges and isolated bushes and may be found by searching; adults advertise existence of nesting group by their calls and so localise search. ♂ calls ♀ off nest to feed her (L Stewart-Brown).

217 **GOLDFINCH**
Carduelis carduelis

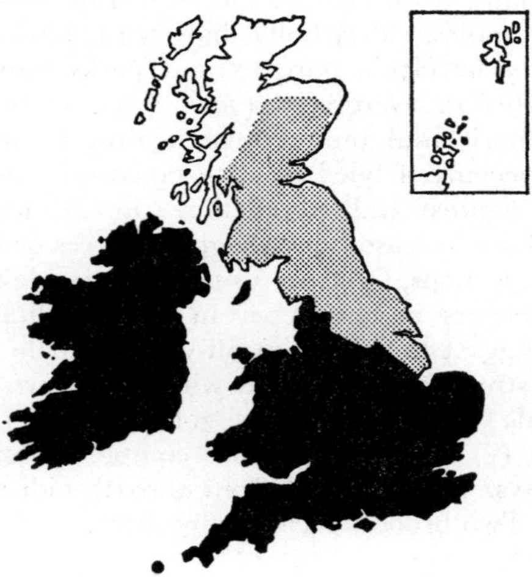

Fairly numerous; breeds all counties England, Wales, Ireland, and Man, but local from Yorkshire north in Scotland to Inverness (probably Skye), occasionally Aberdeen and formerly Ross. Preference for gardens, orchards, parks, avenues and tree-lined streets; also in conifer plantations, bushy hedgerows and scrub patches.

Nest (♀ accompanied by ♂, 5 cm) Neat and compact, of rootlets, dead grass, sometimes much wool, cobwebs, but only a little moss and lichen, lined vegetable down and wool, sometimes a little hair. Favourite site ultimate fork of horizontal or sloping branch, often up to 15 m, of horse chestnut, elm, lime, sycamore, flowering cherries and other avenue trees; in gardens in fruit and other small trees and bushes, especially lilac; in hedges and commons in elders, elms, hawthorns, birches, alders, gorse, occasionally tree lupins and in creepers such as *Clematis vitalba*; in Virginia creeper and ivy on walls; sometimes in conifers, especially larches and yews. Solitary to social. Eggs 5 to 6 (3 to 7) bluish-white with underlying grey marks and scattered spots and streaks of dark chestnut-brown (17 × 13 mm). Incubation (♀) begins before completion of clutch, 12 to 13 days. Fledging (♀♂ from throat) nidicolous, 13 to 15 days. Two broods, perhaps three occasionally.

Methods Being so small and compact, not at all easy to spot by searching; fall of leaves in autumn reveals many unsuspected nests. Fairly easy to find by watching as pair flies together to nest at all stages and often remains close at hand, telling observer whether he is 'warm' or not. But sometimes misleading visits paid to other trees, and in habitats unfavourable for observation pair may vanish completely. ♂ may call ♀ off nest (Whitaker).

218 **SISKIN**

Carduelis spinus

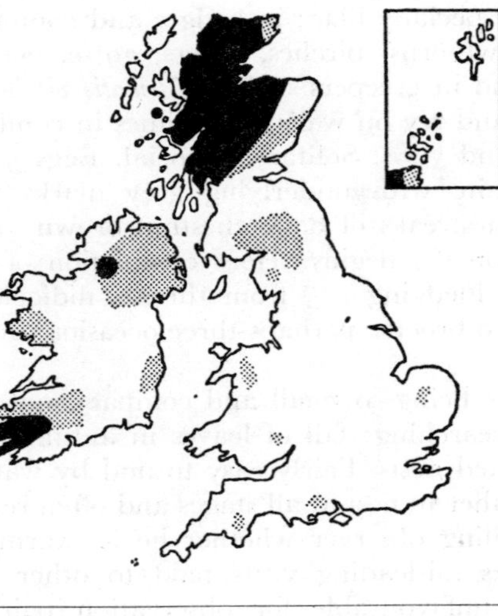

Not scarce; breeds commonly over much of Highlands; much more locally elsewhere in Scotland, including some Inner Hebrides (6 pairs Rum 1970), and in all provinces of Ireland, in parts of Wales and north, south and south-west England and in one area of East Anglia (Connor); singing ♂♂ reported increasingly elsewhere. Distribution essentially connected with open coniferous woodland, including older plantations, and extending into parks, policies, shrubberies, and gardens with spaced out conifers.

Nest (♀ accompanied by ♂, 4 cm) Moss and wool interwoven with small twigs (*Handbook*) lined rootlets, hair, down and a few feathers which may curl over cup. Prefers horizontal branches or leaders of Scots pines, spruces, silver firs, larches; favours trees bordering rides which catch sunlight (Connor); height 5 to 20 m, even more, but may be lower where branches not pruned. Solitary to social. Eggs 4 to 5 (3 to 6) pale blue with red-brown or darker spots and fine streaks (16 × 12 mm). Incubation (♀) begins before completion of clutch, about 12 days. Fledging (♀♂ from throat) nidicolous, about 15 days. Two broods.

Methods Very difficult to find, especially in large areas of open woodland, and almost impossible by cold searching, though Mayer-Gross spotted one 'by scanning every branch'. In gardens and policies, where pairs located more easily, same technique as for Goldfinch; look out also for song-flight of ♂. Essential to know call notes and to be able to follow birds when heard. ♂ feeds ♀ on nest or calls her off (Nethersole-Thompson). He alights at top of tree and drops down through branches to nest, but emerges directly. He may also continue to carry material to nest even when ♀ sitting, though normally does not take part in building (Connor).

219 **LINNET**
Acanthis cannabina

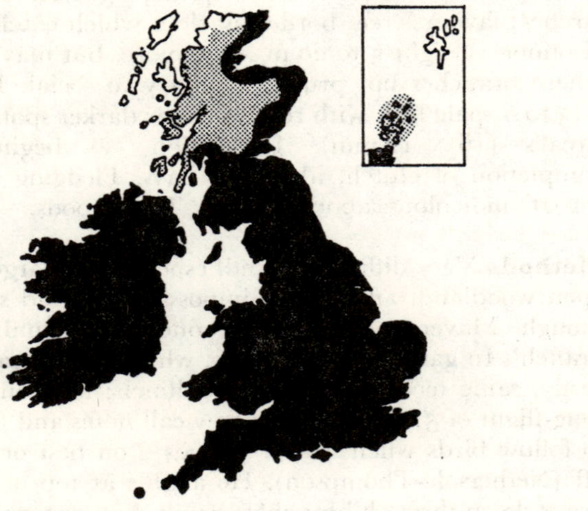

Numerous: breeds throughout Britain and Ireland except Shetland and Outer Hebrides, but very local central and north-west Scotland. Especially gorse-clad commons and heaths, but also rough grassland with thorn bushes, hedgerows in cultivated areas, large gardens, young plantations, coastal dunes and moorland edge.

Nest (♀ accompanied by ♂, 5 cm) Mainly stalks and grass stems, sometimes with moss or twigs, lined wool and hair, sometimes some feathers or down from flowerheads. Usually in bushes up to 3 or 4 m; gorse the traditional site, especially for early nests, generally placed near tops of sprays; also in brambles, thorns, elders, *Clematis* and other hedgerow species, very young conifers, occasionally in heather, even in cabbages and other vegetables; sometimes in stacks, drystone walls, banks and on ground in marram (on dunes), grass tufts and dead bracken. Solitary to social. Eggs 4 to 6 (4 to 7) pale blue or bluish-white with spots and streaks of dark brown (18 × 13 mm). Incubation (mainly ♀) begins before completion of clutch, 10 to 12 days. Fledging (♀♂ from throat) nidicolous, 11 to 13 days. Two, sometimes three broods.

Methods Birds sometimes give site away by plunging together, ♀ with beak full of material, into hedge or bush. Hence easy to watch back when building or feeding young, but in social groups, especially in gorse, proportion of nests can be found by hot or even cold searching. In hedges builds just inside canopy, so easy to see against light. ♂ sometimes calls ♀ off nest in open country (Mayer-Gross). Like other small finches, Linnets are volatile and a flourishing group one year may not be in same place the next season, but is not difficult to rediscover.

220 **TWITE**

Acanthis flavirostris

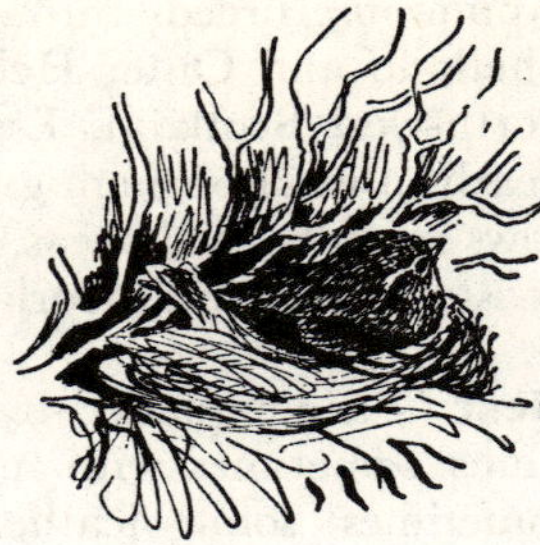

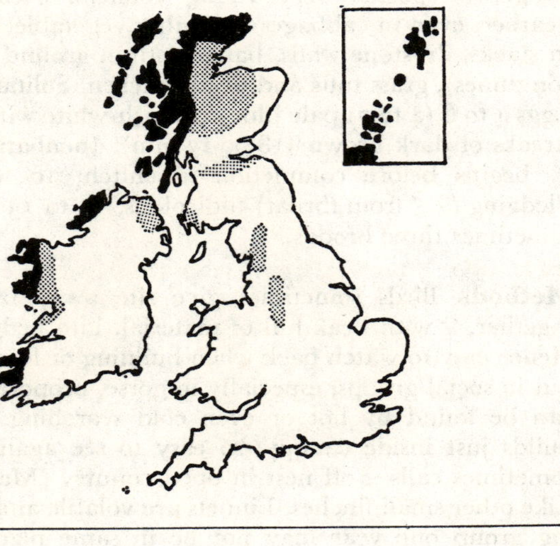

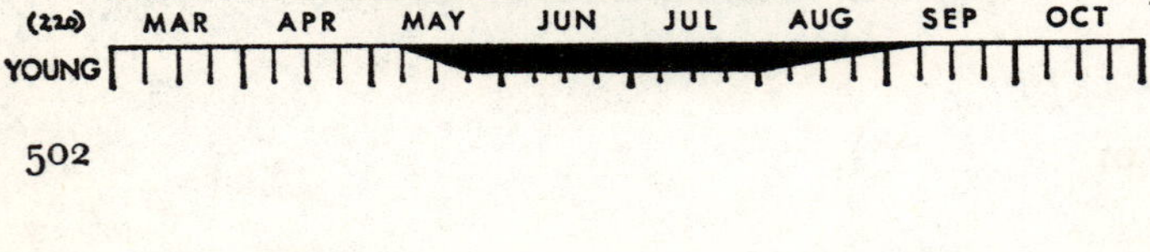

Not scarce; locally common Shetland, Orkney, Scottish Highlands down to Clyde area and Wigtown, and in northern and western Ireland; very local in northern England south to Derby and Stafford. Down to sea level in rocky as well as smooth moorland, rough grassland and bracken slopes; round crofts and in gardens, but away from continuous scrub or woodland; in northern England moorland edge from 300 to 500 m.

Nest (♀ accompanied by ♂, 5 cm) Grass stems, with a few twigs and some moss; conspicuous wool lining, also some hair and feathers. Sites from ground level, even under sod or furrow, up to about 2 m in bushes but most commonly in heather; also in banks, small crags, old walls; usually rather well hidden or at least masked by vegetation, but sometimes very open. Solitary to social. Eggs 5 to 6 (4 to 7) very like Linnet, but deeper blue and usually with more and darker markings (17 × 13 mm). Incubation (♀) usually beginning before clutch complete, 12 to 13 days. Fledging (♀♂ from throat) nidicolous, about 15 days. Two broods not unusual.

Methods Watching best method after preliminary location. Pair visits nest together, especially during building, and may show great excitement when observer near. Searching may be successful where species abundant, when examination of heathery banks is rewarded either by flushing bird or seeing nest (often conspicuous owing to white lining). Desertion risk high before incubation starts. In Pennines ♂ said to sing close to nest; but birds may feed in fields a long way away from breeding area (Mayer-Gross).

221 REDPOLL

Acanthis flammea

Fairly numerous; increasing throughout Britain and Ireland, though still absent or very rare Shetland, Orkney, Outer Hebrides, Pembroke, Cornwall, south-central and southern England (except New Forest). Wide variety of habitats with common denominator small trees or bushes: in south in gardens and parks, tall hedges, osier beds and, in areas of spread, especially young conifer plantations; in highland areas, characteristic of birch, alder, sallow and even low hazel scrub.

Nest (♀ accompanied by ♂, 4·5 cm) Foundation of twigs and rootlets which give recognisable 'roughly-furnished external appearance' (*Handbook*); also moss, bark strips, dead leaves, willow catkins and spider cocoons, and nests in birches may be perfectly blended with lichens; lined copious white vegetable down and some hair, occasionally feathers. Great height range, from timber trees down to tree lupins (Suffolk coast), sea buckthorn (East Lothian) and cabbage plant in Donegal (per Theed Pearse); usually one to 5 m up in bushes and small trees – especially hawthorn, elder, wych elm, birch, willow, sallow, poplar, alder, holly and conifers, and tops of gorse bushes (G Wren, Connor) – and often in ultimate fork or upward-sloping branch, but in gardens and parks may build high up any suitably branched tree. Solitary to social: Gosnell found nine nests in one group of silver poplars. Eggs 4 to 6 (3 to 7) blue, streaked and spotted with red-brown, sometimes in zone (16 × 12 mm). Incubation (♀) about 11 days. Fledging (♀♂ from throat) nidicolous, about 12 days. One, sometimes two broods.

Methods As with other small finches, watching recommended. Essential to recognise stuttering call-notes, very distinctive in this species, and to follow them when heard, but determination of precise breeding area may be difficult, though less so than Siskin. Look out for ♂; Gosnell, who found nests in junipers in Perthshire, described how ♂ flies away, perhaps returning with another ♂, and both dive into own areas. Pair often visits nest together. Searching usually unprofitable except where group breeding, but nests in sallows (North Wales, Kinross) surprisingly conspicuous. Bird may twitter on nest (BC).

222 **SERIN**
Serinus serinus

Bred English south coast counties 1967 and several subsequent years. Habitats have varied from private gardens to wood edges; on Continent, though found in open woodland and copses, associated particularly with parks, gardens, churchyards, orchards, avenues, and cultivated land near villages and towns.

Nest (♀ accompanied by ♂, 4·5 cm) First English nest about 7·5 cm in (presumably external) diameter, 'rather shallow cup built of grass stems' and lined hair and reddish wool, believed to be from cat (*BB* 61: 87–8); on Continent usually of dry grass, weeds or other locally available material such as moss, rootlets and lichens, sometimes bound with spiders' webs and lined with fine rootlets, vegetable down, feathers, hair and even string, the whole more similar to Goldfinch than, say, Greenfinch. First English nest in western red cedar *Thuja plicata*; on Continent most well hidden either in deciduous trees or solitary conifers (among deciduous species) such as lime, beech, maple and hazel, mostly at heights of 2 to 10 m and usually in fork or flat on outer half (often outermost quarter) of horizontal or rising branch. Solitary to social. Eggs 4 (3 to 5) pale bluish spotted and streaked, chiefly at larger end, with purplish and red-brown and almost indistinguishable from Goldfinch (16 × 12 mm), late April to early July. Incubation (♀) about 13 days. Fledging (♀♂ from throat) nidicolous, about 13 up to 17 days. Frequently two broods.

Methods (with special acknowledgement to Viking Olsson, *BB* 61: 213–23) Serins get almost all their food from open weedy ground, flying thence to their wooded breeding areas, where ♂ sings mostly from perches just below tree-tops and utters special, Blue Tit-like calls when near nest. He feeds incubating ♀ at hourly intervals, calling briefly when 20 to 30 m away, ♀ answering with begging call *chichichichi*. Sometimes she leaves nest briefly to defecate before receiving regurgitated food. But at other times breeding birds silent, giving no clue to whereabouts of nest. ♀ broods young closely for several days, passing on food from ♂ every hour or so, intervals shortening as brood develops. At first ♀ cleans up droppings, but after a week they begin to accumulate and nests may then be found by searching beneath trees. At first English nest twittering from young heard about a week before they fledged.

223 **BULLFINCH**

Pyrrhula pyrrhula

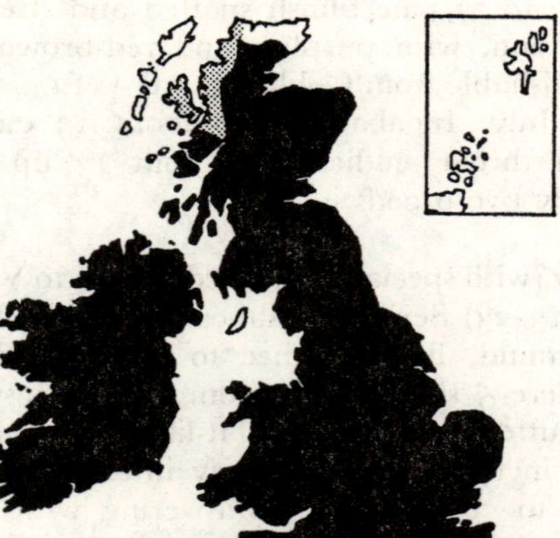

Numerous, breeds every county of Britain and Ireland, except Shetland and Orkney, scarce Caithness; absent Outer Hebrides, Man. Typical southern habitat small woods and thickets with brambles, briars and other thick undergrowth; commonly in gardens, even quite small ones, shrubberies, hedgerows and lanes with good cover; often in young conifer plantations before they are 'cleaned'; in highland districts round habitations and in low scrub, e.g. juniper, and banks or roadsides with long heather.

Nest (♀ accompanied by ♂, 5 cm) Foundation of small twigs like Hawfinch, and cup of fine black or brown rootlets often mixed with hair which may be white. Thick bushes and trees of many kinds favoured, especially evergreens – yew, cypress, box, rhododendron, ivy-covered trunks and stumps, flat branches of firs (Black) – also very commonly in brambles, briars, hawthorn and blackthorn, and snowberry *Symphoricarpa* in some areas; quite often in epicormic shoots of trees (e.g. alder), in long heather on steep banks in highland districts, and exceptionally in sedge tussock (IJF-L) and live bracken (Mayer-Gross). Generally just inside canopy, but sometimes much deeper; normal height range 1 to 2, rarely up to 5 m. Solitary. Eggs 4 to 6 (4 to 7) greenish blue with dark purple-brown streaks usually as zone round big end, rather pointed (19·5 × 14·5 mm). Incubation (♀) 12 to 14 days. Fledging (♀♂ from throat) nidicolous, 12 to 16 days. Two broods.

Methods Watching recommended as for smaller finches, especially when pair visits site during building; risk of desertion high at this stage. Searching of suitable bushes often successful once pair located, as nest shows up well against light. ♀ sits very tight and cannot normally be flushed by tapping.

224 **CROSSBILL**

Loxia curvirostra

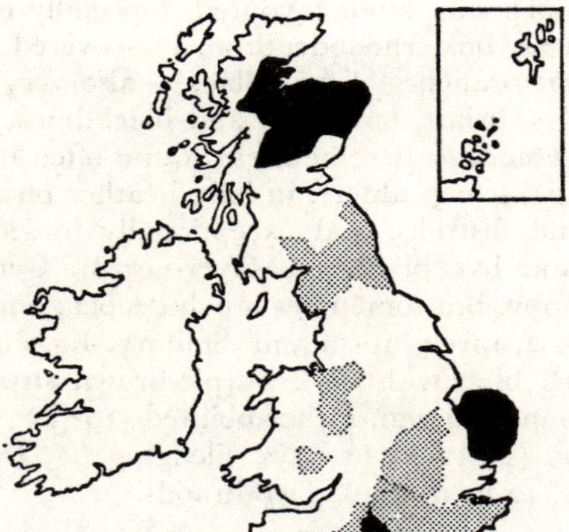

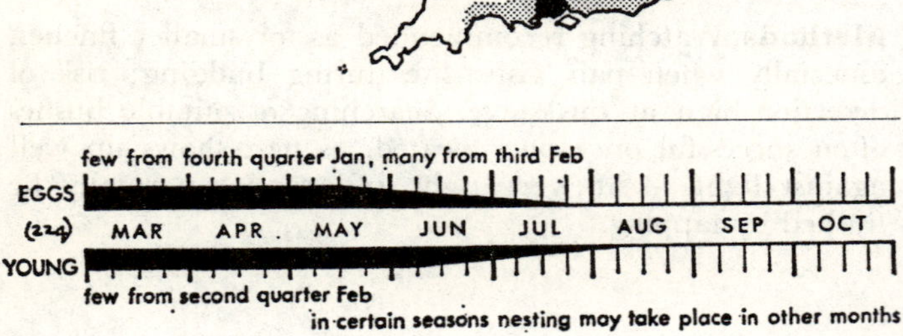

Not scarce; apart from resident Scottish race* in eastern Highlands, and residents of nominate race in East Anglia and Hampshire, sporadic over rest of Britain, but may breed almost regularly in other southern English counties; absent western seaboard of Britain and islands, and in Ireland possible recent breeding records only in Down, Tyrone and Wicklow. Both races chiefly in woods, clumps or tree lines (as in East Anglia) in which Scots pine predominates, but not in closed plantations; Scottish race in larches in Ross (*Handbook*). After invasions may breed in gardens and parks with spaced-out conifers of many species.

Nest (♀ accompanied by ♂, who may help initially, occasionally later, 7·5 cm) Foundation and framework of twigs from nesting or neighbouring trees, with cup of grass, moss, wool, hair, lichen, bark fibres or vegetable down, sometimes string and exceptionally paper (Walpole-Bond); inner lining fine grass, fur, often a few feathers curling over rim. Favourite sites near end of lateral branch or at top of pine or other conifer, but sometimes close to trunk; height range usually 8 to over 20, exceptionally down to 2 m. Solitary to social. Eggs 3 to 4 (2 to 5) indistinguishable from Greenfinch (22 × 16 mm). Incubation (♀) may begin before clutch complete, 12 to 13 days. Fledging (♀♂ from throat) nidicolous, 20 to 25 days. One brood, possibly a second occasionally.

Methods (with special acknowledgement to D Humphrey) Initial location of birds usually by listening for loud *chip chip* flight calls and observing flight lines of ♂♂ or pairs leaving feeding trees. But beware of non-breeding adults in parties. Deeper alarm and anger note *tek tek* heard both from feeding parties and when nest in danger.

* We take the view that the Scottish race should be ascribed to this species and not to Parrot Crossbill.

'Squeaking rattle' of ♂ is 'hot' indication of nest (Gosnell); he utters this when close to building ♀ or may break off to accompany her, as she collects material near at hand or makes longer journeys to find feathers. At this stage birds very tame and one pair flew to tree under which BC was sitting. During incubation, watch for visits of ♂ to feed ♀ on nest at one to two hour intervals, or await her off-nest spells. Some nests can be found by searching lateral branches and small trees (forked tail of ♀ shows over edge of cup). Birds stealthy when feeding brood (at hourly intervals) but in later stages deposit of faeces makes nest more conspicuous. Success needs hard work and luck: on 26 March 1936 Gosnell saw two ♂♂ settle on either side of two ♀♀ on telegraph wires; both fed mates, who dropped to verge, tore off 'beakful of grass' and flew to half-built nests in adjacent pines not 50 m away.

225 **PARROT CROSSBILL**
Loxia pytyopsittacus

Suspected nesting attempt at Wisley, Surrey, in April 1963 (*BB* 57: 497). Breeding habits closely resemble those of Crossbill and Scottish Crossbill.

226 **CHAFFINCH**

Fringilla coelebs

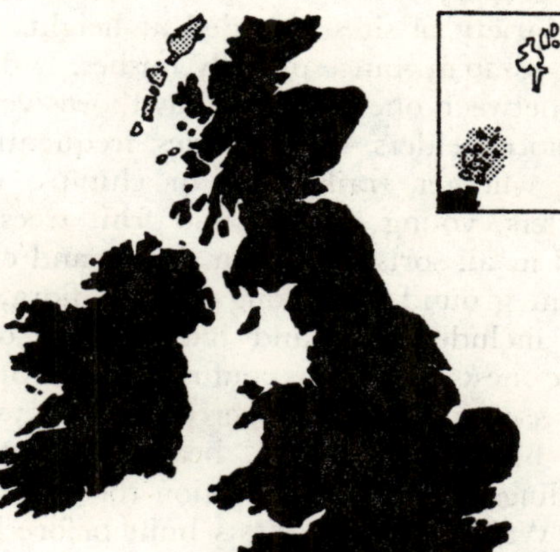

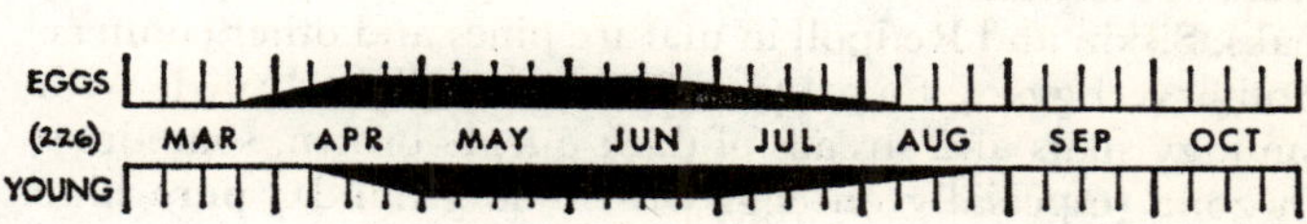

Abundant; breeds all counties of Britain and Ireland and large islands, except Shetland. Tree or bush cover of all kinds, especially hedgerows, gardens (even small ones), orchards, shrubberies, woods large and small, broadleaved and coniferous, plantations at all except initial stages, low scrub and bushy commons.

Nest (♀ sometimes accompanied by ♂ who exceptionally assists, 5 cm) Smooth, bulbous outline characteristic; moss main material with grass, fibres and rootlets interwoven, also often external embellishments of lichen held by spiders webs, birch-bark (*Handbook*), chips from Willow Tit excavation, confetti (C Gallagher) and variety of other man-made scraps; lined with hair and some feathers. Enormous variety of sites recorded at heights from a few centimetres to 20 m, but especially bushes, hedgerows and small trees between one and 4 m; hawthorns very popular, also blackthorns, elders, bird cherries, frequently brambles and briars whether trailing or in clumps, often elms, birches, alders, young conifers and fruit trees, especially apples, and in all sorts of garden shrubs and creepers. No records from ground or among ground flora, but many ledge sites include snags and ivied trunks of big trees (where late nests may be confused with Spotted Flycatcher), tree-roots, creeper-covered walls, haystacks, ferns on side of bridge (Whitaker), beams and other shelves inside buildings, even railway station roof, and old nest of Blackbird (Walpole-Bond). Nests built before leaves open may be close to stock or main stem, but later ones overlap Greenfinch, Redpoll, Linnet and Goldfinch in forks of sloping branches (BC has known Chaffinch evict Goldfinch from chosen site); also overlap Hawfinch in spreading oaks, Siskin and Redpoll in mature pines and other conifers. Solitary. Eggs 4 to 5 (4 to 8) blue or light brown with smudgy spots and streaks of dark purple-brown, sometimes in zone (especially on eggs with blue ground); pure blue clutches not unusual (20 × 15 mm). Incubation (♀) 11 to 13 days. Fledging (♀♂) nidicolous, 13 to 14 days. One brood.

Methods May often be watched building, but high desertion risk then and nests sometimes dismantled and rebuilt elsewhere. *Pink* call advertises site at all stages and monotonous repeated *wheet* of ♂ good clue to incubating ♀ nearby (Simson). Some nests blend so well with lichened or mossy trunks that finding may still be difficult. Methodical search early in season often successful; as foliage thickens, this becomes much harder. Look for bulbous swelling of any stem or branch; greenish-grey colour of nest also stands out among bare branches. Unlike most finches, parents bring insects to young in beak, so can be watched back carrying food (Mayer-Gross).

227 **BRAMBLING**
Fringilla montifringilla

Nest robbed Sutherland 1920; reported to have nested earlier in Perth, Inverness and Easter Ross (*BB* 14: 209–10; *Scottish Naturalist 1920:* 181–2; *Zoologist 1877:* 60). In recent years several ♂♂ reported singing in Scotland and further breeding seems likely. Birch and mixed birch-conifer woodland, also low scrub beyond tree limit in Scandinavia.

Nest (mainly ♀) Similar to Chaffinch but larger and less compact, with stronger foundation of grass stems, decorated with birch bark and lichen; lined with hairs, feathers and down. Usual sites in birch or conifer at heights of 1·5 to 3 m, but Sutherland nest 8 m in fork of Scots pine. Solitary. Eggs 5 to 7 (4 to 9) similar to Chaffinch types but often darker and greener (19·5 × 15 mm); Sutherland nest had 7 eggs by 31 May. Incubation (♀) about 14 days. Young (♀♂) nidicolous, about 14 days. One brood.

Methods Sutherland nest found at building stage. Location by singing ♂ and watching probably most rewarding in relatively open woodland.

228 **CORN BUNTING**
Emberiza calandra

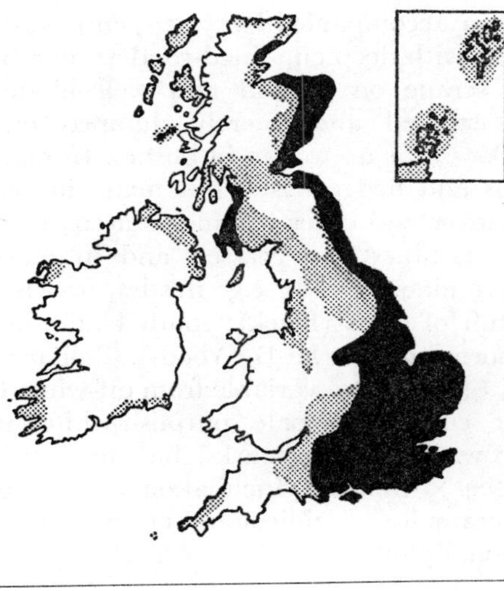

Not scarce; breeds most counties of England and Scotland but commonest down east side and very local in many areas; in Wales regular only Flint, but bred Monmouth 1970 (first record since 1903); in Scotland only small numbers Shetland, Orkney, some Inner and Outer Hebrides where once common; in Ireland confined to coastal areas of, mainly, north and north-east Wexford, Waterford, Kerry and Mayo. Two fairly distinct habitats: inland on downs or arable land, often with large fields and low or no hedges (e.g. Plain of York, parts of Oxfordshire); coastally in cliff-edge tangles or scattered cover of gorse, brambles and scrub; also on *machair*, fields and adjacent fixed dunes in Hebrides and other islands.

Nest (♀ often accompanied by ♂, 7·5 cm) Rather loosely built of grass with deep cup lined rootlets, fine bents, hair; usually in scrape on ground and well hidden, though sometimes exposed and 'merely dumped on the flat' (Walpole-Bond), or up to 2 m in bushes. In marginal land round fields and hedge bases, but many in cereal crops, hayfields, clover and other legumes; on coast in thick low tangles of brambles and grasses, and in marram tufts. Often by prominent weeds, e.g. thistles, or where there is extra big tuft of grass (Black); south Hampshire nests in low hawthorn bushes (H E Woods). Solitary to social. Eggs 3 to 5 (3 to 7) very variable from off-white to reddish-brown but commonly pale purplish-white with bold, blackish-brown scribbling marks, blotches, streaks and a few spots (24 × 18 mm). Incubation (♀) 12 to 13 days. Fledging (normally ♀) nidicolous, 11 to 14 days. One or two, occasionally three broods.

Methods Walpole-Bond, who found well over 500 nests, recommended watching expanse of likely habitat from good vantage point. Building takes place throughout day and ♀, often accompanied by ♂, goes readily to site; but beware of courting ♂ who may carry nest material briefly. During incubation ♀ leaves nest about every hour–half hour to two hours (D Macdonald, *Scottish Birds* 3: 235–46) – usually joined by ♂ who may sing anything from 10 to 150 m away. Feeding may take place 100 to 400 m from nest to which ♀ usually returns in 10 to 15 minutes with long direct flight, alighting on prominent stem where she may preen for half a minute before slanting flight down to nest. Sometimes she flutters over site or uses intermediate perch and, if observer too near nest, will fly agitatedly from perch to perch. ♂ frequently follows ♀, even chasing her back towards nest, then flies off to resume singing. Walpole-Bond pointed out ♀ often more reluctant to return to young than to eggs; she may fly about in vicinity carrying food for some time before going down; ♂ occasionally feeds young too. *Chip* call may be used by birds with eggs or young at all stages, though Walpole-Bond noted 'coarse-sounding *sow*' with nestlings. Stephens recommends using car off road as hide. Some, perhaps many ♂♂ polygamous, with nests 20 to 50 m apart; several song perches used (H H and B H Ryves, *BB* 28: 2–26, 154–164). Gosnell found last two hours of daylight most rewarding, ♀♀ leaving nests more frequently, while there was little activity in afternoon. ♀ may sit very tight and ground must be worked over twice before she rises 'with loud whirr' (Gosnell), but sometimes flutters off, feigning injury. Risk of desertion if disturbed off fresh eggs.

229 **YELLOWHAMMER**
Emberiza citrinella

Abundant; breeds all counties of Britain and Ireland except Shetland; very local Inner Hebrides and Orkney; bred North Uist 1970. A typical roadside bird, generally associated with arable land bounded by hedges, but also commonly on bracken-clad hillsides (e.g. South Wales), in long heather with scattered bushes, young conifer plantations and scrub amounting to open woodland (Scottish Highlands) and on commons and heaths in south.

Nest (♀♂, 6·5 cm) Substantial, of straw, grass, weed stalks, some moss, lined hair and fine grass; often characteristic 'doorstep' built out in front. Typical sites bank or base of hedge, small tree, bush or weed clump where grass has grown up, well inside bramble clumps and under dead bracken; often about 50 cm above ground and sometimes 2 m or more in hedge or bush, even haystack. Solitary. Eggs 3 to 5 (2 to 6) whitish, purple-white or light red-brown with thin or thick dark scribbles and some spots; sometimes almost unmarked (22 × 16 mm). Incubation (♀) 12 to 14 days. Fledging (♀♂ at first from throat) nidicolous, 12 to 13 days. Two, sometimes three broods.

Methods Usually easy to follow when building or feeding young. Though some bank nests quite open, many in bushes extremely well hidden, often right inside leaf canopy, but smoothed entrance, doorstep and protruding stems sometimes give them away. Incubating birds fly off with commotion at range of metre or so and many nests can be found along roadsides from car or bicycle on route traversed regularly, singing ♂♂ being first located. But risk of desertion when eggs fresh, and some shy pairs need careful watching (Mayer-Gross).

230] CIRL BUNTING
Emberiza cirlus

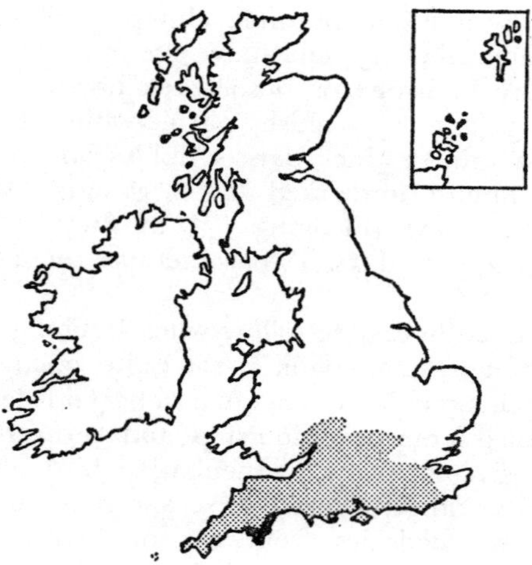

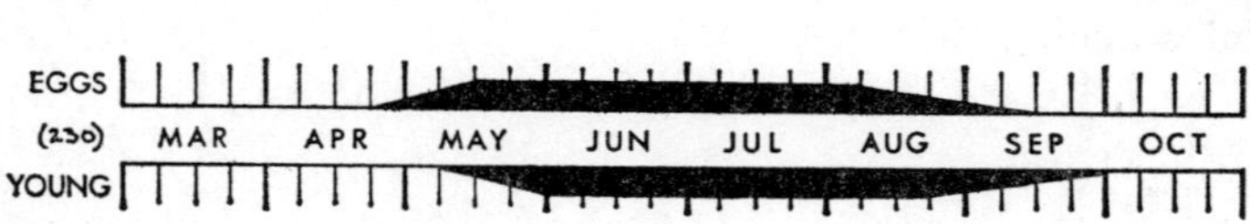

Scarce; now restricted southern England, mainly Sussex to Cornwall, with outlying groups in Worcester (Malvern Hills), Oxford, Buckingham and Hertford (Chilterns); sporadic records much farther north until 1950's. General preference for sheltered slopes in chalk and limestone areas, especially near villages, for arable land with lanes and hedges, sometimes thin and straggly (Gosnell), and for coastal cliff tops (N W Orr); edge of downland often favoured, and quite frequently gardens and parks, and sites of felled woodland (*Handbook*).

Nest (♀♂, 6·5 cm) Resembles Greenfinch rather than Yellowhammer: moss as foundation, with fine roots, grass, sometimes leaves, lined fine grasses and hair. Usually well off ground and higher than Yellowhammer, 40 cm to 1 m, though considerable overlap, from bank level through gorse, brambles, hedges, especially hawthorn and evergreen, to elm suckers and small trees: one Hampshire nest 3 m in spreading yew branch just like Greenfinch. Walpole-Bond listed ricks, rose bushes in gardens, ivy on wall; Gosnell, haystack and, in his own garden, apple, *Cupressus macrocarpa*, hawthorn hedge and thin bramble (September); Lewis recorded Somerset nests among strawberry plants and one suspended 'Reed Warbler fashion' between broad beans at 30 cm. Solitary to social. Eggs 3 to 4 (2 to 5) bluish or greenish-white with markings similar to but usually bolder and more blotched than Yellowhammer (21 × 16 mm). Incubation (♀) 11 to 13 days. Fledging (mainly ♀) nidicolous, 11 to 13 days. Two, sometimes three broods.

Methods More elusive than Yellowhammer. Building, incubation and feeding of young normally by ♀, but Mayer-Gross watched ♂ visit ♀ at hedgerow site where nest subsequently built, Walpole-Bond found ♂ sometimes fed sitting ♀ and BC saw ♂ visit young. Singing ♂, often on high perch, should aid location of pair and may be guide to nest, but also sings up to 200 m or more away. ♂ follows ♀ to nest, but very difficult to watch her back and Walpole-Bond recommended hot searching as only reliable method; ♀ sits very tight, especially on well hidden nests, and may easily be overlooked. Disturbed pairs often utter rattling or squeaky alarm calls near nest.

231 **REED BUNTING**
Emberiza schoeniclus

Fairly numerous; breeds all counties of Britain and Ireland, including most islands, but only odd pairs Shetland. All types of marshy and boggy localities with thick vegetation: fens, reed, osier and *Glyceria maxima* beds, rushy and sedgy areas, bog myrtle and *Molinia* in highland areas; also coastal marram grass and bushy islets in Scottish and Irish lochs. In Ireland has long occupied drier habitats, e.g. rough grassland, gorse heaths, and this now increasingly so in Britain, where colonising downland, hedgerows and young conifer plantations; possible to find Yellowhammer, Corn Bunting and Reed Bunting nesting within a few metres (Stephens).

Nest (normally ♀, 6·5 cm) Substantial, mainly of dry grasses and sedges, lined fine grass and some hair; sometimes reed-flowers (*Handbook*). Usually on ground or slightly raised (up to 1 m) in vegetation, e.g. sedge tussocks, rushes, overgrown stumps, bog myrtle, but sometimes up to 4 m in hawthorns, briars and osier beds (Walpole-Bond); increasingly now in small conifers, gorse and hedgerow thorns; almost always well hidden, often concealed by overhanging grass or sedge tuft, but more open nests recorded on cinders by Cheshire flashes (A W Boyd) and under small bushes on Sussex shingle (E C Arnold). Solitary to social. Eggs 4 to 5 (4 to 6) olive brown or buff, marked with bold dark streaks and smudgy spots (20 × 15 mm). Incubation (♀♂) 13 to 14 days. Fledging (♀♂) nidicolous, 10 to 13 days. Two, perhaps three broods occasionally.

Methods Owing to conspicuous ♂ and confiding habits, initial location easy and a few minutes watching ♀ usually successful at all stages, though nests found when building may be deserted. But birds sit very close and, if hot searching employed, take some flushing, when injury-feigning common. Smoothed entrance to nest sometimes a guide.

232 SNOW BUNTING
Plectrophenax nivalis

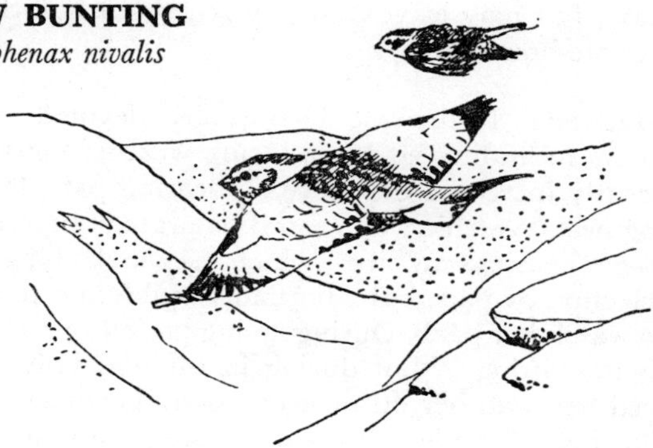

Very scarce; few pairs breed Cairngorm Hills, probably occasionally other Scottish mountains, e.g. Ben Nevis (1954) and Wester Ross. Mountain top detritus and broken rocky outcrops above 900 m.

Nest (♀, often attended by ♂) Typically pad of dark *Rhacomitrium* moss and cup of grasses (especially *Deschampsia flexuosa*) lined finer stems and few to many feathers (mostly Ptarmigan). Generally 25 to 75 cm or more inside boulders of scree, below block of granite or in crevice of outcrop. Solitary. Eggs 4 to 6 (2 to 6) off-white, bluish or greenish, boldly marked red-brown and dark brown spots and blotches with underlying violet marks (21 × 16 mm). Incubation (♀) probably starting before completion of clutch, 12 to 13 days. Fledging (♀♂) nidicolous, 10 to 12 days, but may leave nest sooner. About half Scottish pairs double-brooded.

Methods Nethersole-Thompsons devoted hundreds of hours to finding 38 nests, facing weather conditions which greatly increased difficulty of locating pair, let alone finding nest. Watching by several separated observers advisable to get bearings on birds, which may make long flights. Nest selection by pair, but ♀ normally builds and this is best time to watch her back. During laying period ♂ may perch near lightly sitting ♀, but during incubation visits nest only to feed her, call her off or accompany her back after she has fed herself. When feeding young, parents may forage separately up to 700 m away, but often return to nest together. In Iceland, where bird locally common and commensal with man, J E Griffith found it nesting in stone artefacts resembling natural sites and with more than one entrance; some birds allowed close approach and some ♂♂ helped to line nest, carrying conspicuous white feathers. He also recommends searching round ♂'s favourite perch to flush lightly sitting ♀ off incomplete clutch; later she sits very tight. Monograph: Nethersole-Thompson (1966).

233 **HOUSE SPARROW**
Passer domesticus

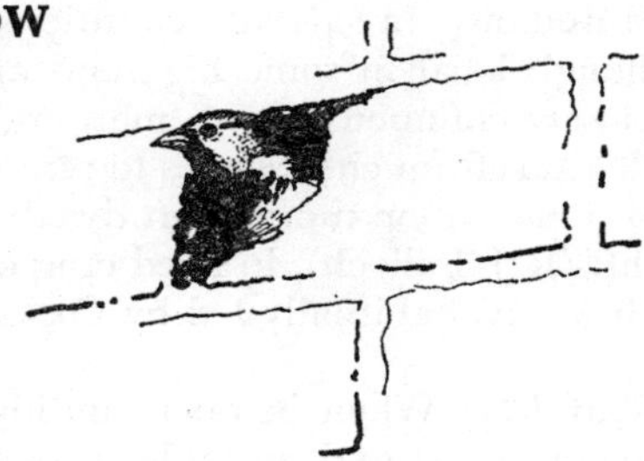

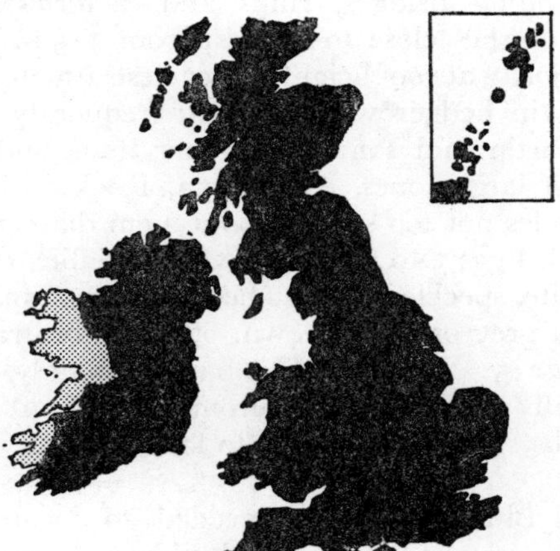

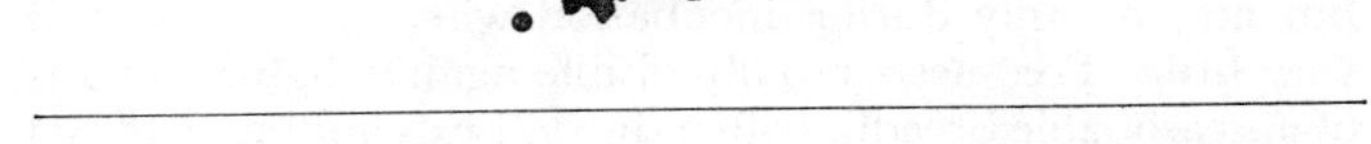

Abundant; breeds all counties of Britain and Ireland, though local in some highland and western coastal areas. Closely commensal with man and found by habitations of all kinds from city centres to remote farms; occasionally up to 1,000 m or more from dwellings, e.g. on Shetland sea cliff (R J Tulloch), in ivied crag on Iona, in conifers where Pheasants habitually fed by Oxfordshire gamekeeper.

Nest (♂♀) When in open, untidy domed structure up to 30 cm across and variable in depth, of straw and grasses (often quite green), lined feathers, some wool and oddments; but in cavity materials much reduced, sometimes only to lining. Sites generally in or on bare or ivied buildings (including bridges, ruins and factories), or cliffs, trees and bushes close to houses; from 1·5 m to at least 20 m (majority at roof height). Tree nests usually in canopy and those in hedgerows also high; frequently takes over House Martin and sometimes other nests and builds in bottoms of larger ones, e.g. Heron, Rook; will use nest-boxes if holes not too small (about 4 cm diameter). Social to colonial. Eggs 3 to 6 (1 to 7) very variable, off-white or bluish-white, speckled or blotched densely or sparsely with grey, dark grey or dark brown, often concentrated round big end (22·5 × 16 mm). Incubation (mainly ♀) 9 to 18 days, usually 12. Fledging (♀♂ from bill or crop) nidicolous, 11 to 19 days, usually 18. One to four broods.

Methods Little experience needed to locate colonies; hidden sites may be found when building or feeding young, but not so easily during incubation when ♀ shows herself very little. Tree nests usually visible against light. Reports of unseasonable breeding often due to birds adding material to nests used as winter roosts. Monograph: Summers-Smith (1963).

234 **TREE SPARROW**

Passer montanus

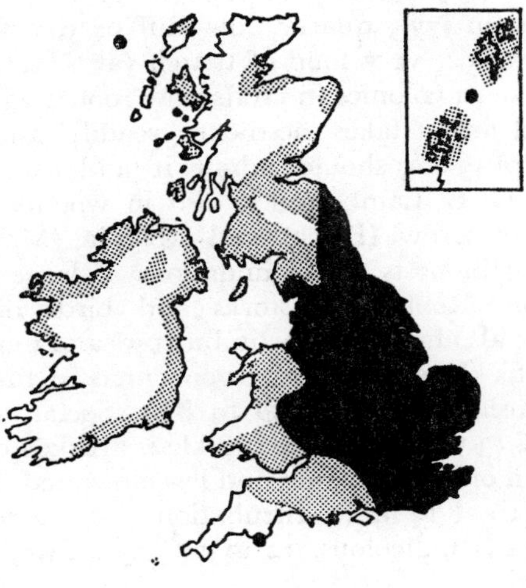

Fairly numerous; breeds most counties of England (very local Devon and absent Cornwall), more locally Wales and Scotland; has recently colonised or re-colonised at least 18 mainly coastal Irish counties and various British islands, e.g. Anglesey, Orkney, Fair Isle, Shetland, St Kilda. Traditional lowland habitats pollard willows along rivers (e.g. East Anglia) and old orchards (e.g. Welsh Border) but also in old trees in hedges, gardens, parks and woods; round buildings, quarries, cliffs, sometimes close to House Sparrow colonies.

Nest (♀♂) Resembles House Sparrow but neater and more flask-shaped when in open: of straws, moss and grass stems, lined feathers. Normally in hole or crevice in building (sometimes in ivy), quarry, low cliff or tree from about 1·5 m upwards; very fond of thatch (also haystacks) and former western colonies in crofts now roofed with slates or corrugated iron; takes nestboxes readily and entrance diameter of 3 cm should admit it and exclude House Sparrow (G C Lambourne); also in woodpecker holes, nest-cups of Crow (Black) and Magpie (Mayer-Gross), House Martin nests and foundations of large structures, e.g. Heron, Rook, and storks and birds of prey on Continent; also in Sand Martin burrows and mole-holes on coastal cliffs (Walpole-Bond); open nests in thick hedges, isolated bushes and trees up to 8 m. Social to colonial. Eggs 4 to 6 (3 to 8) off-white speckled, streaked or blotched dark brown or grey; smaller and less elongated than House Sparrow (19 × 14 mm). Incubation (♀♂) 12 to 14 days. Fledging (♀♂) nidicolous. 12 to 14 days. Two, sometimes three broods.

Methods Large colonies easy to locate but single nests take some finding, though pairs habitually perch near site. They may also be followed when building, which often begins weeks before eggs laid. Like House Sparrows, keep very quiet during incubation and most slip off nest unobtrusively (L Ballard), but some sit tighter and can be flushed by tapping. Searching likely holes where birds seen quite successful, but slim torch essential. With young, parents more in evidence and may scold observer.

Bibliography

ALEXANDER, W B 1945–7 The Woodcock in the British Isles *Ibis* 87: 512–50; 88: 1–24, 159–79, 271–86, 427–44; 89: 1–28

ANON 1969 *Book of British Birds* London

ARMSTRONG, EDWARD A 1955 *The Wren* London

BEEBE, W 1937 *Pheasants: their Lives and Homes* New York

BLACK, J G 1920 *Birdsnesting* Newcastle upon Tyne

BRITISH ORNITHOLOGISTS' UNION 1971 *The Status of Birds in Britain and Ireland* Oxford

BRITISH TRUST FOR ORNITHOLOGY 1971 *A Species List of British and Irish Birds* Tring

BROWN, LESLIE and AMADON, DEAN 1968 *Eagles, Hawks and Falcons of the World*, 2 vols London

BROWN, P E and DAVIES, M G 1949 *Reed-Warblers* East Molesey

BROWN, PHILIP and WATERSTON, GEORGE 1962 *The Return of the Osprey* London (includes chapters on Avocet by Gwen Davies and on Black-tailed Godwit by Peter Conder)

BUB, HANS 3rd revised ed 1971 *Vogelfang und Vogelberingung* Wittenberg

BUXTON, JOHN 1950 *The Redstart* London

CAMPBELL, BRUCE 1953 *Finding Nests* London

DAVIS, PETER G 1965 Notes on the ringing of nestling Passerines (with comment by H Mayer-Gross) *Ringers' Bulletin* 2(8): 5–9

EASTMAN, ROSEMARY 1969 *The Kingfisher* London
FISHER, JAMES 1947, 1951, 1955 *Bird Recognition*, vols 1–3 Harmondsworth
—— —— 1952 *The Fulmar* London
FITTER, R S R 1959 *The Ark in our Midst* London
GORDON, SETON 1955 *The Golden Eagle* London
GOSNELL, H T 1947 *The Science of Birdnesting* Barnston, Wirral
HEADSTROM, RICHARD 1949 *Birds' Nests* New York
LACK, DAVID 1943 *The Life of the Robin* London
—— —— 1956 *Swifts in a Tower* London
LEWIS, STANLEY (ed K M WILLCOX) 1952 *The Breeding Birds of Somerset and their Eggs* Ilfracombe
LOCKLEY, R M 1942 *Shearwaters* London
LOWE, FRANK A 1954 *The Heron* London
MAYER-GROSS, H 1970 The Nest Record Scheme *BTO Field Guide No* 12 Tring
MOUNTFORT, GUY 1957 *The Hawfinch* London
MURTON, R K 1965 *The Wood-Pigeon* London
NETHERSOLE-THOMPSON, DESMOND 1951 *The Greenshank* London
—— —— 1966 *The Snow Bunting* Edinburgh
—— —— 1971 *Highland Birds* Inverness
PARSLOW, J L F 1967–8 Changes in status among breeding birds in Britain and Ireland *British Birds* 60: 2–47, 97–123, 177–202, 261–85, 396–404, 493–508; 61: 49–64, 241–55
RUTTLEDGE, ROBERT F 1966 *Ireland's Birds* London
SAVAGE, C D W 1952 *The Mandarin Duck* London
SEAL, D T, MATTHEWS, J D and WHEELER, R T revised ed 1962 Collection of cones from standing trees *Forestry Commission Forest Record No* 39
SIMSON, CLIVE 1966 *A Bird Overhead* London
SMITH, STUART 1950 *The Yellow Wagtail* London
SNOW, D W 1958 *A Study of Blackbirds* London
SOUTHERN, H N 1970 The natural control of a popula-

tion of Tawny owls (*Strix aluco*) *Journal of Zoology* 162: 197–285
SPENCER, K G 1953 *The Lapwing in Britain* London
STEPHENS, G O 1966 Nestlings at random *Ringers' Bulletin* 2(10): 11–13
SUMMERS-SMITH, J D 1963 *The House Sparrow* London
TINBERGEN, NIKO 1953 *The Herring Gull's World* London
VENABLES, L S V and U M 1955 *Birds and Mammals of Shetland* Edinburgh
WALPOLE-BOND, JOHN 1938 *A History of Sussex Birds*, 3 vols London
WITHERBY, H F *et al.* 1938–41 *The Handbook of British Birds*, 5 vols London

In addition we have consulted the Scottish, Irish and Welsh bird reports, many county and local bird reports and books, and the national journals of ornithology

Index

Entries are confined to the English and scientific names of the birds treated in the 'Accounts of each species' on pages 40–533; the introductory chapters are not indexed. The names are those currently in widest use and follow the British Trust for Ornithology's *A Species List of British and Irish Birds* (1971). The English are indexed under the last word—but note that some names (e.g. 'Skylark') are now written and included here as one word (e.g. *not* 'Lark, Sky')—and the scientific under the generic names.